To Stilia

With all my Love

Jeanne

1000 Recipe Cookbook

1000 Recipe Cookbook

Recipes for all occasions

Edited by
Isabelle Barrett and Jane Harrop

Glossary of cooking terms

Recipes for starred ingredients can be found in the last chapter, Basic Recipes, on pages 403 to 415.

Flour in ingredients is plain and sugar is granulated unless otherwise specified.

Metric measurements are given first, followed by their Imperial equivalent. As a general guide the conversion is as follows:

1.25 ml. spoon = ¼ teaspoon
2.5 ml. spoon = ½ teaspoon
5 ml. spoon = 1 teaspoon
15 ml. spoon = 1 tablespoon
25 g. = 1 oz.
125 g. = 4 oz.
½ kg. = 1 lb.
25 ml. = 1 fl. oz.
300 ml. = 10 fl. oz.

Al dente literally 'to the teeth', ie slightly firm and crunchy, and is used to describe the ideal texture of cooked pasta. The best way to test if pasta is al dente is to extract a strand from the pot and bite

Bake blind to bake without any filling

Beurre manié literally kneaded butter: twice as much flour as butter blended together to form a paste; used to thicken soups, stews, etc.

Blanch plunging vegetables or fruit into boiling water to precook slightly, often to make it easier to skin

Bouquet garni literally bunch of herbs: a sprig of parsley, spray of thyme and a bay leaf tied together

Dégorge method of de-liquefying some vegetables, such as aubergines, courgettes and sometimes cucumbers; sprinkle the vegetables with salt, then leave for 15 minutes to 1 hour. Rinse in cold running water and dry

Flameproof a utensil which can be used on top of the stove as well as in the oven

Fold in used to incorporate a light airy mixture, such as beaten egg whites, into a heavier one, by cutting and folding gently with the side of a metal spoon

Knead pummelling dough by punching it with your hands or knuckles, to distribute the ingredients and incorporate air

Marinate soaking an ingredient, usually meat, in liquid to tenderize; the soaking mixture is called a marinade

Parboil partially cooking vegetables or fruit, before cooking them with other ingredients, in rapidly boiling water for 2 to 5 minutes

Sauté frying quickly in little fat over fairly high heat

Seasoned flour plain flour seasoned with salt and pepper

Sift passing flour, baking powder, some sugars, etc., through a sieve or strainer to remove any lumps and incorporate air

Simmer cooking below boiling point

Stir-fry a method of Chinese cooking involving frying ingredients over moderate to fairly high heat, tossing and turning them constantly to cook evenly

First published 1976 by Octopus Books Limited,
59 Grosvenor Street, London W1
Reprinted 1982

ISBN 0 7064 0531 5

Drawings by Mary Tomlin

© 1976 Octopus Books Limited

Printed in Czechoslovakia

50337/12

Contents

Soups & Starters

Oxtail Soup

1 oxtail, skinned and cut into
   pieces
salt and pepper
50 ml./2 fl. oz. oil
2 onions, sliced
2 carrots, sliced
2 celery stalks, sliced
2 turnips, chopped
2 l./3½ pints water
1 × 400 g./14 oz. can
   tomatoes
2.5 ml./½ teaspoon dried basil
30 ml./2 tablespoons flour
50 ml./2 fl. oz. sherry

Rub the oxtail with the salt and pepper. Heat the oil in a saucepan. Add the oxtail and brown on all sides. Transfer to a plate. Add the onions, carrots, celery and turnips to the pan and fry for 10 minutes. Return the oxtail to the pan, add the water and bring to the boil. Cover and simmer for 4 hours or until the meat is falling off the bone.

Add the tomatoes with the can juice, basil and salt and pepper to taste. Mix the flour with the sherry to form a smooth paste and stir it into the soup. Bring to the boil, stirring constantly, then simmer for a further 10 minutes. Cool, then chill for 8 hours or overnight. Remove any fat from the surface of the soup, then pour it into a saucepan and bring slowly to the boil. Simmer for a further 5 minutes or until it is completely reheated.

Serves 6

Italian Fish Soup

75 ml./3 fl. oz. cooking oil
1 large onion, thinly sliced
1 kg./2 lb. tomatoes, skinned
   and chopped
30 ml./2 tablespoons
   chopped fresh parsley
1 garlic clove, crushed
1 kg./2 lb. mixed white fish
   fillets, chopped
600 ml./1 pint fish stock*
salt and pepper

Heat the oil in a saucepan. When it is hot, add the onion and fry for 5 minutes. Add the tomatoes, parsley and garlic, cover and simmer for 15 minutes. Add the fish pieces and stock, re-cover and bring to the boil. Simmer for 10 to 15 minutes, or until the fish flakes easily. Season to taste.

Serves 6

Cock-a-Leekie

1 × 2 kg./4 lb. chicken
2¼ l./4 pints water
1 kg./2 lb. leeks, chopped
50 g./2 oz. pearl barley,
washed
salt and pepper

Put the chicken, water and three of the leeks in a large saucepan. Cover and bring to the boil, then simmer gently for 1 hour or until the chicken is tender. Remove the chicken from the pan and cool. Skim off the scum from the top of the soup and add the remaining leeks, barley and salt and pepper to taste. Cover and simmer for 30 minutes.

Remove the meat from the chicken and chop it into small pieces. Add the meat to the soup and simmer for a further 5 minutes.

Serves 8

Creamed Kidney Soup

50 g./2 oz. butter
1 onion, finely chopped
4 lambs' kidneys, chopped
400 ml./15 fl. oz. beef stock
25 g./1 oz. flour
150 ml./5 fl. oz. milk
salt and pepper
150 ml./5 fl. oz. single cream
30 ml./2 tablespoons sherry
chopped parsley to garnish

Melt the butter in a saucepan. Add the onion and kidneys and fry until the kidneys are evenly browned. Stir in the stock, cover and simmer for 15 minutes. Blend the flour with the milk and stir into the kidney mixture with salt and pepper to taste. Simmer for 2 to 3 minutes, stirring constantly, or until the soup thickens. Stir in the cream and sherry and heat gently for 2 minutes. Sprinkle over the parsley.

Serves 4

Carrot Soup

675 g./1½ lb. carrots, chopped
900 ml./1½ pints chicken
stock
30 ml./2 tablespoons butter
30 ml./2 tablespoons flour
salt and pepper
10 ml./2 teaspoons tomato
purée
175 ml./6 fl. oz. single cream
15 ml./1 tablespoon chopped
parsley

Put the carrots and stock in a saucepan and bring to the boil. Simmer for 20 minutes or until the carrots are soft. Strain the soup, reserving the stock, and rub the carrots through the strainer to form a purée.

Melt the butter in the saucepan. Stir in the flour to form a smooth paste and gradually stir in the reserved stock. Add the puréed carrots and season to taste. Bring to the boil, add the tomato purée and cream and stir well. Garnish with the parsley.

Serves 4

Cauliflower Soup

50 g./2 oz. butter
1 large onion, sliced
1 garlic clove, crushed
1 cauliflower, broken into
    flowerets
900 ml./1½ pints chicken
    stock
salt and pepper
1.25 ml./¼ teaspoon grated
    nutmeg
50 ml./2 fl. oz. single cream

Melt the butter in a saucepan. Add the onion and garlic and fry for 5 minutes. Add the cauliflower and stock and bring to the boil. Season with salt and pepper to taste and stir in the nutmeg. Cover and simmer for 1 hour. Rub through a strainer or purée in an electric blender. Return to the pan, reheat and stir in the cream.

Serves 6

Mushroom Soup

50 g./2 oz. butter
2 spring onions, finely
    chopped
225 g./8 oz. mushrooms,
    sliced
300 ml./10 fl. oz. chicken
    stock
300 ml./10 fl oz. milk
15 ml./1 tablespoon flour
salt and pepper
150 ml./5 fl. oz. single cream

Melt three-quarters of the butter in a saucepan. Add the spring onions and mushrooms and fry for 3 minutes. Pour in the stock and milk, bring to the boil and simmer, covered, for 20 minutes. Rub through a strainer or purée in an electric blender.

    Melt the remaining butter in the rinsed-out pan. Stir in the flour to form a smooth paste. Gradually stir in the puréed soup and bring to the boil. Season to taste and stir in the cream.

Serves 4

Spinach Soup

25 g./1 oz. butter
1 onion, chopped
675 g./1½ lb. spinach,
    chopped
1¼ l./2 pints chicken stock
1 potato, chopped
2.5 ml./½ teaspoon grated
    nutmeg
30 ml./2 tablespoons lemon
    juice
salt and pepper
75 ml./3 fl. oz. single cream
3 bacon slices, cooked and
    chopped

Melt the butter in a saucepan. Add the onion and fry for 5 minutes. Add the spinach and fry for 3 minutes. Pour in the stock and add the potato, nutmeg, lemon juice and salt and pepper to taste. Bring to the boil and simmer for 20 to 25 minutes or until the potato is soft. Purée in an electric blender, return to the pan and reheat. Stir in the cream and garnish with the chopped bacon.

Serves 6

Vegetable Soup

50 ml./2 fl. oz. oil
2 onions, chopped
3 carrots, chopped
1 swede, chopped
2 potatoes, chopped
3 celery stalks, chopped
1 × 200 g./7 oz. can
   tomatoes, drained
125 g./4 oz. dried butter
   beans, soaked overnight
   and drained
1 bay leaf
salt and pepper
2 l./3 pints beef stock
125 g./4 oz. peas

Heat the oil in a saucepan. Add the onions, carrots, swede, potatoes and celery and fry for 10 minutes. Add the tomatoes, beans and bay leaf and salt and pepper to taste and pour in the stock. Bring to the boil, then simmer for 20 minutes.

Strain the soup and pour the liquid back into the pan along with about half of the vegetables in the strainer. Discard the bay leaf and rub the rest of the vegetables through the strainer to form a purée. Add the puréed vegetables and the peas to the soup and bring to the boil. Simmer for 5 to 10 minutes, or until the peas are tender.

Serves 8

Broad Bean Soup

15 ml./1 tablespoon oil
2 bacon slices, chopped
1 onion, chopped
900 ml./1½ pints chicken
   stock
2 savory sprigs
½ kg./1 lb. shelled broad
   beans, blanched and
   skinned
salt and pepper
5 ml./1 teaspoon arrowroot or
   cornflour
150 ml./5 fl. oz. milk
2.5 ml./½ teaspoon lemon
   juice

Heat the oil in a saucepan. Add the bacon and onion and fry for 5 minutes. Stir in the stock and savory and bring to the boil. Add the beans and simmer for 15 to 20 minutes, or until they are tender. Rub through a strainer or purée in an electric blender. Return to the pan, season to taste and bring to the boil. Simmer for 10 minutes.

Meanwhile, mix the arrowroot or cornflour and milk together and stir into the soup. Bring to the boil and simmer for 2 to 3 minutes, stirring constantly, or until the soup has thickened. Stir in the lemon juice.

Serves 6

Lentil Soup

225 g./8 oz. lentils
1¾ l./2 pints water
45 ml./3 tablespoons cooking
  oil
175 g./6 oz. leeks, chopped
75 g./3 oz. onion, chopped
1 carrot, chopped
1 green pepper, pith and
  seeds removed and
  chopped
1 large tomato, skinned and
  chopped
40 g./1½ oz. butter
45 ml./3 tablespoons flour
3 l./4 pints vegetable or
  chicken stock
10 ml./2 teaspoons salt
10 ml./2 teaspoons vinegar

Put the lentils and water into a saucepan and bring to the boil. Simmer, covered, for 1 hour. Meanwhile, heat the oil in a frying-pan. Add the leeks, onion, carrot, pepper and tomato and fry for 5 minutes. Add the fried vegetables to the lentils. Melt the butter in the same frying-pan and stir in the flour to form a smooth paste. Gradually stir in the stock, salt and vinegar and bring to the boil, stirring constantly until the liquid thickens. Pour the stock mixture into the soup and simmer for 30 minutes, stirring occasionally.

Serves 6

Onion and Pepper Soup

50 g./2 oz. butter
2 large onions, cut into thin
  strips
2 garlic cloves, crushed
1 large green pepper, pith
  and seeds removed and
  cut into thin strips
1 large red pepper, pith and
  seeds removed and cut
  into thin strips
900 ml./1½ pints beef stock
2 large tomatoes, skinned
  and chopped
125 g./4 oz. mushrooms,
  sliced
salt and pepper
50 g./2 oz. cheese, grated

Melt the butter in a large saucepan. Add the onions and garlic and fry for 5 minutes. Add the peppers and fry for 2 minutes. Pour in the stock and bring to the boil. Add the tomatoes and mushrooms and continue cooking for 10 to 15 minutes or until all the vegetables are soft. Season to taste with salt and pepper. Stir in the cheese.

Serves 4-6

Avocado Soup

900 ml./1½ pints chicken
   stock
1 small onion, finely
   chopped
2 avocados, halved
15 ml./1 tablespoon butter,
   softened
10 ml./2 teaspoons lemon
   juice
salt and pepper

Simmer the stock and onion in a covered saucepan for 30 minutes. Meanwhile, rub the avocados through a strainer and mix with the butter and lemon juice. Remove the stock from the heat, blend in the avocado mixture and season to taste with salt and pepper.

Serves 4

Leek and Potato Soup

50 g./2 oz. butter
½ kg./1 lb. leeks, sliced
2 large potatoes, diced
900 ml./1½ pints chicken
   stock
225 g./8 oz. peas
1 bouquet garni
1 mint sprig
salt and pepper
50 ml./2 fl. oz. single cream
pinch of paprika

Melt the butter in a saucepan. Add the leeks and potatoes and fry for 5 minutes. Pour in the stock and bring to the boil. Simmer for 15 minutes. Add the peas, bouquet garni, mint and salt and pepper to taste and simmer for a further 30 minutes. Remove the bouquet garni and rub through a strainer or purée in an electric blender. Return to the pan, stir in the cream and reheat gently. Sprinkle with the paprika.

Serves 4-6

Lettuce Soup

50 g./2 oz. butter
1 onion, finely chopped
1 lettuce, chopped
900 ml./1½ pints chicken
   stock
15 ml./1 tablespoon lemon
   juice
salt and pepper
1.25 ml./¼ teaspoon grated
   nutmeg
75 ml./3 fl. oz. single cream
chopped parsley to garnish

Melt the butter in a saucepan. Add the onion and fry for 5 minutes. Add the lettuce and fry for 2 minutes, then stir in the stock, lemon juice, salt and pepper to taste and nutmeg. Bring to the boil, cover and simmer for 10 minutes. Rub through a strainer or purée in an electric blender. Return to the saucepan, stir in the cream and reheat gently. Sprinkle over the parsley.

Serves 4

Bortsch

15 ml./1 tablespoon cooking
  oil
1 onion, thinly sliced
225 g./8 oz. stewing beef,
  cubed
2 l./3 pints cold water
10 ml./2 teaspoons salt
2.5 ml./½ teaspoon pepper
1 bay leaf
5 ml./1 teaspoon dried thyme
1 garlic clove, crushed
1 carrot, thinly sliced
½ turnip, thinly sliced
¼ cabbage, finely shredded
2 tomatoes, skinned and
  chopped
2 cooked beetroot, peeled
  and grated
300 ml./10 fl. oz. sour cream

Heat the oil in a large saucepan. Add the onion and fry for 7 minutes. Add the meat and brown on all sides. Stir in the water, salt, pepper, bay leaf, thyme and garlic. Bring to the boil, cover and simmer gently for 10 minutes. Add the carrot, turnip and cabbage, return to the boil and simmer for 1 hour. Add the tomatoes and simmer for a further 30 minutes.

Stir in the beetroot 5 minutes before serving, topped with sour cream

Serves 8

Dutch Pea Soup

½ kg./1 lb. dried split peas,
  soaked overnight and
  drained
3½ l./6 pints water
1 knuckle unsalted bacon,
  soaked overnight and
  drained
1 pig's trotter, soaked
  overnight and drained
50 g./2 oz. butter
2 onions, chopped
2 leeks, thinly sliced
2 celery stalks, sliced
salt and pepper
4 frankfurters, sliced

Put the peas and water in a saucepan and bring to the boil. Cover and simmer for 2 hours. Add the bacon and pig's trotter and simmer for a further 2 hours. Cool.

Meanwhile, melt the butter in a frying-pan. Add the vegetables and fry for 5 minutes. Remove the bacon and trotter from the soup. Rub the soup through a strainer or purée in an electric blender. Return to the pan, add the fried vegetables and simmer, covered, for 1 hour.

Remove the meat from the bacon, cut into small pieces and add to the soup. Discard the trotter. Simmer for 5 minutes to reheat the bacon, season to taste with the salt and pepper and dilute with water if necessary. Garnish with the frankfurters.

Serves 8

Turnip Soup

50 g./2 oz. butter
3 turnips, chopped
1 large onion, chopped
1 small potato, chopped
1 l./1¾ pints chicken stock
salt and pepper
1 bay leaf
2.5 ml./½ teaspoon grated
    nutmeg
150 ml./5 fl. oz. single cream
chopped parsley to garnish

Melt the butter in a saucepan. Add the turnips, onion and potato and fry for 5 minutes. Stir in the stock, salt and pepper to taste, bay leaf and nutmeg and bring to the boil. Simmer for 20 minutes or until the vegetables are tender. Remove the bay leaf. Rub the soup through a strainer or purée in an electric blender. Return to the saucepan and reheat. Stir in the cream and heat gently. Garnish with the chopped parsley.

Serves 4

Minestrone

45 ml./3 tablespoons cooking
    oil
2 onions, thinly sliced
2 garlic cloves, crushed
3 bacon slices, chopped
4 tomatoes, skinned and
    chopped
125 g./4 oz. haricot beans,
    soaked overnight and
    drained
2 l./3 pints water
2.5 ml./½ teaspoon dried
    marjoram
2.5 ml./½ teaspoon dried
    thyme
2 carrots, diced
2 potatoes, diced
1 turnip, diced
2 celery stalks, chopped
½ small cabbage, shredded
50 g./2 oz. small pasta such
    as macaroni
15 ml./1 tablespoon chopped
    fresh parsley
salt and pepper
45 ml./3 tablespoons grated
    Parmesan cheese

Heat the oil in a large saucepan. Add the onions, garlic and bacon and fry for 5 minutes. Add the tomatoes, beans, water, marjoram and thyme. Cover and simmer for about 2 hours.

Add the carrots and continue cooking for 10 minutes, then add the potatoes and turnip. Cook for 3 minutes, then add the celery, cabbage and pasta. Cook for 10 to 15 minutes or until the pasta and vegetables are tender. Stir in the parsley, salt and pepper to taste and cheese.

Serves 6

Watercress Soup

225 g./8 oz. potatoes,
  chopped
1 l./1¾ pints chicken stock
salt and pepper
2.5 ml./½ teaspoon grated
  nutmeg
2 bunches of watercress,
  chopped
150 ml./5 fl. oz. single cream

Put the potatoes, stock, salt and pepper to taste into a saucepan and bring to the boil. Cook for 20 minutes or until the potatoes are tender. Reserve about 30 ml./2 tablespoons of the watercress and add the rest to the saucepan. Cook for a further 5 minutes. Rub the soup through a strainer or purée in an electric blender. Return to the saucepan, stir in the cream and reheat gently. Serve hot or cold, garnished with the reserved watercress.

Serves 4

Courgette Soup

50 g./2 oz. butter
1 onion, finely chopped
¼ kg./1 lb. courgettes, grated
1 potato, grated
900 ml./1½ pints chicken
  stock
1.25 ml./¼ teaspoon grated
  nutmeg
50 g./2 oz. Parmesan cheese,
  grated

Melt the butter in a saucepan. Add the onion, courgettes and potato and fry for 5 minutes. Stir in the stock and nutmeg and bring to the boil. Simmer for 15 to 20 minutes or until the vegetables are soft. Stir in the cheese and cook for 1 to 2 minutes or until it has melted.

Serves 4

Bread and Cheese Soup

12 small slices of French
  bread, fried on both sides
12 slices of cheese
2 l./3 pints beef stock

Lay the bread slices on the bottom of an ovenproof soup tureen. Place one slice of cheese on each piece of bread.

Bring the stock to the boil and pour it over the bread and cheese. Put the tureen in the oven preheated to moderate (180°C/350°F or Gas Mark 4) and cook for 10 minutes or until the cheese has melted.

Serves 6

Jerusalem Artichoke Soup

50 g./2 oz. butter
1 kg./2 lb. Jerusalem
  artichokes, chopped
1 large onion, chopped
2 celery stalks, chopped
2 bacon slices, chopped
600 ml./1 pint chicken stock
600 ml./1 pint milk
salt and pepper
pinch of dried mixed herbs
60 ml./4 tablespoons single
  cream (optional)
15 ml./1 tablespoon chopped
  parsley

Melt the butter in a saucepan. Add the artichokes, onion, celery and bacon and fry for 8 minutes. Stir in the stock, milk, seasoning and herbs. Cover and simmer gently for about 30 minutes or until the artichokes are tender. Rub through a strainer or purée in an electric blender. Reheat, then stir in the cream, if used. Garnish with the parsley.

Serves 6

Egg and Lemon Soup

2 l./3 pints chicken stock
75 g./3 oz. rice
4 eggs, well beaten
juice of two lemons
salt and pepper

Put the stock in a saucepan and bring to the boil. Add the rice and simmer for 15 minutes, or until the rice is tender.

    Meanwhile, mix together the eggs and lemon juice. Stir in a few spoonfuls of stock. Stir this mixture into the remaining stock. Cook gently for 3 minutes. Season to taste with salt and pepper.

Serves 6

Cold Tomato Soup

1 kg./2 lb. tomatoes, skinned
  and seeded
1 small onion, chopped
1 bay leaf
6 peppercorns
1 strip lemon rind
1¼ l./2 pints chicken stock
15 ml./1 tablespoon
  arrowroot or cornflour
45 ml./3 tablespoons water
salt and pepper
125 ml./4 fl. oz. orange juice
125 ml./4 fl. oz. single cream
grated orange rind to garnish

Put the tomatoes, onion, bay leaf, peppercorns, lemon rind and stock in a saucepan. Cover and bring to the boil. Simmer for 1 hour. Cool and rub through a strainer or purée in an electric blender. Mix the arrowroot or cornflour and water together. Stir into the soup and bring to the boil. Simmer until the soup thickens. Season to taste with salt and pepper and stir in the orange juice. Cool, then chill thoroughly. Stir in the cream and sprinkle over the orange rind.

Serves 6

Chilled Asparagus and Almond Soup

1 × 450 g./1 lb. can
  asparagus spears, drained
1¼ l./2 pints chicken stock
125 g./4 oz. ground almonds
salt and pepper

Cut off and reserve some of the asparagus tips. Blend the remaining asparagus and half of the stock to a purée in an electric blender. Put the purée, the remaining stock, almonds, salt and pepper to taste in a saucepan. Cover, bring to the boil and simmer for 1 minute. Strain and chill.

Serve in a chilled serving bowl and garnish with the reserved asparagus tips.

Serves 6

Chilled Summer Soup

50 g./2 oz. butter
1 lettuce, shredded
1 bunch of watercress,
  chopped
1 bunch of spring onions,
  chopped
900 ml./1½ pints chicken
  stock
40 g./1½ oz. flour
salt and pepper
300 ml./10 fl. oz. single
  cream
30 ml./2 tablespoons
  chopped fresh parsley

Melt the butter in a saucepan. Add the lettuce, watercress and spring onions and fry for 8 minutes. Stir in all but 45 ml./3 tablespoons of the stock and simmer for a further 10 minutes, or until the vegetables are tender. Blend the flour to a paste with the remaining stock and stir into the soup. Add salt and pepper to taste and continue cooking until the soup has thickened. Rub through a strainer or purée in an electric blender. Cool, then stir in the cream. Sprinkle over the parsley.

Serves 4-6

Iced Cucumber Soup

1 large cucumber, peeled,
  seeded and chopped
225 ml./8 fl. oz. plain yogurt
10 ml./2 teaspoons white
  wine vinegar
5 ml./1 teaspoon olive oil
salt and cayenne pepper
5 ice cubes
15 ml./1 tablespoon chopped
  fresh mint

Blend the cucumber and yogurt together in an electric blender until smooth. Stir in the vinegar and oil, and season to taste with the salt and cayenne. Chill then add the ice cubes and garnish with the chopped mint.

Serves 4

16

Vichyssoise

125 g./4 oz. butter
4 leeks, very thinly sliced
1 large onion, finely chopped
1¼ l./2 pints chicken stock
2 medium potatoes, sliced
15 ml./1 tablespoon chopped
   fresh parsley
1 celery stalk, chopped
salt and pepper
150 ml./5 fl. oz. single
   cream, chilled
chopped chives to garnish

Melt the butter in a large saucepan. Add the leeks and onion and simmer, covered, for 10 minutes, or until the vegetables are soft. Stir in the stock, potatoes, parsley, celery and salt and pepper to taste. Cover and simmer for 20 to 30 minutes or until the potatoes are tender. Cool, then rub through a strainer or purée in an electric blender. Chill. Just before serving, stir in the chilled cream and sprinkle over the chives.

Serves 8

Cold Pumpkin Soup

900 ml./1½ pints beef stock
1 × 200 g./7 oz. can
   tomatoes, drained
1 onion, chopped
1 bay leaf
225 g./8 oz. cooked
   pumpkin, puréed
salt and pepper
300 ml./10 fl. oz. milk
chopped chives to garnish

Put the stock, tomatoes, onion and bay leaf in a saucepan. Cover and simmer for 15 minutes. Remove the bay leaf and cool. Rub the soup through a strainer or purée in an electric blender. Return to the pan and add the pumpkin. Season to taste with salt and pepper and simmer for 2 minutes. Stir in the milk. Chill, then garnish with the chives.

Serves 6

Gazpacho

350 g./12 oz. tomatoes,
   skinned
1 small cucumber, skinned
1 small onion
½ green pepper
½ red pepper
2 celery stalks
1 garlic clove, peeled
300 ml./10 fl. oz. tomato
   juice
50 ml./2 fl. oz. cooking oil
25 ml./1 fl. oz. vinegar
salt and pepper
3-4 drops Tabasco sauce

Roughly chop all the vegetables and reserve about one quarter for garnish. Put the remaining vegetables with the garlic in an electric blender. Add the tomato juice, oil, vinegar, salt and pepper to taste and Tabasco sauce and blend to a purée. Chill.

Blend the reserved vegetables for a few seconds only and add to the soup. Serve chilled.

Serves 4

Cod Chowder

50 g./2 oz. butter
1 onion, finely chopped
1¼ l./2 pints milk
½ kg./1 lb. potatoes, diced
1 kg./2 lb. cod, skinned,
   boned and diced
2.5 ml./½ teaspoon dried
   thyme
salt and pepper
225 ml./8 fl. oz. double
   cream

Melt the butter in a saucepan. Add the onion and fry for 5 minutes. Stir in the milk and potatoes and bring to the boil. Simmer for 5 minutes. Add the cod and thyme and cook for a further 15 to 20 minutes or until the potatoes and fish are tender. Season to taste with salt and pepper and stir in the cream.

Serves 4

Corn Chowder

2 potatoes, chopped
1 × 450 g./1 lb. can
   sweetcorn, drained
300 ml./10 fl. oz. chicken
   stock
300 ml./10 fl. oz. milk
25 g./1 oz. butter
1 onion, finely chopped
30 ml./2 tablespoons flour
salt and pepper
150 ml./5 fl. oz. double
   cream

Put the potatoes, sweetcorn, stock and milk into a saucepan and bring to the boil. Simmer for 10 minutes.

Meanwhile, melt the butter in a frying-pan. Add the onion and fry for 5 minutes. Stir in the flour to form a smooth paste. Gradually add a few spoonfuls of the hot stock. When the mixture is smooth add it to the soup. Bring to the boil and simmer for a further 10 minutes. Stir in salt and pepper to taste and the cream.

Serves 4

Cheese and Anchovy Sandwiches

4 slices Mozzarella cheese
4 slices white bread, crusts
   removed and halved
   diagonally
8 anchovy fillets
pepper
125 ml./4 fl. oz. cooking oil

Place a slice of cheese on four of the pieces of bread. Lay two anchovy fillets over each piece of cheese and sprinkle with pepper to taste. Cover with the remaining pieces of bread to form sandwiches. Heat the oil in a frying-pan. Add the sandwiches and fry for 3 to 5 minutes or until they are brown on one side and the cheese has melted. Turn over and fry until they are brown on the other side.

Serves 4

Shellfish Chowder

½ kg./1 lb. prawns
600 ml./1 pint water
125 g./4 oz. salt pork, diced
1 onion, finely chopped
½ kg./1 lb. new potatoes
300 ml./10 fl. oz. single
   cream

Shell the prawns and put the shells in a saucepan with the water. Cover, bring to the boil and simmer for 15 minutes. Strain the cooking liquid and make it up to 600 ml./1 pint with water. Dice the prawns.

Fry the salt pork for 5 minutes or until it has rendered most of its fat. Transfer to a plate. Add the onion to the pan and fry for 5 minutes. Add the potatoes and fry for 2 minutes. Stir in the reserved cooking liquid and return the salt pork to the pan. Cover and simmer for 15 to 20 minutes, or until the potatoes are tender.

Stir in the prawns and cream and heat gently for 3 to 5 minutes or until they are heated through.

Serves 6

Clam Chowder

75 g./3 oz. salt pork, diced
2 onions, finely chopped
175 ml./6 fl. oz. water
225 ml./8 fl. oz. milk
4 medium potatoes, chopped
1 × 450 g./1 lb. can clams,
   chopped
1.25 ml./¼ teaspoon cayenne
   pepper
salt and pepper
150 ml./5 fl. oz. double
   cream

Fry the salt pork in a saucepan for 5 minutes, or until it has rendered most of its fat. Add the onions and fry for 5 minutes. Pour in the water and milk, add the potatoes and bring to the boil. Simmer for 10 to 15 minutes or until the potatoes are tender. Add the clams and can juice, cayenne and salt and pepper to taste. Bring to the boil, then stir in the cream.

Serves 4

Glazed Radishes

25 g./1 oz. butter
½ kg./1 lb. radishes, peeled
   and halved
10 ml./2 teaspoons sugar
300 ml./10 fl. oz. water
2.5 ml./½ teaspoon salt
chopped fresh parsley to
   garnish

Melt the butter in a frying-pan. Add the radishes, sprinkle over the sugar and fry for 3 minutes. Stir in the water and salt, and cook for a further 10 minutes, or until most of the water has evaporated and the radishes are tender. Garnish with the chopped parsley.

Serves 4

Palm Heart Cocktail

4 lettuce leaves, shredded
1 × 400 g./14 oz. can palm
  hearts, drained and sliced
15 ml./1 tablespoon lemon
  juice
paprika to garnish
Dressing
150 ml./5 fl. oz.
  mayonnaise*
pinch of curry powder
30 ml./2 tablespoons double
  cream, lightly whipped
5 ml./1 teaspoon
  Worcestershire sauce
3-4 drops Tabasco sauce
salt and pepper

Put an equal quantity of shredded lettuce into each of four serving glasses. Arrange the palm heart slices on top and sprinkle over the lemon juice. Combine all the dressing ingredients together and season to taste with the salt and pepper. Spoon over the palm hearts. Sprinkle a little paprika over the top.

Serves 4

Chicken Livers on Toast

30 ml./2 tablespoons cooking
  oil
30 ml./2 tablespoons finely
  chopped onion
2 fresh sage leaves
225 g./8 oz. chicken livers,
  finely chopped
pepper
4 slices lightly toasted bread

Heat the oil in a frying-pan. Add the onion and sage leaves and fry for 5 minutes. Remove the sage. Add the livers and pepper to taste and simmer for 10 to 15 minutes or until the livers are cooked through. Spread the mixture over the toast.

Serves 4

Mushrooms in Marinade

150 ml./5 fl. oz. cooking oil
juice of 2 lemons
90 ml./6 tablespoons water
2 garlic cloves, crushed
6 peppercorns
1 bay leaf
2.5 ml./½ teaspoon salt
½ kg./1 lb. mushrooms

Put the oil, lemon juice, water, garlic, peppercorns, bay leaf and salt into a saucepan and bring slowly to the boil. Strain the liquid, return to the pan and bring to the boil again. Add the mushrooms and simmer for 5 minutes. Remove the pan from the heat and cool the mushrooms in the marinade. Drain before serving.

Serves 4

Spinach Stuffed Eggs

4 hard-boiled eggs, halved
50 g./2 oz. ricotta or cream
  cheese
30 ml./2 tablespoons grated
  Parmesan cheese
30 ml./2 tablespoons cooked
  spinach, finely chopped
salt and pepper
pinch of grated nutmeg
1.25 ml./¼ teaspoon cayenne
  pepper

Remove the yolks from the eggs and put in a small mixing bowl. Add the cheeses and spinach. Beat the mixture until it is smooth. Season to taste with salt, pepper and nutmeg and then pile back into the egg whites. Sprinkle over the cayenne.

Serves 4

Tuna Stuffed Tomatoes

4 large firm tomatoes,
  halved and seeded
2 hard-boiled eggs, finely
  chopped
1 × 200 g./7 oz. can tuna,
  drained and flaked
10 ml./2 teaspoons capers
5 ml./1 teaspoon chopped
  fresh parsley
45 ml./3 tablespoons
  mayonnaise*
pepper
4 stuffed olives, halved

Turn the tomato shells upside down to drain. Meanwhile, place all the remaining ingredients, except the olives, in a small bowl and mix well. Pile the mixture into the tomato shells and garnish with the olives.

Serves 4

Prawn Cocktail

350 g./12 oz. prawns, shelled
lemon wedges and parsley
  sprigs to garnish
Sauce
125 ml./4 fl. oz. tomato
  ketchup
75 ml./3 fl. oz. lemon juice
3-4 drops Tabasco sauce
15 ml./1 tablespoon
  horseradish sauce
50 ml./2 fl. oz. single cream
salt and pepper

Chop the prawns if they are very large and put an equal quantity into each of six glasses. Mix all the sauce ingredients together and pour over the prawns. Serve chilled, garnished with the lemon wedges and parsley.

Serves 6

Smoked Trout with Devilled Sauce

8 lettuce leaves
2 smoked trout, heads
   removed and split down
   the centre
2 hard-boiled eggs, sliced
¼ cucumber, thinly sliced
Sauce
30 ml./2 tablespoons single
   cream
15 ml./1 tablespoon
   horseradish sauce
5 ml./1 teaspoon lemon juice
pinch of curry powder
dash of Tabasco sauce

Arrange the lettuce leaves on four small serving plates and place a trout half on each plate. In a small bowl, mix together all the sauce ingredients. Spread the sauce over the trout and garnish with egg and cucumber slices.

Note: Smoked mackerel can be served in the same way.

Serves 4

Salmon Eggs

8 lettuce leaves
4 hard-boiled eggs, halved
15 g./½ oz. butter, softened
2.5 ml./½ teaspoon lemon
   juice
salt and pepper
50 g./2 oz. smoked salmon,
   chopped
4 thin slices lemon, twisted

Arrange the lettuce leaves on four small serving plates. Remove the yolks from the eggs and mash them in a small bowl with the butter, lemon juice, salt and pepper to taste and salmon. Pile back into the egg whites, top with the lemon slices and serve on the lettuce leaves.

Note: Fresh or canned salmon can be used instead.

Serves 4

Savoury Melon with Ham

8 lettuce leaves
150 ml./5 fl. oz. natural
   yogurt
10 ml./2 teaspoons
   horseradish sauce
5 ml./1 teaspoon mustard
4 slices lean ham
1 small melon, peeled,
   seeded and cut into thin
   strips

Arrange the lettuce leaves on four small serving plates. In a small mixing bowl, mix together the yogurt, horseradish and mustard. Spread over one side of each ham slice and roll up. Arrange the ham and melon on the lettuce.

Serves 4

Avocado with Crab Mousse

125 g./4 oz. fresh or canned
    crabmeat, flaked
30 ml./2 tablespoons
    mayonnaise*
15 ml./1 tablespoon lemon
    juice
30 ml./2 tablespoons single
    cream
1.25 ml./¼ teaspoon cayenne
    pepper
2.5 ml./½ teaspoon salt
2 avocados
1 lemon, cut into 4 wedges

Put the crabmeat, mayonnaise, lemon juice, cream and seasoning in a small mixing bowl and beat thoroughly. Halve the avocados, remove the stones and spoon the mixture into the centres. Garnish with the lemon wedges.

Serves 4

Cucumber and Pineapple Hors D'Oeuvre

1 small pineapple, peeled,
    cored and cubed
1 medium cucumber, peeled
    and cubed
50 g./2 oz. blanched
    almonds, toasted
Dressing
125 ml./4 fl. oz. single cream
50 ml./2 fl. oz. lemon juice
salt and pepper

Put the pineapple and cucumber cubes in a serving bowl with the almonds. Mix the dressing ingredients together and pour over the mixture. Serve chilled.

Note: This hors d'oeuvre may also be served as an accompaniment to curries.

Serves 4

Stuffed Peaches

175 g./6 oz. cream cheese
25 g./1 oz. sultanas, soaked
    in boiling water and
    drained
25 g./1 oz. walnuts, chopped
4 canned peach halves
4 lettuce leaves
watercress sprigs to garnish

Mix the cheese, sultanas and nuts together. Chill for a few minutes to firm. Arrange each of the peach halves on a lettuce leaf, spoon an equal amount of the cheese mixture into the centre and garnish with the watercress.

Serves 4

Pâtés & Savoury Mousses

French Pork Pâté

50 g./2 oz. butter
1 shallot, finely chopped
2 garlic cloves, crushed
25 g./1 oz. flour
150 ml./5 fl. oz. beef stock
10 ml./2 teaspoons freshly
    chopped sage
salt and pepper
pinch of grated nutmeg
½ kg./1 lb. pig's liver, finely
    chopped
225 g./8 oz. lean pork meat,
    finely chopped
225 g./8 oz. belly of pork,
    finely chopped
1 bay leaf
½ kg./1 lb. bacon slices

Melt the butter in a large saucepan. Add the shallot and garlic and toss lightly for a few minutes. Stir in the flour to form a smooth paste. Gradually add the stock, stirring constantly, and bring to the boil. Add the sage, seasoning and nutmeg. Add the meat, and, if you wish each type of meat to be distinct, stir very little. Put the bay leaf on the bottom of the terrine or ovenproof dish, then line the bottom and sides with two-thirds of the bacon. Spoon in the meat mixture and place the remaining bacon on top. Cover with aluminium foil and put on a lid. Put the dish in a roasting pan half filled with boiling water and put the pan into the oven preheated to warm (170°C/325°F or Gas Mark 3). Cook for 1½ hours or until firm. Remove the dish from the water, place a small weight over the foil and cool.

Serves 8-10

24

Thrifty Pâté

675 g./1½ lb. lean belly of
pork, boned and diced
225 g./8 oz. pig's liver,
chopped
125 g./4 oz. bacon slices
125 g./4 oz. onion, chopped
1 garlic clove
salt and pepper
25 g./1 oz. butter, melted

Mince the pork, liver, bacon, onion and garlic together three times. Stir in salt and pepper to taste. Turn into a 1¼ l./2 pint terrine or ovenproof dish and cover with foil and a lid. Put in a roasting pan half-filled with water and put the pan into the oven preheated to cool (150°C/300°F or Gas Mark 2). Cook for 1½ hours or until firm. Remove the lid and place a weight over the foil until the pâté has cooled completely. Pour the melted butter over the pâté and chill.

Serves 6

Speedy Spiced Pâté

225 g./8 oz. liver sausage
125 g./4 oz. cream cheese
30 ml./2 tablespoons
mayonnaise*
45 ml./3 tablespoons cream
5 ml./1 teaspoon
Worcestershire sauce
2.5 ml./½ teaspoon curry
powder
5 ml./1 teaspoon brandy
(optional)
salt and pepper

Mix together the liver sausage, cheese, mayonnaise, cream, Worcestershire sauce, curry powder and brandy, if used. Season to taste. Place in a pâté mould lined with aluminium foil, or in individual pots, cover with clear plastic wrap or aluminium foil and chill. Serve in individual pots or turn out of the mould and serve in slices with hot, crisp toast.

Serves 6-8

Turkey Pâté

125 g./4 oz. butter
225 g./8 oz. cooked turkey,
minced
15 ml./1 tablespoon sherry
2.5 ml./½ teaspoon lemon
juice
2-3 drops Tabasco sauce
pinch of ground cloves
salt and pepper
50 g./2 oz. butter, melted

Cream the butter and mix in the turkey. Add the sherry, lemon juice, Tabasco sauce and cloves and stir well to mix. Season to taste with the salt and pepper. Put into individual pots, smooth the surface and pour over the melted butter. Cover with aluminium foil and chill.
Note: This recipe is equally good with cooked goose instead of turkey.

Serves 4

Rabbit Pâté

½ kg./1 lb. rabbit meat,
   chopped
½ kg./1 lb. belly of pork,
   minced
225 g./8 oz. pig's liver,
   minced
½ kg./1 lb. pork sausagemeat
225 g./8 oz. garlic sausage,
   minced
125 g./4 oz. onion, finely
   chopped
45 ml./3 tablespoons sherry
30 ml./2 tablespoons
   chopped fresh parsley
15 ml./1 tablespoon dried
   sage
salt and pepper
½ kg./1 lb. bacon slices

Mix the rabbit pieces with the pork, liver, sausagemeat, garlic sausage and onion. Stir in the sherry, parsley and sage and season well. Line a large terrine or ovenproof dish with the bacon slices, allowing some of them to hang over the sides of the dish. Turn the meat mixture into the dish and fold the bacon slices over the top. Cover with foil and a lid and put into a roasting pan half-filled with boiling water. Put the pan into the oven preheated to warm (170°C/325°F or Gas Mark 3) and cook for 3 hours or until firm. Remove the lid and place a weight over the foil. Cool.

Serves 16

Smoked Trout Pâté

2 large smoked trout,
   skinned and boned
225 g./8 oz. butter, softened
50 ml./2 fl. oz. double cream
30 ml./2 tablespoons lemon
   juice
salt and pepper
parsley sprigs to garnish

Mash the trout and butter together with a fork, then gradually mix in the cream and lemon juice. Season to taste with the salt and pepper. Chill, then garnish with the parsley sprigs.

Serves 6

Kipper Pâté

30 ml./2 tablespoons white
   wine
125 g./4 oz. raw kipper
   fillets, skinned
pepper
125 g./4 oz. butter, softened

Pour the wine over the kipper fillets and leave to marinate for 8 hours or overnight. Put the kipper fillets in a mortar and mash with a pestle until smooth. Alternatively, purée in an electric blender. Season with pepper to taste and beat in the softened butter. Divide between four individual serving dishes and serve with hot toast.

Serves 4

Chopped Chicken Livers

1 onion, finely chopped
50 g./2 oz. chicken fat
½ kg./1 lb. chicken livers
2 hard-boiled eggs, finely
    chopped
salt and pepper
8 lettuce leaves
1 egg yolk, sieved

Gently fry the onion in the melted chicken fat until soft. Add the chicken livers and fry for 3 minutes. Cool, then mince the livers and onion. Add the eggs and salt and pepper to taste, and mix well.

Place a lettuce leaf on each of eight serving plates and put a portion of pâté on each leaf. Sprinkle over the egg yolk and serve.

Note: Chicken fat may be purchased at most delicatessen stores. This is a traditional Jewish dish which is served as a first course.

Serves 8

Smoked Haddock Pâté

125 g./4 oz. smoked
    haddock, skinned and
    boned
125 g./4 oz. butter
1 shallot, finely chopped
5 ml./1 teaspoon lemon juice
1.25 ml./¼ teaspoon curry
    powder
pepper
chopped parsley to garnish

Mash the haddock and butter together with a fork, then mix in the shallot, lemon juice, curry powder and pepper to taste. Chill, then garnish with the parsley.

Serves 4

Chicken Liver Pâté

175 g./6 oz. butter
2 onions, finely chopped
2 garlic cloves, crushed
½ kg./1 lb. chicken livers,
  chopped
15 ml./1 tablespoon finely
  chopped fresh parsley
1 bay leaf
pinch of thyme
salt and pepper
15 ml./1 tablespoon brandy
  (optional)

Melt 125 g./4 oz. of the butter in a frying-pan. Add the onions and garlic and fry until they are soft. Add the chicken livers and fry for a further 3 minutes. Add the parsley, bay leaf, thyme and salt and pepper to taste. Cook for a further 2 minutes. Remove the bay leaf. Cool and pound the mixture with a wooden spoon or purée in an electric blender.

Melt the remaining butter and add to the mixture together with the brandy, if used. Pack into a pâté mould lined with aluminium foil, cover with plastic wrap or aluminium foil and chill.

Serves 8

Smoked Mackerel Pâté

2 large smoked mackerel,
  skinned and boned
275 g./10 oz. butter, softened
75 g./3 oz. cream cheese
25 ml./1 fl. oz. lemon juice
salt and pepper
watercress sprigs to garnish

Mash the mackerel and butter together with a fork, then mix in the cheese and lemon juice. Season to taste with salt and pepper. Chill, then garnish with the watercress sprigs.

Serves 6

28

Taramasalata

225 g./8 oz. smoked cod's
  roe, skinned
1 garlic clove, crushed
2 slices white bread, crusts
  removed
30 ml./2 tablespoons milk
125 ml./4 fl. oz. olive oil
30 ml./2 tablespoons lemon
  juice
salt and pepper

Mash the roe and garlic in a mortar or bowl with a pestle or fork until smooth. Soak the bread in the milk, then squeeze out as much milk as possible. Add the bread to the roe and continue mashing. Beat in the oil a little at a time. Stir in the lemon juice and season to taste with the salt and pepper. Serve chilled.

Serves 4

Terrine Maison

225 g./8 oz. streaky bacon
  slices
225 g./8 oz. lean veal,
  minced
225 g./8 oz. pork, minced
225 g./8 oz. lamb's liver,
  minced
50 g./2 oz. butter
1 small onion, finely
  chopped
1 garlic clove, crushed
175 g./6 oz. chicken livers
30 ml./2 tablespoons brandy
15 ml./1 tablespoon lemon
  juice
15 ml./1 tablespoon chopped
  fresh herbs
1 egg, beaten
30 ml./2 tablespoons double
  cream (optional)
salt and pepper
1 bay leaf

Line a terrine or straight-sided ovenproof dish with overlapping slices of bacon. Allow some of slices to hang over the sides so you can fold them over the top later.

Mix the veal, pork and lamb's liver together. Melt the butter in a frying-pan. Add the onion and garlic and fry for 5 minutes. Drain and add to the meat. Fry the whole chicken livers for 3 minutes. Drain and set aside. Add the brandy and lemon juice to the pan, stir to loosen sediment and add to the meat with the herbs, egg and cream, if used. Season with salt and pepper to taste. Mix well. Place half the meat mixture in the terrine, press down firmly and smooth the top. Cut the chicken livers into quarters and place in a row down the centre of the meat. Cover with the remaining meat mixture. Smooth the top, cover with the bacon slices and place the bay leaf on top. Cover with foil and then with a tightly fitting lid. Put in a roasting pan half-filled with boiling water and put the pan into the oven preheated to moderate (180°C/350°F or Gas Mark 4). Cook for 2 hours or until firm. Remove the lid and place a weight over the foil until the pâté has cooled completely. Serve at room temperature, in thick slices.

Serves 12

Terrine of Chicken

1 × 1½ kg./3½ lb. roasting
chicken, giblets reserved
425 ml./15 fl. oz. water
1 onion
1 bouquet garni
salt and pepper
225 g./8 oz. veal
350 g./12 oz. bacon slices
225 g./8 oz. pork
sausagemeat
30 ml./2 tablespoons
chopped fresh parsley

Cut all the meat from the chicken. Take great care when removing the breast as this needs to be cut later into neat slices. Put the bones and giblets into a saucepan with the water, whole onion and bouquet garni. Season well. Cover and simmer for about 30 minutes. Remove the lid and boil rapidly until the liquid is reduced to about 60 ml./4 tablespoons of really strong stock. Remove the liver and strain the stock.

Put the cooked chicken liver, all the dark meat, the veal and two bacon slices through a mincer. Season and mix with the sausagemeat and half of the reserved stock. Slice the breast neatly, put in a dish, add the remaining stock and parsley and season lightly.

Line the bottom of a terrine or ovenproof dish with half the remaining bacon slices. Put a thick layer of the minced meat mixture over the bacon, then add some of the sliced chicken breast. Continue filling the dish like this, ending with a layer of the minced meat. Arrange the remaining bacon slices over the top, cover with aluminium foil and a lid. Put the dish in a roasting pan half-filled with boiling water and put the pan into the oven pre-heated to warm (170°C/325°F or Gas Mark 3). Cook for about 1½ hours, or until firm. Remove the lid and place a weight over the foil until the pâté has cooled completely.

Serves 10

Simple Terrine

225 g./8 oz. bacon slices
225 g./8 oz. pork, minced
225 g./8 oz. veal, minced
225 g./8 oz. sausagemeat
225 g./8 oz. lamb's liver,
  minced
1 onion, finely chopped
15 ml./1 tablespoon chopped
  fresh herbs
175 g./6 oz. fresh
  breadcrumbs
1 egg, beaten
salt and pepper
1 bay leaf

Line a terrine, or straight-sided ovenproof dish, with overlapping slices of bacon, reserving a few slices for the top. Mix together the remaining ingredients, except the bay leaf. Fill the terrine or dish with the mixture, press down firmly, and smooth the surface. Cover with the remaining bacon slices and place the bay leaf on top. Cover with a piece of aluminium foil and the lid of the terrine or dish and put in a roasting pan half-filled with boiling water. Put the pan into the oven pre-heated to moderate (180°C/350°F or Gas Mark 4) and cook for 1 to 1½ hours or until firm. Remove the lid and place a weight over the foil until the pâté has cooled completely. Serve at room temperature, cut in thick slices.

Serves 12

Duck Terrine

1 × 3 kg./6 lb. duck, skinned
  and boned
125 ml./4 fl. oz. brandy
225 g./8 oz. veal, minced
½ kg./1 lb. lean pork, minced
2 hard-boiled eggs, finely
  chopped
salt and pepper
2 garlic cloves, crushed
50 g./2 oz. butter
125 g./4 oz. chicken livers,
  finely chopped
350 g./12 oz. unsalted pork
  fat, thinly sliced

Remove and discard the duck fat and cut the meat into thin strips. Pour over half the brandy and leave to marinate for 1 hour. Mix together the veal, pork, eggs, salt and pepper to taste, garlic and the remaining brandy.

Melt the butter in a frying pan. Add the livers and fry for 3 minutes. Add the livers to the veal and pork mixture. Line a large terrine or ovenproof dish with half of the pork fat. Spread one-third of the veal and pork mixture over the bottom. Cover with one-third of the duck meat and spoon over a little of the brandy used for marinating. Lay a thin layer of the remaining pork fat over the duck and make two more layers in the same way. Finish with a layer of pork fat. Cover the terrine with foil and a lid and put in a roasting pan half filled with boiling water. Put the pan into the oven preheated to moderate (180°C/350°F or Gas Mark 4) and cook for 1½ hours or until firm. Remove the lid and place a weight over the foil. Leave until the pâté has cooled completely. Serve in thick wedges.

Serves 10

Egg Mousse

6 hard-boiled eggs, finely
    chopped
15 ml./1 tablespoon finely
    chopped onion
15 ml./1 tablespoon finely
    chopped parsley
2.5 ml./½ teaspoon anchovy
    essence
125 ml./4 fl. oz.
    mayonnaise *
150 ml./5 fl. oz. sour cream
1 × 275 g./10 oz. can
    consommé
10 ml./2 teaspoons gelatine
30 ml./2 tablespoons water
salt and pepper

Mix together the eggs, onion, parsley, anchovy essence, mayonnaise, sour cream and two-thirds of the consommé. Soften the gelatine in the water, then set over a saucepan of gently simmering water until it has dissolved. Stir it into the egg mixture. Season to taste with the salt and pepper. Turn into a serving dish and chill. Chill the remaining consommé. When the consommé is set, chop and use to decorate the mousse. Serve with bread and butter.

Serves 6-8

Salmon Mousse

1 × 225 g./8 oz. can red
    salmon
125 ml./4 fl. oz.
    mayonnaise *
2.5 ml./½ teaspoon anchovy
    essence
150 ml./5 fl. oz. double
    cream, lightly whipped
salt and pepper
10 ml./2 teaspoons gelatine
30 ml./ tablespoons water
cucumber slices and parsley
    sprigs to garnish

Mash the salmon and can juice with the mayonnaise and anchovy essence. Fold in the cream and season to taste. Soften the gelatine in the water, then set over a saucepan of gently simmering water until it has dissolved. Stir it into the salmon mixture. Turn into six small moulds, or into one large dish, and chill until set. Turn out of the moulds by dipping quickly into very hot water, then invert on to a plate. Garnish with the cucumber and parsley.

Serves 6

Prawn, Cheese and Cucumber Mousse

½ cucumber, peeled and
  diced
salt
45 ml./3 tablespoons wine
  vinegar
350 g./12 oz. cream cheese
125 ml./4 fl. oz. double
  cream
175 ml./6 fl. oz.
  mayonnaise*
2.5 ml./½ teaspoon paprika
pepper
30 ml./2 tablespoons
  chopped chives
15 g./½ oz. gelatine
50 ml./2 fl. oz. hot water
225 g./8 oz. shelled prawns

Put the cucumber in a colander and sprinkle with salt and vinegar. Leave for 1 hour. Press to remove any liquid and set aside. Beat the cheese until soft and creamy. Fold in the cream and mayonnaise. Add the paprika, pepper to taste and chives. Dissolve the gelatine in the water and mix into the cheese mixture. Fold in the prawns and cucumber. Pour into a lightly oiled 900 ml./1½ pint mould. Chill for 1 hour or until set.

Serves 8

Blue Cheese Mousse

175 g./6 oz. blue cheese,
  such as Dolcelatte or
  Roquefort
225 g./8 oz. cream cheese
5 ml./1 teaspoon anchovy
  essence
pinch of cayenne pepper
30 ml./2 tablespoons
  chopped spring onions
15 g./½ oz. gelatine
50 ml./2 fl. oz. hot water
175 ml./6 fl. oz.
  mayonnaise*
175 ml./6 fl. oz. double
  cream

Rub the blue cheese through a strainer and mix with the cream cheese, anchovy essence, cayenne and spring onions. Beat well. Dissolve the gelatine in the water and mix into the cheese mixture. Fold in the mayonnaise and cream. Pour into a lightly oiled 900 ml./1½ pint mould. Chill for 1 hour or until set.

Serves 8

Meat-Beef

Beef and Vegetable Casserole

675 g./1½ lb. stewing beef,
  cubed
25 g./1 oz. seasoned flour
50 ml./2 fl. oz. oil
2 onions, sliced
2 carrots, sliced
1 turnip, chopped
2 celery stalks, chopped
600 ml./1 pint beef stock
salt and pepper
125 g./4 oz. peas
2 tomatoes, skinned and
  chopped
chopped parsley to garnish

Coat the beef cubes in the seasoned flour. Heat the oil in a frying-pan. Add the onions and fry for 5 minutes. Transfer to a plate. Add the meat to the pan and fry for 5 to 8 minutes or until evenly browned. Add the carrots, turnip and celery and return the onions to the pan. Cook for 2 minutes. Gradually stir in the stock and seasoning to taste. Bring to the boil, stirring occasionally. Transfer to an ovenproof casserole, cover tightly and put into the oven preheated to warm (170°C/325°F or Gas Mark 3). Cook for 1½ to 1¾ hours, or until the beef is tender. About 20 minutes before the end of the cooking time, add the peas and tomatoes. Garnish with the parsley.

Serves 4

Minced Meat Pie

15 ml./1 tablespoon oil
1 onion, chopped
¼ kg./1 lb. beef, minced
2 tomatoes, skinned and
    chopped
45 ml./3 tablespoons tomato
    purée
30 ml./2 tablespoons
    chopped fresh parsley
salt and pepper
350 g./12 oz. shortcrust or
    rough puff pastry*
1 egg, beaten

Heat the oil in a saucepan. Add the onion and fry for 5 minutes. Add the beef and fry for a further 5 minutes or until it loses its pinkness. Add the tomatoes, tomato purée, parsley and salt and pepper to taste. Cover and simmer for 45 minutes.

Divide the dough in half. Roll out one half to a circle large enough to line a 23 cm./9 in. pie plate. Place the meat filling in the shell. Roll out the remaining dough to a circle large enough to enclose the filling and place it on top of the meat. Trim and dampen the edges and press to seal. Make a slit in the centre of the dough and glaze the top with the egg. Put the pie plate in the oven preheated to hot (220°C/425°F or Gas Mark 7) and bake for 15 minutes. Reduce the oven temperature to moderate (180°C/350°F or Gas Mark 4) and bake for a further 15 to 30 minutes, or until the filling is cooked and the pastry is brown.

Serves 4-6

Steak and Kidney Pie

675 g./1½ lb. stewing steak,
    cubed
225 g./8 oz. ox kidney, cubed
25 g./1 oz. seasoned flour
1 onion, finely chopped
    (optional)
300 ml./10 fl. oz. water
225 g./8 oz. rough puff
    pastry*
1 egg, beaten
300 ml./10 fl. oz. hot beef
    stock

Coat the steak and kidney pieces with the seasoned flour. Put the meat in a 1l./1¾ pint pie dish, and sprinkle over the onion, if used. Place a pie funnel in the centre of the meat and add the water. Roll out the dough to a circle slightly larger than the dish. Cut a 1 cm./½ in. border and press it on to the dampened rim of the pie dish. Brush the strip with cold water. Place the rest of the dough on top and press to seal. Use any scraps for decoration. Brush the pie with the egg. Place on a baking sheet and put into the oven preheated to hot (220°C/425°F or Gas Mark 7). Bake for 30 minutes, then cover loosely with foil, turning it under the pie dish to seal. Reduce the oven temperature to moderate (180°C/350°F or Gas Mark 4) and bake for a further 1½ hours. To serve, cut away a portion of pastry and dilute the thick gravy with some hot, strong beef stock.

Serves 4-6

Beef Meat Loaf

1 thick slice of bread, crusts
    removed
50 ml./2 fl. oz. milk
675 g./1½ lb. lean beef,
    minced
30 ml./2 tablespoons
    Worcestershire sauce
50 g./2 oz. fruit chutney
1 beef stock cube, dissolved
    in 30 ml./2 tablespoons
    boiling water
salt and pepper
1 celery stalk, finely chopped

Soak the bread in the milk for 10 minutes. Mix together with the beef and the remaining ingredients. Place the mixture in a greased 1 kg./2 lb. loaf tin, lined with foil, and smooth the top. Put the tin into the oven preheated to fairly hot (190°C/375°F or Gas Mark 5) and bake for 1 hour. Serve hot or cold. To serve cold, allow the loaf to cool for 1 hour in the tin before turning it out.

Serves 4-6

Steak au Poivre

½ kg./1 lb. rump steak
15 ml./1 tablespoon black
    peppercorns, crushed
75 g./3 oz. butter
15 ml./1 tablespoon brandy

Trim and cut the steak into two pieces. Beat with a rolling pin. Press the peppercorns into the steaks on both sides and leave for 1 hour. Melt the butter in a large frying-pan. Add the steaks and fry for 2 minutes on each side. Reduce the heat to low and fry for a further 2 minutes. This will produce rare steaks—double the time for well-done steak. Transfer the steaks to a heated serving plate. Stir the brandy into the pan juices and bring to the boil. Pour over the steaks.

Serves 2

Steak Diane

350 g./12 oz. fillet steak,
    pounded thin and cut into
    two pieces
1 garlic clove, crushed
salt and pepper
25 g./1 oz. butter
15 ml./1 tablespoon
    Worcestershire sauce
15 ml./1 tablespoon chopped
    fresh parsley
30 ml./2 tablespoons double
    cream

Rub the steaks with the garlic and season with salt and pepper to taste. Melt the butter in a frying-pan. Add the steaks and fry for 2 minutes on each side. Add the Worcestershire sauce, reduce the heat to low and fry for a further 2 minutes. This will produce rare steaks—double the time for well-done. Transfer the steaks to a heated serving plate and sprinkle over the chopped parsley. Stir the cream into the pan juices, heat gently and pour over the steaks.

Serves 2

Oriental Beef with Vegetables

5 ml./1 teaspoon finely
   chopped fresh ginger
15 ml./1 tablespoon sherry
5 ml./1 teaspoon sugar
10 ml./2 teaspoons soy sauce
15 ml./1 tablespoon
   cornflour
30 ml./2 tablespoons oil
1 garlic clove
225 g./8 oz. rump steak, cut
   into thin strips
150 ml./5 fl. oz. beef stock
1 × 150 g./5 oz. can bamboo
   shoot, drained and cut into
   thin strips
6 water chestnuts, thinly
   sliced
1 onion, cut into 8 pieces
2 celery stalks, sliced
1 carrot, sliced
salt and pepper

Mix together the ginger, sherry, sugar, soy sauce and cornflour. Heat the oil in a frying-pan. Add the garlic and fry for 2 minutes, then remove. Add the beef and stir-fry for 5 minutes until it is evenly browned. Add the soy sauce mixture, stock, prepared vegetables and salt and pepper to taste. Bring to the boil, stirring constantly. Simmer for 5 minutes.

Serves 4

Cottage Pie

30 ml./2 tablespoons oil
1 onion, finely chopped
½ kg./1 lb. beef, minced
150 ml./5 fl. oz. beef stock
30 ml./2 tablespoons tomato
   ketchup
10 ml./2 teaspoons
   Worcestershire sauce
5 ml./1 teaspoon dried mixed
   herbs
15 ml./1 tablespoon chopped
   fresh parsley
salt and pepper
675 g./1½ lb. potatoes,
   cooked and mashed
15 g./½ oz. butter, cut into
   small pieces

Heat the oil in a frying-pan. Add the onion and fry for 5 minutes. Add the beef and fry for 5 minutes or until it loses its pinkness. Add the stock, tomato ketchup, Worcestershire sauce, herbs, parsley and salt and pepper to taste. Cover and simmer for 45 minutes. Transfer to a greased 1¼ l./2 pint pie dish. Top with the mashed potatoes and dot over the butter pieces. Put the dish on a baking sheet and put the sheet into the oven preheated to fairly hot (190°C/375°F or Gas Mark 5). Bake for 30 minutes or until the top is golden brown.

Serves 4-6

Braised Beef Neapolitan

675 g./1½ lb. lean braising
  steak
salt and pepper
½ kg./1 lb. tomatoes, skinned
  and chopped
2 small onions, chopped
2 garlic cloves, crushed
1 bay leaf
pinch of dried mixed herbs

Divide the meat into four steaks and cut off any excess fat. Season well with the salt and pepper. Grill for 5 minutes on each side, or until the meat is lightly browned. Transfer to an ovenproof casserole. Mix together the tomatoes, onions, garlic, herbs and seasoning to taste and spoon over the meat. Put the dish into the oven preheated to moderate (180°C/350°F or Gas Mark 4) and bake for 1½ to 2 hours, or until the meat is tender. The cooking time will depend on the thickness and quality of the meat.

Serves 4

Meat Loaf

15 g./½ oz. butter
50 g./2 oz. dry breadcrumbs
1 kg./2 lb. beef, minced
1 medium onion, finely
  chopped
salt and pepper
½ beef stock cube, dissolved
  in 15 ml./1 tablespoon
  boiling water
pinch of dried mixed herbs
30 ml./2 tablespoons tomato
  purée
1 egg, beaten

Grease a 1 kg./2 lb. loaf tin with the butter, then coat with some of the breadcrumbs. Put the remaining ingredients into a bowl and mix well. Pack the mixture into the loaf tin and put the tin into the oven preheated to fairly hot (190°C/375°F or Gas Mark 5). Bake for 1¼ hours. Serve either hot or cold. If serving hot, allow to stand for 10 minutes before slicing.

Serves 6-8

Goulash

50 g./2 oz. butter
675 g./1½ lb. lean, tender beef
2 large onions, sliced into
  rings
salt and pepper
15 ml./1 tablespoon paprika
½ kg./1 lb. tomatoes, skinned
  and chopped
50 ml./2 fl. oz. beef stock
150 ml./5 fl. oz. sour cream
chopped fresh parsley

Melt the butter in a saucepan. Add the meat and fry for 5 to 8 minutes, or until it is evenly browned. Stir in the onions, salt and pepper to taste and paprika. Add the tomatoes and stock, cover and simmer for 1½ to 2 hours, or until the meat is tender. If necessary, add a little liquid during cooking. Top with sour cream and parsley.

Serves 4

Beef-stuffed Peppers

4 green peppers
½ kg./1 lb. lean beef, minced
1 garlic clove crushed
1 onion, finely chopped
125 g./4 oz. mushrooms,
    chopped
pinch of dried mixed herbs
salt and pepper
300 ml./10 fl. oz. tomato
    juice

Slice the tops off the stalk end of the peppers and reserve them. Remove and discard the pith and seeds. Mix together the beef, garlic, onion, mushrooms, herbs and seasoning to taste. Spoon the mixture into the peppers and cover with the reserved tops. Arrange the peppers upright in a saucepan and pour over the tomato juice. Cover and simmer for 1 hour. Serve hot with the cooking liquid.

Serves 4

Chilli con Carne

30 ml./2 tablespoons oil
1 large onion, chopped
2 garlic cloves, crushed
125 g./4 oz. bacon slices,
    chopped
½ kg./1 lb. beef, minced
1 × 400 g./14 oz. can
    tomatoes
1 × 400 g./14 oz. can red
    kidney beans, drained
2 teaspoons chilli powder
salt

Heat the oil in a saucepan. Add the onion, garlic and bacon and fry for 5 minutes. Add the beef and fry for a further 5 minutes or until it loses its pinkness. Stir in all the remaining ingredients. Cover and simmer for 1 hour.

Serves 4

Beef and Vegetable Stew

675 g./1½ lb. stewing steak,
    cubed
25 g./1 oz. seasoned flour
50 ml./2 fl. oz. oil
8 small onions, whole
600 ml./1 pint beef stock
8 small carrots
3 celery stalks, chopped
125 g./4 oz. button
    mushrooms
1 bouquet garni
salt and pepper
chopped fresh parsley to
    garnish

Coat the meat in the seasoned flour. Heat the oil in a large saucepan. Add the onions and meat and fry for 5 to 8 minutes, or until the meat is evenly browned. Gradually stir in the stock and bring to the boil. Add the remaining vegetables, herbs and salt and pepper to taste. Cover and simmer for 2¼ to 2½ hours, or until the meat is tender. Remove the bouquet garni and garnish with the parsley.

Serves 4

Steak and Kidney Pudding

675 g./1½ lb. stewing steak,
cubed
225 g./8 oz. ox kidney, diced
50 g./2 oz. seasoned flour
2 onions, finely chopped
(optional)
beef stock
Pastry
275 g./10 oz. self-raising
flour
pinch of salt
150 g./5 oz. shredded suet
water

Coat the steak and kidney pieces in the seasoned flour. To make the pastry, sift the flour and salt into a bowl. Add the suet and enough cold water to mix to a soft rolling consistency. Roll out the dough and cut off and reserve a quarter. Use the remaining dough to line a 2 l./3 pint basin. Mix the onions, if used, with the meat and put the mixture into the basin. Add just enough stock to come half way up the meat mixture. Dampen the edges of the dough. Arrange the remaining dough on top to form a lid, pressing the edges together firmly to seal. Cover with greased greaseproof paper and foil, making a pleat in the centre to allow room for the pudding to rise. Steam or boil for 4 to 5 hours or until the meat is tender. Serve in the basin. Make a gravy to serve with the pudding, or, when you cut out the first portion, add a little hot beef stock and use this as gravy.

Serves 6

Beef in Red Wine

50 g./2 oz. butter
30 ml./2 tablespoons oil
2 large onions, finely
chopped
2 garlic cloves, crushed
4 celery stalks, chopped
175 g./6 oz. streaky bacon,
chopped
1½ kg./3 lb. braising steak,
cubed
45 ml./3 tablespoons flour
300 ml./10 fl. oz. red wine
425 ml./15 fl. oz. water
15 ml./1 tablespoon tomato
purée
1 bouquet garni
salt and pepper

Heat the butter and oil in a large saucepan. Add the onions, garlic, celery and bacon and fry for 5 minutes. Add the meat and fry for a further 10 minutes. Stir in the flour and cook for 2 minutes. Gradually stir in the wine and water and bring to the boil. Add the tomato purée, bouquet garni and seasoning to taste. Cover and simmer for 2 hours, or until the beef is tender.

Serves 6-8

Beef, Sausage and Corn Stew

50 ml./2 fl. oz. oil
2 onions, chopped
1 red pepper, pith and seeds
   removed and chopped
675 g./1½ lb. stewing steak,
   cubed
10 ml./2 teaspoons paprika
1 l./1¾ pints beef stock
1 × 125 g./4 oz. can butter
   beans, drained
2 bacon slices, chopped
225 g./8 oz. garlic sausage,
   sliced
salt and pepper
1 × 225 g./8 oz. can
   sweetcorn, drained

Heat the oil in a large saucepan. Add the onions, pepper and beef and fry for 5 to 8 minutes, or until the meat is evenly browned. Gradually stir in the paprika and stock. Add the butter beans, bacon, garlic sausage and salt and pepper to taste. Bring to the boil, cover and simmer for 2 hours. Add the sweetcorn and simmer for a further 30 minutes.

Serves 4-6

Rolled Braised Beef

1 kg./2 lb. stewing steak, in
   one piece
50 g./2 oz. butter
2 onions, thinly sliced and
   pushed into rings
1 garlic clove, crushed
3 celery stalks, chopped
125 ml./4 fl. oz. beef stock
Marinade
125 ml./4 fl. oz. wine vinegar
1 bay leaf
2.5 ml./½ teaspoon crushed
   black peppercorns
salt

Slice the beef in half horizontally so that you have two equal slices. Pound each slice until it is thin. Roll the meat up and secure with string at 2.5 cm./1 in. intervals. Put the rolls in a shallow dish. Mix the marinade ingredients together and pour over the beef rolls. Marinate for 2 hours, basting occasionally. Remove the rolls, strain and reserve the marinade.

Melt the butter in a large frying-pan. Add the rolls and fry for 10 minutes, or until the meat is evenly browned. Remove the rolls and set aside. Add the onions, garlic and celery and fry for 5 minutes. Return the meat to the pan and pour in the stock and reserved marinade. Bring to the boil, cover and simmer for 1 to 1½ hours, or until the beef is cooked through. Serve with the cooking liquid.

Serves 6

Cold Baked Silverside of Beef

$1 \times 2\frac{1}{2}$ kg./5 lb. silverside of
  beef, soaked in water for 2
  hours and drained
2 carrots, chopped
2 onions, chopped
1 garlic clove, crushed
1 bay leaf
6 peppercorns
2 cloves
300 ml./10 fl. oz. beer or red
  wine

Place the beef in a large ovenproof casserole. Add the remaining ingredients and sufficient water just to cover the beef. Cover and put into the oven preheated to moderate (180°C/350°F or Gas Mark 4). Cook for 3 to 4 hours, or until the meat is tender. Remove the beef from the casserole and place in a bowl. Put a plate or board and a heavy weight on top. Leave to stand for eight hours or overnight. Serve cold, in thin slices.

Serves 10-12

Boeuf Bourguignonne

30 ml./2 tablespoons oil
225 g./8 oz. streaky bacon,
  sliced into strips
675 g./1½ lb. stewing steak,
  cubed
15 g./½ oz. flour
300 ml./10 fl. oz. beef stock
150 ml./5 fl. oz. red wine
1 bay leaf
2.5 ml./½ teaspoon dried
  mixed herbs
15 ml./1 tablespoon chopped
  fresh parsley
salt and pepper
125 g./4 oz. small pickling
  onions
125 g./4 oz. button
  mushrooms

Heat the oil in a frying-pan. Add the bacon and fry for 5 minutes or until it is evenly browned. Drain on kitchen towels and transfer to a large ovenproof dish. Add the beef to the pan and fry for 5 to 8 minutes or until it is evenly browned. Add to the bacon. Pour off all but 30 ml./2 tablespoons of the fat and stir in the flour to form a smooth paste. Gradually stir in the stock and wine and bring to the boil. Simmer for 5 minutes, stirring constantly, or until the liquid has thickened. Add the bay leaf, herbs, parsley and salt and pepper to taste and pour over the meat. Cover the dish and put into the oven preheated to warm (170°C/325°F or Gas Mark 3). Cook for 1½ hours. Add the onions and mushrooms to the casserole and cook for a further 1 hour, or until the meat is cooked through and tender.

Serves 6

Beef and Apricot Stew

600 ml./1 pint beef stock
18 dried apricots
675 g./1½ lb. stewing steak,
  cubed
25 g./1 oz. seasoned flour
50 ml./2 fl. oz. oil
grated rind and juice of 1
  lemon
10 ml./2 teaspoons sugar
1 × 125 g./4 oz. can
  tomatoes, drained

Bring the stock to the boil, pour over the apricots and leave to soak for about 12 hours. Coat the beef cubes with the seasoned flour. Heat the oil in a large saucepan. Add the beef and fry for 5 to 8 minutes or until it is evenly browned. Strain the stock from the apricots and add to the meat. Bring to the boil and simmer until the liquid has thickened. Add the lemon rind and juice, sugar and about six finely chopped apricots. Cover the pan and simmer for about 1¾ hours. Add the remaining apricots and simmer for a further 15 minutes. Stir in the tomatoes and cook for 15 minutes, or until the meat is cooked through and tender.

Serves 4

Quick Beef in Beer

675 g./1½ lb. cooked lean
  beef, minced
1 onion, grated
1 garlic clove, crushed
200 ml./7 fl. oz. beer
salt and pepper

Put all the ingredients in a dish and leave for 30 minutes. Transfer to a saucepan and simmer for 15 to 20 minutes, or until completely heated through. Season to taste with salt and pepper.

Serves 4

Barbecued Beef Saté

1 kg./2 lb. rump steak, cubed
Marinade
30 ml./2 tablespoons soy
  sauce
15 ml./1 tablespoon clear
  honey
2 garlic cloves, crushed
5 ml./1 teaspoon ground
  coriander
5 ml./1 teaspoon caraway
  seeds
1.25 ml./¼ teaspoon chilli
  powder
30 ml./2 tablespoons oil

Put the meat in a large bowl. Mix all the marinade ingredients together and pour over the meat. Marinate for 1 hour, basting occasionally. Thread the meat on to six skewers. Grill or barbecue over hot charcoal for 10 minutes, or until the meat is cooked to taste. Baste occasionally with the marinade during the cooking period.

Serves 6

Beef Cutlets

25 g./1 oz. butter
25 g./1 oz. flour
150 ml./5 fl. oz. beef stock
50 g./2 oz. fresh
   breadcrumbs
pinch of dried mixed herbs
salt and pepper
½ kg./1 lb. cooked beef,
   minced
1 egg, beaten
125 g./4 oz. dry breadcrumbs
75 ml./3 fl. oz. oil

Melt the butter in a saucepan and stir in the flour to form a smooth paste. Gradually add the stock and bring to the boil, stirring. Stir in the fresh breadcrumbs, herbs and seasoning to taste. Stir the mixture into the meat and cool. Form the mixture into eight small cutlet shapes. Coat in the beaten egg, then in the dry breadcrumbs. Heat the oil in a large frying-pan. Add the cutlets, a few at a time, and fry for 8 to 10 minutes or until they are golden brown. Drain on kitchen towels and serve hot or cold.

Serves 4

Beef Stew with Cheese

1 kg./2 lb. brisket of beef,
   cubed
45 ml./3 tablespoons
   mustard
2 garlic cloves, crushed
50 ml./2 fl. oz. oil
1 kg./2 lb. leeks, sliced
5 ml./1 teaspoon sugar
30 ml./2 tablespoons
   Worcestershire sauce
225 ml./8 fl. oz. beef stock
225 g./8 oz. cheese, grated

Mix together the beef, mustard and garlic. Heat the oil in a flameproof casserole. Add the meat and fry for 5 to 8 minutes, or until evenly browned. Add the leeks, sugar and Worcestershire sauce. Pour over the stock and bring to the boil. Cover and put the casserole into the oven preheated to moderate (180°C/350°F or Gas Mark 4). Cook for 2 hours. Sprinkle over the cheese and cook, uncovered, for a further 10 to 15 minutes, or until the cheese is golden brown.

Serves 4

Meat Pudding

pinch of grated nutmeg
300 ml./10 fl. oz. Yorkshire
   pudding batter*
675 g./1½ lb. beef, minced
1 small onion, finely
   chopped
15 ml./1 tablespoon chopped
   fresh parsley
1 garlic clove, crushed
salt and pepper
25 ml./1 fl. oz. oil

Stir the nutmeg into the batter. Mix together the beef, onion, parsley, garlic and salt and pepper to taste. Heat the oil in a small baking tin and pour in half the batter. Quickly spread over the meat mixture. Pour over the remaining batter. Put the tin into the oven preheated to fairly hot (200°C/400°F or Gas Mark 6) and bake for 20 minutes. Reduce the oven temperature to moderate (180°C/350°F or Gas Mark 4) and bake for a further 30 minutes or until the pudding is golden brown.

Serves 4

Beef Ribs with Peppers

1 × 1½ kg./3 lb. top rib of beef
salt and pepper
25 g./1 oz. butter
12 spring onions, finely
  chopped
2 large red peppers, pith and
  seeds removed and
  chopped
300 ml./10 fl. oz. beef stock
50 ml./2 fl. oz. red wine

Rub the meat with the salt and pepper and lay in a shallow ovenproof dish. Put the dish into the oven preheated to hot (220°C/425°F or Gas Mark 7) and cook for 30 minutes, turning once. Meanwhile, melt the butter in a frying-pan. Add the spring onions and peppers and fry for 3 minutes. Pour in the stock and wine and bring to the boil. Reduce the oven temperature to moderate (180°C/350°F or Gas Mark 4) and pour the stock mixture over the meat. Cover and cook, basting occasionally, for a further 2 hours, or until the meat is tender. Serve with the cooking juices.

Serves 4-6

Red Beef and Bean Casserole

25 g./1 oz. seasoned flour
2.5 ml./½ teaspoon ground
  ginger
1 kg./2 lb. stewing beef,
  cubed
50 ml./2 fl. oz. oil
1 red pepper, pith and seeds
  removed and chopped
1 × 425 g./15 oz. can red
  kidney beans, drained
Sauce
5 ml./1 teaspoon chilli
  powder
1 × 200 g./7 oz. can
  tomatoes
125 g./4 oz. mushrooms,
  sliced
15 ml./1 tablespoon
  Worcestershire sauce
30 ml./2 tablespoons brown
  sugar
30 ml./2 tablespoons wine
  vinegar
2 garlic cloves, crushed
1 bay leaf

Mix the seasoned flour with the ginger and coat the beef cubes in the mixture. Heat the oil in a large frying-pan. Add the beef cubes and fry for 5 to 8 minutes or until they are evenly browned. Transfer to a large ovenproof dish. Combine all the sauce ingredients and pour over the meat. Cover and put the dish into the oven preheated to warm (170°C/325°F or Gas Mark 3). Cook for about 2 hours, or until the meat is tender. Add the red pepper and kidney beans 30 minutes before the end of the cooking time. Remove the bay leaf before serving.

Serves 6

Beef and Vegetable Pie

15 ml./1 tablespoon oil
1 onion, finely chopped
1 kg./2 lb. beef, minced
125 g./4 oz. mushrooms,
    sliced
125 g./4 oz. carrots,
    parboiled and sliced
1 × 400 g./14 oz. can
    peas, drained
15 ml./1 tablespoon
    Worcestershire sauce
salt and pepper
30 ml./2 tablespoons tomato
    ketchup
675 g./1½ lb. potatoes,
    cooked and mashed
25 g./1 oz. butter, cut into
    pieces

Heat the oil in a frying-pan. Add the onion and fry for 5 minutes. Add the meat and fry for a further 5 minutes or until it loses its pinkness. Add the mushrooms, carrots, peas, Worcestershire sauce, salt and pepper to taste and tomato ketchup. Cook for 5 minutes. Transfer to an ovenproof dish and spoon over the mashed potato. Dot the butter over the potatoes and put into the oven preheated to moderate (180°C/350°F or Gas Mark 4). Bake for 40 minutes, or until the top is crisp and golden brown.

Serves 6

Beef and Sweetcorn Pie

45 ml./3 tablespoons oil
2 onions, sliced
1 red chilli, seeded and finely
    chopped
1 garlic clove, crushed
675 g./1½ lb. beef, minced
salt
5 ml./1 teaspoon ground
    cumin
2.5 ml./½ teaspoon cayenne
    pepper
15 ml./1 tablespoon flour
125 g./4 oz. sultanas, soaked
    in water for 10 minutes
    and drained
Topping
30 ml./2 tablespoons oil
1 onion, finely chopped
1 × 350 g./12 oz. can
    sweetcorn, drained and
    puréed
salt and pepper

Heat the oil in a frying-pan. Add the onions, chilli and garlic and fry for 5 minutes. Add the beef and fry for 5 minutes or until it loses its pinkness. Stir in salt to taste, cumin, cayenne, flour and sultanas. Spoon into a shallow greased 1¼ l./2 pint baking dish.

To make the topping, heat the oil in a frying-pan. Add the onion and fry for 5 minutes. Add the sweetcorn and salt and pepper to taste and cook for 5 minutes. Spoon over the meat. Put the dish into the oven preheated to fairly hot (190°C/375°F or Gas Mark 5) and cook for 20 minutes, or until the top is golden brown.

Serves 4

Beef and Aubergine Meatballs

675 g./1½ lb. beef, minced
2 medium aubergines,
    peeled, chopped and
    dégorged
30 ml./2 tablespoons
    chopped fresh parsley
50 g./2 oz. fresh
    breadcrumbs
1 egg, lightly beaten
2.5 ml./½ teaspoon dried
    marjoram
1 small onion, finely
    chopped
salt and pepper
50 ml./2 fl. oz. oil
425 ml./15 fl. oz. tomato
    sauce *

Mix together the beef, aubergines, parsley, bread-crumbs, egg, marjoram, onion and salt and pepper to taste. Shape into small balls. Heat the oil in a frying-pan. Add the balls and fry for 5 to 8 minutes or until they are evenly browned. Pour off most of the fat and pour in the tomato sauce. Simmer for 10 to 15 minutes or until the meatballs are cooked through.

Serves 4

Beef with Pineapple

1 kg./2 lb. topside of beef,
    thinly sliced
50 g./2 oz. butter
2 onions, chopped
125 g./4 oz. mushrooms,
    sliced
1 green pepper, pith and
    seeds removed and thinly
    sliced
1 × 450 g./16 oz. can
    pineapple chunks, drained
50 g./2 oz. chutney, chopped
Marinade
75 ml./3 fl. oz.
    Worcestershire sauce
75 g./3 oz. tomato purée
salt and pepper
1 garlic clove, crushed

Mix together the marinade ingredients in a shallow dish. Add the beef slices and marinate for 30 minutes, basting occasionally. Drain and reserve any remaining marinade. Melt the butter in a frying-pan. Add the onions, mushrooms and pepper and fry for 5 minutes. Stir in the pineapple, chutney and reserved marinade and fry for a further 10 minutes. Grill the beef slices for 5 minutes on each side, then transfer to a warmed serving dish. Spoon the fruit and vegetables around the meat.

Serves 4

Hamburgers

1½ kg./3 lb. steak, minced
25 g./1 oz. chopped fresh
  parsley
15 ml./1 tablespoon
  Worcestershire sauce
1 small onion, finely
  chopped
salt and pepper

Blend all the ingredients together and form into flat cakes. (The less handling the uncooked mixture receives, the more tender the hamburgers will be.) Grill slowly for 5 to 10 minutes on each side, according to taste. Serve between sesame seed buns or with salad.

Serves 6-8

Hot Pot

1 kg./2 lb. topside of beef,
  cubed
salt and pepper
2 large onions, sliced
350 g./12 oz. carrots, sliced
675 g./1½ lb. potatoes, sliced
300 ml./10 fl. oz. beef stock

Put the beef in a deep ovenproof dish and season with salt and pepper to taste. Arrange the onions, carrots and potatoes in thin layers over the meat, ending with a layer of potatoes arranged in overlapping slices. Pour over the stock, cover and put the dish into the oven preheated to warm (170°C/325°F or Gas Mark 3). Cook for 2 to 2½ hours, or until the meat is just tender. Increase the oven temperature to fairly hot (200°C/400°F or Gas Mark 6), uncover and cook for a further 30 minutes or until the top layer of potatoes is browned.

Serves 4

Greek Meatballs

675 g./1½ lb. beef, minced
1 onion, finely chopped
1 garlic clove, crushed
30 ml./2 tablespoons
  chopped fresh parsley
30 ml./2 tablespoons rice
salt and pepper
750 ml./1¼ pints beef stock
Sauce
4 eggs
45 ml./3 tablespoons water
125 ml./4 fl. oz. lemon juice
salt

Mix together the beef, onion, garlic, parsley, rice and salt and pepper to taste. Shape into small balls. Pour the stock into a saucepan and bring to the boil. Add the meatballs, cover and simmer for 45 minutes. To make the sauce, beat the eggs and water in a heatproof bowl over a saucepan of simmering water until the mixture is light and fluffy. Gradually beat in 50 ml./2 fl. oz. of the stock from the meatballs. Add the lemon juice and continue whisking until the sauce thickens. Stir in salt to taste and leave for 10 minutes. Remove the meatballs from the saucepan and put in a serving dish. Pour over the lemon sauce.

Serves 6

Meatballs in Sour Cream Sauce

1 egg
150 ml./5 fl. oz. milk
salt and pepper
50 g./2 oz. dry breadcrumbs
½ small onion, finely chopped
½ kg./1 lb. beef, minced
15 g./½ oz. butter
15 ml./1 tablespoon flour
125 ml./4 fl. oz. tomato
   sauce*
150 ml./5 fl. oz. sour cream
few small black olives

Beat the egg, milk, salt and pepper to taste and breadcrumbs together. Add about 1.25 ml./¼ teaspoon of the chopped onion and set aside for a few minutes. Stir in the meat, then shape the mixture into small balls. Cover and chill until firm.

Melt the butter in a frying-pan. Add the meat balls and fry for 5 minutes or until they are browned. Drain on kitchen towels and keep warm. Add the remaining onion to the pan and cook for 5 minutes. Stir in the flour to form a smooth paste. Gradually add the tomato sauce and bring to the boil, stirring constantly. Return the meatballs to the pan and simmer for 10 minutes. Stir in the sour cream and olives and cook for a further 2 minutes.

Serves 4

Beef Stew with Chick Peas

4 streaky bacon slices,
   chopped
1 kg./2 lb. stewing beef,
   cubed
25 ml./1 fl. oz. oil
1 large onion, thinly sliced
1 garlic clove, crushed
15 ml./1 tablespoon flour
600 ml./1 pint water
300 ml./10 fl. oz. beef stock
15 ml./1 tablespoon tomato
   purée
225 g./8 oz. tomatoes,
   skinned and chopped
2.5 ml./½ teaspoon dried basil
salt and pepper
125 g./4 oz. chick peas,
   soaked for 12 hours,
   cooked and drained

Cook the bacon in a large frying-pan for 5 minutes or until it has rendered most of its fat. Transfer to a deep ovenproof dish. Add the meat to the pan and fry for 5 to 8 minutes or until it is evenly browned. Add to the bacon. Pour the oil into the pan. When it is hot, add the onion and garlic, and fry for 5 minutes. Stir in the flour to form a smooth paste. Gradually add the water and stock and bring to the boil, stirring constantly. Cook for 2 to 3 minutes, stirring constantly, or until the sauce thickens. Add the tomato purée, tomatoes, basil and salt and pepper to taste. Pour over the beef and bacon. Cover and put into the oven preheated to warm (170°C/325°F or Gas Mark 3). Cook for 2 hours. Add the chick peas and cook for a further 30 minutes, or until the meat is cooked through and tender.

Serves 6

Beef Rolls with Bacon

1 kg./2 lb. top rump of beef,
   thinly sliced and pounded
salt and pepper
½ kg./1 lb. bacon slices
25 g./1 oz. butter
1 large onion, finely chopped
25 g./1 oz. flour
350 ml./12 fl. oz. red wine

Rub the beef slices with the salt and pepper and lay a bacon slice on each one. Roll up and secure with a toothpick or skewer. Melt the butter in a frying-pan. Add the beef rolls and fry for 10 minutes or until evenly browned. Transfer to a plate. Add the onion to the pan and fry for 5 minutes. Stir in the flour to make a smooth paste. Gradually add the wine and bring to the boil, stirring constantly. Cook for 2 to 3 minutes, stirring constantly, or until the sauce thickens. Return the beef rolls to the pan, cover and simmer for 1 hour, or until the meat is tender.

Serves 6

Corned Beef and Egg Hash

1 × 350 g./12 oz. can corned
   beef, flaked
225 g./8 oz. potatoes, cooked
   and mashed
salt and pepper
little milk
50 g./2 oz. butter
4 eggs
2 tomatoes, sliced

Mix the beef with the potatoes, salt and pepper to taste and enough milk to make a soft consistency. Form the mixture into four rounds and hollow out the centres. Melt the butter in a frying-pan. Add the beef and potato rounds and fry for 5 minutes or until the rounds are evenly browned. Spoon a little of the hot fat into the centres and break an egg into each hollow. Continue cooking for a few minutes or until the egg whites have set. Lift out carefully and garnish with the tomato slices.

Serves 4

Steak Tartare

225 g./8 oz. fillet steak,
   minced
30 ml./2 tablespoons finely
   chopped onion
15 ml./1 tablespoon capers
15 ml./1 tablespoon chopped
   fresh parsley
salt and pepper
2 egg yolks

Mix together the minced steak, onion, capers, parsley and salt and pepper to taste. Shape the mixture into two rounds and slightly hollow the middle. Put an egg yolk in the centre of each.

Serves 2

Steaks au Poivre Vert

*1 × 75 g./3 oz. can green
  peppercorns, rinsed and
  drained*
*30 ml./2 tablespoons
  mustard*
4 fillet steaks
50 g./2 oz. butter
225 ml./8 fl. oz. single cream
salt and pepper

Put the peppercorns in a mortar and crush with a pestle. Mix with the mustard and spread over the steaks. Melt the butter in a large frying-pan. Add the steaks and fry quickly for 2 minutes on each side. Reduce the heat and fry for a further 2 minutes on each side. This will produce rare steaks—double the time if you prefer them well done. Transfer the steaks to a warmed serving dish and keep hot. Add the cream and salt and pepper to taste to the pan and heat gently. Pour over the steaks.

Serves 4

Beef Stroganoff

50 g./2 oz. butter
1 onion, chopped
*1 kg./2 lb. fillet steak, cut into
  very thin strips*
*225 g./8 oz. mushrooms,
  sliced*
150 ml./5 fl. oz. sour cream
salt and pepper

Melt the butter in a large frying-pan. Add the onion and fry for 5 minutes. Add the meat and fry for 8 minutes, or until it is almost cooked. Add the mushrooms and fry for 3 minutes. Stir in the sour cream, season to taste and heat through gently.

Serves 6

Hash

50 ml./2 fl. oz. oil
1 onion, chopped
*1 red pepper, pith and seeds
  removed and chopped*
*1 kg./2 lb. potatoes, cooked
  and chopped*
*1 kg./2 lb. cooked roast beef,
  cubed*
salt and pepper
*10 ml./2 teaspoons
  Worcestershire sauce*
*15 ml./1 tablespoon chopped
  fresh parsley*
*150 ml./5 fl. oz. double
  cream*

Heat the oil in a frying-pan. Add the onion and pepper and fry for 5 minutes. Add the potatoes and fry for 10 minutes or until they are evenly browned. Stir in the beef, salt and pepper to taste, Worcestershire sauce and parsley and cook for 3 minutes. Stir in the cream. Press the hash down firmly to form a cake. Cook over low heat for 12 minutes, or until a crust has formed on the base.

Serves 4

Cornish Pasties

½ kg./1 lb. rump steak, diced
2 potatoes, diced
2 onions, chopped
1 small swede, diced
30 ml./2 tablespoons beef
  stock
salt and pepper
½ kg./1 lb. shortcrust pastry *
1 egg, beaten

Mix together the beef, potatoes, onions and swede. Add the stock and season with salt and pepper. Roll out the dough thinly and cut into four circles. Put one quarter of the filling in the centre of each one, dampen the edges with water and fold in half to form a semi-circle. Flute the edges with your fingers. Lift the pasties on to a lightly greased baking sheet and brush with the beaten egg. Put the sheet into the oven preheated to hot (220°C/425°F or Gas Mark 7) and bake for 15 to 20 minutes, or until the pastry is golden brown. Reduce the oven temperature to moderate (180°C/350°F or Gas Mark 4) and bake for a further 20 minutes.

Serves 4

Beef and Beans in Vinegar Sauce

1 × 2 kg./4 lb. brisket of beef,
  boned and rolled
½ kg./1 lb. carrots, sliced
2 large onions, chopped
salt and pepper
1 kg./2 lb. runner beans,
  sliced
Sauce
175 ml./6 fl. oz. malt vinegar
75 g./3 oz. brown sugar
75 g./3 oz. cornflour

Put the beef, carrots, onions and salt and pepper to taste in a large saucepan. Add enough water to cover and bring to the boil. Cover and simmer for 2½ to 3 hours, or until the meat is tender. About 20 minutes before the end of the cooking time add the beans.

Meanwhile prepare the sauce. Mix together the vinegar, sugar and cornflour to form a smooth paste. Add 90 ml./6 tablespoons of the cooking liquid to the paste and stir well. Take the beef out of the pan, cut into thick slices and place on a warmed serving dish. Keep hot. Pour the vinegar mixture into the saucepan and bring to the boil, stirring constantly until the liquid thickens. Pour the sauce and beans over the beef.

Serves 10

52

Spiced Fillet of Beef

1 × 1 kg./2 lb. fillet of beef
salt and pepper
4 ham slices, cut into strips
2 garlic cloves, halved
50 g./2 oz. butter
300 ml./10 fl. oz. red wine
10 ml./2 teaspoons ground
  cinnamon
2.5 ml./½ teaspoon grated
  nutmeg
25 g./1 oz. beurre manié*

Rub the beef with salt and pepper. Make four slits about halfway down the meat and insert a quarter of the ham strips and half a garlic clove in each one. Roll up the meat so that the slits are on the inside and secure with string. Melt the butter in a small roasting pan. Add the fillet and fry for 10 minutes, or until the meat is evenly browned. Mix the wine with the cinnamon and nutmeg and pour into the roasting pan. Transfer to the oven preheated to very hot (230°C/450°F or Gas Mark 8) and cook for 25 to 30 minutes or until the meat is tender. Transfer the beef to a warmed serving dish and keep hot. Bring the cooking liquid to the boil. Add the beurre manié, piece by piece, to the cooking liquid and simmer until the sauce has thickened. Serve with the beef.

Serves 4-6

Carbonnade

125 g./4 oz. butter
1½ kg./3 lb. chuck steak,
  cubed
2 large onions, sliced
30 ml./2 tablespoons flour
1 garlic clove, crushed
600 ml./1 pint beer
600 ml./1 pint beef stock
salt and pepper
1 bouquet garni
pinch of grated nutmeg
5 ml./1 teaspoon sugar
6-8 pieces bread, crusts
  removed
French mustard

Melt the butter in a large frying-pan. Add the meat and fry for 5 to 8 minutes, or until it is evenly browned. Transfer to a plate. Add the onions to the pan and fry for 5 minutes. Stir in the flour to form a smooth paste. Add the garlic, beer and stock and bring to the boil, stirring constantly. Season with salt and pepper and add the bouquet garni, nutmeg and sugar. Return the meat to the pan and turn into an ovenproof casserole. Cover and put the casserole into the oven preheated to warm (170°C/325°F or Gas Mark 3). Cook for 2 hours, or until the meat is tender. Skim off any surface fat. Spread the bread squares lightly with mustard and place on top of the casserole, pushing down to ensure that they are well soaked with gravy. Return to the oven and cook, uncovered, for a further 10 to 15 minutes or until the bread crisps on top.

Serves 6-8

Easy Sukiyaki

675 g./1½ lb. chuck steak, cut
  into very thin strips
50 ml./2 fl. oz. oil
1 onion, sliced
50 g./2 oz. beans, sliced
125 g./4 oz. mushrooms,
  sliced
3 celery stalks, sliced
½ bunch of watercress,
  chopped
5 ml./1 teaspoon arrowroot or
  cornflour
Marinade
150 ml./5 fl. oz. beef stock
5 ml./1 teaspoon sugar
15 ml./1 tablespoon soy
  sauce
30 ml./2 tablespoons sherry
salt and pepper

Put the beef strips in a bowl. Combine all the
marinade ingredients and pour over the meat.
Leave for 2 hours, basting occasionally. Drain and
reserve the marinade.

Heat the oil in a saucepan. Add the meat and
onion and fry for 10 minutes. Add the remaining
vegetables and cook for a further 5 minutes. Mix
the arrowroot or cornflour with a little water and
stir into the meat with the reserved marinade.
Bring to the boil and cook for a further 3 minutes,
or until the liquid thickens.

Serves 4

Beef Olives

75 g./3 oz. butter
4 small onions, finely
  chopped
75 g./3 oz. fresh
  breadcrumbs
30 ml./2 tablespoons
  chopped fresh parsley
2.5 ml./½ teaspoon dried
  thyme
salt and pepper
little milk
1 kg./2 lb. skirt steak, cut into
  thin slices
3 carrots, chopped
1 small turnip, chopped
1 celery stalk, chopped
425 ml./15 fl. oz. beef stock
1 bouquet garni
15 ml./1 tablespoon beurre
  manié *

Melt 25 g./1 oz. of the butter in a saucepan. Add
one of the onions and fry for 5 minutes. Remove
from the heat and stir in the breadcrumbs, herbs,
salt and pepper to taste and just enough milk to
bind the mixture together. Spread a layer of the
mixture over each slice of meat. Roll up each slice
and secure with string. Melt the remaining butter
in the saucepan. Add the rest of the vegetables and
fry for 10 minutes. Pour over the stock and add the
meat rolls and bouquet garni. Bring to the boil,
cover and simmer for 1½ to 2 hours, or until the
meat is cooked through and tender. Transfer the
meat to a serving dish and remove the string. Stir
the beurre manié, in small pieces, into the cooking
liquid. Simmer until the gravy thickens. Remove
the bouquet garni and pour over the meat.

Serves 6

Beef Cakes with Beetroot

675 g./1¼ lb. beef, minced
½ kg./1 lb. potatoes, cooked
and mashed
salt and pepper
4 small pickled beetroot,
chopped
1 onion, finely chopped
5 ml./1 teaspoon dried mixed
herbs
50 g./2 oz. butter

Mix together the beef, potatoes and salt and pepper to taste. Stir in the beetroot, onion and herbs. Roll the mixture into eight balls and flatten slightly to make cakes. Melt half the butter in a frying-pan. Add half the cakes and fry for 20 minutes or until they are evenly browned and cooked through. Drain on kitchen paper. Cook the remaining cakes in the same way.

Serves 4

Indonesian Meatballs

25 g./1 oz. butter
1 small onion, finely
chopped
2 garlic cloves, crushed
½ kg./1 lb. lean beef, minced
1.25 ml./¼ teaspoon grated
nutmeg
salt and pepper
4 spring onions, finely
chopped
½ kg./1 lb. potatoes, cooked
and mashed
2 eggs, separated
oil for deep-frying

Melt the butter in a frying-pan. Add the onion and garlic and fry for 5 minutes. Add the meat, nutmeg and salt and pepper to taste and fry for 5 minutes or until the meat loses its pinkness. Add the spring onions with their tops, stir well and simmer for 15 to 20 minutes, or until the meat is cooked. Combine the mashed potatoes, the meat mixture and egg yolks. Form into small balls and chill for 1 hour to firm. Beat the egg whites very lightly with a fork. Dip the meatballs in the egg whites and deep-fry for 2 to 3 minutes or until they are golden brown. Drain on kitchen towels.

Serves 4

Spiced Steak

50 g./2 oz. butter
2 onions, thinly sliced
½ kg./1 lb. rump steak, cut
into thin strips
Sauce
15 ml./1 tablespoon flour
10 ml./2 teaspoons soy sauce
5 ml./1 teaspoon
Worcestershire sauce
300 ml./10 fl. oz. beef stock
10 ml./2 teaspoons curry
powder
pinch of cayenne pepper

To make the sauce, mix the flour with the soy and Worcestershire sauces to form a smooth paste. Gradually stir in the stock, curry powder and cayenne.

Melt the butter in a saucepan. Add the onions and fry for 5 minutes. Add the steak and fry for 2 to 3 minutes, or until evenly browned. Pour over the sauce and cook for 10 to 15 minutes, or until the steak is tender and the sauce very hot.

Serves 4

Boiled Beef with Dumplings

1 × 1½–2 kg./3–4 lb. salted
   silverside
1 bouquet garni
6 peppercorns
1 onion, stuck with 2 cloves
6 small onions
6 carrots, quartered
2 small turnips, quartered
Dumplings
225 g./8 oz. flour
5 ml./1 teaspoon baking
   powder
pinch of salt
125 g./4 oz. shredded suet
water

Put the meat into a large saucepan and cover with cold water. Bring slowly to the boil, skimming the surface several times. Add the bouquet garni, peppercorns and onion. Half cover and simmer for 1¼ hours. Remove the bouquet garni and onion and skim again. Add the onions, carrots and turnips and simmer for about 20 minutes or until the vegetables are tender.

Meanwhile prepare the dumplings. Sift the flour, baking powder and salt into a bowl. Add the suet and enough water to make a light dough. Divide into small pieces and roll into balls. Drop into the boiling stock about 15 minutes before the end of the cooking time. Serve the meat on a large dish surrounded with the vegetables and dumplings.

Serves 6-8

Steak Kebabs

1 kg./2 lb. rump steak, cubed
2 medium onions, halved
1 red pepper, pith and seeds
   removed and cut into
   squares
1 green pepper, pith and
   seeds removed and cut
   into squares
4 mushroom caps
50 g./2 oz. butter, melted
Marinade
15 ml./1 tablespoon oil
45 ml./3 tablespoons red
   wine
15 ml./1 tablespoon lemon
   juice
15 ml./1 tablespoon soy
   sauce
1 garlic clove, crushed
pinch of mustard
pinch of dried thyme
1 small onion, chopped

Put the beef cubes in a shallow bowl. Combine all the marinade ingredients and pour over the beef. Cover and marinate for 8 hours or overnight, basting occasionally.

Thread the vegetables and meat on to four skewers. Grill for 10 to 15 minutes or until they are cooked to taste, brushing occasionally with the remaining marinade and melted butter.

Serves 4

Stuffed Vine Leaves

1 × 425 g./15 oz. can vine
  leaves, (or fresh cabbage
  leaves)
½ kg./1 lb. beef, minced
75 g./3 oz. rice
30 ml./2 tablespoons
  chopped fresh parsley
2 onions, chopped
salt and pepper
1 × 425 g./15 oz. can
  mushroom soup

Rinse the vine leaves and drain them. (If you are using cabbage leaves, blanch them in boiling water for 3 minutes.) Combine the meat, rice, parsley, onions and salt and pepper to taste. Place a little of the mixture in the centre of each leaf and fold into neat parcels. If the leaves are small, put two together. Arrange the parcels in an ovenproof dish and pour over the mushroom soup. Cover and put the dish into the oven preheated to warm (170°C/325°F or Gas Mark 3). Bake for 1½ to 2 hours, or until the leaves and filling are tender. Add a little water to the dish, if necessary, during cooking.

Serves 4

Tournedos Chasseur

50 ml./2 fl. oz. oil
50 g./2 oz. butter
4 thick slices white bread,
  crusts removed and cut
  into rounds
4 tournedos steaks
salt and pepper
Sauce
150 ml./5 fl. oz. beef stock
15 ml./1 tablespoon tomato
  purée
40 g./1½ oz. butter
225 g./8 oz. mushrooms,
  sliced
2 spring onions, finely
  chopped
salt and pepper
10 ml./2 teaspoons cornflour
30 ml./2 tablespoons
  Madeira

Heat the oil and butter in a frying-pan. Add the bread and fry for 5 minutes or until crisp and golden brown. Keep warm on a serving plate in the oven. Add the steaks to the pan and fry quickly for 2 minutes on each side. Reduce the heat and fry for a further 2 minutes on each side. This will produce rare steaks—double the time for well done. Remove from the pan and season with salt and pepper to taste. Place each steak on a round of fried bread and keep warm in the oven until the sauce is made.

Pour off most of the fat from the frying-pan. Pour in the stock and stir in the tomato purée. Boil rapidly. Melt the butter in a second pan and fry the mushrooms for 3 minutes. Add the spring onions, salt and pepper to taste and cook for a further 1 minute. Remove from the heat. Blend the cornflour with the Madeira and stir into the stock mixture. Boil for 1 minute, stirring constantly. Add the mushroom mixture to the sauce, and cook for 2 minutes more, or until the sauce thickens. Pour the sauce over the steaks.

Serves 4

Roast Fillet of Beef

1 × 1–1½ kg./2–3 lb. fillet of
*   beef*
salt and pepper
125 g./4 oz. butter, melted
little water

Rub the beef with salt and pepper and put on a rack in a roasting pan. Pour over the melted butter and put the pan into the oven preheated to hot (220°C/425°F or Gas Mark 7). Roast for 5 minutes. Reduce the oven temperature to moderate (180°C/350°F or Gas Mark 4) and continue roasting until done to taste. (Allow 10 minutes per ½ kg./1 lb. for rare meat and 20 minutes per ½ kg./1 lb. for medium; allow a little longer for well done.) Transfer the fillet to a warmed serving dish, turn off the oven and allow the meat to sit in the oven for 10 minutes; this will make it easier to carve. Boil up the pan juices, adding a little water and seasoning. Slice the meat thickly and spoon over the pan juices.

Serves 6

Ragoût of Beef with Prunes

600 ml./1 pint beef stock
18 prunes
675 g./1½ lb. braising steak,
*   cubed*
25 g./1 oz. seasoned flour
50 ml./2 fl. oz. oil
15 ml./1 tablespoon tomato
*   purée*
2 bay leaves
4–5 tomatoes, skinned

Bring the stock to the boil, pour over the prunes and soak for about 12 hours. Coat the beef cubes with the seasoned flour. Heat the oil in a saucepan. Add the beef and fry for 5 to 8 minutes or until it is evenly browned. Strain the stock from the prunes and add to the meat. Bring to the boil and cook, stirring occasionally, until the liquid has thickened. Add the tomato purée, about six finely chopped prunes and the bay leaves. Cover the saucepan and simmer for 1¾ hours. Add the rest of the prunes and cook for 15 minutes. Stir in the tomatoes and cook for another 15 minutes. Remove the bay leaves.

Serves 4

Beef Wellington

1 × 1¼ kg./2½ lb. fillet of beef
125 g./4 oz. butter, softened
1 small onion, finely
   chopped
125 g./4 oz. mushrooms,
   thinly sliced
50 g./2 oz. pâté de foie gras
salt and pepper
450 g./1 lb. rough puff
   pastry*
1 egg yolk
300 ml./10 fl. oz. beef stock
30 ml./2 tablespoons red
   wine

Spread the beef with 25 g./1 oz. of the softened butter and put in a roasting pan. Put the pan into the oven preheated to hot (220°C/425°F or Gas Mark 7) and roast for 10 to 15 minutes or until the fillet is evenly browned. Remove from the oven and allow to cool completely. Reserve the pan juices.

Melt another 25 g./1 oz. of butter in a saucepan. Add the onion and mushrooms and fry for 5 minutes. Allow to cool.

Combine the remaining butter with the pâté, and salt and pepper to taste. Spread the pâté mixture over the top of the beef and top with the onion and mushroom mixture. Roll out the dough very thinly. Place the fillet carefully in the centre and wrap the dough round it, like a parcel; dampen and press the edges neatly and firmly together to seal. Make sure any overlapping edges of dough are not too thick. Using a sharp knife, make a few slits in the dough. Place the fillet in a baking dish and brush with the egg yolk. Put the baking dish into the oven preheated to very hot (230°C/450°F or Gas Mark 8) and bake for 10 minutes. Reduce the oven temperature to hot (220°C/425°F or Gas Mark 7) and bake for a further 10 to 15 minutes, or until the pastry is a rich golden brown. Keep the fillet warm while you make the sauce.

Add the stock and wine to the reserved pan juices and boil until slightly reduced. Strain. Cut the fillet into thick slices and serve with the sauce.

Serves 6

Beef Creole

4 minute (very thin) steaks
salt and pepper
2–3 drops of Tabasco sauce
75 g./3 oz. butter
1 onion, finely chopped
1 green pepper, pith and
   seeds removed and
   chopped
150 ml./5 fl. oz. beef stock

Flatten the steaks with a rolling pin and season with the salt, pepper and Tabasco sauce. Melt the butter in a frying-pan. Add the onion and fry for 2 minutes. Add the steaks and pepper and fry for 2 minutes. Add the stock, bring to the boil and simmer for 5 minutes.

Serves 4

Carpetbag Steak

1 × 1 kg. /2 lb. rump steak,
  about 6 cm./2½ in. thick
salt and pepper
1 small jar oysters, drained
125 g./4 oz. butter

Cut a large pocket in the steak with a sharp knife. Season with salt and pepper. Stuff the oysters into the pocket and secure with small skewers. Melt the butter in a frying-pan. Add the steak and fry quickly for 2 minutes on each side. Reduce the heat and fry for a further 2 minutes on each side. This will produce a rare steak—double the time for well done. Cut the steak into four pieces and transfer to a warmed serving dish. Pour over the pan juices.

Serves 4

Steak in Red Wine Sauce

125 g./4 oz. butter
1 kg./2 lb. fillet steak, cut into
  4 pieces
Sauce
300 ml./10 fl. oz. red wine
30 ml./2 tablespoons
  chopped chives
salt and pepper
50 g./2 oz. butter
juice of ½ lemon
30 ml./2 tablespoons
  chopped fresh parsley

Melt the butter in a frying-pan. Add the steaks and fry quickly for 2 minutes on each side. Reduce heat and fry for a further 2 minutes. This will produce rare steaks—double the time for well done. Transfer the steaks to a warm serving dish and keep hot.

Pour the wine into a saucepan and add the chives. Boil until reduced by half. Season with salt and pepper to taste and stir in the butter, lemon juice, parsley and steak pan juices. Cook over high heat, stirring constantly, until the sauce is hot and bubbles. Pour over the steaks.

Serves 4

Basic Beef Casserole

675 g./1½ lb. stewing steak,
  cubed
25 g./1 oz. seasoned flour
50 ml./2 fl. oz. oil
1 onion, sliced
1 carrot, sliced
600 ml./1 pint beef stock

Coat the beef cubes with the seasoned flour. Heat the oil in a frying-pan. Add the onion and fry for 5 minutes. Transfer to a plate. Add the beef and fry for 5 to 8 minutes or until it is evenly browned. Add the carrot and return the onion to the pan. Gradually pour in the stock, stirring constantly. Bring to the boil then transfer to an ovenproof casserole. Cover tightly and put into the oven preheated to warm (170°C/325°F or Gas Mark 3). Cook for 1½ to 1¾ hours, or until the beef is cooked through and tender.

Serves 4

Meat-Lamb & Mutton

Crown Roast of Lamb

1 × 16-chop crown roast of lamb
450-675 g./1-1½ lb. stuffing
salt and pepper

Put the roast into a roasting pan and carefully spoon the stuffing into the centre. Cover the tops of the chop bones with aluminium foil and sprinkle with salt and pepper to taste.

Put into the oven preheated to moderate (180°C/350°F or Gas Mark 4) and roast for about 20 minutes per ½ kg./1 lb. plus 20 minutes over, or until the chops are cooked through.

Note: Any traditional stuffing such as herb, sage and onion*, or bread* would be suitable for a crown roast.

Serves 8

Lamb with Coriander

1 × 2 kg./4 lb. leg of lamb
3 garlic cloves, halved
15 ml./1 tablespoon crushed coriander seeds
salt and pepper
25 g./1 oz. butter, cut into small pieces

Make six small incisions all over the lamb, and insert the garlic halves and a little crushed coriander. Rub the joint all over with salt and pepper.

Put the lamb into a roasting pan and dot with the butter pieces. Put into the oven preheated to fairly hot (200°C/400°F or Gas Mark 6) and roast for 20 minutes. Reduce the oven temperature to warm (170°C/325°F or Gas Mark 3) and continue to roast for a further 1½ hours, or until the juices run out clear when the meat is pierced by a knife. Cool slightly before carving into thin slices.

Note: Mint sauce or redcurrant jelly are the traditional accompaniments to roast leg of lamb.

Serves 8

Boiled Lamb with Caper Sauce

1 × 2 kg./4 lb. breast of
  lamb, trimmed of excess
  fat and tied into shape
12 peppercorns
1 bouquet garni
15 ml./1 tablespoon chopped
  fresh rosemary
3 carrots, chopped
1 turnip, chopped
4 potatoes, chopped
Caper Sauce
40 g./1½ oz. butter
40 g./1½ oz. flour
300 ml./10 fl. oz. milk
salt and pepper
2.5 ml./½ teaspoon vinegar
25 ml./1½ tablespoons
  chopped capers

Put the lamb and seasonings into a large saucepan and add just enough water to cover. Bring to the boil, skimming off any scum. Cover and simmer for 1½ hours. Add the vegetables, re-cover and continue to simmer for 1 hour, or until the lamb is cooked through. Transfer the lamb and vegetables to a warmed serving dish and keep hot. Strain the cooking liquid and reserve 300 ml./10 fl. oz.

To make the sauce, melt the butter in a saucepan. Stir in the flour to form a smooth paste, then gradually stir in the milk and reserved cooking liquid. Bring to the boil and cook for 2 to 3 minutes, stirring constantly, or until the sauce thickens. Stir in the salt and pepper to taste, vinegar and capers and simmer for 1 minute. Serve with the meat.

Serves 6

Shoulder of Lamb Chasseur

50 g./2 oz. butter
1 onion, chopped
225 g./8 oz. pork
  sausagemeat
125 g./4 oz. walnuts, finely
  chopped
15 ml./1 tablespoon chopped
  fresh parsley
1.25 ml./¼ teaspoon dried
  mixed herbs
15 ml./1 tablespoon finely
  grated orange rind
salt and pepper
1 egg, beaten
1 × 1½ kg./3 lb. shoulder of
  lamb, chined

Melt half the butter in a frying-pan. Add the onion and fry for 5 minutes. Stir in the sausagemeat, walnuts, parsley, herbs, orange rind and salt and pepper and fry until the meat loses its pinkness. Remove from the heat and beat in the egg.

Lay the meat with the cut side towards you and fill with the stuffing. Secure at 5 cm./2 in. intervals with string or thread.

Put the meat in a roasting pan and spread with the remaining butter. Put into the oven preheated to hot (220°C/425°F or Gas Mark 7) and roast for 20 minutes. Reduce the oven temperature to fairly hot (190°C/375°F or Gas Mark 5) and continue to roast for 1¼ hours, or until the lamb is cooked through. Baste the meat occasionally during the cooking period.

Serves 4-6

Roast Lamb Bonne Femme

1 × 2 kg./4 lb. leg of lamb
2 garlic cloves, halved
salt and pepper
25 g./1 oz. butter, cut into
  small pieces
1 kg./2 lb. potatoes, thinly
  sliced
15 ml./1 tablespoon chopped
  fresh sage
½ kg./1 lb. onions, thinly
  sliced

Make four small incisions all over the lamb, and insert the garlic halves. Rub the joint all over with salt and pepper.

Put the lamb into a roasting pan and dot with the butter pieces. Put into the oven preheated to fairly hot (200°C/400°F or Gas Mark 6) and roast for 20 minutes. Arrange about half the potatoes in a layer around the meat and sprinkle over half the sage. Top with a layer of half the onions and season to taste with salt and pepper. Continue making layers until the ingredients are finished. Reduce the oven temperature to warm (170°C/325°F or Gas Mark 3) and continue to roast for a further 1½ hours, or until the juices run clear when the meat is pierced by a knife.

Cool slightly before carving into thin slices. Serve with the potatoes and onions.

Serves 8

Lamb in Pastry

1 × 2 kg./4 lb. leg of lamb
3 garlic cloves, halved
salt and pepper
5 ml./1 teaspoon dried
  rosemary
25 g./1 oz. butter, cut into
  small pieces
450 g./1 lb. shortcrust
  pastry*
1 egg, beaten with 15 ml./1
  tablespoon milk

Make six small incisions all over the lamb, and insert the garlic halves. Rub the joint all over with the salt and pepper and rosemary.

Put the lamb in a roasting pan and dot with the butter pieces. Put into the oven preheated to moderate (180°C/350°F or Gas Mark 4) and roast for 1 hour.

Roll out the dough until it is large enough to enclose the lamb completely. Cover the lamb with the dough, with the join underneath, and return it to the roasting pan. Prick the dough with a fork, then brush it with the beaten egg mixture. Put into a fairly hot oven (190°C/375°F or Gas Mark 5) and continue to roast for a further 45 minutes, or until the pastry is deep golden brown and the lamb is cooked through. Cool slightly before carving into thin slices.

Serves 8

Lamb with Cherry Sauce

1 × 2 kg./4 lb. leg of lamb
4 rosemary sprigs
4 strips of lemon rind
25 g./1 oz. butter, melted
15 ml./1 tablespoon lemon
   juice
Sauce
425 ml./15 fl. oz. chicken or
   lamb stock
40 g./1½ oz. flour
1 × 400 g./14 oz. can black
   cherries
150 ml./5 fl. oz. port
salt and pepper
25 g./1 oz. butter, cut into
   small pieces
5 ml./1 teaspoon chopped
   fresh mint

Make four small incisions all over the lamb, and insert the rosemary sprigs and strips of lemon rind. Mix together the melted butter and lemon juice and brush all over the lamb.

Put the lamb into a roasting pan, pour over any remaining melted butter and put into the oven preheated to fairly hot (200°C/400°F or Gas Mark 6). Roast for 20 minutes, then reduce the oven temperature to warm (170°C/325°F or Gas Mark 3). Continue to roast for a further 1½ hours, or until the juices run clear when the meat is pierced.

Transfer the lamb to a carving board and allow to cool slightly before carving into thin slices.

Meanwhile to make the sauce, mix a little of the stock with the flour to form a smooth paste. Put the remaining stock into a saucepan and bring to the boil. Stir in the flour mixture and cook for 2 to 3 minutes, stirring constantly, or until the sauce thickens. Stir in the cherries and can juice and all the remaining ingredients. Simmer for 2 to 3 minutes, or until the cherries are heated through. Serve with the lamb.

Serves 8

Lamb in Barbecue Sauce

4 large lamb cutlets, boned
50 g./2 oz. seasoned flour
25 g./1 oz. butter
1 onion, chopped
1 garlic clove, crushed
2.5 ml./½ teaspoon grated
   lemon rind
10 ml./2 teaspoons lemon
   juice
15 ml./1 tablespoon brown
   sugar
5 ml./1 teaspoon prepared
   mustard
salt and pepper

Roll each cutlet up and secure with a wooden toothpick. Roll in the seasoned flour. Melt the butter in a saucepan. Add the meat rolls and brown on all sides. Transfer each roll to a double thickness of foil, about 25 cm./10 in. square.

Add the onion and garlic to the pan and fry for 5 minutes. Stir in the remaining ingredients and bring to the boil. Simmer the sauce for 5 minutes, stirring constantly.

Spoon the sauce over the lamb rolls, then fold over the foil. Put the parcels on a baking sheet and put into the oven preheated to warm (170°C/325°F or Gas Mark 3). Cook for 45 minutes, or until the lamb is tender.

Serves 4

Lamb Shoulder with Spring Vegetables

1 × 1½ kg./3 lb. shoulder of
    lamb, chined
125 g./4 oz. sage and onion
    stuffing *
50 g./2 oz. butter
30 ml./2 tablespoons flour
425 ml./15 fl. oz. chicken or
    lamb stock
2 carrots, quartered
2 turnips, quartered
8 small potatoes
1 bouquet garni
salt and pepper

Lay the meat with the cut side towards you and fill with the stuffing. Secure at 5 cm./2 in. intervals with string or thread.

Melt the butter in a roasting tin. Add the meat and brown on all sides. Transfer to a plate. Stir the flour into the fat in the tin to form a smooth paste. Gradually stir in the stock and bring to the boil. Cook for 2 minutes, stirring constantly, or until the sauce thickens. Return the meat to the tin and add the vegetables, bouquet garni and salt and pepper to taste.

Put into the oven preheated to hot (220°C/425°F or Gas Mark 7) and roast for 20 minutes. Reduce the oven temperature to fairly hot (190°C/375°F or Gas Mark 5) and continue to roast for 1¼ hours, or until the lamb is cooked through. Baste the meat occasionally during the cooking period.

Serves 4-6

Lamb Cassoulet

45 ml./3 tablespoons cooking
    oil
1 kg./2 lb. lamb chops, cut
    into pieces
1 large onion, sliced
1 garlic clove, crushed
600 ml./1 pint chicken stock
1 × 225g./8 oz. can tomato
    purée
350 g./12 oz. dried haricot
    beans, soaked overnight
    and drained
2 carrots, sliced
2 parsnips, sliced
2 celery stalks, sliced
1 bouquet garni
salt and pepper
15 ml./1 tablespoon chopped
    fresh parsley

Heat the oil in a saucepan. Add the lamb, onion and garlic and fry until the lamb is evenly browned. Pour in a little stock, then stir in the tomato purée. Add the remaining stock, the beans, carrots, parsnips, celery, bouquet garni and salt and pepper to taste. Bring to the boil, cover and simmer for 2½ hours or until the lamb is cooked through. Garnish with the parsley.

Serves 4-6

Crumbed Lamb Chops

50 g./2 oz. flour
salt and pepper
5 ml./1 teaspoon chopped
  fresh rosemary
1.25 ml./¼ teaspoon cayenne
  pepper
8 small lamb chops
2 eggs, beaten
125 g./4 oz. dry breadcrumbs
75 g./3 oz. butter
15 ml./1 tablespoon chopped
  fresh parsley

Mix the flour, salt and pepper to taste, rosemary and cayenne together. Coat the chops in the flour mixture, then in the beaten eggs and finally in the breadcrumbs. Melt the butter in a frying-pan. Add the chops and brown on all sides. Fry for 10 to 12 minutes, or until the chops are cooked through and tender. Garnish with the parsley.

Serves 4

Irish Stew

1 kg./2 lb. potatoes, sliced
2 large onions, sliced
salt and pepper
15 ml./1 tablespoon dried
  thyme
1 kg./2 lb. lamb chops

Put about half the potatoes on the bottom of a large casserole. Cover with half the onions, then sprinkle with salt and pepper and half the thyme. Add the chops, then continue to make layers with the remaining onions, salt and pepper, thyme and the remaining potatoes. Add just enough water to cover. Cover tightly and put into the oven pre-heated to warm (170°C/325°F or Gas Mark 3). Cook for 2 to 2½ hours, or until the chops are cooked through.

Serves 4

Lemon and Ginger Chops

125 ml./4 fl. oz. cooking oil
grated rind of 2 lemons
60 ml./4 tablespoons lemon
  juice
30 ml./2 tablespoons brown
  sugar
15 ml./1 tablespoon ground
  ginger
salt and pepper
4 large lamb chops

Mix the oil, lemon rind and juice, sugar, ginger, salt and pepper to taste together in a large, shallow dish. Add the chops and leave to marinate at room temperature for 4 hours.

Put the chops on the rack in the grill pan. Grill until the chops are browned on both sides. Brush generously with the marinade, reduce the heat to moderate and continue to grill, basting occasionally with the marinade, for a further 12 to 20 minutes, or until the chops are cooked through.

Serves 4

Hawaiian Lamb

4 large lamb chops
salt and pepper
25 g./1 oz. butter, cut into
  small pieces
1 × 225 g./8 oz. can
  pineapple rings
25 g./1 oz. butter, melted
5 ml./1 teaspoon ground
  ginger
15 ml./1 tablespoon finely
  chopped preserved ginger

Put the chops on the rack in the grill pan and sprinkle over salt and pepper to taste. Dot over the butter. Grill until the chops are browned on both sides. Reduce the heat and continue to grill for a further 5 minutes.

Arrange the pineapple rings over the chops. Mix the melted butter and ground ginger together and brush over the rings. Continue to grill for 7 to 15 minutes, or until the chops are cooked through. Transfer the chops and pineapple rings to a warmed serving dish. Put the pineapple can juice and preserved ginger into a saucepan and bring to the boil, stirring constantly. Pour over the chops.

Serves 4

Braised Garlic Lamb

50 g./2 oz. bacon fat
4 large lamb chops
salt and pepper
10 garlic cloves
15 ml./1 tablespoon flour
150 ml./5 fl. oz. chicken
  stock
45 ml./3 tablespoons tomato
  purée

Melt the bacon fat in a frying-pan. Add the chops and brown on both sides. Season with the salt and pepper and arrange the garlic cloves around them. Simmer gently for 3 minutes. Sprinkle over the flour, pour in the stock and add the tomato purée. Stir to mix, then simmer for 15 minutes, or until the chops are cooked through. Remove the garlic before serving.

Serves 4

Mixed Grill

4 lamb chops
8 sausages
4 tomatoes, halved
12 mushroom caps
salt and pepper
30 ml./2 tablespoons butter,
  melted
4 lean bacon slices

Put the chops, sausages, tomato halves and mushrooms on the rack in the grill pan. Sprinkle over salt and pepper to taste and melted butter. Grill until the chops are brown on both sides. Reduce the heat to moderate and continue to grill for a further 12 minutes. Remove the vegetables from the pan and keep hot. Add the bacon slices and grill for a further 2 to 8 minutes, or until the chops are cooked through.

Serves 4

Devilled Lamb Chops

4 large lamb chops
salt and pepper
50 ml./2 fl. oz. cooking oil
1 × 275 g./10 oz. can tomato
  soup
10 ml./2 teaspoons mustard
15 ml./1 tablespoon brown
  sugar
15 ml./1 tablespoon
  Worcestershire sauce
15 ml./1 tablespoon lemon
  juice
30 ml./2 tablespoons sherry
1 onion, finely chopped
2 celery stalks, finely
  chopped
1 garlic clove, crushed

Rub the lamb chops with the salt and pepper. Heat the oil in a deep frying-pan. Add the chops and brown on both sides. Pour off the oil from the pan and set the chops aside, in the pan.

Put the remaining ingredients in a saucepan and bring to the boil, stirring constantly. Cook for 2 minutes. Pour the mixture over the chops, cover and simmer for 20 minutes or until the chops are cooked through and tender.

Serves 4

Lamb Noisettes Milanaise

6 lamb noisettes (boned
  lamb chops)
salt and pepper
125 g./4 oz. butter
½ kg./1 lb. hot cooked
  spaghetti
Sauce
30 ml./2 tablespoons cooking
  oil
1 onion, chopped
1 garlic clove, crushed
125 g./4 oz. button
  mushrooms, sliced
1 × 400 g./14 oz. can
  tomatoes
50 g./2 oz. tomato purée
5 ml./1 teaspoon sugar
15 ml./1 tablespoon dried
  basil
150 ml./5 fl. oz. red wine or
  beef stock
salt and pepper

To make the sauce, heat the oil in a saucepan. Add the onion and garlic and fry for 5 minutes. Stir in the mushrooms and fry for 3 minutes. Stir in all the remaining sauce ingredients and bring to the boil. Cover and simmer for 30 minutes, or until the sauce is thick.

Meanwhile, rub the noisettes with salt and pepper. Melt the butter in a frying-pan. Add the noisettes and fry for 10 to 12 minutes, or until they are cooked through and tender.

Put the spaghetti in a large, warmed serving bowl. Arrange the noisettes on top and cover with the sauce.

Serves 4-6

Mexican Lamb Chops

15 ml./1 tablespoon cooking
oil
15 ml./1 tablespoon vinegar
15 ml./1 tablespoon tomato
purée
15 ml./1 tablespoon prepared
mustard
salt and pepper
1.25 ml./¼ teaspoon garlic
salt
4 large lamb chops
4 tomatoes, halved

Mix the oil, vinegar, tomato purée, mustard, salt and pepper to taste and garlic salt together. Put the lamb chops on the rack in the grill pan. Brush with the oil mixture and grill until the chops are lightly browned. Add the tomato halves to the pan. Reduce the heat to moderate and continue to grill, basting occasionally with the oil mixture, for a further 12 to 20 minutes, or until the chops are cooked through.

Serves 4

Tipsy Chops

8 small lamb chops
salt and pepper
15 ml./1 tablespoon finely
grated orange rind
15 ml./1 tablespoon orange
juice
50 ml./2 fl. oz. red wine

Arrange the chops in a shallow ovenproof dish. Sprinkle over salt and pepper to taste, the orange rind and juice and the red wine. Cover the dish with foil and put it into the oven preheated to fairly hot (190°C/375°F or Gas Mark 5). Cook for 25 minutes, or until the chops are cooked through.

Serves 4

Italian Lamb Casserole

50 ml./2 fl. oz. cooking oil
1 kg./2 lb. lean lamb, cubed
2 onions, chopped
2 garlic cloves, crushed
15 ml./1 tablespoon chopped
fresh basil
15 ml./1 tablespoon chopped
fresh oregano
225 ml./8 fl. oz. stock
1 × 400 g./14 oz. can Italian
plum tomatoes
50 g./2 oz. Parmesan cheese,
grated

Heat the oil in a saucepan. Add the lamb cubes and fry for 5 to 8 minutes, or until they are evenly browned. Add the onions and garlic and fry for 5 minutes. Stir in the basil, oregano, stock and tomatoes with the can juice. Bring to the boil, cover and simmer for 1¼ hours, or until the lamb is tender. Stir in half the grated Parmesan and cook until it has melted. Serve with the remaining grated Parmesan.

Serves 4-6

Lamb Chops in Pastry Cases

6 large lamb chops
50 g./2 oz. butter
salt and pepper
2 tomatoes, skinned and
    chopped
175 g./6 oz. mushrooms,
    minced
125 g./4 oz. cooked ham,
    minced
15 ml./1 tablespoon finely
    chopped fresh parsley
450 g./1 lb. puff pastry*
2 egg yolks
30 ml./2 tablespoons water

Lay the chops on the rack in the grill pan. Dot with half the butter, cut into small pieces, and sprinkle over salt and pepper to taste. Grill the chops until they are browned on both sides.

Meanwhile, mix the tomatoes, mushrooms, ham, parsley and salt and pepper to taste together. Melt the remaining butter and stir into the mixture.

Roll out the dough into six rectangles, each large enough to enclose a chop. Put a tablespoon of the tomato mixture in the centre of each dough piece and top with a chop. Spoon the remaining tomato mixture over the top.

Beat the egg yolks and water together and brush around the edges of the dough. Fold and seal the edges to enclose the chop. Transfer to a baking sheet. Brush with the remaining egg mixture. Put into the oven preheated to hot (220°C/425°F or Gas Mark 7) and bake for 20 to 25 minutes, or until the pastry is puffed up and golden brown.

Serves 6

Lamb Saté

675 g./1½ lb. lean lamb,
    cubed
50 g./2 oz. butter, melted
Peanut Sauce
15 ml./1 tablespoon butter
1 small onion, chopped
1 garlic clove, crushed
5 ml./1 teaspoon crushed red
    chillis
300 ml./10 fl. oz. water
50 g./2 oz. peanut butter
25 ml./1½ tablespoons soy
    sauce
2.5 ml./½ teaspoon sugar
15 ml./1 tablespoon lemon
    juice

Thread the meat on to six skewers and brush with a little melted butter. Put the skewers on the rack in the grill pan. Brush again with melted butter and grill for 5 minutes. Reduce the heat to moderate and continue to grill, basting occasionally with melted butter, for 8 to 10 minutes, or until the lamb cubes are cooked through.

Meanwhile to make the sauce, melt the butter in a small saucepan. Add the onion and garlic and fry for 5 minutes. Stir in the chillis, water and peanut butter and bring slowly to the boil. Cook for 2 minutes, stirring constantly, or until the sauce becomes smooth and thick. Stir in the remaining ingredients. Serve the kebabs, with the peanut sauce.

Serves 4-6

Lamb Kebabs with Herb Sauce

½ kg./1 lb. lean lamb, cubed
1 green pepper, pith and
   seeds removed and
   chopped
12 button mushrooms
4 small tomatoes
12 pickling onions
25 g./1 oz. butter, melted
Sauce
300 ml./10 fl. oz. tomato
   juice
10 ml./2 teaspoons mustard
150 ml./5 fl. oz. plain yogurt
pinch of cayenne pepper
10 ml./2 teaspoons finely
   chopped fresh mint
10 ml./2 teaspoons chopped
   spring onions

Mix all the sauce ingredients together. Stir in the lamb and leave to marinate at room temperature for 4 hours. Drain and reserve the sauce.

Thread the meat and vegetables on to four skewers, then brush the vegetables with the melted butter. Put the skewers on the rack in the grill pan. Brush the meat with the reserved sauce. Grill for 5 minutes. Reduce the heat to moderate and continue to grill, basting with the marinade occasionally, for 8 to 10 minutes, or until the lamb cubes are cooked through. Gently heat the sauce until it is hot and serve with the kebabs.

Serves 4

Shashlik

50 ml./2 fl. oz. cooking oil
50 ml./2 fl. oz. lemon juice
salt and pepper
2.5 ml./½ teaspoon dried
   thyme
2.5 ml./½ teaspoon dried
   rosemary
675 g./1½ lb. lean lamb,
   cubed
12 large mushroom caps
2 green peppers, pith and
   seeds removed and cut
   into wedges
4 small tomatoes, halved
2 lean bacon slices,
   quartered
1 lemon, thinly sliced

Mix the oil, lemon juice, salt and pepper to taste, thyme and rosemary together in a shallow dish. Stir in the lamb and mushrooms and leave to marinate at room temperature for 4 hours. Remove the meat and mushrooms from the marinade and reserve the marinade.

Thread the meat and mushrooms on the skewers with the remaining vegetables and bacon pieces. Put the skewers on the rack in the grill pan. Brush with the reserved marinade. Grill for 5 minutes. Reduce the heat to moderate and grill, basting occasionally with the marinade, for 8 to 10 minutes, or until the lamb cubes are cooked through. Garnish with the lemon slices.

Serves 4

Lamb Stew

1 kg./2 lb. lamb chops
50 g./2 oz. seasoned flour
50 ml./2 fl. oz. cooking oil
2 onions, chopped
2 carrots, chopped
1 parsnip, chopped
2 celery stalks, chopped
1 large cooking apple, cored
    and chopped
600 ml./1 pint chicken stock
15 ml./1 tablespoon plum
    jam
salt and pepper

Coat the lamb chops with the seasoned flour. Heat the oil in a saucepan. Add the chops and brown on both sides. Add the onions, carrots, parsnip, celery and apple and fry for 5 minutes. Add the stock, jam and salt and pepper, and bring to the boil, stirring constantly. Cover and simmer for 1¼ hours, or until the lamb is cooked.

If you wish to thicken the gravy, blend 15 ml./1 tablespoon of flour with 15 ml./1 tablespoon of water and stir it into the stew. Cook for 2 or 3 minutes, or until the gravy has thickened a little.

Serves 4

Lamb Stew with Dumplings

1 kg./2 lb. lean lamb, cubed
50 g./2 oz. seasoned flour
50 ml./2 fl. oz. cooking oil
2 onions, chopped
3 carrots, chopped
3 potatoes, chopped
1 bay leaf
5 ml./1 teaspoon dried thyme
salt and pepper
425 ml./15 fl. oz. chicken
    stock
150 ml./5 fl. oz. tomato
    sauce*
15 ml./1 tablespoon flour
15 ml./1 tablespoon water
Dumplings
125 g./4 oz. self-raising flour
2.5 ml./½ teaspoon salt
10 ml./2 teaspoons butter
15 ml./1 tablespoon chopped
    fresh parsley
50-75 ml./2-3 fl. oz. milk

Coat the lamb cubes with the seasoned flour. Heat the oil in a saucepan. Add the lamb cubes and brown on all sides. Add the vegetables and fry for 5 minutes. Stir in the bay leaf, thyme, salt and pepper to taste, stock and tomato sauce. Bring to the boil, cover and simmer for 1 hour.

To make the dumplings, sift the flour and salt together. Rub in the butter, then stir in the parsley. Add enough milk to make a soft dough. Drop heaped tablespoonsful of the dumpling mixture into the stew. Cover and simmer for 15 to 20 minutes, or until the lamb is tender. Blend the flour and water together and stir into the stew. Cook for 2 minutes, stirring constantly, or until the sauce thickens.

Serves 4-6

Lamb Stew with Chutney

1 kg./2 lb. lean lamb, cubed
50 g./2 oz. seasoned flour
50 ml./2 fl. oz. cooking oil
1 onion, chopped
2 garlic cloves, crushed
10 ml./2 teaspoons chopped
  fresh root ginger
1 green pepper, pith and
  seeds removed and
  chopped
50 g./2 oz. sultanas
50 g./2 oz. mixed chutney
15 ml./1 tablespoon curry
  powder
15 ml./1 tablespoon finely
  grated lemon rind
15 ml./1 tablespoon lemon
  juice
15 ml./1 tablespoon vinegar
300 ml./10 fl. oz. chicken
  stock
150 ml./5 fl. oz. double
  cream

Coat the lamb cubes with the seasoned flour. Heat the oil in a saucepan. Add the lamb cubes and brown on all sides. Transfer to a plate. Add the onion, garlic, ginger and green pepper to the pan and fry for 5 minutes. Stir in the sultanas, chutney and curry powder, then add the lemon rind, lemon juice, vinegar and stock. Bring to the boil. Cover and simmer for 1¼ hours, or until the lamb is tender. Stir in the cream and cook gently for 1 to 2 minutes or until it is heated through.

Serves 4-6

Cranberry Lamb Stew

50 ml./2 fl. oz. cooking oil
1 kg./2 lb. lean lamb, cubed
1 onion, chopped
2 garlic cloves, crushed
salt and pepper
225 ml./8 fl. oz. red wine
1 × 175 g./6 oz. can tomato
  purée
225 ml./8 fl. oz. chicken
  stock
175 ml./6 fl. oz. cranberry
  sauce (bottled or canned)
10 ml./2 teaspoons ground
  ginger

Heat the oil in a saucepan. Add the lamb cubes and brown on all sides. Transfer to a plate. Add the onion and garlic to the pan and fry for 5 minutes. Stir in salt and pepper to taste, the wine, tomato purée and stock and bring to the boil. Return the lamb cubes to the pan and simmer for 45 minutes.

Stir in the remaining ingredients, cover and simmer for a further 30 minutes, or until the lamb is tender.

Serves 4-6

Lamb Daube

1 kg./2 lb. lean lamb, cubed
175 g./6 oz. streaky bacon,
    chopped
2 onions, sliced
2 carrots, sliced
175 g./6 oz. mushrooms,
    sliced
300 ml./10 fl. oz. chicken
    stock
Marinade
300 ml./10 fl. oz. dry white
    wine
30 ml./2 tablespoons cooking
    oil
1 bouquet garni
2 garlic cloves, crushed
1 onion, chopped
10 peppercorns
15 ml./1 tablespoon chopped
    fresh parsley
15 ml./1 tablespoon finely
    grated orange rind
3 cloves

Mix all the marinade ingredients together. Add the lamb cubes and leave to marinate at room temperature for 8 hours or overnight. Remove the cubes from the marinade and dry. Reserve the marinade.

Arrange about one-third of the bacon on the bottom of a deep flameproof casserole. Cover with half the lamb cubes and vegetables. Continue to make layers until the ingredients are finished. Pour over the stock and reserved marinade. Bring to the boil, cover and put into the oven preheated to warm (170°C/325°F or Gas Mark 3). Cook for 3 hours, or until the lamb is tender.

Serves 4-6

Lamb Curry I

50 ml./2 fl. oz. cooking oil
1 kg./2 lb. lean lamb, cubed
2 onions, chopped
2 garlic cloves, crushed
5 ml./1 teaspoon chopped
    fresh root ginger
15 ml./1 tablespoon hot curry
    powder
1 × 400 g./14 oz. can
    tomatoes
25 g./1 oz. desiccated
    coconut

Heat the oil in a saucepan. Add the lamb cubes and brown on all sides. Add the onions, garlic and ginger and fry for 5 minutes. Stir in the curry powder and fry for 1 minute. Stir in the tomatoes and can juice and bring to the boil. Cover and simmer for 1 hour. Stir in the coconut and simmer for a further 15 minutes, or until the lamb is tender.

Serves 4-6

Lamb Curry II

150 ml./5 fl. oz. sour cream
10 ml./2 teaspoons garam
  masala
15 ml./1 tablespoon curry
  powder
1 kg./2 lb. lean lamb, cubed
125 g./4 oz. butter
30 ml./2 tablespoons slivered
  almonds
50 g./2 oz. sultanas
50 g./2 oz. dried apricots,
  sliced
2 garlic cloves, crushed
10 ml./2 teaspoons finely
  chopped fresh root ginger
2 onions, sliced
salt and pepper
15 ml./1 tablespoon lemon
  juice

Mix the sour cream, garam masala and curry powder together in a shallow dish. Add the lamb cubes and leave to marinate at room temperature for 4 hours.

Melt the butter in a saucepan. Add the almonds and fry until they are browned. Transfer to a plate. Add the sultanas and apricots to the pan and fry until they are lightly browned and have plumped slightly. Transfer to the plate.

Add the garlic, ginger and onions to the pan and fry for 5 minutes. Stir in the lamb with its marinade, salt and pepper to taste and lemon juice and fry for 5 minutes. Return the sultanas and apricots to the pan and mix well. Bring to the boil, cover and simmer for 1¼ hours, or until the lamb is tender. Add a little water if the mixture becomes too dry. Sprinkle over the almonds.

Serves 4-6

Moroccan Lamb Casserole

2.5 ml./½ teaspoon cumin
2.5 ml./½ teaspoon ground
  saffron
1.25 ml./¼ teaspoon ground
  ginger
salt and pepper
15 ml./1 tablespoon finely
  grated lemon rind
1 kg./2 lb. lean lamb, cubed
50 g./2 oz. butter
30 ml./2 tablespoons cooking
  oil
2 onions, chopped
1 garlic clove, crushed
water or stock
juice of ½ lemon
125 g./4 oz. flaked almonds

Mix the cumin, saffron, ginger, salt and pepper to taste and lemon rind together. Coat the lamb cubes with the mixture. Heat the butter and oil in a saucepan. Add the lamb cubes and brown on all sides. Add the onions and garlic and just enough water or stock to prevent the mixture from becoming too dry. Fry for 10 minutes. Then add a little more liquid, cover and simmer, adding more liquid from time to time, for 1 hour, or until the meat is tender. (At the end of the cooking time, there should be no excess liquid but the meat and vegetables should be very moist.)

Squeeze the lemon juice into the mixture, then stir in the almonds. Simmer for a further 5 minutes.

Serves 4-6

French Lamb Stew

1 kg./2 lb. lean lamb, cubed
2 onions, chopped
2 carrots, chopped
2 small turnips, chopped
1 celery stalk, chopped
5 ml./1 teaspoon dried
   rosemary
salt and pepper
1 bouquet garni
600 ml./1 pint chicken stock
600 ml./1 pint water
175 g./6 oz. mushrooms,
   halved
40 g./1½ oz. butter
40 g.1½ oz. flour
1 large egg yolk
125 ml./4 fl. oz. single cream

Put the lamb, onions, carrots, turnips, celery, rosemary, salt and pepper to taste, bouquet garni, stock and water into a saucepan. Bring to the boil, then simmer for 1¼ hours. Stir in the mushrooms and simmer for a further 15 minutes, or until the meat and vegetables are tender. Transfer the meat and vegetables to a warmed serving dish and keep hot.

Boil the cooking liquid over high heat until it reduces to about 600 ml./1 pint. Strain. Melt the butter in a saucepan. Stir in the flour to form a smooth paste. Gradually stir in the cooking liquid and bring to the boil. Cook for 3 minutes, stirring constantly, or until the sauce thickens. Mix the egg yolk and cream together, then add a little of the sauce. Return the egg yolk mixture to the sauce and stir to blend. Heat gently for 1 minute, taking care not to boil. Pour the sauce over the vegetables and meat.

Serves 4-6

Lamb Goulash

1 kg./2 lb. lean lamb, cubed
50 g./2 oz. seasoned flour
50 ml./2 fl. oz. cooking oil
1 large onion, chopped
1 garlic clove, crushed
125 g./4 oz. mushrooms,
   sliced
30 ml./2 tablespoons paprika
1 × 400 g./14 oz. can
   tomatoes
5 ml./1 teaspoon caraway
   seeds
salt and pepper
4 potatoes, quartered
150 ml./5 fl. oz. sour cream

Coat the lamb cubes with the seasoned flour. Heat the oil in a saucepan. Add the onion, garlic and mushrooms and fry for 5 minutes. Add the meat and brown on all sides. Stir in the paprika.

Add the tomatoes and can juice, caraway seeds, salt and pepper and bring to the boil. Cover and simmer for 45 minutes. Add the potatoes and continue to simmer for 30 minutes, or until the lamb is tender. Stir in the sour cream.

Serves 4-6

Italian Lamb Stew

1 kg./2 lb. lean lamb, cubed
50 g./2 oz. seasoned flour
45 ml./3 tablespoons cooking
   oil
2 onions, chopped
1 garlic clove, crushed
4 celery stalks, chopped
salt and pepper
5 ml./1 teaspoon sugar
300 ml./10 fl. oz. chicken
   stock
30 ml./2 tablespoons tomato
   purée
150 ml./5 fl. oz. dry white
   wine
5 ml./1 teaspoon dried
   rosemary
125 g./4 oz. mushrooms,
   sliced
15 ml./1 tablespoon chopped
   fresh parsley

Coat the lamb cubes with the seasoned flour. Heat the oil in a saucepan. Add the lamb cubes and brown on all sides. Transfer to a plate. Add the onions, garlic, celery, salt and pepper to taste and sugar to the pan and fry for 5 minutes. Stir in the stock, tomato purée, wine and rosemary and bring to the boil. Cover and simmer for 1 hour.

Add the mushrooms, re-cover and continue to simmer for 15 minutes, or until the lamb is tender. Garnish with the parsley.

Serves 4-6

Navarin de Mouton

50 ml./2 fl. oz. cooking oil
1 kg./2 lb. lean mutton,
   trimmed of excess fat and
   cubed
400 ml./15 fl. oz. hot water
50 g./2 oz. tomato purée
salt and pepper
1 bouquet garni
1 garlic clove, crushed
8 pickling onions
4 small carrots, halved
1 small turnip, quartered
4 celery stalks, quartered
8 small new potatoes

Heat the oil in a saucepan. Add the mutton and brown on all sides. Transfer to a plate. Mix the water and tomato purée together, then add to the pan. Sprinkle over salt and pepper to taste and add the bouquet garni. Bring to the boil, then return the mutton to the pan. Cover and simmer for 1 hour.

Add all the remaining ingredients, re-cover the pan and continue to simmer for 1 hour, or until the mutton is cooked through. Transfer the meat and vegetables to a warmed serving dish. Strain a little of the cooking liquid over the meat and vegetables.

Serves 4

Spanish Lamb Stew

50 ml./2 fl. oz. cooking oil
1 kg./2 lb. lean lamb, cubed
2 onions, chopped
2 red peppers, pith and seeds
  removed and chopped
2.5 ml./½ teaspoon ground
  saffron dissolved in 15
  ml./1 tablespoon water
salt and pepper
350 ml./12 fl. oz. stock
45 ml./3 tablespoons dry
  sherry
50 g./2 oz. olives, chopped

Heat the oil in a saucepan. Add the lamb cubes and brown on all sides. Transfer to a plate. Add the onions and peppers to the pan and fry for 5 minutes. Stir in the saffron mixture, salt and pepper and stock. Return the lamb cubes to the pan, cover and simmer for 1 hour. Stir in the sherry and olives, re-cover and simmer for 15 minutes, or until the lamb is tender.

Serves 4-6

Swedish Lamb Stew

50 g./2 oz. butter
1 kg./2 lb. lean lamb, cubed
1 onion, chopped
½ kg./1 lb. mushrooms,
  chopped
salt and pepper
5 ml./1 teaspoon paprika
175 ml./6 fl. oz. chicken
  stock
225 ml./8 fl. oz. sour cream
15 ml./1 tablespoon chopped
  fresh dill

Melt the butter in a saucepan. Add the lamb cubes and brown on all sides. Transfer to a plate. Add the onion to the pan and fry for 5 minutes. Stir in the mushrooms, salt and pepper to taste, paprika and stock and bring to the boil. Return the lamb cubes to the pan and stir well. Cover and simmer for 1¼ hours, or until the lamb is tender.

Stir in the sour cream and cook gently for 1 or 2 minutes, or until it is heated through. Sprinkle over the dill.

Serves 4-6

Bobotee

50 g./2 oz. butter
2 onions, chopped
3 tomatoes, skinned and
  chopped
575 g./1¼ lb. minced lamb
150 ml./5 fl. oz. beef stock
15 ml./1 tablespoon curry
  powder
45 ml./3 tablespoons flaked
  almonds
salt and pepper
2 eggs, beaten
300 ml./10 fl. oz. milk

Melt the butter in a saucepan. Add the onions and tomatoes and fry for 5 minutes. Stir in the lamb and fry until it loses its pinkness. Stir in the stock and curry powder and bring to the boil. Simmer for 25 minutes. Stir in the almonds and simmer for 5 minutes, then transfer the mixture to a casserole.

Mix the remaining ingredients together and pour over the lamb. Put into the oven preheated to warm (170°C/325°F or Gas Mark 3) and bake for 45 to 50 minutes or until the topping is firm and set.

Serves 4

Lamb Ratatouille

3 tablespoons olive oil
1 kg./2 lb. lean lamb, cubed
2 onions, chopped
2 garlic cloves, crushed
675 g./1½ lb. tomatoes,
    skinned and chopped
2 small green peppers, pith
    and seeds removed and
    chopped
1 large aubergine, chopped
    and dégorged
4 courgettes, cut into 2.5
    cm./1 in. slices
15 ml./1 tablespoon chopped
    fresh parsley
salt and pepper

Heat the oil in a saucepan. Add the lamb, onions and garlic and fry until the meat is evenly browned. Stir in all the remaining ingredients and bring to the boil. Cover and simmer for 1¼ hours, or until the meat is tender.

Serves 4-6

Lamb with Bean Sprouts

15 ml./1 tablespoon soy
    sauce
30 ml./2 tablespoons vinegar
30 ml./2 tablespoons brown
    sugar
5 ml./1 teaspoon finely
    chopped fresh ginger
salt and pepper
15 ml./1 tablespoon
    cornflour
30 ml./2 tablespoons cooking
    oil
½ kg./1 lb. lean lamb, cut into
    thin strips
3 spring onions, sliced
1 × 450 g./1 lb. can bean
    sprouts, drained

Mix the soy sauce, vinegar, sugar, ginger, salt and pepper and cornflour with 150 ml./5 fl. oz. of water. Set aside. Heat the oil in a saucepan. Add the lamb strips and brown on all sides. Stir in the cornflour mixture and spring onions and bring to the boil. Simmer, stirring constantly, for 2 minutes. Add the bean sprouts and cook, stirring constantly, for 3 minutes longer.

Serves 4

Savoury Lamb

1 kg./2 lb. lamb, cubed
50 g./2 oz. seasoned flour
45 ml./3 tablespoons cooking oil
2 onions, chopped
1 × 425 g./15 oz. can condensed tomato soup
300 ml./10 fl. oz. beef stock
30 ml./2 tablespoons sherry
15 ml./1 tablespoon brown sugar
15 ml./1 tablespoon lemon juice
15 ml./1 tablespoon Worcestershire sauce
10 ml./2 teaspoons dry mustard
salt and pepper
2 carrots, chopped
1 turnip, chopped
4 celery stalks, chopped
1 red pepper, pith and seeds removed and chopped
1 green pepper, pith and seeds removed and chopped

Coat the lamb cubes with the seasoned flour. Heat the oil in a saucepan. Add the lamb cubes and onions and fry until the lamb is evenly browned. Add all the remaining ingredients, except the vegetables, and bring to the boil. Cover and simmer for 1 hour.

Stir in the vegetables, re-cover and continue to simmer for 30 to 45 minutes, or until the lamb is tender and the vegetables are cooked.

Serves 4-6

Lancashire Hot Pot

8 small lamb chops
50 g./2 oz. seasoned flour
2 onions, sliced
4 lambs' kidneys, halved
125 g./4 oz. mushrooms, sliced
salt and pepper
10 ml./2 teaspoons dried thyme
675 g./1½ lb. potatoes, cut into thick slices
350 ml./12 fl. oz. well-seasoned beef stock
15 g./½ oz. butter, cut into small pieces

Coat the lamb chops with the seasoned flour. Layer the chops, onions, kidneys and mushrooms in a deep ovenproof casserole, seasoning each layer with salt and pepper and thyme. Cover with the potato slices, then pour in the stock. Scatter the butter pieces over the potato slices. Cover the casserole and put it into the oven preheated to moderate (180°C/350°F or Gas Mark 4). Cook for 2 hours. Uncover and cook for a further 30 minutes, or until the potatoes are golden brown and the chops are cooked and tender.

Serves 4

Lamb and Cabbage Hot Pot

25 g./1 oz. butter, melted
1½ kg./3 lb. lean lamb, cubed
1 small cabbage, cut into
   thick segments
50 g./2 oz. flour
salt and pepper
2 carrots, sliced
900 ml./1½ pints chicken
   stock
15 ml./1 tablespoon chopped
   fresh parsley

Pour the butter into a flameproof casserole. Put about one-third of the lamb cubes into the casserole and top with about one-third of the cabbage. Sprinkle over flour, salt and pepper. Continue making layers until all the ingredients are used up, finishing with the cabbage. Cover with the carrots, then pour over the stock. Bring to the boil and put into the oven preheated to warm (170°C/325°F or Gas Mark 3). Cook for 1½ to 2 hours, or until the lamb is tender. Garnish with the parsley.

Serves 6

Welsh Hot Pot

675 g./1½ lb. potatoes, thinly
   sliced
salt and pepper
½ kg./1 lb. leeks, sliced into
   rings
3 large carrots, sliced
1 kg./2 lb. middle end of
   neck of lamb, chopped
15 ml./1 tablespoon chopped
   fresh sage
150 ml./5 fl. oz. water
25 g./1 oz. butter, cut into
   small pieces

Put about one-third of the potato slices on the bottom of a deep casserole and sprinkle over salt and pepper to taste. Cover with half the leeks and half the carrots and season well. Cover with half the lamb and half the sage. Continue to make layers until all the ingredients are finished. Pour over the water and dot with the butter pieces. Put into the oven preheated to moderate (180°C/350°F or Gas Mark 4) and cook for 2 hours. Cover and cook for a further 30 minutes, or until the chops are tender.

Serves 4

Moussaka

125 ml./4 fl. oz. cooking oil
1 onion, chopped
1 garlic clove, crushed
675 g./1½ lb. minced lamb
1 × 400 g./14 oz. can
    tomatoes
5 ml./1 teaspoon dried
    rosemary
salt and pepper
2 aubergines, sliced and
    dégorged
Topping
175 g./6 oz. ricotta or cottage
    cheese
2 eggs, beaten
125 ml./4 fl. oz. single cream

Heat half the oil in a saucepan. Add the onion and garlic and fry for 5 minutes. Add the lamb and cook until it loses its pinkness. Add the tomatoes and can juice, rosemary and salt and pepper to taste, and stir well. Bring to the boil, then simmer for 20 minutes.

Meanwhile, heat the remaining oil in a frying-pan. When it is hot, add the aubergine slices and brown on both sides. Add a little more oil if necessary. Drain the slices on kitchen towels. Mix all the topping ingredients together.

Pour the lamb mixture into a casserole. Cover with the aubergine slices, then pour over the topping. Put the casserole into the oven preheated to fairly hot (190°C/375°F or Gas Mark 5) and bake for 40 minutes or until the topping is set and golden.

Serves 4

Lamb Ragoût

1 kg./2 lb. lean lamb, cubed
50 g./2 oz. seasoned flour
60 ml./4 tablespoons cooking
    oil
½ kg./1 lb. onions, chopped
2 garlic cloves, crushed
1 bay leaf
salt and pepper
600 ml./1 pint red wine
150 g./5 oz. tomato purée
½ kg./1 lb. potatoes, quartered

Coat the lamb cubes with the seasoned flour. Heat the oil in a saucepan. Add the lamb cubes, onions and garlic and fry until the meat is evenly browned. Stir in the bay leaf, salt and pepper to taste, wine and tomato purée, and bring to the boil. Cover and simmer for 1 hour. Stir in the potatoes and continue to simmer, uncovered, for 1 hour, or until the lamb is very tender.

Serves 4-6

Lamb Fondue

1 kg./2 lb. lean boned leg of
    lamb, cut into 2.5 cm./1 in.
    cubes
oil for fondue frying
dip and sauces (see note
    below)
Marinade
30 ml./2 tablespoons wine
    vinegar
50 ml./2 fl. oz. oil
50 ml./2 fl. oz. dry white
    wine
½ garlic clove, crushed
1 shallot, chopped
6 peppercorns, crushed
1 rosemary sprig
5 ml./1 teaspoon finely
    chopped mint

Mix all the marinade ingredients together in a
shallow dish. Add the lamb cubes and leave to
marinate at room temperature for 8 hours.

Drain the meat from the marinade and dry. Fill
the fondue pot half-full with oil and heat. Spear the
lamb cubes with fondue forks and carefully lower
them, a few at a time, into the oil. Fry for 5 minutes
or until the lamb is cooked to taste. Serve with dips
and sauces.

Note: Béarnaise sauce*, mint sauce*, Chinese
plum sauce* and chutney butter* are particularly
recommended as dips for Lamb Fondue.

Serves 4-6

Lamb Rissoles

25 g./1 oz. butter
25 g./1 oz. flour
150 ml./5 fl. oz. milk
50 g./2 oz. fresh
    breadcrumbs
350 g./12 oz. cooked lamb,
    minced or very finely
    chopped
salt and pepper
1.25 ml./¼ teaspoon cayenne
    pepper
5 ml./1 teaspoon dried thyme
50 g./2 oz. seasoned flour
2 eggs, beaten
50 g./2 oz. dry breadcrumbs
oil for deep frying

Melt the butter in a saucepan. Stir in the flour to
form a smooth paste, then gradually stir in the
milk. Bring to the boil and cook for 2 to 3 minutes,
stirring constantly, or until the sauce thickens. Stir
in the fresh breadcrumbs, lamb, salt and pepper to
taste, cayenne and thyme and cook for 2 minutes.
Set aside to cool.

Form the mixture into about eight small cakes.
Coat first in the seasoned flour, then in the eggs
and finally in the dry breadcrumbs. Set aside for 10
minutes.

Deep-fry for 5 minutes, or until golden brown.
Drain on kitchen towels.

Serves 4

Lamb and Raisin Patties

25 g./1 oz. butter
25 g./1 oz. flour
150 ml./5 fl. oz. beef stock
75 g./3 oz. raisins
15 ml./1 tablespoon chopped
 fresh parsley
½ kg./1 lb. minced lamb
salt and pepper
50 g./2 oz. fresh
 breadcrumbs
50 g./2 oz. seasoned flour
2 eggs, beaten
75 g./3 oz. dry breadcrumbs
125 ml./4 fl. oz. cooking oil

Melt the butter in a frying-pan. Stir in the flour to form a smooth paste, then gradually stir in the stock. Bring to the boil, then cook for 2 minutes, stirring constantly, or until the sauce thickens. Stir in the raisins, parsley and lamb and cook for 2 minutes. Stir in salt and pepper to taste and the fresh breadcrumbs and set aside to cool.

Form the mixture into about eight small patties and chill in the refrigerator for 30 minutes or until firm. Dip the patties in the seasoned flour, then in the beaten eggs and finally in the dry breadcrumbs. Set aside for 10 minutes.

Heat the oil in a frying-pan. Add the patties and fry for 10 to 15 minutes, or until they are cooked through and tender.

Serves 4

Turkish Lamb Shanks

4 lamb shanks
50 g./2 oz. seasoned flour
125 ml./4 fl. oz. olive oil
2 onions, chopped
2 garlic cloves, crushed
2 green peppers, pith and
 seeds removed and
 chopped
10 ml./2 teaspoons cumin
 seeds
10 ml./2 teaspoons crushed
 black peppercorns
2 × 425 g./15 oz. cans
 tomato juice
juice of 1 lemon
salt and pepper

Ask your butcher to chop through the bone in the shanks. Roll the shanks in the seasoned flour. Heat the oil in a saucepan. Add the lamb shanks and brown on all sides. Add the remaining ingredients and bring to the boil. Cover and simmer for 3 hours, or until the meat is falling off the bone.

Serves 4

Shepherd's Pie

675 g./1½ lb. potatoes
30 ml./2 tablespoons cooking
  oil
1 onion, chopped
125 g./4 oz. mushrooms,
  sliced
575 g./1¼ lb. cooked lamb,
  minced
45 ml./3 tablespoons tomato
  ketchup
2.5 ml./½ teaspoon dry
  mustard
salt and pepper
150 ml./5 fl. oz. well-
  seasoned gravy
25 g./1 oz. butter

Cook the potatoes in boiling, salted water for 15 to 20 minutes, or until they are tender. Meanwhile, heat the oil in a saucepan. Add the onion and mushrooms and fry for 5 minutes. Stir in the lamb, tomato ketchup, mustard, salt and pepper to taste. Pour over the gravy and bring to the boil. Simmer for 5 minutes, then transfer to a pie dish.

Drain the potatoes, then mash with the butter and salt and pepper to taste. Spoon over the mixture in the dish, then put into the oven preheated to moderate (180°C/350°F or Gas Mark 4). Bake for 20 to 25 minutes, or until the potatoes are browned.

Serves 4-6

Spiced Lamb with Vegetables

2 eggs
45 ml./3 tablespoons
  cornflour
½ kg./1 lb. lean lamb, cut into
  thin strips
oil for deep frying
1 red pepper, pith and seeds
  removed and cut into
  wedges
1 onion, cut into wedges
15 ml./1 tablespoon soy
  sauce
5 ml./1 teaspoon finely
  chopped fresh ginger
1 garlic clove, crushed
1.25 ml./¼ teaspoon salt
3 celery stalks, diagonally
  sliced
1 × 150 g./5 oz. can bamboo
  shoot, diagonally sliced

Mix the eggs and 30 ml./2 tablespoons of cornflour together. Add the lamb strips and stir well to coat. Deep-fry the strips for 3 minutes or until they are golden brown. Drain on kitchen towels.

Cook the red pepper and onion wedges in boiling water for 5 minutes, then drain. Mix the soy sauce, ginger, garlic, salt and remaining cornflour with 150 ml./5 fl. oz. water in a saucepan and bring to the boil, stirring constantly. Add the celery, bamboo shoot, red pepper and onion and simmer for 4 minutes. Stir in the lamb strips and reheat for 2 minutes.

Serves 4

Sweet and Sour Meatballs

675 g./1½ lb. minced lamb
3 spring onions, very finely
    chopped
10 ml./2 teaspoons ground
    ginger
salt and pepper
5 ml./1 teaspoon brown
    sugar
30 ml./2 tablespoons soy
    sauce
25 g./1 oz. dry breadcrumbs
15 ml./1 tablespoon water
125 ml./4 fl. oz. cooking oil
Sauce
1 × 400 g./14 oz. can
    pineapple chunks
15 ml./1 tablespoon soy
    sauce
40 ml./2½ tablespoons brown
    sugar
15 ml./1 tablespoon cooking
    oil
30 ml./2 tablespoons vinegar
salt and pepper
2 carrots, thinly sliced
½ cucumber, thinly sliced
2 celery stalks, thinly sliced
25 ml./1½ tablespoons
    cornflour

Mix the lamb, spring onions, ginger, salt and pepper to taste, sugar, soy sauce, breadcrumbs and water together. Form into small balls and chill in the refrigerator for 30 minutes.

Heat the oil in a frying-pan. Add the meat balls, a few at a time, and fry for 10 to 15 minutes, or until they are cooked through. Keep hot. Meanwhile combine all the sauce ingredients (including the pineapple can juice) together in a large saucepan and bring to the boil. Cook for 2 to 3 minutes, stirring constantly, or until the sauce thickens and becomes translucent. Add the meat balls and simmer for 1 to 2 minutes.

Serves 4

Meat-Pork

Pork Rissoles

25 ml./1 fl. oz. oil
1 large onion, finely chopped
1 kg./2 lb. cooked pork,
   minced
2 eggs
30 ml./2 tablespoons sour
   cream
5 ml./1 teaspoon paprika
30 ml./2 tablespoons
   chopped fresh parsley
50 g./2 oz. fresh
   breadcrumbs
salt and pepper
50 g./2 oz. butter

Heat the oil in a frying-pan. Add the onion and fry for 5 minutes. Transfer to a bowl and add the pork, one egg, sour cream, paprika, parsley, half the breadcrumbs and salt and pepper to taste. Mix well and form the mixture into 12 thick rissoles. Lightly beat the remaining egg. Coat the rissoles first in the beaten egg and then in the remaining breadcrumbs.

Melt the butter in a frying-pan. Add the rissoles, a few at a time, and cook for 10 minutes or until they are evenly browned and cooked through. Drain on kitchen towels.

Serves 6

Salt Pork Stew

1 kg./2 lb. salt pork, cubed
2 onions, chopped
2.5 ml./½ teaspoon brown
   sugar
½ kg./1 lb. okra
1 × 450 g./1 lb. can
   sweetcorn, drained
1 × 200 g./7 oz. can
   tomatoes, chopped
1 large green pepper, pith
   and seeds removed and
   chopped
300 ml./10 fl. oz. beef stock
pinch of dried sage
salt and pepper

Put the salt pork in a saucepan and cook, stirring, for 10 to 15 minutes, or or until the pork is evenly browned and has rendered most of its fat. Transfer to a plate. Pour off all but 30 ml./2 tablespoons of the fat and add the onions and sugar. Fry for 5 minutes then stir in the okra, sweetcorn, tomatoes and can juice and the pepper. Return the salt pork to the pan and cook for 5 minutes. Pour over the stock and stir in the sage and salt and pepper to taste. Bring to the boil and simmer for 20 minutes, or until the pork and vegetables are tender.

Serves 4-6

Pork Chops with Coriander

15 ml./1 tablespoon
  coriander seeds
5 peppercorns, crushed
50 ml./2 fl. oz. soy sauce
2 garlic cloves, crushed
5 ml./1 teaspoon sugar
4 pork chops

Mix together the coriander seeds, peppercorns, soy sauce, garlic and sugar. Put the chops on a plate and spoon the coriander mixture over them. Leave for 30 minutes, turning once. Reserve the marinade. Grill the chops for 2 minutes on each side. Reduce the heat and grill for a further 8 minutes on each side, basting occasionally with the marinade, or until the pork is cooked through and tender.

Serves 4

Spareribs with Maple Syrup Sauce

1 × 2 kg./4 lb. sparerib of
  pork, cut into 2-rib pieces
Sauce
175 ml./6 fl. oz. maple syrup
2 garlic cloves, crushed
30 ml./2 tablespoons tomato
  purée
30 ml./2 tablespoons lemon
  juice
15 ml./1 tablespoon mustard

Put the spareribs in a roasting pan and put into the oven preheated to fairly hot (200°C/400°F or Gas Mark 6). Bake for 30 minutes, turning once. Mix together all the sauce ingredients. Drain off the fat from the roasting pan and pour the sauce over the spareribs. Reduce the oven temperature to moderate (180°C/350°F or Gas Mark 4) and roast for a further 45 minutes, basting occasionally, or until the ribs are tender and glazed.

Serves 4-6

Peppered Pork Steaks

1 kg./2 lb. pork fillets, cut
  into four steaks
salt
30 ml./2 tablespoons crushed
  black peppercorns
50 g./2 oz. butter
125 g./4 oz. mushrooms,
  sliced
150 ml./5 fl. oz. single cream

Rub the pork steaks with the salt and press in the crushed peppercorns. Melt the butter in a frying-pan. Add the steaks and fry for 10 minutes on each side. Reduce the heat and fry for a further 10 minutes on each side, or until the pork is evenly browned and cooked through. Transfer to a warmed serving dish and keep hot.

Add the mushrooms to the pan and fry for 5 minutes. Stir in the cream and cook for a further 3 minutes. Pour the sauce over the pork.

Serves 4

Swiss Pork

1 kg./2 lb. pork fillets
salt and pepper
50 g./2 oz. butter
10 ml./2 teaspoons dried
  sage
225 g./8 oz. Gruyère cheese,
  cut into 12 slices
30 ml./2 tablespoons
  mustard
150 ml./5 fl. oz. single cream

Rub the fillets with salt and pepper. Melt the butter in a frying-pan. Add the fillets, sprinkle over the sage and fry for 8 minutes, or until the pork is evenly browned. Cover and cook for 40 minutes. Remove the pork from the pan and make 12 deep cuts along it. Spread the cheese slices with three-quarters of the mustard and insert one slice into each cut. Return the pork to the pan and cook, uncovered, for a further 7 minutes or until the cheese has melted. Transfer to a warmed serving plate and keep hot.

Stir the remaining mustard and cream into the cooking juices and cook gently until the cream is warmed through. Pour the sauce over the fillets.

Serves 4

Pork Kebabs

1 kg./2 lb. pork fillets, cubed
Marinade
3 garlic cloves, crushed
10 ml./2 teaspoons grated
  orange rind
5 ml./1 teaspoon dried sage
5 ml./1 teaspoon dried
  marjoram
5 ml./1 teaspoon sugar
30 ml./2 tablespoons oil
30 ml./2 tablespoons sherry
salt and pepper

Mix together all the marinade ingredients in a bowl. Add the pork cubes and coat well. Marinate for 2 hours, basting occasionally.

Thread the meat cubes on to skewers and brush with some of the reserved marinade. Grill for 10 to 15 minutes or until the meat is cooked through. Baste occasionally with the marinade during the cooking period.

Serves 6

Pork with Juniper Berries

4 pork chops
2 garlic cloves, halved
salt and pepper
10 ml./2 teaspoons juniper
   berries, crushed
50 ml./2 fl. oz. oil

Rub each chop with half a garlic clove and then with salt and pepper. Press the juniper berries into the meat. Brush lightly with oil and grill for 10 minutes on each side or until the meat is cooked through.

Serves 4

Pork Chops with Plums

½ kg./1 lb. plums, stoned
50 g./2 oz. sugar
pinch of ground allspice
225 ml./8 fl. oz. red wine
4 pork chops
salt and pepper

Put the plums in a saucepan with the sugar, allspice and wine and bring to the boil. Simmer for 10 to 15 minutes or until tender.

Meanwhile, rub the chops with salt and pepper and grill for 4 minutes on each side or until lightly browned. Transfer the chops to an ovenproof serving dish.

Rub the plum mixture through a strainer and pour over the chops. Cover and put the dish into the oven preheated to moderate (180°C/350°F or Gas Mark 4). Cook for 45 minutes to 1 hour, or until the chops are tender.

Serves 4

Roast Pork with Apples

1 × 1 kg./2 lb. loin of pork,
   boned and rolled
2 cooking apples, sliced
salt and pepper
25 g./1 oz. butter
1 onion, chopped
300 ml./10 fl. oz. water
15 ml./1 tablespoon flour
5 ml./1 teaspoon mustard
150 ml./5 fl. oz. sour cream

Make about 10 slits on both sides of the pork and insert half of the apple slices into the slits. Rub the pork with the salt and pepper. Melt the butter in a deep flameproof dish. Add the pork, onion and remaining apple slices and fry for 8 to 10 minutes or until the meat is evenly browned. Add the water and bring to the boil. Simmer for about 1¼ hours, or until the meat is cooked through. Transfer the pork to a warmed serving dish and keep hot.

Stir the flour and mustard into the cooking juices and cook for 3 minutes, stirring constantly, or until the liquid thickens. Stir in the cream, heat gently and serve with the pork.

Serves 4

Pork with Peaches

1 × 2 kg./4 lb. leg of pork
salt
175 ml./6 fl. oz. wine vinegar
175 ml./6 fl. oz white wine
5 ml./1 teaspoon ground
　allspice
8 canned peach halves,
　syrup reserved
10 ml./2 teaspoons cornflour
Marinade
125 ml./4 fl. oz. oil
2 garlic cloves, crushed
salt and pepper
5 ml./1 teaspoon mustard
5 ml./1 teaspoon dried sage

Combine all the marinade ingredients in a shallow dish and add the pork. Marinate for 2 hours, basting occasionally. Drain the pork and make small cuts in the thickest parts of the meat. Rub the salt into the pork and place it on a rack in a roasting pan. Put the pan into the oven preheated to fairly hot (190°C/375°F or Gas Mark 5) and roast for 2 to 2½ hours, or until the meat is tender.

Meanwhile, pour the vinegar and wine into a saucepan and stir in the allspice. Simmer for 30 minutes. Put the peach halves in a large shallow dish and pour over the vinegar mixture.

When the pork is cooked, transfer it to a warmed serving dish and arrange the peach halves around the meat. Keep hot. Skim off any fat from the cooking juices in the roasting pan and pour into a saucepan. Add the wine and vinegar mixture and bring to the boil. Mix the cornflour to a paste with 15 ml./1 tablespoon of the reserved peach syrup and add to the sauce. Cook, stirring constantly, until the sauce thickens. Serve with the pork.

Serves 6

Pork with Spicy Orange Sauce

675 g./1½lb. pork fillet, cubed
45 ml./3 tablespoons
　seasoned flour
25 g./1 oz. butter
1 small onion, chopped
1 green pepper, pith and
　seeds removed and cut
　into thin strips
juice of 2 oranges
2.5 ml./½ teaspoon grated
　orange rind
15 ml./1 tablespoon
　Worcestershire sauce
150 ml./5 fl. oz. beef stock
1 orange, peeled and
　separated into segments

Coat the pork cubes in the seasoned flour. Melt the butter in a saucepan. Add the onion and pepper and fry for 5 minutes. Add the pork cubes and fry for a further 5 to 8 minutes or until they are evenly browned. Stir in the orange juice and rind, Worcestershire sauce and stock. Bring to the boil then simmer for 30 minutes. Stir in the orange segments just before serving.

Serves 4

Braised Pork with Sour Cream Sauce

75 g./3 oz. butter
1 × 1½ kg./3 lb. loin of pork, boned and rolled
2 onions, chopped
15 ml./1 tablespoon paprika
300 ml./10 fl. oz. chicken stock
75 ml./3 fl. oz. white wine
salt and pepper
25 g./1 oz. beurre manié*
225 ml./8 fl. oz. sour cream
15 ml./1 tablespoon caraway seeds

Melt the butter in a large flameproof dish. Add the pork and fry for 8 to 10 minutes or until it is browned on all sides. Remove the pork from the dish and set aside. Add the onions and fry for 5 minutes. Stir in the paprika, stock, wine and salt and pepper to taste. Bring to the boil. Return the pork to the dish, cover and put into the oven pre-heated to moderate (180°C/350°F or Gas Mark 4). Cook for 1½ hours, or until the pork is cooked through. Transfer the pork to a warmed serving dish and keep hot.

Strain the cooking juices into a saucepan and bring to the boil. Boil until the liquid is reduced by about one-quarter. Simmer and add the beurre manié, a piece at a time, stirring constantly until the sauce thickens. Stir in the sour cream and caraway seeds. Heat gently and serve with the pork.

Serves 6

Fried Pork with Aubergines

125 ml./4 fl. oz. oil
1 kg./2 lb. pork fillet, cut into thin strips
1 onion, sliced
1 red pepper, pith and seeds removed and chopped
½ kg./1 lb. tomatoes, skinned and chopped
30 ml./2 tablespoons tomato purée
300 ml./10 fl. oz. chicken stock
salt and pepper
10 ml./2 teaspoons cornflour
30 ml./2 tablespoons lemon juice
1 large aubergine, sliced and dégorged
1 egg, lightly beaten
50 g./2 oz. dry breadcrumbs

Heat half the oil in a frying-pan. Add the pork and fry for 5 minutes, or until it is evenly browned. Transfer to a plate. Add the onion and pepper to the pan and fry for 5 minutes. Stir in the tomatoes, tomato purée, stock and salt and pepper to taste. Mix the cornflour and lemon juice together and add to the pan. Bring to the boil, stirring constantly. Cook for 2 minutes or until the mixture thickens. Return the pork to the pan, cover and simmer for 30 minutes or until the meat is cooked through. Transfer to a warmed serving dish and keep hot.

Dip the aubergine slices in the egg and then in the breadcrumbs. Heat the remaining oil in a frying-pan. Add the aubergine slices, a few at a time and fry for 8 minutes or until they are evenly browned and cooked through. Arrange over the pork.

Serves 4

Pork with Bean Sprouts and Almonds

15 ml./1 tablespoon soy
   sauce
30 ml./2 tablespoons chicken
   stock
5 ml./1 teaspoon sugar
30 ml./2 tablespoons oil
350 g./12 oz. lean pork,
   cubed
50 g./2 oz. blanched
   almonds, halved
2 spring onions, thinly sliced
1 × 450 g./1 lb. can bean
   sprouts, drained
1 pineapple ring, chopped
salt and pepper

Mix together the soy sauce, stock and sugar. Heat the oil in a frying-pan. Add the pork and fry for 5 to 8 minutes or until it is evenly browned. Add the almonds and spring onions and fry for 4 minutes. Pour off any oil. Stir in the soy sauce mixture, bean sprouts and chopped pineapple. Season with salt and pepper to taste, and mix well. Cover and simmer for 2 minutes before serving.

Serves 3-4

Pork Chops with Mixed Fruit Sauce

4 pork chops
1 egg, beaten
125 g./4 oz. prepared dry
   sage and onion stuffing*
Sauce
15 ml./1 tablespoon
   cornflour
1 × 400 g./14 oz. can fruit
   cocktail
25 g./1 oz. butter
1 onion, chopped
1 green pepper, pith and
   seeds removed and
   chopped
125 g./4 oz. mushrooms,
   thinly sliced
50 ml./2 fl. oz. tomato
   ketchup
squeeze of lemon juice
pinch of mustard
15 ml./1 tablespoon brown
   sugar

Dip each chop in the egg, then coat in the stuffing. Place on a rack in a roasting pan and put into the oven preheated to moderate (180°C/350°F or Gas Mark 4). Bake for 1 hour, or until the meat is tender and the stuffing crisp.

While the chops are cooking, make the sauce. Mix the cornflour with the juice from the can of fruit cocktail. Set aside and reserve the fruit. Melt the butter in a frying-pan. Add the onion and pepper and fry for 5 minutes. Add the mushrooms and fry for a further 3 minutes. Stir in the tomato ketchup, lemon juice, mustard, sugar and cornflour paste and bring to the boil, stirring constantly. Simmer for 10 minutes, then stir in the reserved fruit. Cook for 2 minutes or until the fruit is warmed through. Spoon the sauce over the chops.

Serves 4

Pork and Olive Loaf

350 g./12 oz. pork, minced
275 g./10 oz. bacon, minced
50 g./2 oz. fresh
  breadcrumbs
pinch of dried sage
pinch of dried oregano
1 egg, lightly beaten
10 stuffed olives, sliced
salt and pepper
3 hard-boiled eggs, sliced
2 bacon slices

Mix together the pork, bacon, breadcrumbs, sage, oregano, egg and olives and season with salt and pepper. Spoon half the mixture into a greased 1 kg./2 lb. loaf tin. Arrange the hard-boiled eggs in a row on top. Cover with the remaining meat mixture and press down firmly. Lay the bacon slices on the top. Put in a roasting pan half-filled with hot water and put the pan into the oven preheated to moderate (180°C/350°F or Gas Mark 4). Bake for 1 hour. Pour off the fat and leave to cool, then cover with foil and chill.

Serves 4-6

Toad in the Hole

15 g./$\frac{1}{2}$ oz. butter
$\frac{1}{2}$ kg./1 lb. pork sausages
Batter
125 g./4 oz. flour
pinch of salt
1 egg
300 ml./10 fl. oz. milk

To make the batter, sift the flour and salt into a bowl. Beat in the egg and gradually add enough milk to form a stiff batter. Set aside for 10 minutes. Add the remaining milk, stirring constantly.

Melt the butter in a flameproof baking dish and add the sausages. Put the dish into the oven preheated to hot (220°C/425°F or Gas Mark 7) and cook for 10 minutes, or until evenly browned. Pour over the batter, reduce the oven temperature to moderate (180°C/350°F or Gas Mark 4) and bake for 30 minutes, or until the batter is golden brown and has risen.

Serves 4

Pork Chops in Cream Sauce

4 pork chops
salt and pepper
50 g./2 oz. butter
225 g./8 oz. mushrooms,
  sliced
30 ml./2 tablespoons flour
300 ml./10 fl. oz. white wine
pinch of dried mixed herbs
150 ml./5 fl. oz. single cream

Season the chops with salt and pepper. Grill for 20 minutes, or until the chops are evenly browned. Reserve the juices in the grill pan. Put the chops on a serving dish and keep hot.

Melt the butter in a frying-pan. Add the mushrooms and fry for 5 minutes. Stir in the flour to form a smooth paste. Stir in the juices from the grill pan, the wine and herbs. Simmer for 2 minutes, stirring constantly. Add the cream and heat gently. Pour the sauce over the chops.

Serves 4

Pork Chops in Devilled Sauce

45 ml./3 tablespoons oil
4 pork chops
Sauce
30 ml./2 tablespoons lemon
  juice
15 ml./1 tablespoon chilli
  sauce
15 ml./1 tablespoon
  Worcestershire sauce
10 ml./2 teaspoons dry
  mustard
1 small onion, finely
  chopped
45 ml./3 tablespoons brown
  sugar
salt and pepper
125 ml./4 fl. oz. water

Heat the oil in a frying-pan. Add the chops and fry for 5 to 8 minutes, or until evenly browned. Mix together all the sauce ingredients and pour over the chops. Cover and simmer for 45 minutes, or until the pork is cooked through.

Serves 4

Pork Fillet with Vermouth

1 kg./2 lb. pork fillets, cut
  into four pieces
salt
50 g./2 oz. butter
1 garlic clove, crushed
pepper
300 ml./10 fl. oz. vermouth
10 ml./2 teaspoons cornflour
30 ml./2 tablespoons water
150 ml./5 fl. oz. sour cream
15 ml./1 tablespoon chopped
  fresh parsley

Rub the pork fillets with salt. Melt the butter in a frying-pan. Add the fillets and fry for 5 to 8 minutes or until they are evenly browned. Transfer to an ovenproof dish. Sprinkle over the garlic and pepper and pour in the vermouth. Cover and put into the oven preheated to moderate (180°C/350°F or Gas Mark 4). Bake for 45 minutes, or until the meat is cooked through. Remove the fillets from the dish, arrange on a warmed serving plate and keep hot.

Skim off any fat from the surface of the cooking liquid, then strain it into a small saucepan and bring to the boil. Mix the cornflour and water to a paste and add to the saucepan. Cook, stirring constantly, for 2 to 3 minutes, or until it thickens. Stir in the sour cream and parsley. Pour the sauce over the pork.

Serves 4

Ginger Pork Spareribs

2 kg./4 lb. pork spareribs
Sauce
60 ml./4 tablespoons soy
   sauce
175 ml./6 fl. oz. water
60 ml./4 tablespoons orange
   marmalade
1 garlic clove, crushed
juice of ½ lemon
pepper
2.5 ml./½ teaspoon ground
   ginger
10 ml./2 teaspoons grated
   fresh ginger

Place the spareribs, meaty side down, in a well-greased shallow baking dish. Put the dish into the oven preheated to hot (220°C/425°F or Gas Mark 7) and roast for 30 minutes. Turn the spareribs over, reduce the oven temperature to moderate (180°C/350°F or Gas Mark 4) and roast for a further 30 minutes. Pour off the excess fat from the pan. Combine all the sauce ingredients and pour over the spareribs. Roast for a further 45 minutes, basting frequently with the sauce.

Serves 6

Pork Chops in Mustard Sauce

25 g./1 oz. butter
4 pork chops
2 dessert apples, peeled and
   sliced
10 ml./2 teaspoons flour
15 ml./1 tablespoon mustard
30 ml./2 tablespoons tomato
   ketchup
150 ml./5 fl. oz. single cream
salt and pepper

Melt the butter in a large frying-pan. Add the chops and fry for about 20 minutes, or until they are cooked through. Transfer to a warmed serving dish and keep hot.

Pour away all but 30 ml./2 tablespoons of the fat, add the apple slices and cook for 5 minutes, or until they are golden brown. Arrange around the pork. Stir the flour into the fat in the pan to form a smooth paste, then add the mustard, tomato ketchup and cream. Season well and cook for 2 to 3 minutes, stirring constantly, or until it thickens. Spoon the sauce over the chops and serve.

Serves 4

Pork Chops in Orange Sauce

4 pork chops
salt and pepper
40 g./1½ oz. butter
grated rind and juice of 1
  orange
15 ml./1 tablespoon mustard
125 g./4 oz. brown sugar

Rub the pork chops with salt and pepper. Melt the butter in a frying-pan. Add the chops and fry for 5 to 8 minutes or until they are evenly browned. Transfer to an ovenproof dish. Mix together the orange rind and juice, mustard and sugar. Pour over the chops and cover the dish with foil. Put into the oven preheated to moderate (180°C/350°F or Gas Mark 4) and bake for 1 to 1½ hours or until the pork is cooked through. Remove the foil for the last 45 minutes of the cooking time. Serve the chops with the cooking juices.

Serves 4

Scotch Eggs

½ kg./1 lb. pork sausagemeat
10 ml./2 teaspoons
  Worcestershire sauce
15 ml./1 tablespoon flour
2.5 ml./½ teaspoon dried sage
salt and pepper
4 hard-boiled eggs
1 large egg, beaten
75 g./3 oz. dry breadcrumbs
oil for deep frying

Mix together the sausagemeat, Worcestershire sauce, flour, sage, and salt and pepper to taste. Divide the mixture into four equal portions. Carefully mould the portions around the eggs to form balls. Coat the balls in the egg, and then in the breadcrumbs. Deep fry for 5 minutes, or until golden brown. Drain on kitchen towels.

Serves 4

Roast Loin of Pork with Prunes

1 × 2 kg./4 lb. loin of pork,
  boned and scored
salt and pepper
125 g./4 oz. prunes, stoned
1 large cooking apple,
  chopped
lemon juice
50 g./2 oz. butter

Make a pocket in the loin by cutting with a sharp knife to within 1 cm./½ in. of both ends. Sprinkle with salt and pepper. Mix together the prunes and apple and sprinkle with lemon juice. Stuff the pocket with the prune and apple mixture. Roll the meat firmly around the filling and secure with string. Rub the scored crackling with salt. Melt the butter in a flameproof baking dish. Add the pork and put the dish into the oven preheated to moderate (180°C/350°F or Gas Mark 4). Roast for 1½ to 2 hours, or until the meat is cooked through and golden brown.

Serves 8

Pork Veronique

40 g./1½ oz. butter
6 loin pork chops
1 onion, finely chopped
300 ml./10 fl. oz. white wine
salt and pepper
125 g./4 oz. white grapes,
* peeled, seeded and halved*
45 ml./3 tablespoons double
* cream*

Melt the butter in a large saucepan. Add the chops and fry for 5 to 8 minutes, or until evenly browned. Transfer to an ovenproof casserole. Add the onion to the pan and fry for 5 minutes. Stir in the wine and salt and pepper to taste and bring to the boil. Pour over the chops. Try to keep the skin of the pork above the wine so that it crisps when cooking. Put the casserole into the oven preheated to moderate (180°C/350°F or Gas Mark 4) and cook for 40 to 45 minutes, or until the pork is cooked through. Transfer the chops to a warmed serving dish and pour the cooking liquid into a saucepan. Add the grapes and stir in the cream. Heat gently for a few minutes. Season if required and spoon over the chops.

Serves 6

Pork with Mushrooms and Cream

675 g./1½ lb. lean stewing
* pork, cubed*
50 g./2 oz. seasoned flour
50 ml./2 fl. oz. oil
1 onion, sliced
1 garlic clove, crushed
600 ml./1 pint chicken stock
225 g./8 oz. mushrooms,
* sliced*
25 g./1 oz. butter
30 ml./2 tablespoons brandy
* (optional)*
50 ml./2 fl. oz. double cream
chopped fresh parsley to
* garnish*

Coat the pork cubes with the seasoned flour. Heat the oil in a saucepan. Add the onion and garlic and fry for 5 minutes. Add the pork and fry for 5 to 8 minutes or until it is evenly browned. Gradually add the stock and bring to the boil, stirring occasionally. Season to taste and cover tightly. Simmer for 1¾ to 2 hours, or until the meat is cooked through.

About 40 minutes before the end of the cooking time, fry the mushrooms in the butter for 5 minutes. Add the mushrooms to the pork and re-cover. Just before serving, stir in the brandy, if used, and cream. Heat gently and garnish with the parsley.

Serves 4

Pork and Apple Stew

50 ml./2 fl. oz. oil
1 large onion, sliced
675 g./1½ lb. lean stewing
    pork, cubed
45 ml./3 tablespoons flour
300 ml./10 fl. oz. chicken
    stock
300 ml./10 fl. oz. dry cider
5 ml./1 teaspoon dried sage
salt and pepper
2 dessert apples, peeled and
    sliced
chopped fresh parsley to
    garnish

Heat the oil in a saucepan. Add the onion and fry for 5 minutes. Add the pork and fry for 5 to 8 minutes or until the meat is evenly browned. Sprinkle the flour over the pork, then stir to form a smooth paste. Gradually add the stock and cider and bring to the boil, stirring constantly. Cook for 1 minute. Stir in the sage and salt and pepper to taste and cover tightly. Simmer for 1¾ to 2 hours, or until the meat is cooked through. About 30 minutes before the end of the cooking time, add the apples. Sprinkle over the parsley.

Serves 4

Crisp Chinese Pork

½ kg./1 lb. lean pork, cubed
425 ml./15 fl. oz. water
30 ml./2 tablespoons soy
    sauce
15 ml./1 tablespoon sugar
1 clove star anise
15 ml./1 tablespoon sherry
pinch of salt
oil for deep frying
Batter
125 g./4 oz. self-raising flour
pinch of salt
1 egg
150 ml./5 fl. oz. water

Put the pork cubes in a saucepan with the water, soy sauce, sugar, star anise, sherry and salt. Simmer for 45 minutes, or until the meat is cooked through. Drain well.

To make the batter, sift the flour and salt into a bowl. Make a well in the centre, drop in the egg and mix with a wooden spoon, gradually bringing in the flour from around the edges. Add the water gradually, beating constantly. Add the pork pieces and stir to coat. Deep-fry the pork for 3 to 5 minutes or until crisp and golden. Drain well on kitchen towels.

Serves 4

Pork and Prune Stew

600 ml./1 pint chicken stock
about 18 prunes
675 g./1½ lb. lean stewing
   pork, cubed
25 g./1 oz. seasoned flour
50 ml./2 fl. oz. oil
2 bay leaves
salt and pepper
30 ml./2 tablespoons
   redcurrant jelly
chopped fresh parsley to
   garnish

Bring the stock to the boil, pour over the prunes and leave to soak for about 12 hours. Coat the pork cubes with the seasoned flour. Heat the oil in a saucepan. Add the pork and fry for 5 to 8 minutes or until it is evenly browned. Strain the stock from the prunes and gradually add it to the meat. Bring to the boil, stirring occasionally. Add the bay leaves, season to taste and cover tightly. Simmer for 1½ to 1¾ hours, or until the meat is just tender. Add the prunes and cook for a further 15 minutes. Stir in the redcurrant jelly and remove the bay leaves. Sprinkle over the parsley.

Serves 4

Pork and Cabbage Stew

25 g./1 oz. butter
1 onion, chopped
125 g./4 oz. bacon, chopped
  and with rinds reserved
225 g./8 oz. carrots, thinly
   sliced
2 celery stalks, chopped
675 g./1½ lb. lean pork, cubed
225 g./8 oz. Italian salami,
   chopped
1 bay leaf
salt and pepper
15 ml./1 tablespoon flour
300 ml./10 fl. oz. white wine
1 firm white cabbage, about
   1 kg./2 lb. in weight,
   chopped, blanched for 5
   minutes and drained

Melt the butter in a large saucepan. Add the onion, bacon, carrots and celery and fry for 5 minutes. Add the pork, salami, bacon rind, bay leaf, salt and pepper to taste, and flour. Stir well. Gradually add the wine and, if there is not enough liquid to cover the contents of the pan, add some water. Cover and simmer for 1 hour.

Add the cabbage and cook for a further 30 minutes. Remove and discard the bacon rind and bay leaf.

Serves 4-5

Roast Leg of Pork

1 × 2-2½ kg./4-5 lb. leg of
pork, on the bone, scored
salt
ground ginger

Place the pork in a well-oiled roasting pan and rub the skin with a generous amount of salt and a little ground ginger. The salt will ensure crisp crackling. Put the pan into the oven preheated to hot (220°C/425°F or Gas Mark 7) and roast for 20 minutes.

Reduce the oven temperature to moderate (180°C/350°F or Gas Mark 4) and continue to roast for a further 25 minutes per ½ kg./1 lb. or until the meat is cooked through and well browned. Baste occasionally during the cooking period with the cooking juices.

Serves 6-8

Pork with Beans and Bacon

675 g./1½ lb. lean stewing
pork, cubed
45 ml./3 tablespoons
seasoned flour
50 ml./2 fl. oz. oil
1 large onion, sliced
4 bacon slices, chopped
1 × 400 g./14 oz. can kidney
beans, drained
2.5 ml./½ teaspoon cayenne
pepper
600 ml./1 pint chicken stock

Coat the pork cubes with the seasoned flour. Heat the oil in a frying-pan. Add the onion and bacon and fry for 5 minutes. Add the pork and fry for 5 to 8 minutes or until it is evenly browned. Add the kidney beans and cayenne. Gradually add the stock and bring to the boil, stirring occasionally. Transfer to a casserole and cover tightly. Put into the oven preheated to moderate (180°C/350°F or Gas Mark 4) and cook for 1 to 1½ hours, or until the pork is cooked through.

Serves 4

Pork Chops with Fennel

50 g./2 oz. butter
4 pork chops
salt and pepper
1 garlic clove, crushed
150 ml./5 fl. oz. red wine
15 ml./1 tablespoon tomato
purée
2.5 ml./½ teaspoon fennel
seeds

Melt the butter in a large frying-pan. Season the chops with the salt and pepper and add to the pan. Fry for 5 to 8 minutes, or until evenly browned, then reduce the heat and cook gently for 20 minutes, or until the meat is cooked through. Remove the chops from the pan and keep hot.

Put the garlic in the pan and allow it to brown. Add the remaining ingredients, stir well and cook for 6 minutes. Strain the sauce over the chops and serve hot.

Serves 4

Barbecued Pork with Bean Sprouts

2.5 ml./½ teaspoon ground
 ginger
60 ml./4 tablespoons soy
 sauce
30 ml./2 tablespoons sherry
1 spring onion, finely
 chopped
1 garlic clove, crushed
½ kg./1 lb. lean pork, cut into
 thin strips
30 ml./2 tablespoons clear
 honey
15 ml./1 tablespoon oil
5 ml./1 teaspoon finely
 chopped fresh ginger
2.5 ml./½ teaspoon salt
1 × 450 g./1 lb. can bean
 sprouts, drained
15 ml./1 tablespoon water
5 ml./1 teaspoon sugar

Mix together the ginger, soy sauce, sherry, spring onion and garlic in a large dish. Add the pork strips, coat with the marinade, and set aside for 4 to 6 hours, basting occasionally. Drain the pork and rub it with the honey. Place on a greased rack in a roasting pan over 2.5 cm./1 in. water. Put the pan into the oven preheated to moderate (180°C/350°F or Gas Mark 4) and cook for 25 minutes.

Heat the oil in a saucepan. Add the chopped ginger and salt and fry for 2 minutes. Add the bean sprouts with the water and sugar. Heat gently, stirring. Add the pork, cover and heat through.

Serves 4

Sweet and Sour Spareribs

300 ml./10 fl. oz. vinegar
1¼ kg./3 lb. pork spareribs,
 cut into individual ribs
75 g./3 oz. cornflour
30 ml./2 tablespoons clear
 honey
15 ml./1 tablespoon soy
 sauce
oil for frying
150 ml./5 fl. oz. syrup from a
 can of pineapple, fruit
 reserved
150 ml./5 fl. oz. water
30 ml./2 tablespoons brown
 sugar
2.5 ml./½ teaspoon salt
1 onion, chopped
1 red pepper, pith and seeds
 removed and chopped

Half fill a large saucepan with water, add 60 ml./4 tablespoons of the vinegar and bring to the boil. Add the spareribs and simmer for 20 minutes. Drain.

Put the cornflour, honey and soy sauce in a bowl and mix well. Coat the spareribs in this mixture. Heat about 2.5 cm./1 in. of oil in a large frying-pan and fry the ribs until they are golden brown. Drain well on kitchen towels. Put the pineapple syrup in a large saucepan with the water, sugar, salt and the remaining vinegar. Bring to the boil, add the spareribs, cover and simmer for 30 minutes, turning occasionally. Add the reserved pineapple, onion and pepper 5 minutes before the end of cooking time.

Serves 4-6

Somerset Pork

675 g./1½ lb. pork fillet
30 ml./2 tablespoons flour
50 g./2 oz. butter
1 large onion, finely chopped
175 g./6 oz. mushrooms,
* sliced*
300 ml./10 fl. oz. dry cider
salt and pepper
60 ml./4 tablespoons double
* cream*
chopped fresh parsley to
* garnish*

Cut the pork fillet into eight pieces. Place each piece between two sheets of greaseproof paper and beat with a meat mallet or rolling pin until very thin. Coat the pork lightly with the flour. Melt the butter in a frying-pan. Add the pork and fry for 6 to 8 minutes or until the slices are evenly browned. Transfer to a plate. Add the onion and mushrooms to the pan and cook for 5 minutes. Stir in the remaining flour to form a smooth paste. Gradually add the cider and bring to the boil, stirring constantly. Cook for 2 to 3 minutes, stirring, or until the liquid thickens. Return the pork to the pan with seasoning to taste, then stir in the cream. Heat gently for a further 2 to 3 minutes. Garnish with the parsley.

Serves 4

Spareribs of Pork with Barbecue Sauce

30 ml./2 tablespoons oil
4 sparerib pork chops
2 medium onions, chopped
30 ml./2 tablespoons tomato
* purée*
50 ml./2 fl. oz. water
30 ml./2 tablespooons brown
* sugar*
30 ml./2 tablespoons vinegar
5 ml./1 teaspoon
* Worcestershire sauce*
5 ml./1 teaspoon dry mustard
pinch of dried mixed herbs
salt and pepper

Heat the oil in a saucepan. Add the meat and fry for 5 to 8 minutes, or until it is evenly browned. Transfer to a plate. Add the onions to the pan and fry for 5 minutes. Stir in the remaining ingredients and bring to the boil. Return the chops to the saucepan. Cover and simmer for 20 minutes.

Serves 4

Pork Ratatouille

1 kg./2 lb. belly of pork, diced
30 ml./2 tablespoons oil
2 onions, chopped
2 garlic cloves, crushed
675 g./1½ lb. tomatoes,
*   skinned and chopped*
2 green peppers, pith and
*   seeds removed and*
*   chopped*
1 large aubergine, chopped
*   and dégorged*
4 courgettes, thinly sliced
30 ml./2 tablespoons
*   chopped fresh parsley*
salt and pepper

Fry the pork in a large saucepan for 5 minutes or until it has rendered most of its fat. Transfer to a plate. Add the oil to the pan with the onions and garlic and fry for 5 minutes. Add the tomatoes, peppers, aubergine, courgettes, parsley and salt and pepper to taste. Cover and simmer for 25 minutes. Return the pork to the pan and mix well. Cover and simmer for a further 25 to 30 minutes or until the pork is cooked through.

Serves 4

Pork Fillet in Wine

25 ml./1 fl. oz. oil
1 kg./2 lb. pork fillet, diced
50 g./2 oz. butter
225 g./8 oz. onions, chopped
225 g./8 oz. button
*   mushrooms*
15 g./½ oz. flour
300 ml./10 fl. oz. beef stock
150 ml./5 fl. oz. white wine
salt and pepper

Heat the oil in a large saucepan. Add the pork and fry for 5 to 8 minutes or until it is evenly browned. Transfer to a plate. Add the butter to the pan. When it has melted, add the onions and fry for 5 minutes. Add the mushrooms and cook for a further 1 minute. Stir in the flour to form a smooth paste and gradually add the stock and wine. Bring to the boil, stirring constantly. Cook for 2 to 3 minutes, stirring constantly, or until the liquid thickens. Return the pork to the pan and season with salt and pepper. Cover and simmer for 45 minutes or until the pork is cooked through.

Serves 6

Plain Pork Casserole

50 ml./2 fl. oz. oil
1 onion, sliced
675 g./1½ lb. lean stewing
*   pork, cubed*
45 ml./3 tablespoons flour
600 ml./1 pint chicken stock
salt and pepper

Heat the oil in a frying-pan. Add the onion and fry for 5 minutes. Add the pork and fry for 5 to 8 minutes or until it is evenly browned. Sprinkle over the flour and stir to form a smooth paste. Gradually add the stock, season with the salt and pepper, and bring to the boil, stirring. Transfer to a casserole and cover tightly. Put into the oven preheated to moderate (180°C/350°F or Gas Mark 4) and cook for 1 to 1½ hours, or until the pork is cooked through.

Serves 4

Cold Loin of Pork Oriental

1 × 2¼ kg./5 lb. loin of pork,
*   boned and rolled*
30 ml./2 tablespoons dry
*   mustard*
225 g./8 oz. redcurrant jelly
30 ml./2 tablespoons sherry
30 ml./2 tablespoons soy
*   sauce*
Marinade
125 ml./4 fl. oz. sherry
125 ml./4 fl. oz. soy sauce
10 ml./2 teaspoons ground
*   ginger*
3 garlic cloves, crushed

Rub the pork with the mustard and put in a bowl. Mix together the marinade ingredients and pour over the pork. Marinate for 2 hours, basting occasionally. Place the pork on a rack in a roasting pan, pour over the marinade and put the pan into the oven preheated to moderate (180°C/350°F or Gas Mark 4). Cook for 2½ to 3 hours, or until the meat is cooked through. Baste occasionally with the marinade during the cooking period.

Melt the redcurrant jelly slowly in a saucepan. Stir in the sherry and soy sauce and heat for 1 minute. Spoon the jelly over the pork and cool.

Serves 8-10

Pork Supreme

75 g./3 oz. butter
2 onions, chopped
2 carrots, sliced
2 celery stalks, chopped
1 small green pepper, pith
*   and seeds removed and*
*   chopped*
½ kg./1 lb. lean pork, diced
50 g./2 oz. seasoned flour
600 ml./1 pint milk
1 bay leaf

Melt the butter in a large saucepan. Add the onions, carrots, celery and pepper and fry for 5 minutes. Coat the pork in the seasoned flour, then add to the vegetables. Fry for 8 minutes, or until the pork is evenly browned. Gradually blend in the milk and stir over low heat until the liquid forms a smooth thick sauce. Add the bay leaf. Cover the pan and simmer for 1¼ to 1½ hours, or until the pork is cooked through. Remove the bay leaf.

Serves 4

Meat-Ham & Gammon

Slipper of Ham in Beer

1 kg./2 lb. slipper of ham,
soaked in cold water for
12 hours and drained
1 onion, chopped
50 g./2 oz. brown sugar
2.5 ml./½ teaspoon dried
mixed herbs
300 ml./10 fl. oz. beer

Put the ham, onion, 15 ml./1 tablespoon of the sugar and the herbs in a large saucepan. Add enough water to cover and bring to the boil. Cover and simmer for 1 hour or until the ham is tender. Drain the ham and place in a shallow ovenproof dish. Sprinkle over the remaining sugar and pour over the beer. Put into the oven preheated to fairly hot (200°C/400°F or Gas Mark 6) and bake for 30 minutes, or until the beer is reduced by half. Baste occasionally during the cooking period. Pour the cooking juices into a warmed sauceboat and serve with the ham.

Serves 4-6

Ham With Vegetables

50 g./2 oz. butter
675 g./1½ lb. cooked ham,
sliced
2 red or green peppers, pith
and seeds removed and
chopped
4 tomatoes, skinned and
sliced
2 onions, sliced
1 garlic clove, crushed
juice of ½ lemon
salt and pepper

Melt the butter in a frying-pan. Add the ham slices and fry for 2 minutes on each side. Transfer to a shallow ovenproof dish. Sprinkle over the chopped peppers and tomatoes. Add the onions and garlic to the pan and fry for 5 minutes. Spoon over the peppers and tomatoes and sprinkle over the lemon juice and salt and pepper to taste. Put into the oven preheated to moderate (180°C/350°F or Gas Mark 4) and bake for 20 minutes.

Serves 4

Ham in Madeira Sauce

50 g./2 oz. butter
1 small onion, finely
   chopped
675 g./1½ lb. cooked ham,
   sliced
25 g./1 oz. flour
350 ml./12 fl. oz. chicken
   stock
50 ml./2 fl oz. Madeira
50 ml./2 fl. oz. double cream
salt and pepper

Melt the butter in a frying-pan. Add the onion and fry for 5 minutes. Add the ham slices and fry for 2 minutes on each side. Transfer to a warmed serving dish and keep hot. Stir the flour into the butter in the pan to form a smooth paste. Gradually stir in the stock and Madeira and bring to the boil. Cook for 2 to 3 minutes, stirring constantly, or until the sauce thickens. Stir in the cream and season with salt and pepper to taste. Heat gently, then pour the sauce over the ham.

Serves 4

Ham and Asparagus Rolls

1 × 425 g./15 oz. can
   asparagus spears, drained
6 large slices cooked ham
225 ml./8 fl. oz. mornay
   sauce*

Take three or four asparagus spears and roll these inside a slice of ham. Arrange the rolls neatly in the bottom of an ovenproof dish. Pour the sauce over the rolls and put into the oven preheated to moderate (180°C/350°F or Gas Mark 4). Cook for 15 minutes.

Serves 6

Ham-Stuffed Peppers

4 large green peppers
50 ml./2 fl. oz. oil
1 small aubergine, finely
   chopped
1 large onion, finely chopped
25 g./1 oz. flour
350 g./12 oz. cooked ham,
   diced
2.5 ml./½ teaspoon dried
   marjoram
300 ml./10 fl. oz. chicken
   stock
30 ml./2 tablespoons tomato
   purée
salt and pepper

Cut off the top of the wider end of each pepper. Remove and discard the pith and seeds and set aside.

Heat the oil in a frying-pan. Add the aubergine and onion and fry for 5 minutes. Stir in the flour to form a smooth paste and gradually stir in the remaining ingredients. Bring to the boil, stirring, and simmer until the mixture thickens. Spoon equal amounts into each pepper and stand them upright in a greased baking dish. Cover with a piece of foil and put into the oven preheated to moderate (180°C/350°F or Gas Mark 4). Bake for 10 minutes or until the peppers are soft.

Serves 4

Gammon Slices with Pineapple and Corn Sauce

4 lean gammon slices
50 g./2 oz. butter, melted
4 canned pineapple rings,
    drained and cut in half,
    syrup reserved
Sauce
25 g./1 oz. butter
1 onion, finely chopped
25 g./1 oz. flour
300 ml./10 fl. oz. milk
salt and pepper
60 ml./4 tablespoons canned
    sweetcorn, drained
30 ml./2 tablespoons
    chopped fresh parsley

Snip the fat edges of the gammon at intervals. Brush on one side with melted butter and grill for 5 minutes. Turn, brush with more butter and grill for 5 minutes, or until the gammon is golden brown. (Do not preheat the grill as this causes the gammon to curl.) When the gammon is nearly cooked, add the pineapple halves to the grill pan. Brush with the remainder of the butter and heat thoroughly. Transfer to a warmed serving plate and keep hot.

To make the sauce, melt the butter in a frying-pan. Add the onion and fry for 5 minutes. Stir in the flour to form a smooth paste. Gradually stir in the milk and bring to the boil. Cook for 2 to 3 minutes, stirring constantly, or until the sauce thickens. Season with the salt and pepper, and stir in the sweetcorn and parsley. Whisk 30 ml./2 tablespoons of the pineapple can juice into the sauce and simmer for 5 minutes. Serve the sauce with the gammon steaks.

Serves 4

Baked Ham

30 ml./2 tablespoons dry
    mustard
2½ kg./5 lb. leg of ham,
    skinned
20 cloves
300 ml./10 fl. oz. cider
50 g./2 oz. brown sugar
1 × 200 g./7 oz. can
    pineapple slices, drained
maraschino cherries to
    garnish

Rub the mustard over the ham and stud the fat side with cloves. Place the ham on a rack in a roasting pan and put into the oven preheated to hot (220°C/425°F or Gas Mark 7). Bake for 20 minutes, then reduce the oven temperature to moderate (180°C/350°F or Gas Mark 4). Pour the cider over the ham and bake for a further 1 hour 20 minutes. Baste occasionally during the cooking period.

Sprinkle half of the sugar over the ham and bake for a further 30 minutes without basting. During the last 15 minutes, place the pineapple rings around the ham and sprinkle the remaining sugar over them. Serve the ham garnished with the glazed pineapple rings and maraschino cherries.

Serves 10-12

Glazed Baked Bacon

2 kg./4 lb. joint of smoked
   bacon, soaked for 6 hours,
   drained and skinned
20 cloves
1 onion, chopped
1 carrot, chopped
2 celery stalks, chopped
600 ml./1 pint cider
30 ml./2 tablespoons brown
   sugar
1 × 425 g./15 oz. can apricot
   halves, drained
10 maraschino cherries
sprigs of watercress to
   garnish

Place the bacon on a rack in a roasting pan and stud the fat side with cloves. Add the vegetables to the pan and pour over the cider. Sprinkle over the sugar. Cover with aluminium foil and put into the oven preheated to moderate (180°C/350°F or Gas Mark 4). Bake for 1½ hours.

Remove the foil and arrange the apricot halves and cherries on the bacon, securing with small wooden sticks. Baste well and cook, uncovered, for a further 20 to 30 minutes, basting occasionally. Cool, then garnish with the sprigs of watercress.

Serves 10-12

Ham and Chicken Rolls

4 chicken breasts, halved
30 ml./2 tablespoons
   seasoned flour
50 g./2 oz. butter
8 slices cooked ham
125 g./4 oz. Bel Paese
   cheese, cut into 8 slices
50 ml./2 fl. oz. white wine
15 ml./1 tablespoon grated
   Parmesan cheese

Coat the chicken pieces in the seasoned flour. Melt the butter in a frying-pan. Add the chicken and brown on all sides. Cool, then wrap each chicken piece in a slice of ham. Lay the rolls in a shallow ovenproof dish. Cover each roll with a slice of cheese. Pour over the wine and sprinkle over the grated cheese. Put into the oven preheated to warm (170°C/325°F or Gas Mark 3) and bake for 20 minutes, or until the cheese has melted and is golden brown.

Serves 4

Gammon with Honey Sauce

1½ kg./3 lb. leg of gammon,
  soaked in cold water for
  12 hours and drained
Sauce
30 ml./2 tablespoons sugar
60 ml./4 tablespoons water
30 ml./2 tablespoons clear
  honey
10 ml./2 teaspoons cornflour
60 ml./4 tablespoons sherry

Put the gammon in the top part of a steamer set over boiling water and steam for 2¼ to 2½ hours, or until tender. Cool, then cut into thin slices and arrange on a heatproof serving dish. Keep hot.

To make the sauce, dissolve the sugar in the water in a saucepan. Stir in the honey and mix well. Mix the cornflour to a smooth paste with the sherry and add to the honey mixture. Bring to the boil, stirring constantly until the sauce thickens. Pour over the gammon slices and put the dish over the steamer. Steam for 3 more minutes.

Serves 6

Gammon Steaks in Tomato Sauce

4 thick gammon steaks
5 ml./1 teaspoon dried sage
Sauce
50 ml./2 fl. oz. oil
1 large onion, finely chopped
1 garlic clove, crushed
1 red pepper, pith and seeds
  removed and chopped
2 × 400 g./14 oz. can
  tomatoes, drained and
  chopped
50 ml./2 fl. oz. tomato purée
salt and pepper
pinch of sugar
2.5 ml./½ teaspoon dried basil

Make small cuts at intervals around the fat edges of the steaks, rub with sage and set aside while you make the sauce.

Heat the oil in a frying-pan. Add the onion and garlic and fry for 5 minutes. Add the pepper and fry for a further 3 minutes. Stir in the tomatoes, tomato purée, salt and pepper to taste, sugar and basil. Cover and simmer for 30 minutes.

Grill the gammon steaks for 10 minutes or until they are cooked through. Place on a warmed serving dish and pour over the sauce.

Serves 4

Meat-Veal

Cold Veal with Lemon

1 × 1½ kg./3 lb. boned leg of
  veal
salt and pepper
10 ml./2 teaspoons grated
  nutmeg
150 ml./5 fl. oz. chicken
  stock
rind and juice of 3 lemons

Secure the boned veal at 2.5 cm./1 in. intervals with string. Rub all over with the salt, pepper and nutmeg. Put into a flameproof casserole and add the stock. Cover and simmer for 30 minutes. Add the lemon rind and juice, re-cover and continue to simmer for 1½ hours, or until the veal is cooked.

Transfer the veal to a serving dish. Skim off any scum from the cooking liquid and pour over the veal. Set aside to cool. Carve the veal into thick slices.

Serves 6-8

Herbed Shoulder of Veal

1 × 2 kg./4 lb. boned
  shoulder of veal
salt and pepper
300 ml./10 fl. oz. chicken
  stock
25 g./1 oz. butter, cut into
  small pieces
Stuffing
25 g./1 oz. butter
1 small onion, chopped
125 g./4 oz. fresh
  breadcrumbs
30 ml./2 tablespoons
  chopped fresh parsley
15 ml./1 tablespoon finely
  grated lemon rind
5 ml./1 teaspoon dried mixed
  herbs
salt and pepper
1 egg

To make the stuffing, melt the butter in a pan. Add the onion and fry for 5 minutes. Stir in the breadcrumbs, parsley, lemon rind, herbs and salt and pepper to taste. Beat in the egg to bind.

Rub the veal with salt and pepper. Fill with the stuffing, then tie into shape with string. Put into a roasting pan, pour over the stock and dot with the butter pieces. Put into the oven preheated to moderate (180°C/350°F or Gas Mark 4) and roast for 2 hours, or until the veal is cooked. Baste with the cooking liquid every 20 minutes during the cooking period.

Serves 6-8

Vitello Tonnato

1 × 1½ kg./3 lb. boned leg of
    veal
6 anchovy fillets, halved
3 bay leaves
1 onion, sliced
2 carrots, sliced
2 celery stalks, sliced
3 parsley sprigs
2 cloves
425 ml./15 fl. oz. dry white
    wine
salt and pepper
Tuna Sauce
1 × 200 g./7 oz. can tuna,
    drained
5 anchovy fillets
5 ml./1 teaspoon capers
30 ml./2 tablespoons lemon
    juice
1.25 ml./¼ teaspoon white
    pepper
150 ml./5 fl. oz. mayonnaise

Secure the boned veal at 2.5 cm/1 in. intervals with string. Make small incisions all over the surface of the meat and insert the anchovy pieces into them. Put the veal into a flameproof casserole, then add the bay leaves, vegetables, flavourings, wine and salt and pepper to taste. Pour over just enough water to cover the meat.

Put the casserole over low heat and bring to the boil. Cover and simmer for 2 hours, or until the veal is cooked and tender. Skim off any scum that rises to the surface. Remove from the heat and leave to cool.

Meanwhile to make the tuna sauce, mash the tuna, anchovies, capers, lemon juice and pepper together to form a smooth paste. Stir in the mayonnaise, then purée the sauce in a blender or put it through a food mill. If the sauce is too thick, thin with a little of the veal stock.

Remove the veal from the stock, dry on kitchen towels and cut into thin slices. Arrange on a serving dish and cover with the sauce.

Serves 6-8

Veal Pot Roast

1 × 2 kg./4 lb. veal rump,
    boned and rolled
salt and pepper
50 ml./2 fl. oz. cooking oil
2 small onions, finely
    chopped
2 celery stalks, chopped
6 carrots, chopped
1 small turnip, chopped
350 ml./12 fl. oz. veal or
    chicken stock
25 ml./1½ tablespoons
    cornflour dissolved in 30
    ml./2 tablespoons water

Rub the veal with the salt and pepper. Heat the oil in a large saucepan. Add the veal and brown on all sides. Transfer to a plate. Add the vegetables to the pan and fry for 5 minutes. Stir in the stock and bring to the boil. Return the veal to the pan, cover and simmer for 2½ hours, or until the veal is cooked.

Transfer the veal and vegetables to a warmed serving dish and keep hot. Boil the cooking liquid until it has reduced by about one-third, then stir in the cornflour mixture. Cook for 2 to 3 minutes, stirring constantly, or until the sauce has thickened. Serve with the veal.

Serves 8

Stuffed Loin of Veal

1 × 2 kg./4 lb. loin of veal,
  boned and trimmed
salt and pepper
225 g./8 oz. sage and onion
  stuffing*
50 g./2 oz. butter
425 ml./15 fl. oz. veal or
  chicken stock
15 ml./1 tablespoon finely
  grated orange rind
5 ml./1 teaspoon dried sage
30 ml./2 tablespoons
  cornflour dissolved in 30
  ml./2 tablespoons stock

Lay out the veal, fat side down, and rub with salt and pepper. Spread over the stuffing, roll up and secure at 2.5 cm./1 in. intervals with string.

Melt the butter in a flameproof casserole. Add the veal and brown on all sides. Pour over the stock and bring to the boil. Cover and put into the oven preheated to fairly hot (190°C/375°F or Gas Mark 5). Braise for 2 to 2½ hours, or until the veal is cooked through.

Transfer the veal to a carving board and keep hot. Boil the cooking liquid until it has reduced by about one-third. Gradually stir in all the remaining ingredients. Cook for 2 to 3 minutes, stirring constantly, or until the sauce has thickened. Serve with the meat.

Serves 8

Shoulder of Veal with Rice Stuffing

1 × 2 kg./4 lb. boned
  shoulder of veal
salt and pepper
125 g./4 oz. butter, cut into
  small pieces
Stuffing
225 g./8 oz. cooked long-
  grain rice
25 g./1 oz. sultanas
30 ml./2 tablespoons
  chopped almonds
5 ml./1 teaspoon ground
  ginger
2.5 ml./½ teaspoon turmeric
2.5 ml./½ teaspoon grated
  nutmeg
2.5 ml./½ teaspoon ground
  cumin
1.25 ml./¼ teaspoon cayenne
  pepper
1 egg, beaten

Mix all the stuffing ingredients together. Rub the veal with salt and pepper. Fill with the stuffing, then tie into shape with string. Put into a roasting pan and dot with the butter pieces. Put into the oven preheated to moderate (180°C/350°F or Gas Mark 4) and roast for 2 hours, or until the veal is cooked. Baste with the juices in the pan occasionally during the cooking period.

Serves 6-8

Veal Chops with Chestnut Purée

4 veal chops

25 g./1 oz. butter, cut into small pieces

1 × 225 g./8 oz. can unsweetened chestnut purée

beef stock to blend

1 lemon, thinly sliced

Marinade

30 ml./2 tablespoons olive oil

30 ml./2 tablespoons wine vinegar or white wine

1 garlic clove, crushed

15 ml./1 tablespoon chopped fresh parsley

Mix all the marinade ingredients together in a shallow dish. Add the veal chops and leave to marinate at room temperature for 3 hours.

Remove the chops from the marinade and transfer to an ovenproof dish (do not drain). Dot with the butter pieces and put into the oven pre-heated to moderate (180°C/350°F or Gas Mark 4). Cook for 40 minutes or until the chops are tender.

Meanwhile, put the chestnut purée into a saucepan and stir in enough stock to make a thick sauce. Simmer gently until very hot.

Garnish the chops with lemon slices and serve with the purée.

Serves 4

Country-Style Veal Chops

50 g./2 oz. butter

4 veal chops

1 onion, chopped

5 ml./1 teaspoon grated lemon rind

15 ml./1 tablespoon lemon juice

300 ml./10 fl. oz. dry cider

7.5 ml./1½ teaspoons cornflour dissolved in 1 tablespoon cider

salt and pepper

75 ml./3 fl. oz. single cream

2 hard-boiled eggs, chopped

Cabbage

25 g./1 oz. butter

1 small white cabbage, blanched and shredded

2 apples, peeled, cored and chopped

salt and pepper

Melt the butter in a saucepan. Add the chops and brown on both sides. Transfer to a plate. Add the onion and lemon rind to the pan and fry for 5 minutes. Add the lemon juice and cider and bring to the boil. Return the chops to the pan and simmer for 35 to 40 minutes or until the chops are tender.

Meanwhile, to prepare the cabbage, melt the butter in a saucepan. Add the cabbage and apples and fry for 5 minutes. Stir in salt and pepper to taste, then simmer for 25 minutes or until the cabbage is cooked. Transfer the cabbage to a large warmed serving dish. Arrange the veal chops on top and keep hot.

Stir the cornflour mixture into the chops' cooking liquid and bring to the boil. Simmer for 3 minutes, stirring constantly, or until the sauce has thickened. Stir in salt and pepper to taste and the cream, and reheat gently. Pour the sauce over the chops and garnish with the chopped eggs.

Serves 4

Veal Chops Bonne Femme

50 g./2 oz. butter
4 veal chops
1 lean bacon slice, chopped
12 pickling onions
125 g./4 oz. button
   mushrooms, sliced
15 ml./1 tablespoon flour
125 ml./4 fl. oz. dry white
   wine
300 ml./10 fl. oz. veal stock
1 bouquet garni
5 ml./1 teaspoon dried sage
salt and pepper
8 small new potatoes

Melt the butter in a saucepan. Add the chops and brown on both sides. Transfer to a plate. Add the bacon, onions and mushrooms to the pan and fry for 5 minutes. Stir in the flour, wine, stock, bouquet garni, sage and seasoning to taste and bring to the boil. Return the chops to the pan and simmer for 10 minutes.

Add the potatoes and continue to simmer for 25 to 30 minutes or until the chops are tender.

Serves 4

Veal Chops with Mushrooms and Onions

125 g./4 oz. butter
6 veal chops
12 pickling onions, par-
   boiled
175 g./6 oz. small button
   mushrooms
salt and pepper
150 ml./5 fl. oz. dry white
   wine or chicken stock
75 ml./3 fl. oz. double cream
chopped parsley to garnish

Melt the butter in a frying-pan. Add the chops and brown on both sides. Transfer to a plate. Add the onions, mushrooms and salt and pepper to taste to the pan, then stir in the wine or stock. Return the chops to the pan and simmer for 35 to 40 minutes, or until they are tender.

Stir in the cream and heat gently for 2 minutes. Garnish with the parsley.

Serves 6

Veal with Blue Cheese

50 g./2 oz. butter, softened
25 g./1 oz. blue cheese
4 veal escalopes
50 g./2 oz. seasoned flour
1 egg, beaten
50 g./2 oz. dry breadcrumbs
50 ml./2 fl. oz. cooking oil
1 lemon, cut into wedges

Mix the butter and cheese together. Spread generously over both sides of the escalopes. Coat the escalopes in the seasoned flour, then the egg and finally the breadcrumbs. Chill in the refrigerator for 1 hour.

Heat the oil in a frying-pan. Add the escalopes and fry for 4 to 6 minutes, or until they are golden brown and cooked through. Garnish with lemon wedges.

Serves 4

Escalopes à la Crème

4 veal escalopes
salt and pepper
50 g./2 oz. flour
75 g./3 oz. butter
2 shallots, chopped
175 g./6 oz. button
  mushrooms, sliced
200 ml./7 fl. oz. dry white
  wine
45 ml./3 tablespoons beurre
  manié*
50 ml./2 fl. oz. double cream

Rub the escalopes with the salt and pepper, then coat them in the flour. Melt the butter in a frying-pan. Add the escalopes and fry for 4 to 6 minutes, or until they are golden brown and cooked through. Transfer to a plate.

Add the shallots and mushrooms to the pan and fry for 3 minutes. Pour in the wine and bring to the boil. Stir in the beurre manié, a little at a time, until the sauce thickens. Bring to the boil again. Return the escalopes to the pan and simmer for 1 minute to heat through. Stir in the cream.

Serves 4

Dutch Veal

4 veal escalopes
salt and pepper
50 g./2 oz. seasoned flour
50 ml./2 fl. oz. cooking oil
4 thin slices of Gouda cheese
4 lean bacon slices
150 ml./5 fl. oz. double
  cream
2.5 ml./½ teaspoon finely
  grated lemon rind
1.25 ml./¼ teaspoon curry
  powder
10 ml./2 teaspoons tomato
  purée

Rub the escalopes with the salt and pepper, then coat in the seasoned flour. Heat the oil in a frying-pan. Add the escalopes and brown on both sides. Transfer to an ovenproof dish. Top each escalope with a slice of cheese and bacon. Put into the oven preheated to moderate (180°C/350°F or Gas Mark 4) and bake for 10 to 15 minutes or until the cheese has melted.

Meanwhile, put all the remaining ingredients into a saucepan and stir to mix. Heat gently until hot but not boiling. Pour over the veal.

Serves 4

Scalloppine Limone

4 veal escalopes
salt and pepper
75 ml./3 fl. oz. lemon juice
50 g./2 oz. seasoned flour
50 g./2 oz. butter
30 ml./2 tablespoons sherry
5 ml./1 teaspoon finely
  grated lemon rind

Rub the escalopes with the salt and pepper. Sprinkle over half the lemon juice, then set aside for 15 minutes. Coat the escalopes in the seasoned flour. Melt the butter in a frying-pan. Add the escalopes and fry for 4 to 6 minutes, or until they are golden brown and cooked through. Stir in the remaining ingredients and simmer gently for 2 minutes.

Serves 4

Veal with Apples and Cream

4 veal escalopes
salt and pepper
50 g./2 oz. flour
75 g./3 oz. butter
2 spring onions, finely
    chopped
125 g./4 oz. apple sauce
2.5 ml./½ teaspoon grated
    nutmeg
50 ml./2 fl. oz. dry cider
50 ml./2 fl. oz. double cream

Rub the escalopes with the salt and pepper, then coat them in the flour. Melt the butter in a frying-pan. Add the escalopes and fry for 4 to 6 minutes, or until they are golden brown and cooked through. Transfer to a warmed serving dish and keep hot.

Add the spring onions to the pan and fry for 3 minutes. Stir in the apple sauce, nutmeg and cider and bring to the boil. Boil for 1 minute. Stir in the cream and heat gently. Pour the sauce over the escalopes.

Serves 4

Escalopes Marsala

4 veal escalopes
salt and pepper
50 g./2 oz. seasoned flour
75 g./3 oz. butter
10 ml./2 teaspoons finely
    grated lemon rind
125 ml./4 fl. oz. Marsala
15 ml./1 tablespoon lemon
    juice

Rub the escalopes with the salt and pepper then coat them in the seasoned flour. Melt the butter in a frying-pan. Add the escalopes and fry for 4 to 6 minutes, or until they are golden brown and cooked through. Transfer to a plate.

Add all the remaining ingredients to the pan and bring to the boil, stirring constantly. Return the escalopes to the pan and simmer for 2 minutes.

Serves 4

Escalopes with Orange

4 veal escalopes
salt and pepper
65 g./2½ oz. flour
75 g./3 oz. butter
125 ml./4 fl. oz. medium
    sherry
125 ml./4 fl. oz. veal stock
2 large oranges
15 ml./1 tablespoon chopped
    fresh parsley

Rub the escalopes with the salt and pepper, then coat them in 50 g./2 oz. of the flour. Melt the butter in a frying-pan. Add the escalopes and brown on both sides. Transfer to a plate. Stir the remaining flour into the fat in the pan to form a smooth paste. Gradually stir in the sherry and stock and bring to the boil. Cook for 2 minutes, stirring constantly, or until the sauce has thickened. Stir in the juice and finely grated rind of 1 orange.

Return the escalopes to the pan and simmer for 5 minutes. Meanwhile cut the remaining orange into wedges and use to garnish the escalopes, with the parsley.

Serves 4

Veal Parmesan

4 veal escalopes
salt and pepper
50 g./2 oz. flour
1 egg
50 g./2 oz. dry breadcrumbs
50 g./2 oz. Parmesan cheese,
    grated
5 ml./1 teaspoon grated
    lemon rind
75 g./3 oz. butter
Sauce
30 ml./2 tablespoons cooking
    oil
1 onion, finely chopped
125 g./4 oz. button
    mushrooms, sliced
1 × 275 g./10 oz. can tomato
    purée
50 ml./2 fl. oz. dry sherry
salt and pepper

Rub the escalopes with the salt and pepper. Dip the escalopes in the flour, then in the beaten egg. Mix the breadcrumbs, grated cheese and lemon rind together, then dip the escalopes in the mixture. Chill in the refrigerator for 30 minutes.

Melt the butter in a frying-pan. Add the escalopes and fry for 4 to 6 minutes, or until they are golden brown and cooked through. Transfer to a warmed serving dish and keep hot.

Heat the oil in a saucepan. Add the onion and mushrooms and fry for 5 minutes. Add all the remaining ingredients and bring to the boil, stirring constantly. Simmer the sauce for 3 minutes. Serve with the escalopes.

Serves 4

Veal Paupiettes

4 veal escalopes
salt and pepper
4 lean bacon slices
2 hard-boiled eggs, halved
    lengthwise
75 g./3 oz. butter
30 ml./2 tablespoons flour
300 ml./10 fl. oz. veal stock
5 ml./1 teaspoon paprika
75 ml./3 fl. oz. double cream
15 ml./1 tablespoon chopped
    fresh parsley

Rub the escalopes with the salt and pepper. Lay a slice of bacon on top of each escalope and place an egg half in the centre. Roll each escalope up and secure it with a wooden toothpick. Melt the butter in a frying-pan. Add the escalope rolls and brown on all sides. Transfer to a plate.

Stir the flour into the fat in the pan until it forms a smooth paste. Gradually stir in the stock and bring to the boil. Stir in the paprika and cook for 2 minutes, stirring constantly, or until thickened. Return the veal rolls to the sauce and simmer for 15 minutes, or until the rolls are cooked through.

Transfer the rolls to a warmed serving dish and remove the toothpicks. Stir the cream into the sauce and heat for 1 minute. Pour the sauce over the veal rolls and garnish with the parsley.

Serves 4

Escalopes Palermo

4 veal escalopes
salt and pepper
50 g./2 oz. plus 15 ml./1
    tablespoon flour
75 g./3 oz. butter
125 ml./4 fl. oz. red wine
150 ml./5 fl. oz. veal stock
10 ml./2 teaspoons tomato
    purée
5 ml./1 teaspoon dried
    rosemary

Rub the escalopes with the salt and pepper, then coat them in 50 g./2 oz. of the flour. Melt the butter in a frying-pan. Add the escalopes and brown on both sides. Pour in the wine, heat for 1 minute, then ignite it. When the flames die away, transfer the escalopes to a plate. Stir in all the remaining ingredients, including the remaining flour, and bring to the boil. Cook for 2 minutes, stirring constantly, or until the sauce thickens.

Return the escalopes to the sauce and simmer for 2 minutes.

Serves 4

Saltimbocca

4 veal escalopes
salt and pepper
4 slices cooked ham, cut to
    the same size as the
    escalopes
4 large sage leaves
75 g./3 oz. butter
125 ml./4 fl. oz. Marsala

Rub the escalopes with the salt and pepper. Lay a slice of ham on top of each escalope and place a sage leaf in the centre. Roll each escalope up and secure it with a wooden toothpick.

Melt the butter in a frying-pan. Add the escalope rolls and brown on all sides. Pour in the Marsala, cover the pan and simmer for 10 to 12 minutes or until the rolls are cooked through. Transfer the escalope rolls to a warmed serving dish and remove the toothpicks. Pour over the pan juices.

Serves 4

Wiener Schnitzel

4 veal escalopes
salt and pepper
10 ml./2 teaspoons paprika
50 g./2 oz. flour
1 egg, beaten
75 g./3 oz. dry breadcrumbs
75 g./3 oz. butter
2 lemons, cut into wedges

Rub the escalopes with the salt, pepper and paprika. Set aside for 10 minutes. Dip the escalopes in the flour, then in the beaten egg, and finally in the breadcrumbs.

Melt the butter in a frying-pan. Add the escalopes and fry for 4 to 6 minutes, or until they are golden brown and cooked through. Garnish with the lemon wedges.

Serves 4

Piquant Veal Escalopes

4 veal escalopes
salt and pepper
50 g./2 oz. flour
75 g./3 oz. butter
6 spring onions, finely
    chopped
1 lemon, thinly sliced
10 ml./2 teaspoons dried
    rosemary
1.25 ml./¼ teaspoon Tabasco
    sauce
150 ml./5 fl. oz. vermouth
15 ml./1 tablespoon chopped
    fresh parsley

Rub the escalopes with the salt and pepper, then coat them with the flour. Melt the butter in a frying-pan. Add the escalopes and brown on both sides. Transfer to a plate.

Add the spring onions to the pan and fry for 3 minutes. Add the lemon, rosemary, Tabasco and vermouth and bring to the boil. Return the escalopes to the pan and simmer for 2 minutes. Garnish with the parsley.

Serves 4

Veal and Ham Pie

675 g./1½ lb. lean veal, cubed
125 g./4 oz. cooked ham,
    chopped
1 small onion, chopped
15 ml./1 tablespoon chopped
    fresh parsley
15 ml./1 tablespoon finely
    grated lemon rind
salt and pepper
about 600 ml./1 pint chicken
    stock
225 g./8 oz. puff pastry*
little milk or beaten egg to
    glaze

Put the veal, ham and onion into a deep ovenproof dish, in layers, seasoning each one with a little parsley, lemon rind and salt and pepper to taste. Add enough stock to fill the dish three-quarters full.

Roll out the dough until it is about 2.5 cm./1 in. larger than the pie dish. Trim the edges all round, then wet the edges of the dish and line with a strip of the dough trimmings. Lay the dough piece on top to cover the filling completely and crimp the edges to seal. Make a slit in the top or use a pie funnel. Brush with a little milk or beaten egg.

Put into the oven preheated to hot (220°C/425°F or Gas Mark 7) and bake for 30 minutes. Cover the pastry with foil or dampened greaseproof paper, reduce the oven temperature to warm (170°C/325°F or Gas Mark 3) and bake for a further 1 hour, or until the veal is cooked through.

Heat the remaining stock until it is very hot, then funnel about 125 ml./4 fl. oz. of it through the slit in the pastry.

Serves 4-6

Veal Marengo

1 kg./2 lb. lean veal, cubed
50 g./2 oz. seasoned flour
50 g./2 oz. butter
1 garlic clove, crushed
25 g./1 oz. flour
150 ml./5 fl. oz. dry white
  wine or stock
600 ml./1 pint chicken stock
30 ml./2 tablespoons tomato
  purée
12 pickling onions, parboiled
2 tomatoes, skinned and
  chopped
225 g./8 oz. mushrooms,
  sliced
chopped parsley to garnish

Roll the veal cubes in the seasoned flour. Melt the butter in a flameproof casserole. Add the cubes and brown on all sides. Transfer to a plate. Add the garlic to the casserole and fry for 1 minute, then stir in the flour to form a smooth paste. Gradually stir in the wine and stock and bring to the boil. Cook for 2 to 3 minutes, stirring constantly, or until the sauce has thickened. Stir in the tomato purée and cook until the sauce has reduced by about one-third.

Return the meat to the casserole, cover and put into the oven preheated to moderate (180°C/350°F or Gas Mark 4). Cook for 1 hour. Stir in the onions, tomatoes and mushrooms and continue to cook for 15 minutes, or until the veal is cooked. Garnish with the parsley.

Serves 4

Swiss Veal

8 large veal escalopes, cut
  into strips about 5 cm./2 in.
  × .75 cm./¼ in.
50 g./2 oz. seasoned flour
175 g./6 oz. butter
2 onions, finely chopped
225 ml./8 fl. oz. dry white
  wine
225 g./8 oz. mushrooms,
  sliced
225 ml./8 fl. oz. double
  cream, lightly whipped
15 ml./1 tablespoon chopped
  fresh parsley
2.5 ml./½ teaspoon paprika

Roll the veal strips in the seasoned flour. Melt 125 g./4 oz. of the butter in a frying-pan. Add the veal and onions and fry for 5 minutes, or until the veal is cooked through. Stir in the wine and cook for a further 2 minutes.

Meanwhile, cook the mushrooms in the remaining butter in another frying-pan. Stir into the veal mixture, with all the remaining ingredients. Heat gently for 2 minutes.

Serves 8-10

Blanquette of Veal

675 g./1½ lb. lean veal, cubed
1 onion, chopped
2 carrots, chopped
2 celery stalks, chopped
2 bay leaves
5 ml./1 teaspoon dried thyme
salt and pepper
15 ml./1 tablespoon lemon
   juice
600 ml./1 pint veal stock
600 ml./1 pint water
225 g./8 oz. mushrooms,
   sliced
40 g./1½ oz. butter
40 g./1½ oz. flour
1 large egg yolk
125 ml./4 fl. oz. single cream

Put the veal in a large saucepan, cover with cold water and bring to the boil. Drain and return the meat to the saucepan. Add the onion, carrots, celery, bay leaves, thyme, salt and pepper to taste, lemon juice, stock and water and bring to the boil. Simmer for 1¼ hours.

Add the mushrooms and simmer for a further 30 minutes, or until the meat and vegetables are cooked. Transfer the meat and vegetables to a warmed serving dish and keep hot.

Boil the liquid in the saucepan until it reduces to about 600 ml./1 pint. Strain and set aside. Melt the butter in a saucepan. Stir in the flour to form a smooth paste. Gradually add the strained cooking liquid. Cook for 2 to 3 minutes, stirring constantly, or until the sauce thickens. Mix the egg yolk and cream together, then add a little of the sauce to the mixture. Return the egg yolk mixture to the sauce and stir to blend. Heat gently for 1 minute, but do not boil. Pour the sauce over the veal and vegetables.

Serves 4

Creamy Veal Curry

50 ml./2 fl. oz. cooking oil
1 kg./2 lb. lean veal, cubed
2 onions, chopped
1 garlic clove, crushed
2 green apples, cored and
   chopped
15 ml./1 tablespoon curry
   powder
425 ml./15 fl. oz. chicken
   stock
25 g./1 oz. sultanas
salt and pepper
75 ml./3 fl. oz. double cream

Heat the oil in a saucepan. Add the veal cubes and brown on all sides. Transfer to a plate. Add the onions, garlic and apples to the pan and fry for 5 minutes. Stir in the curry powder, stock, sultanas and salt and pepper to taste, and bring to the boil.

Return the veal cubes to the pan and stir well. Cover and simmer for 1¼ to 1½ hours, or until the veal is cooked. Stir in the cream and heat gently for 2 minutes.

Serves 4

Veal and Mushroom Ragoût

50 g./2 oz. butter
1 kg./2 lb. lean veal, cubed
2 onions, chopped
15 ml./1 tablespoon paprika
1 × 425 g./15 oz. can cream
   of mushroom soup
350 ml./12 fl. oz. chicken
   stock
salt and pepper
2 green or red peppers, pith
   and seeds removed and
   thinly sliced
125 g./4 oz. mushrooms,
   thinly sliced

Melt the butter in a saucepan. Add the veal cubes and brown on all sides. Transfer to a plate. Add the onions to the pan and fry for 5 minutes. Stir in the paprika, soup, stock, and salt and pepper and bring to the boil, stirring constantly.

Return the veal cubes to the pan and stir well. Cover and simmer for 1 to 1¼ hours. Stir in the peppers and mushrooms, re-cover and continue to simmer for 15 minutes or until the veal is cooked.

Serves 4

Osso Buco

1½ kg./3 lb. veal knuckle, cut
   into 7.5 cm./3 in. pieces
50 g./2 oz. seasoned flour
50 g./2 oz. butter
2 carrots, sliced
2 celery stalks, sliced
1 onion, sliced
2 garlic cloves, crushed
15 ml./1 tablespoon flour
150 ml./5 fl. oz. dry white
   wine
300 ml./10 fl. oz. veal stock
1 × 400 g./14 oz. can
   tomatoes
1 bay leaf
10 ml./2 teaspoon dried basil
salt and pepper
50 g./2 oz. black olives,
   chopped
Garnish
grated rind of 1 lemon
30 ml./2 tablespoons
   chopped fresh parsley
1 garlic clove, crushed

Roll the knuckle pieces in the seasoned flour. Melt the butter in a frying-pan. Add the knuckle pieces and brown lightly on all sides. Transfer to a casserole. Fry the carrots, celery, onion and garlic in the butter remaining in the pan for 5 minutes. Transfer to the casserole.

Stir the flour into the pan juices to form a smooth paste. Gradually, stir in the wine and stock and bring to the boil. Add all the remaining ingredients, except the garnish, and mix well. Cook for 2 minutes, stirring constantly. Pour the sauce over the meat and vegetables, cover the casserole and put it into the oven preheated to warm (170°C/325°F or Gas Mark 3). Cook for 3 hours, or until the meat is almost falling off the bone.

Mix the garnish ingredients together and stir into the Osso Buco.

Serves 4-6

Veal Goulash

50 g./2 oz. butter
1 kg./2 lb. lean veal, cubed
2 onions, chopped
1 garlic clove, crushed
25 ml./1½ tablespoons
  paprika
5 ml./1 teaspoon dried dill
1 × 400 g./14 oz. can
  sauerkraut, drained
150 ml./5 fl. oz. chicken
  stock
salt and pepper
150 ml./5 fl. oz. sour cream

Melt the butter in a saucepan. Add the veal cubes and brown on all sides. Transfer to a plate. Add the onions and garlic to the pan and fry for 5 minutes. Stir in the paprika and dill. Add the sauerkraut, stock and salt and pepper to taste, and stir to mix. Bring to the boil. Return the veal cubes to the pan and stir well. Cover and simmer for 1¼ to 1½ hours, or until the veal is cooked.

Stir in the sour cream and heat gently for 2 minutes.

Serves 4

Spanish Veal Stew

1 kg./2 lb. lean veal, cubed
50 g./2 oz. seasoned flour
50 ml./2 fl. oz. cooking oil
2 onions, sliced
2 celery stalks, sliced
15 ml./1 tablespoon finely
  grated orange rind
10 ml./2 teaspoons dried
  rosemary
425 ml./15 fl. oz. orange
  juice
30 ml./2 tablespoons beurre
  manié*

Roll the veal cubes in the seasoned flour. Heat the oil in a saucepan. Add the veal cubes and brown on all sides. Transfer to a plate. Add the onions and celery to the pan and fry for 5 minutes. Stir in the orange rind and rosemary and pour over the juice. Return the veal to the pan and bring to the boil. Cover and simmer for 1¼ to 1½ hours, or until the veal is cooked.

Stir in the beurre manié, a little at a time, until the sauce has thickened.

Serves 4-6

Veal Meat Loaf

675 g./1½ lb. minced veal
1 onion, grated
2 hard-boiled eggs, finely
  chopped
salt and pepper
10 ml./2 teaspoons paprika
1 egg, beaten
150 ml./5 fl. oz. sour cream
175 g./6 oz. button
  mushrooms, sliced
125 g./4 oz. butter

Mix the veal, onion, eggs, seasoning, paprika, egg and sour cream together. Spoon the mixture into a well-greased loaf tin and put the tin into a baking tin half-filled with hot water. Put into the oven pre-heated to moderate (180°C/350°F or Gas Mark 4) and bake for 1 to 1¼ hours, or until a knife inserted into the centre comes out clean.

Meanwhile, fry the mushrooms in the butter for 5 minutes. Pour over the loaf.

Serves 4

Fricadelles with Sour Cream

675 g./1½ lb. minced veal
25 g./1 oz. butter, melted
75 g./3 oz. dry breadcrumbs
1 egg, beaten
2.5 ml./½ teaspoon dried sage
5 ml./1 teaspoon finely
   grated lemon rind
50 g./2 oz. flour
75 ml./3 fl. oz. cooking oil
Sauce
25 g./1 oz. butter
30 ml./2 tablespoons flour
225 ml./8 fl. oz. chicken or
   veal stock
300 ml./10 fl. oz. sour cream

Mix the minced veal, melted butter, breadcrumbs, egg, sage and lemon rind together until they are thoroughly blended. Shape into about eight patties and coat them in the flour. Set aside for 10 minutes.

Heat the oil in a frying-pan. Add the patties and fry for 10 to 15 minutes, or until they are evenly browned and cooked through.

Meanwhile to make the sauce, melt the butter in a saucepan. Stir in the flour to form a smooth paste, then gradually stir in the stock. Bring to the boil and cook for 2 to 3 minutes, stirring constantly, or until the sauce has thickened. Stir in the sour cream and heat gently for 2 minutes. Pour over the patties.

Serves 4

Émincé de Veau

50 ml./2 fl. oz. cooking oil
1 large onion, sliced
1 garlic clove, crushed
1 red pepper, pith and seeds
   removed and sliced
1 × 400 g./14 oz. can
   tomatoes
salt and pepper
30 ml./2 tablespoons lemon
   juice
2.5 ml./½ teaspoon cayenne
   pepper
½ kg./1 lb. cooked veal, cut
   into strips

Heat the oil in a frying-pan. When it is hot, add the onion, garlic and red pepper and fry for 5 minutes. Stir in the tomatoes and can juice, salt and pepper to taste, lemon juice and cayenne, and bring to the boil. Simmer for 15 minutes. Stir in the veal strips and simmer gently for 5 minutes or until they are heated through.

Serves 3-4

Meat-Offal

Kidneys with Bordelaise Sauce

12 lambs' kidneys, halved
75 g./3 oz. seasoned flour
75 g./3 oz. butter
2 onions, chopped
3 lean bacon slices, chopped
15 ml./1 tablespoon chopped
   fresh parsley
300 ml./10 fl. oz. beef stock
150 ml./5 fl. oz. red wine
30 ml./2 tablespoons
   cornflour, blended with 30
   ml./2 tablespoons water

Roll the kidneys in the seasoned flour. Melt the butter in a saucepan. Add the kidneys and brown on all sides. Transfer to a plate. Add the onions, bacon and parsley to the pan and fry for 5 minutes. Stir in the stock and wine and bring to the boil. Return the kidneys to the liquid, cover and simmer for 15 to 20 minutes, or until the kidneys are cooked through.

Stir in the cornflour mixture and simmer for 2 to 3 minutes, stirring constantly, or until the sauce has thickened.

Serves 6

Kidneys Chasseur

8 lambs' kidneys, sliced
salt and pepper
125 g./4 oz. butter
15 ml./1 tablespoon chopped
   spring onion
15 ml./1 tablespoon flour
300 ml./10 fl. oz. white wine
125 g./4 oz. mushrooms,
   sliced
15 ml./1 tablespoon chopped
   fresh parsley

Rub the kidneys with the salt and pepper. Melt half the butter in a saucepan. Add the kidneys and brown on all sides. Transfer to a plate. Add the spring onion and flour to the pan and stir to form a paste. Gradually stir in the wine and bring to the boil. Return the kidneys to the pan and simmer for 10 minutes.

Meanwhile, fry the mushrooms in the remaining butter for 3 minutes. Add the mushrooms to the kidneys and stir to mix. Simmer for a further 5 minutes. Garnish with the parsley.

Serves 4

Kidney Kebabs with Barbecue Sauce

8 pickling onions, blanched
   for 4 minutes in boiling
   water, then drained
4 lamb's kidneys, halved
4 skinless chipolata
   sausages, halved
4 small tomatoes, halved
10 ml./2 teaspoons tomato
   purée
10 ml./2 teaspoons
   Worcestershire sauce
30 ml./2 tablespoons cooking
   oil
Sauce
25 g./1 oz. butter
1 onion, very finely chopped
150 ml./5 fl. oz. tomato
   ketchup
5 ml./1 teaspoon
   Worcestershire sauce
30 ml./2 tablespoons clear
   honey
30 ml./2 tablespoons lemon
   juice
salt and pepper

Thread the onions, kidneys, sausages and tomatoes on to four skewers. Mix the tomato purée, Worcestershire sauce and oil together. Line the grill pan with foil and lay the kebabs on the rack. Brush the kebabs generously with the purée mixture. Grill for 12 to 15 minutes or until the kebabs are cooked through and tender. Baste with the tomato purée mixture from time to time during cooking.

Meanwhile, melt the butter in a saucepan. Add the onion and fry for 5 minutes. Add all the remaining sauce ingredients and stir to mix. Bring to the boil, then simmer for 5 minutes, stirring occasionally.

Transfer the kebabs to a warmed serving dish and serve with the sauce.

Serves 4

Milanaise Kidneys

45 ml./3 tablespoons cooking
   oil
8 lambs' kidneys, sliced
2 onions, thinly sliced
1 garlic clove, crushed
1 × 400 g./14 oz. can
   tomatoes
150 ml./5 fl. oz. beef stock
15 ml./1 tablespoon chopped
   fresh parsley
salt and pepper
15 ml./1 tablespoon
   cornflour dissolved in 30
   ml./2 tablespoons water

Heat the oil in a frying-pan. Add the kidneys and brown on all sides. Transfer to a plate. Add the onions and garlic to the pan and fry for 5 minutes. Stir in the tomatoes and can juice, stock, parsley and salt and pepper to taste. Bring to the boil, then return the kidneys to the pan. Cover and simmer for 15 to 20 minutes, or until the kidneys are cooked through and tender.

Transfer the kidneys to a serving dish. Stir the cornflour mixture into the sauce and bring to the boil. Simmer for 2 to 3 minutes, stirring constantly, or until the sauce is thick. Pour over the kidneys.

Serves 4

Creamed Kidneys

8 lambs' kidneys, halved
50 g./2 oz. seasoned flour
50 g./2 oz. butter
1 green pepper, pith and
   seeds removed and
   chopped
1 red pepper, pith and seeds
   removed and chopped
225 g./8 oz. long-grain rice
45 ml./3 tablespoons sherry
150 ml./5 fl. oz. single cream

Roll the kidneys in the seasoned flour. Melt the butter in a saucepan. Add the peppers and fry for 5 minutes. Stir in the kidneys and fry for 15 to 20 minutes, or until they are cooked through.

Meanwhile, cook the rice in boiling, salted water for 15 to 20 minutes, or until it is cooked and the liquid has been absorbed. Mix the sherry and cream together. Stir into the pan with the kidneys and heat gently for 3 minutes. Arrange the rice in a serving dish, then pour over the creamed kidneys.

Serves 4

Devilled Kidneys

8 lambs' kidneys
50 g./2 oz. seasoned flour
50 g./2 oz. butter
125 g./4 oz. mushrooms,
   sliced
30 ml./2 tablespoons flour
1 × 225 ml./8 fl. oz. can
   consommé
10 ml./2 teaspoons dry
   mustard
5 ml./1 teaspoon
   Worcestershire sauce
50 ml./2 fl. oz. single cream

Roll the kidneys in the seasoned flour. Melt the butter in a frying-pan. Add the kidneys and brown on all sides. Add the mushrooms and fry for 3 minutes. Stir in the flour to form a smooth paste. Gradually stir in the consommé, mustard and Worcestershire sauce. Bring to the boil. Simmer for 15 to 20 minutes, or until the kidneys are cooked through.

Transfer the kidneys to a warmed serving dish. Stir the cream into the sauce and heat gently for 2 minutes. Pour the sauce over the kidneys.

Serves 4

Lemon Garlic Kidneys

8 lambs' kidneys, sliced
salt and pepper
50 g./2 oz. butter
2 garlic cloves, crushed
juice of 1 lemon
2.5 ml./½ teaspoon finely
   grated lemon rind

Rub the kidneys with the salt and pepper. Melt the butter in a frying-pan. Add the kidney slices and garlic and brown the kidneys on all sides. Stir in the lemon juice and rind. Continue to fry for a further 8 to 10 minutes, or until the kidneys are cooked through.

Serves 4

Kidney Kebabs with Orange Sauce

12 pickling onions, blanched
    for 4 minutes in boiling
    water and drained
4 lambs' kidneys, halved
12 mushrooms
4 lean bacon slices, halved
    and rolled up
50 g./2 oz. butter, melted
5 ml./1 teaspoon dried mixed
    herbs
salt and pepper
Sauce
300 ml./10 fl. oz. beef stock
25 g./1 oz. cornflour
25 g./1 oz. butter
finely grated rind and juice
    of 2 oranges
5 ml./1 teaspoon sugar

Thread the onions, kidneys, mushrooms and bacon rolls on to four skewers. Line the grill pan with foil and lay the kebabs on the rack. Mix the melted butter, mixed herbs and salt and pepper to taste together and brush generously over the kebabs. Grill for 12 to 15 minutes or until the kebabs are cooked through and tender. Baste with the melted butter occasionally during the cooking period. To make the sauce, mix a little of the stock with the cornflour to make a smooth paste. Put the remaining stock into a saucepan and bring to the boil. Stir in the cornflour mixture and all the remaining sauce ingredients and cook for 2 to 3 minutes, stirring constantly, or until the sauce thickens.

Transfer the kebabs to a warmed serving dish and serve with the sauce. .

Serves 4

Kidneys with Sherry

50 g./2 oz. butter
1 large onion, chopped
8 lambs' kidneys, sliced
25 g./1 oz. flour
125 ml./4 fl. oz. dry sherry
225 ml./8 fl. oz. beef stock
5 ml./1 teaspoon dried thyme
5 ml./1 teaspoon grated
    lemon rind
salt and pepper
Garnish
2 large slices white bread,
    crusts removed, and
    quartered
30 ml./2 tablespoons olive oil
15 ml./1 tablespoon chopped
    fresh parsley

Melt the butter in a saucepan. Add the onion and fry for 5 minutes. Add the kidneys and brown on all sides. Transfer to a plate. Stir the flour into the butter remaining in the pan to form a smooth paste. Gradually stir in the sherry, stock, thyme, lemon rind and salt and pepper to taste. Bring to the boil, then simmer for 2 minutes, stirring constantly, or until the sauce thickens. Return the kidneys and onion to the pan and simmer for 15 to 20 minutes, or until the kidneys are cooked through and tender.

Meanwhile to make the garnish, fry the bread quarters in the oil for 3 to 5 minutes, or until they are deep brown. Transfer the kidney mixture to a warmed serving dish and arrange the fried bread quarters around the edge. Garnish with the parsley.

Serves 4

Kidneys in Sour Cream

8 lambs' kidneys, chopped
50 g./2 oz. seasoned flour
75 g./3 oz. butter
1 onion, chopped
1 garlic clove, crushed
1 red pepper, pith and seeds
 removed and chopped
125 g./4 oz. green beans,
 chopped
25 g./1 oz. flaked almonds
150 ml./5 fl. oz. sour cream
5 ml./1 teaspoon caraway
 seeds
5 ml./1 teaspoon dried dill

Roll the kidneys in the seasoned flour. Melt the butter in a saucepan. Add the kidneys and brown on all sides. Transfer to a plate. Add the onion, garlic, vegetables and almonds to the pan and fry for 5 minutes. Return the kidneys to the pan and simmer for 15 minutes. Stir in the remaining ingredients and continue to simmer for a further 5 minutes, or until the kidneys are cooked through and tender.

Serves 4

Kidneys in Wine

50 g./2 oz. butter
8 lambs' kidneys, sliced
4 bacon slices, chopped
1 onion, chopped
1 celery stalk, chopped
15 ml./1 tablespoon flour
300 ml./10 fl. oz. red wine
75 ml./3 fl. oz. beef stock
30 ml./2 tablespoons tomato
 purée
1 bay leaf
2.5 ml./½ teaspoon dried
 thyme
225 g./8 oz. mushrooms,
 sliced
30 ml./2 tablespoons dry
 breadcrumbs
30 ml./2 tablespoons grated
 cheese
15 ml./1 tablespoon chopped
 fresh parsley

Melt half the butter in a frying-pan. Add the kidneys and brown on all sides. Transfer to a plate. Add the bacon, onion and celery to the pan and fry for 5 minutes. Stir in the flour to form a smooth paste, then gradually stir in the wine, stock, tomato purée, bay leaf and thyme. Bring to the boil. Return the kidney slices to the pan and simmer for 15 minutes.

Meanwhile, fry the mushrooms in the remaining butter for 5 minutes. Transfer the kidney mixture to a flameproof dish and stir in the mushrooms. Sprinkle the breadcrumbs and cheese over the top and grill for 5 minutes, or until the top is golden brown. Garnish with the parsley.

Serves 4

Liver with Apples and Onion

½ kg./1 lb. calf's liver, thinly
   sliced
50 g./2 oz. seasoned flour
125 g./4 oz. butter
2 red apples, cored and
   thinly sliced
1 onion, thinly sliced into
   rings

Coat the liver slices in the seasoned flour. Melt half the butter in a frying-pan. Add the liver slices and cook for 3 to 5 minutes, or until the liver is cooked through and tender. Transfer to a warmed serving dish and keep hot.

Melt the remaining butter in the pan. Add the apples and onion and fry for 5 minutes, or until they are tender. Arrange the apples and onion slices on the liver and pour over the pan juices.

Serves 4

Liver Cream Loaf

½ kg./1 lb. calf's liver
½ kg./1 lb. cooked ham
1 onion
225 g./8 oz. pork
   sausagemeat
45 ml./3 tablespoons tomato
   purée
2 eggs, beaten
1 large slice of white bread,
   crusts removed, shredded
   and soaked in 150 ml./5
   fl. oz. beef stock for 15
   minutes
salt and pepper

Put the liver, ham and onion in a fine mincer or blender and reduce to a smooth purée. Beat in the sausagemeat, tomato purée and eggs. Beat the bread mixture until smooth, then stir into the liver mixture with salt and pepper to taste. Spoon into a well-greased loaf tin and cover with greased foil. Put in a deep baking tin half-filled with hot water and bake in the oven preheated to warm (170°C/325°F or Gas Mark 3) for 1½ hours or until a knife inserted into the centre comes out clean. Cool in the tin before serving.

Serves 8

Liver Paupiettes

4 lean bacon slices
4 thin slices calf's liver
salt and pepper
15 ml./1 tablespoon lemon
  juice
8 thyme sprigs
50 g./2 oz. butter
10 ml./2 teaspoons flour
75 ml./3 fl. oz. Marsala
4 tomatoes, skinned and
  chopped
50 ml./2 fl. oz. beef stock
1 lemon, thinly sliced

Put the bacon slices on the liver and season with the salt and pepper. Sprinkle over the lemon juice and put two thyme sprigs in the centre of each slice. Roll up the slices and secure them with wooden toothpicks.

Melt the butter in a frying-pan. Add the liver rolls and fry for 4 minutes. Stir in the flour to form a smooth paste with the butter. Gradually stir in the Marsala and bring to the boil. Add the tomatoes and stock and stir to mix. Cover and simmer for 8 minutes, or until the liver rolls are cooked through. Garnish with the lemon slices.

Serves 4

Venetian Liver

½ kg./1 lb. calf's liver, thinly
  sliced
50 g./2 oz. seasoned flour
50 g./2 oz. butter
2 onions, thinly sliced in
  rings
15 ml./1 tablespoon chopped
  fresh parsley

Coat the liver slices in the seasoned flour. Melt the butter in a frying-pan. Add the liver slices and cook for 3 to 5 minutes, or until the liver is cooked through and tender. Transfer to a warmed serving dish and keep hot.

Add the onion rings to the pan and fry for 5 to 8 minutes, or until they are crisp and brown. Arrange them on the liver and garnish with the parsley.

Serves 4

Calf's Liver in Wine Sauce

½ kg./1 lb. calf's liver, thinly
  sliced
50 g./2 oz. seasoned flour
50 g./2 oz. butter
1 onion, chopped
50 g./2 oz. cooked ham,
  chopped
45 ml./3 tablespoons finely
  chopped fresh parsley
150 ml./5 fl. oz. red wine

Coat the liver slices in the seasoned flour. Melt the butter in a frying-pan. Add the liver slices and fry for 3 to 5 minutes, or until they are cooked through and tender. Transfer to a warmed serving dish and keep hot.

Add all the remaining ingredients to the pan and cook for 5 minutes. Boil the sauce for a further 2 minutes, or until it has reduced a little. Pour over the liver.

Serves 4

Chicken Livers with Almonds

½ kg./1 lb. chicken livers
2 spring onions, chopped
30 ml./2 tablespoons soy
   sauce
30 ml./2 tablespoons dry
   sherry
1 garlic clove, crushed
5 ml./1 teaspoon finely
   chopped fresh ginger
2.5 ml./½ teaspoon salt
15 ml./1 tablespoon brown
   sugar
50 ml./2 fl. oz. cooking oil
1 × 150 g./5 oz. can bamboo
   shoot, drained and sliced
50 g./2 oz. flaked almonds
40 g./1½ oz. flour
150 ml./5 fl. oz. chicken
   stock
15 ml./1 tablespoon
   cornflour dissolved in 15
   ml./1 tablespoon stock

Put the chicken livers in a saucepan and add enough water to cover. Boil for 2 minutes, then drain. Mix the spring onions, soy sauce, sherry, garlic, ginger, salt and sugar together in a shallow dish. Add the livers, baste well and leave to marinate for 1½ hours. Drain the livers and reserve the marinade.

Heat the oil in a frying-pan. Add the bamboo shoot and almonds and fry for 2 minutes. Meanwhile, quickly roll the livers in the flour. Add the livers to the pan and fry for 5 to 8 minutes or until they are cooked through. Transfer to a plate.

Add the stock, cornflour and reserved marinade to the pan and bring to the boil. Simmer for 2 minutes, stirring constantly, or until the sauce thickens. Return the livers to the pan and simmer for 2 minutes or until they are thoroughly reheated.

Serves 4

Chicken Liver Scramble

125 g./4 oz. butter
½ kg./1 lb. chicken livers,
   chopped
1 onion, chopped
1 green pepper, pith and
   seeds removed and
   chopped
1 × 225 g./8 oz. can
   sweetcorn, drained
salt and pepper
5 ml./1 teaspoon paprika
6 eggs, beaten
30 ml./2 tablespoons single
   cream

Melt the butter in a frying-pan. Add the livers, onion and green pepper and fry for 5 minutes. Stir in the sweetcorn, salt and pepper to taste and paprika and cook for 1 minute. Mix the eggs and cream together and stir into the pan. Cook for 2 to 3 minutes, stirring constantly, or until the eggs have set and the livers are cooked through and tender.

Serves 3-4

Chicken Liver Pie

½ kg./1 lb. chicken livers,
    halved
50 g./2 oz. seasoned flour
50 ml./2 fl. oz. cooking oil
2 bacon slices, chopped
1 onion, chopped
175 g./6 oz. mushrooms
3 carrots, chopped
30 ml./1 tablespoon flour
300 ml./10 fl. oz. red wine or
    beef stock
15 ml./1 tablespoon chopped
    fresh parsley
salt and pepper
675 g./1½ lb. cooked
    potatoes, mashed
25 g./1 oz. butter
50 g./2 oz. Cheddar cheese,
    grated

Roll the livers in the seasoned flour. Heat the oil in a frying-pan. Add the livers and brown on all sides. Add the bacon, onion, mushrooms and carrots and fry for 5 minutes. Stir in the flour to form a paste. Gradually stir in the wine or stock, parsley and salt and pepper to taste. Bring to the boil and cook for 2 minutes, stirring constantly, or until the sauce thickens. Transfer to a baking dish.

Mix the potatoes, butter and half the cheese together and season with salt and pepper. Spread over the liver mixture and sprinkle over the remaining cheese. Put the dish into the oven preheated to moderate (180°C/350°F or Gas Mark 4) and bake for 15 to 20 minutes or until the top is brown.

Serves 4

Liver Casserole

½ kg./1 lb. lamb's liver, cut
    into 5 cm./2 in. pieces
50 g./2 oz. seasoned flour
50 ml./2 fl. oz. cooking oil
1 onion, chopped
1 garlic clove, crushed
175 g./6 oz. mushrooms,
    sliced
1 × 400 g./14 oz. can
    tomatoes
30 ml./2 tablespoons tomato
    purée
15 ml./1 tablespoon chopped
    fresh parsley
salt and pepper
25 g./1 oz. black olives,
    chopped

Roll the liver pieces in the seasoned flour. Heat the oil in a flameproof casserole. Add the liver and brown on all sides. Add the onion, garlic and mushrooms and fry for 5 minutes. Stir in the tomatoes and can juice and all the remaining ingredients and bring to the boil. Put the casserole into the oven preheated to moderate (180°C/350°F or Gas Mark 4) and cook for 35 to 40 minutes, or until the liver is cooked through and tender.

Serves 4

Liver with Orange

½ kg./1 lb. lamb's liver, thinly
   sliced
50 g./2 oz. seasoned flour
15 ml./1 tablespoon finely
   grated orange rind
125 g./4 oz. butter
50 ml./2 fl. oz. fresh orange
   juice

Coat the liver slices in the seasoned flour. Sprinkle over half the orange rind. Melt the butter in a large frying-pan. Add the liver slices and fry for 5 to 8 minutes, or until they are cooked through and tender. Transfer to a warmed serving dish.

Pour the orange juice into the pan, then stir in the remaining orange rind. Bring to the boil, then pour over the liver.

Serves 4

Liver Ragoût

30 ml./2 tablespoons cooking
   oil
2 onions, chopped
2 carrots, chopped
2 celery stalks, chopped
1 turnip, chopped
350 ml./12 fl. oz. beef stock
15 ml./1 tablespoon
   Worcestershire sauce
salt and pepper
½ kg./1 lb. lamb's liver, sliced
300 ml./10 fl. oz. milk

Heat the oil in a saucepan. Add the onions, carrots, celery and turnip and fry for 5 minutes. Pour in the stock and Worcestershire sauce and season with the salt and pepper. Bring to the boil and simmer for 30 minutes.

Meanwhile, soak the liver slices in the milk for 10 minutes. Drain the slices, then cut them into strips. Stir the strips into the vegetable mixture, cover and simmer for 5 to 8 minutes, or until the liver is cooked.

Serves 4

Liver Ragoût Sicilienne

675 g./1½ lb. ox liver, cut into
   strips
50 g./2 oz. seasoned flour
50 ml./2 fl. oz. cooking oil
3 onions, thinly sliced in
   rings
1 garlic clove, crushed
300 ml./10 fl. oz. beef stock
300 ml./10 fl. oz. cider or red
   wine
15 ml./1 tablespoon
   redcurrant jelly
2.5 ml./½ teaspoon grated
   lemon rind
45 ml./3 tablespoons stoned
   green olives

Roll the liver strips in the seasoned flour. Heat the oil in a saucepan. Add the onions and garlic and fry for 5 minutes. Add the liver and brown on all sides. Stir in all the remaining ingredients and bring to the boil. Cover and simmer for 2 hours, or until the liver is cooked through and tender.

Serves 4-6

Braised Liver and Onions

*30 ml./2 tablespoons cooking
  oil*
4 bacon slices, chopped
3 onions, sliced
25 g./1 oz. flour
300 ml./10 fl. oz. beef stock
*15 ml./1 tablespoon chopped
  fresh parsley*
*½ kg./1 lb. lamb's liver, thinly
  sliced*
salt and pepper

Heat the oil in a saucepan. Add the bacon and fry for 5 minutes. Transfer to a plate. Add the onions to the pan and fry for 5 minutes. Stir in the flour to form a smooth paste. Gradually stir in the stock and bring to the boil. Stir in the parsley and cook for 3 minutes, stirring constantly, or until the sauce thickens.

Season the liver slices with salt and pepper and add them to the sauce, with the bacon. Cover and simmer for 8 to 10 minutes or until the liver is cooked through and tender.

Serves 4

Liver Stroganoff

*½ kg./1 lb. lamb's liver, cut
  into strips*
50 g./2 oz. seasoned flour
75 g./3 oz. butter
1 onion, finely chopped
1 garlic clove, crushed
*125 g./4 oz. mushrooms,
  sliced*
15 ml./1 tablespoon paprika
salt and pepper
150 ml./5 fl. oz. sour cream

Roll the liver strips in the seasoned flour. Heat 50 g./2 oz. of the butter in a frying-pan. Add the liver strips and brown on all sides. Transfer to a plate.

Add the remaining butter to the pan with the onion, garlic and mushrooms and fry for 5 minutes. Stir in the paprika until it is thoroughly blended, then salt and pepper to taste. Stir in the sour cream and return the liver strips to the pan. Simmer gently for 2 to 3 minutes, or until the liver is cooked through and tender.

Serves 4

Normandy Liver

½ kg./1 lb. lamb's liver, cut
   into strips
50 g./2 oz. seasoned flour
75 g./3 oz. butter
2 dessert apples, cored and
   thinly sliced in rings
1 large onion, thinly sliced in
   rings
225 ml./8 fl. oz. cider
15 ml./1 tablespoon chopped
   green olives
15 ml./1 tablespoon chopped
   black olives
675 g./1½ lb. hot cooked
   potatoes, mashed
salt and pepper
30 ml./2 tablespoons double
   cream

Roll the liver strips in the seasoned flour. Melt half the butter in a frying-pan. Add the liver strips and brown lightly on all sides. Transfer to a plate. Add the remaining butter to the pan with the apple and onion rings. Brown lightly on both sides. Stir in the cider and olives and bring to the boil. Simmer for 5 minutes, then stir in the liver strips. Continue to simmer for a further 5 minutes, or until they are cooked through and tender.

Mix the potatoes, salt and pepper to taste and cream together. Arrange on the bottom of a warmed serving dish. Spoon over the liver mixture.

Serves 4

Lemon-Flavoured Lamb's Brawn

1 lamb's head, cleaned in
   cold water
2 extra lambs' tongues,
   cleaned
rind and juice of 1 lemon
2 bay leaves
4 pickling onions
1 bouquet garni
2 pig's trotters
salt and pepper

Put all the ingredients, except the lemon juice, into a very large saucepan and cover with cold water. Bring slowly to the boil, removing any scum which rises to the surface. Cover and simmer for 2 hours, or until the meat is cooked through and tender.

Remove the head, tongues and trotters from the liquid and set aside until they are cool enough to handle. Reserve the cooking liquid. Cut all the meat from the head, tongues and trotters and arrange in a 1½ l./3 pint mould. Add the lemon juice to the reserved liquid and boil rapidly until it has reduced to about 400 ml./15 fl. oz. Strain over the meat and set aside to cool. Chill in the refrigerator until set.

To serve, dip the bottom of the mould in hot water and invert over a serving dish, giving it a sharp tap.

Serves 8

Brains in Black Butter

3 sets of calves' brains,
    soaked in cold salted
    water for 1 hour, drained
    and with the membrane
    and veins removed
50 g./2 oz. seasoned flour
175 g./6 oz. butter
juice of 1 lemon
5 ml./1 teaspoon chopped
    capers
15 ml./1 tablespoon chopped
    fresh parsley

Poach the brains in boiling, salted water for 10 minutes. Drain the brains, then cut them into large cubes. Roll the cubes in the seasoned flour. Melt half of the butter in a frying-pan. Add the brains and fry for 6 to 8 minutes, or until they are evenly browned and cooked through. Transfer to a plate.

Add the remaining butter to the pan and heat until it is deep golden brown. Stir in the lemon juice and capers, then pour over the brains. Sprinkle with chopped parsley.

Serves 4

Brains in Lemon Sauce

3 sets of calves' brains,
    soaked in cold salted
    water for 1 hour, drained,
    and with membrane and
    veins removed
50 g./2 oz. seasoned flour
2 eggs, beaten
125 g./4 oz. Parmesan or
    Cheddar cheese, grated
oil for deep frying
Lemon Sauce
6 egg yolks, beaten
125 ml./4 fl. oz. lemon juice
75 ml./3 fl. oz. chicken stock

Poach the brains in boiling, salted water for 10 minutes. Drain the brains, then cut them into bite-sized pieces. Roll the pieces in the seasoned flour, then dip the pieces first in the eggs, then in the grated cheese.

Carefully deep-fry the brain pieces in oil for 3 minutes or until they are golden brown. Drain on kitchen paper towels. Keep hot while you make the sauce.

Mix the egg yolks and lemon juice together in a small saucepan. Gradually add the chicken stock, beating constantly. Simmer the sauce over low heat, beating constantly, for 3 minutes or until it is thick. Do not boil or the sauce will curdle. Arrange the brains on a serving dish and pour over the sauce.

Serves 4

Sweetbread Fricassee

675 g./1½ lb. sweetbreads,
  soaked in cold salted
  water for 3 hours, drained
  and with the skin and
  membrane removed
300 ml./10 fl. oz. chicken
  stock
1 onion, quartered
1 bouquet garni
pared rind of 1 lemon
6 peppercorns
25 g./1 oz. butter
25 g./1 oz. flour
15 ml./1 tablespoon chopped
  fresh parsley
50 ml./2 fl. oz. double cream

Put the sweetbreads, stock, onion, bouquet garni, lemon rind and peppercorns in a saucepan and simmer for 30 to 35 minutes, or until the sweetbreads are cooked through and tender. Strain and transfer the sweetbreads to a plate. Reserve about 225 ml./8 fl. oz. of the cooking liquid.

Melt the butter in a saucepan. Stir in the flour to form a smooth paste, then gradually stir in the reserved cooking liquid and parsley. Bring to the boil and cook for 2 to 3 minutes, stirring constantly, or until the sauce thickens. Stir in the cream and return the sweetbreads to the sauce. Simmer gently for 2 to 3 minutes or until they are heated through.

Serves 4

Sweetbreads à la King

675 g./1½ lb. sweetbreads,
  soaked in cold salted
  water for 3 hours, drained
  and with the skin and
  membrane removed
75 g./3 oz. butter
125 g./4 oz. mushrooms,
  sliced
2 green peppers, pith and
  seeds removed and
  chopped
45 ml./3 tablespoons sherry
15 ml./1 tablespoon flour
300 ml./10 fl. oz. milk
salt and pepper
4 slices of hot buttered toast

Poach the sweetbreads in boiling, salted water for 10 minutes. Drain and cut into cubes. Melt 50 g./2 oz. of butter in a saucepan. Add the mushrooms and peppers and fry for 5 minutes. Stir in the sherry and simmer for 3 minutes. Add the sweetbreads.

Meanwhile, melt the remaining butter in a saucepan. Stir in the flour to form a smooth paste, then gradually stir in the milk. Bring to the boil and cook the sauce for 2 minutes, stirring constantly, or until it thickens. Stir in the sweetbread mixture and season to taste. Continue to simmer for 10 minutes, or until the sweetbreads are cooked through and tender. Spoon over hot buttered toast.

Serves 4

Glazed Tongue

1 ox tongue, soaked for 24
   hours and drained
1 onion, sliced
6 peppercorns
1 bouquet garni
1 carrot, sliced
15 ml./1 tablespoon gelatine,
   dissolved in 30 ml./2
   tablespoons boiling water
600 ml./1 pint water
15 ml./1 tablespoon wine
   vinegar
3 cloves
3 strips pared lemon rind
10 ml./2 teaspoons lemon
   juice
5 ml./1 teaspoon salt

Put the tongue in a saucepan and cover with cold water. Add the onion, peppercorns, bouquet garni and carrot and bring to the boil. Cover and simmer for about 3 hours (allow between ¾ and 1 hour per pound), or until the tongue is cooked through and tender. Set aside until cool enough to handle, then drain and skin the tongue. Pack into a tongue press or large bowl.

Put all the remaining ingredients into a saucepan and bring to the boil, stirring constantly. Cool, then strain this aspic through a double thickness of cheesecloth. Pour in just enough aspic to cover the tongue completely. Put a saucer or plate to cover, then place a weight on top. Set aside to cool, then chill in the refrigerator overnight, or until the aspic has set. Just before serving, invert the press or bowl over a serving dish, giving the bottom a sharp tap.

Serves 8-10

Tongue Florentine

675 g./1½ lb. cooked tongue,
   sliced
125 ml./4 fl. oz. milk
675 g./1½ lb. hot cooked
   spinach
25 g./1 oz. butter
salt and pepper
15 ml./1 tablespoon
   cornflour
pinch of grated nutmeg
15 ml./1 tablespoon chopped
   fresh parsley

Put the tongue in a large, wide saucepan and pour over the milk. Simmer gently for 5 to 10 minutes, or until the tongue is thoroughly heated through.

Mix the spinach with half the butter and salt and pepper to taste. Arrange decoratively around the edge of a warmed serving dish. Drain the tongue slices, reserving the cooking liquid. Arrange the slices in the centre of the dish and keep hot. Make the reserved liquid up to about 300 ml./10 fl. oz. with water or stock. Melt the remaining butter in a saucepan. Stir in the cornflour to form a smooth paste, then gradually stir in the reserved liquid. Bring to the boil, then stir in the nutmeg and cook for 2 to 3 minutes, stirring constantly, or until the sauce thickens. Pour over the tongue slices and garnish with the parsley.

Serves 4

Tongue with Cherry Sauce

chicken stock
1 × 225 g./8 oz. can red
   cherries
25 ml./1½ tablespoons
   cornflour blended with 30
   ml./2 tablespoons water
25 g./1 oz. butter
675 g./1½ lb. hot cooked
   tongue, sliced

Add enough stock to the cherry can liquid to make 300 ml./10 fl. oz. Put into a saucepan and bring to the boil. Stir in the cornflour mixture and butter. Cook for 2 to 3 minutes, stirring constantly, or until the sauce thickens. Stir in the cherries and simmer for a further 1 minute, or until they are heated through. Arrange the tongue slices on a serving dish and pour over the sauce.

Serves 4

Tongue Niçoise

300 ml./10 fl. oz. tomato
   juice
15 ml./1 tablespoon
   cornflour, dissolved in 15
   ml./1 tablespoon water
5 ml./1 teaspoon garlic salt
30 ml./2 tablespoons
   medium sherry
675 g./1½ lb. cooked tongue,
   chopped

Put the tomato juice into a saucepan and bring to the boil. Stir in the cornflour, garlic salt and sherry and cook for 2 to 3 minutes, stirring constantly, or until the sauce thickens. Stir in the chopped tongue and simmer for a further 2 to 3 minutes, or until it is heated through.

Serves 4

Tongue with Raisin Sauce

50 g./2 oz. butter
25 g./1 oz. flour
425 ml./15 fl. oz. beef stock
salt and pepper
5 ml./1 teaspoon finely
   grated lemon rind
15 ml./1 tablespoon lemon
   juice
5 ml./1 teaspoon brown
   sugar
2.5 ml./½ teaspoon ground
   ginger
125 g./4 oz. raisins
675 g./1½ lb. hot cooked
   tongue, sliced

Melt the butter in a saucepan. Stir in the flour to form a smooth paste. Gradually stir in the stock, salt and pepper to taste, lemon rind and juice, sugar and ginger and bring to the boil. Cook for 2 to 3 minutes, stirring constantly, or until the sauce has thickened. Stir in the raisins and simmer for a further 3 minutes.

Arrange the tongue slices on a serving plate and pour over the sauce.

Serves 4

Tripe Bordelaise

25 g./1 oz. butter
2 onions, chopped
1 garlic clove, crushed
675 g./1½ lb. tripe, parboiled
  and cut into pieces
3 tomatoes, skinned and
  chopped
30 ml./2 tablespoons tomato
  purée
175 ml./6 fl. oz. chicken
  stock
salt and pepper
1 bouquet garni

Melt the butter in a saucepan. Add the onions and garlic and fry for 5 minutes. Stir in all the remaining ingredients and bring to the boil. Cover and simmer for 1½ to 2 hours, or until the tripe is tender. Remove the bouquet garni before serving.

Serves 4

Tripe and Onions

675 g./1½ lb. tripe, parboiled
  and cut into pieces
3 large onions, chopped
750 ml./1¼ pints milk
salt and pepper
5 ml./1 teaspoon dried thyme
25 g./1 oz. butter
25 g./1 oz. flour

Put the tripe, onions, milk, salt and pepper to taste and thyme in a saucepan. Bring to the boil, then cover and simmer for 1½ to 2 hours, or until the tripe is tender. Transfer the tripe and onions to a warmed serving bowl. Reserve the cooking liquid.

Melt the butter in a saucepan. Stir in the flour to form a smooth paste, then gradually stir in the cooking liquid. Bring to the boil and cook for 2 to 3 minutes, stirring constantly, or until the sauce thickens. Stir the sauce into the tripe and onions.

Serves 4

Tripe with Parsley Sauce

675 g./1½ lb. tripe, parboiled
  and cut into strips
50 g./2 oz. butter
25 g./1 oz. flour
300 ml./10 fl. oz. milk or
  single cream
30 ml./2 tablespoons
  chopped fresh parsley
salt and pepper

Put the tripe into a saucepan and add enough water to cover. Bring to the boil, then cover and simmer for 1½ to 2 hours, or until the tripe is tender. Drain the tripe.

Melt the butter in a saucepan. Stir in the flour to form a smooth paste, then gradually stir in the milk or cream. Bring to the boil and cook for 2 to 3 minutes, stirring constantly, or until the sauce thickens. Stir in the parsley, salt and pepper to taste and the tripe. Simmer for 3 minutes before serving.

Serves 4

Tripe French-Style

45 ml./3 tablespoons cooking oil
2 onions, chopped
2 carrots, chopped
125 g./4 oz. mushrooms, sliced
15 ml./1 tablespoon flour
300 ml./10 fl. oz. beef stock
675 g./1½ lb. tripe, parboiled and cut into pieces
salt and pepper
5 ml./1 teaspoon paprika
50 ml./2 fl. oz. single cream
30 ml./2 tablespoons brandy

Heat the oil in a saucepan. Add the vegetables and fry for 5 minutes. Stir in the flour to form a paste, then gradually stir in the stock. Bring to the boil. Stir in the tripe, salt and pepper to taste, and paprika. Cover and simmer for 1½ to 2 hours, or until the tripe is tender.

Mix the cream and brandy together and stir into the tripe. Heat gently for 2 to 3 minutes.

Serves 4

Hotch Potch

50 ml./2 fl. oz. cooking oil
1½ kg./3 lb. oxtail, cut into 5 cm./2 in. pieces and trimmed of excess fat
3 onions, chopped
4 large carrots, chopped
1¼ l./2 pints beef stock
finely grated rind of 1 lemon
1 bouquet garni
salt and pepper
40 g./1½ oz. cornflour
Dumplings
125 g./4 oz. self-raising flour, sifted
7.5 ml./1½ teaspoons dry mustard
50 g./2 oz. shredded suet
water to blend

Heat the oil in a large saucepan. Add the oxtail pieces and brown on all sides. Transfer to a plate. Add the onions and half the carrots to the pan and fry for 5 minutes. Stir in the stock, lemon rind, bouquet garni and salt and pepper to taste and bring to the boil. Return the oxtail pieces to the pan, cover and simmer for 1½ hours. Stir in the remaining carrots and continue to simmer for a further 1 hour. Cool, then chill in the refrigerator overnight.

Remove the fat from the top of the pan and bring to the boil. Cover and simmer for 1 hour. Meanwhile to make the dumplings, mix all the ingredients together until they are blended to a fairly soft dough. Shape into about eight balls and drop into the oxtail mixture. Cover and simmer for 30 minutes, or until the meat comes away easily from the bones. Mix the cornflour with a little of the pan liquid, then stir into the pan. Simmer for 2 to 3 minutes, stirring constantly, or until the sauce is thick.

Serves 6

Oxtail Casserole I

1½ kg./3 lb. oxtail, cut into 5
   cm./2 in. pieces, and
   trimmed of excess fat
75 g./3 oz. seasoned flour
50 ml./2 fl. oz. cooking oil
2 streaky bacon slices,
   chopped
2 onions, chopped
3 carrots, chopped
1 turnip, chopped
2 celery stalks, chopped
1 bay leaf
3 parsley sprigs
10 ml./2 teaspoons crushed
   black peppercorns
salt and pepper
900 ml./1½ pints beef stock

Roll the oxtail pieces in the seasoned flour. Heat the oil in a large saucepan. Add the oxtail pieces and brown on all sides. Transfer to a plate. Add the bacon, vegetables and flavourings to the pan and fry for 5 minutes, or until the bacon is crisp. Pour in the stock and bring to the boil. Return the oxtail pieces to the pan, cover and simmer for 4 hours, or until the meat comes away easily from the bones. Transfer the oxtail pieces to a warmed serving dish and keep hot. Boil the stock over high heat until it has reduced by about half. Strain over the oxtail.

Serves 6

Oxtail Casserole II

1½ kg./3 lb. oxtail, cut into 5
   cm./2 in. pieces and
   trimmed of excess fat
75 g./3 oz. seasoned flour
75 ml./3 fl. oz. cooking oil
2 large onions, chopped
2 large carrots, chopped
15 ml./1 tablespoon brown
   sugar
60 ml./4 tablespoons flour
6 tomatoes, skinned and
   chopped
3 garlic cloves, crushed
1 bay leaf
5 ml./1 teaspoon dried thyme
1½ l./3 pints beef stock
salt and pepper
1 × 400 g./14 oz. can cream
   of tomato soup
175 g./6 oz. dried haricot
   beans, soaked in cold
   water overnight and
   drained

Roll the oxtail pieces in the seasoned flour. Heat the oil in a large flameproof casserole. Add the oxtail pieces and brown on all sides. Transfer to a plate. Add the onions and carrots to the casserole and fry for 5 minutes. Drain off any excess oil in the casserole. Return the oxtail pieces to the casserole and sprinkle over the brown sugar and flour. Add all the remaining ingredients, except the haricot beans, and stir to mix. Bring to the boil.

Cover the casserole and put it into the oven preheated to cool (150°C/300°F or Gas Mark 2). Cook for 3 hours. Remove from the oven, cool and chill in the refrigerator overnight.

Cook the haricot beans in boiling, salted water for 1 hour, or until they are tender. Meanwhile, remove the fat from the top of the casserole. Put the casserole into the oven preheated to cool (150°C/300°F or Gas Mark 2) and cook for 45 minutes. Drain the haricot beans and add them to the casserole. Continue to cook for a further 15 minutes, or until the meat comes away easily from the bones.

Serves 6

Heart Casserole

75 ml./3 fl. oz. cooking oil
4 lambs' hearts, cleaned,
    soaked in cold salted
    water for 2 hours, and
    chopped
2 onions, chopped
1 garlic clove, crushed
3 carrots, chopped
1 small turnip, chopped
125 g./4 oz. green beans,
    sliced
150 ml./5 fl. oz. red wine
150 ml./5 fl. oz. beef stock
15 ml./1 tablespoon finely
    grated orange rind
15 ml./1 tablespoon orange
    juice
salt and pepper
5 ml./1 teaspoon grated
    nutmeg
15 ml./1 tablespoon beurre
    manié*

Heat the oil in a flameproof casserole. Add the hearts and vegetables and fry for 5 to 8 minutes, or until they are browned. Stir in the wine, stock, orange rind and juice, salt and pepper to taste and nutmeg, and bring to the boil. Cover the casserole and put into the oven preheated to warm (170°C/325°F or Gas Mark 3). Cook for 2 to 2½ hours, or until the hearts are cooked and tender. Stir in the beurre manié, a little at a time, until the sauce thickens a little.

Serves 4

Stuffed Hearts

4 lambs' hearts, cleaned and
    soaked in cold salted
    water for 2 hours
50 g./2 oz. seasoned flour
50 ml./2 fl. oz. cooking oil
425 ml./15 fl. oz. chicken
    stock
Filling
50 g./2 oz. dry breadcrumbs
50 g./2 oz. cooked ham, very
    finely chopped
1 onion, grated
45 ml./3 tablespoons melted
    butter
5 ml./1 teaspoon dried mixed
    herbs
salt and pepper

To make the filling, mix all the ingredients together until they are thoroughly blended. Spoon into the hearts and secure with string. Gently coat with seasoned flour.

Heat the oil in a flameproof casserole. Add the hearts and brown on all sides. Pour in the stock and bring to the boil. Cover the casserole and put it into the oven preheated to moderate (180°C/350°F or Gas Mark 4). Bake for 2 to 2½ hours, or until the hearts are cooked through and tender.

Serves 4

Poultry & Game

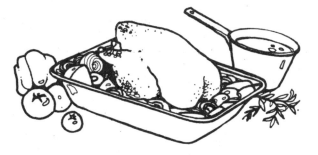

Oriental Chicken

1 × 2 kg./4 lb. chicken
425 ml./15 fl. oz. chicken
  stock
30 ml./2 tablespoons
  cornflour
30 ml./2 tablespoons sherry
25 ml./1 fl. oz. cooking oil
Stuffing
125 g./4 oz. bean sprouts
125 g./4 oz. cooked ham,
  finely chopped
1 × 50 g./2 oz. can water
  chestnuts, drained and
  ·chopped
25 g./1 oz. chopped almonds
30 ml./2 tablespoons
  chopped preserved ginger

To make the stuffing, mix all the ingredients together. Fill the cavity of the chicken with the stuffing, then secure with string or skewers. Mix the stock and cornflour together, then pour into a roasting pan. Bring to the boil, stirring constantly until it thickens. Stir in the sherry. Put the chicken in the pan, brush with the oil and put into the oven preheated to moderate (180°C/350°F or Gas Mark 4). Braise for 2 hours, or until the chicken is cooked through. Baste occasionally during the cooking period. Serve with the pan juices.

Serves 4-6

Roast Chicken with Parsley and Thyme Stuffing

1 × 1½ kg./3 lb. chicken
salt and pepper
350 g./12 oz. parsley and
  thyme stuffing*
25 g./1 oz. butter, melted
15 ml./1 tablespoon cooking
  oil

Rub the chicken with the salt and pepper. Fill the cavity with the stuffing, then secure with string or skewers. Put the chicken in a roasting pan and brush all over first with the butter, then the oil. Put into the oven preheated to hot (220°C/425°F or Gas Mark 7) and roast for 15 minutes. Reduce the oven temperature to moderate (180°C/350°F or Gas Mark 4) and continue to roast for 1 to 1¼ hours, or until the chicken is cooked through. Baste frequently with the melted butter and oil during the cooking period.

Serves 4

Chicken with Apricots

1 × 1½ kg./3 lb. chicken, cut
  into serving pieces
50 g./2 oz. seasoned flour
50 ml./2 fl. oz. cooking oil
15 ml./1 tablespoon flour
350 g./12 oz. dried apricots,
  soaked overnight in 600
  ml./1 pint water
12 pickling onions
5 ml./1 teaspoon sugar
salt and pepper

Roll the chicken pieces in the seasoned flour. Heat the oil in a saucepan. Add the chicken pieces and brown on all sides. Transfer to a plate. Add the flour to the oil in the pan and stir to form a smooth paste. Drain the cooking liquid from the apricots and gradually stir it into the paste. Bring to the boil.

Return the chicken pieces to the sauce, then add the apricots and all the other ingredients. Mix well, cover and simmer for 40 to 45 minutes or until the chicken is cooked through.

Serves 4

Chicken Marengo

50 g./2 oz. butter
4 chicken joints, skinned
2 garlic cloves, crushed
125 g./4 oz. mushrooms,
  sliced
150 ml./5 fl. oz. white wine
1 × 400 g./14 oz. can
  tomatoes
1 bouquet garni
salt and pepper

Melt the butter in a saucepan. Add the chicken joints and brown on all sides. Transfer to a plate. Add the garlic and mushrooms to the pan and fry for 3 minutes. Pour in the wine, tomatoes and can juice, bouquet garni and salt and pepper. Bring to the boil, stirring constantly. Return the chicken pieces to the saucepan and simmer for 45 minutes or until the chicken is cooked through.

Serves 4

Chicken Casserole

4 chicken joints, skinned
salt and pepper
125 g./4 oz. butter
1 onion, chopped
10 ml./2 teaspoons paprika
45 ml./3 tablespoons flour
350 ml./12 fl. oz. chicken
   stock
150 ml./5 fl. oz. sour cream
1 × 400 g./14 oz. can
   artichoke hearts, drained

Rub the chicken joints with the salt and pepper. Melt the butter in a flameproof casserole. Add the chicken joints and brown on all sides. Transfer to a plate. Add the onion to the casserole and fry for 5 minutes. Stir in the paprika and flour to form a smooth paste. Gradually stir in the stock. Bring to the boil, stirring constantly. Cook the sauce for 2 minutes, then stir in the sour cream.

Return the chicken joints to the casserole and add the artichoke hearts. Stir to mix, then cover and put into the oven preheated to moderate (180°C/350°F or Gas Mark 4). Cook for 40 minutes, or until the chicken is cooked through.

Serves 4

Coq Au Vin

50 g./2 oz. bacon fat
1 × 2 kg./4 lb. chicken, cut
   into serving pieces
3 bacon slices, chopped
2 celery stalks, chopped
1 garlic clove, crushed
30 ml./2 tablespoons flour
425 ml./15 fl. oz. red wine
1 bouquet garni
1 bay leaf
salt and pepper
175 g./6 oz. mushrooms,
   sliced
12 pickling onions
50 g./2 oz. butter

Melt the bacon fat in a flameproof casserole. Add the chicken pieces and brown on all sides. Transfer to a plate. Add the bacon, celery and garlic to the casserole and fry until the bacon is crisp. Stir in the flour until it forms a paste. Gradually add the wine, bouquet garni, bay leaf and salt and pepper. Bring to the boil.

Return the chicken to the casserole, cover and put into the oven preheated to warm (170°C/325°F or Gas Mark 3). Cook for 45 minutes.

Meanwhile, fry the mushrooms and onions in the butter for 5 minutes. Add to the casserole and stir to mix. Re-cover and continue to cook for 45 minutes, or until the chicken is cooked through.

Serves 4-6

Creole Chicken

1 × 1½ kg./3 lb. chicken, cut
   into serving pieces
50 g./2 oz. seasoned flour
2 eggs, beaten
75 g./3 oz. dry breadcrumbs
50 ml./2 fl. oz. cooking oil
1 large onion, chopped
1 garlic clove, crushed
1 green pepper, pith and
   seeds removed and
   chopped
125 g./4 oz. mushrooms,
   sliced
1 × 400 g./14 oz. can
   tomatoes
15 ml./1 tablespoon mild
   chilli powder
45 ml./3 tablespoons flaked
   almonds

Roll the chicken pieces in the seasoned flour then dip them in the eggs, then the breadcrumbs. Heat the oil in a saucepan. Add the chicken pieces and brown on all sides. Transfer to a plate. Add the onion, garlic and green pepper to the pan and fry for 5 minutes. Add the mushrooms and cook for 3 minutes. Stir in the tomatoes and can juice, and chilli and bring to the boil.

Return the chicken pieces to the sauce and simmer for 40 to 45 minutes or until the chicken is cooked through. Stir in the flaked almonds and heat for 1 minute.

Serves 4

Curried Chicken

50 ml./2 fl. oz. cooking oil
4 chicken joints, skinned
2 onions, chopped
1 garlic clove, crushed
25 g./1 oz. flour
15 ml./1 tablespoon hot curry
   powder
300 ml./10 fl. oz. chicken
   stock
30 ml./2 tablespoons mango
   chutney
45 ml./3 tablespoons
   sultanas
1 apple, cored and chopped
2 hard-boiled eggs, chopped
Garnish
30 ml./2 tablespoons
   desiccated coconut
1 lemon, cut into wedges

Heat the oil in a saucepan. Add the chicken joints and brown on all sides. Transfer to a plate. Add the onions and garlic to the pan and fry for 5 minutes. Stir the flour and curry powder into the oil remaining in the pan to form a smooth paste. Gradually add the chicken stock and bring to the boil, stirring constantly. Add the chutney and simmer the sauce for 3 minutes or until it has thickened.

Return the chicken joints to the pan, cover and simmer for 40 minutes. Stir in the sultanas, apple and eggs and continue to simmer for 5 minutes or until the chicken is cooked through. Garnish with the coconut and lemon wedges.

Serves 4

...waiian Chicken

...l./4 tablespoons soy
   sauce
150 ml./5 fl. oz. white wine
juice of 1 lemon
1 garlic clove, crushed
2.5 ml./½ teaspoon curry
   powder
2.5 ml./½ teaspoon ground
   ginger
1.25 ml./¼ teaspoon black
   pepper
1 × 2 kg./4 lb. chicken, cut
   into serving pieces
50 g./2 oz. seasoned flour
125 g./4 oz. butter
2 onions, sliced
1 red pepper, pith and seeds
   removed and chopped
1 × 450 g./1 lb. can
   pineapple rings, drained
   and halved
50 g./2 oz. slivered almonds
350 g./12 oz. cooked rice

Mix the soy sauce, half the wine, the lemon juice, garlic, curry powder, ginger and pepper together in a large, shallow dish. Add the chicken pieces and marinate at room temperature for 4 hours. Drain the chicken pieces, reserving the marinating liquid. Dry the chicken, then roll in the seasoned flour.

Melt 75 g./3 oz. of the butter in a large saucepan. Add the chicken pieces and brown on all sides. Add the onions to the pan and fry for 5 minutes. Add the reserved marinade and stir to mix. Bring to the boil, cover and simmer for 30 minutes. Uncover the pan and continue to simmer for 10 to 15 minutes, or until the chicken is cooked through.

Meanwhile, melt the remaining butter in a saucepan. Add the red pepper and fry for 3 minutes. Add the pineapple, almonds and rice and cook for 3 to 5 minutes, or until they are heated through. Transfer to a large, warmed serving dish. Arrange the chicken pieces on top. Add the remaining white wine to the chicken cooking liquid and bring to the boil. Pour the juices over the chicken.

Serves 4-6

Normandy Chicken

50 ml./2 fl. oz. cooking oil
1 × 1½ kg./3 lb. chicken, cut
   into serving pieces
1 onion, chopped
1 garlic clove, crushed
3 streaky bacon slices,
   chopped
25 g./1 oz. flour
425 ml./15 fl. oz. dry cider
2 red apples, cored and
   chopped
150 ml./5 fl. oz. double
   cream
15 ml./1 tablespoon chopped
   fresh parsley

Heat the oil in a saucepan. Add the chicken pieces and brown on all sides. Transfer to a plate. Add the onion, garlic and bacon to the pan and fry for 5 minutes. Stir in the flour to form a smooth paste. Gradually stir in the cider. Bring to the boil, then simmer the sauce for 2 minutes.

Return the chicken pieces to the pan and simmer for 40 minutes, or until the chicken is cooked through. Stir in the apples and cream and heat for 3 minutes, without bringing to the boil. Garnish with the parsley.

Serves 4

Lemon Chicken

4 chicken joints, skinned
salt and pepper
25 g./1 oz. butter
1 bouquet garni
peeled rind and juice of 2
   lemons
2.5 ml./½ teaspoon dried sage
225 ml./8 fl. oz. chicken
   stock
15 ml./1 tablespoon chopped
   fresh parsley
Sauce
25 g./1 oz. butter
25 g./1 oz. flour
salt and pepper
5 ml./1 teaspoon finely
   grated lemon rind
150 ml./5 fl. oz. single cream

Rub the chicken joints with salt and pepper and put in a shallow baking dish. Spread the butter over the joints, and add the bouquet garni, peeled lemon rind and sage. Mix the lemon juice and stock together and pour into the dish. Put into the oven preheated to moderate (180°C/350°F or Gas Mark 4) and cook for 40 minutes, or until the chicken is cooked through.

Transfer the chicken to a warmed serving dish and keep hot. Strain the cooking liquid and reserve. Melt the butter in a saucepan. Stir in the flour to form a smooth paste. Gradually stir in the strained cooking liquid, salt and pepper and lemon rind. Bring to the boil, then cook the sauce for 2 minutes or until it has thickened. Stir in the cream. Pour the sauce over the chicken and garnish with the parsley.

Serves 4

Satin Chicken

30 ml./2 tablespoons soy
   sauce
2 cloves star anise
15 ml./1 tablespoon sherry
2.5 ml./½ teaspoon salt
5 ml./1 teaspoon finely
   chopped fresh ginger
1 garlic clove, crushed
1 × 2 kg./4 lb. chicken, cut
   into serving pieces
50 ml./2 fl. oz. cooking oil
1 × 150 g./5 oz. can bamboo
   shoot, sliced
150 ml./5 fl. oz. chicken
   stock
15 ml./1 tablespoon
   cornflour
2.5 ml./½ teaspoon sugar

Mix the soy sauce, star anise, sherry, salt, ginger and garlic together. Rub the mixture over the chicken pieces and set aside for 1½ hours.

Heat the oil in a saucepan. Add the chicken pieces and brown on all sides. Add the bamboo shoot and stock and bring to the boil. Cover and simmer for 45 minutes or until the chicken is cooked through. Remove from the heat.

Remove the chicken from the pan and remove the meat from the bones. Cut the meat into long shreds. Mix the cornflour and sugar with 30 ml./2 tablespoons of water. Return the pan to the heat and add the cornflour mixture. Bring to the boil, stirring constantly. Return the chicken to the pan and simmer for 5 minutes or until it is thoroughly reheated and the sauce is thick and translucent.

Serves 4-6

Chicken Provençal

1 × 2 kg./4 lb. chicken, cut
   into serving pieces
50 g./2 oz. seasoned flour
50 ml./2 fl. oz. cooking oil
1 onion, chopped
2 garlic cloves, crushed
1 × 400 g./14 oz. can
   tomatoes
10 ml./2 teaspoons chopped
   fresh basil
2.5 ml./½ teaspoon grated
   lemon rind
12 black olives, stoned

Roll the chicken pieces in the seasoned flour. Heat the oil in a saucepan. Add the chicken pieces and brown on all sides. Transfer to a plate. Add the onion and garlic to the pan and fry for 5 minutes. Add the tomatoes and can juice, basil and lemon rind, and mix well. Bring to the boil.

Return the chicken pieces to the sauce and simmer for 40 to 45 minutes, or until the chicken is cooked through. Stir in the olives and heat for 1 minute.

Serves 4-6

Chicken Breasts with Asparagus

4 boned chicken breasts
50 g./2 oz. seasoned flour
2 eggs, beaten
75 g./3 oz. Parmesan cheese,
   grated
50 g./2 oz. butter
12 cooked asparagus spears,
   kept hot

Roll the chicken breasts in the seasoned flour. Mix the eggs and half the grated cheese together, then dip the chicken breasts in this mixture. Melt the butter in a frying-pan. Add the chicken breasts and fry for 15 minutes or until they are cooked through.

Transfer the chicken to a flameproof dish and arrange a few asparagus spears over each one. Sprinkle over the remaining grated cheese. Grill for 2 to 3 minutes or until the cheese melts.

Serves 4

Chicken with Herbs

4 boned chicken breasts
50 g./2 oz. seasoned flour
50 g./2 oz. butter
15 ml./1 tablespoon flour
150 ml./5 fl. oz. white wine
2.5 ml./½ teaspoon chopped
   fresh thyme
2.5 ml./½ teaspoon chopped
   fresh rosemary
15 ml./1 tablespoon chopped
   fresh parsley
15 ml./1 tablespoon chopped
   fresh chives

Roll the chicken breasts in the seasoned flour. Melt the butter in a frying-pan. Add the chicken breasts and brown on all sides. Transfer to a plate. Stir the flour into the pan to form a smooth paste. Gradually add the wine, stirring constantly. Stir in the herbs and bring to the boil. Return the chicken breasts to the sauce and simmer for 25 to 30 minutes, or until the chicken is cooked through.

Serves 4

Paprika Chicken

1 × 1½ kg./3 lb. chicken, cut
    into serving pieces
50 g./2 oz. seasoned flour
50 g./2 oz. butter
2 onions, chopped
2 garlic cloves, crushed
1 large green pepper, pith
    and seeds removed and
    chopped
25 ml./1½ tablespoons
    paprika
350 ml./12 fl. oz. chicken
    stock
5 ml./1 teaspoon caraway
    seeds
salt and pepper
1 × 400 g./14 oz. can
    tomatoes
15 ml./1 tablespoon
    cornflour dissolved in 15
    ml./1 tablespoon water
150 ml./5 fl. oz. sour cream

Roll the chicken pieces in the seasoned flour. Melt the butter in a saucepan. Add the chicken pieces and brown on all sides. Transfer to a plate. Add the onions, garlic and green pepper to the pan and fry for 5 minutes. Stir in the paprika, stock, caraway seeds, salt and pepper, and tomatoes and can juice. Bring to the boil.

Return the chicken pieces to the pan and simmer for 40 to 45 minutes, or until the chicken is cooked through. Transfer the chicken pieces to a warmed serving dish and keep hot. Stir the cornflour mixture into the sauce and cook, stirring constantly, for 2 minutes or until the sauce has thickened. Stir in the sour cream and pour over the chicken.

Serves 4

Chicken in White Wine

4 chicken joints, skinned
50 g./2 oz. seasoned flour
50 ml./2 fl. oz. cooking oil
2 celery stalks, sliced
1 carrot, grated
1 bay leaf
15 ml./1 tablespoon chopped
    fresh parsley
2.5 ml./½ teaspoon dried
    thyme
425 ml./15 fl. oz. dry white
    wine
175 g./6 oz. mushrooms,
    sliced
8 pickling onions

Roll the chicken joints in the seasoned flour. Heat the oil in a saucepan. Add the chicken joints and brown on all sides. Add the celery, carrot, bay leaf, parsley and thyme, and stir to mix. Cook for 5 minutes. Stir in the wine and bring to the boil. Add the mushrooms and onions and simmer for 35 to 40 minutes, or until the chicken is cooked through.

Serves 4

Chicken in Foil

4 chicken breasts, skinned
salt and pepper
50 g./2 oz. butter
25 g./1 oz. flour
225 ml./8 fl. oz. chicken
  stock
1.25 ml./¼ teaspoon cayenne
  pepper
150 g./5 oz. mushrooms,
  sliced

Rub the chicken breasts with the salt and pepper. Melt the butter in a saucepan. Add the chicken breasts and brown on all sides. Cut out four double thicknesses of aluminium foil large enough to enclose the chicken breasts completely, and place one breast on each piece of foil.

Stir the flour into the butter remaining in the pan to form a smooth paste. Gradually add the chicken stock, stirring constantly. Bring to the boil, then simmer for 2 minutes. Stir in the cayenne and mushrooms. Simmer the sauce for 10 to 15 minutes, or until it is very thick and smooth.

Spoon the sauce over the four chicken breasts, then wrap up the foil to make parcels. Put the parcels on a baking sheet and put into the oven preheated to fairly hot (200°C/400°F or Gas Mark 6). Bake for 40 minutes, or until the chicken is cooked through.

Serves 4

Barbecued Chicken

1 × 2 kg./4 lb. chicken, cut
  into serving pieces
salt and pepper
Barbecue Sauce
45 ml./3 tablespoons cooking
  oil
45 ml./3 tablespoons
  Worcestershire sauce
45 ml./3 tablespoons tomato
  purée
1 spring onion, finely
  chopped
45 ml./3 tablespoons chicken
  stock
2.5 ml./½ teaspoon cayenne
  pepper
salt and pepper
7.5 ml./1½ teaspoons brown
  sugar

Rub the chicken pieces with the salt and pepper. Line the grill pan with foil and put the chicken pieces on the rack. Mix all the sauce ingredients together and brush over the chicken. Grill the chicken for 25 to 30 minutes or until it is cooked through. Baste with the sauce from time to time during the cooking period.

Transfer the chicken pieces to a warmed serving dish. Pour any cooking juices into a saucepan and add the remaining barbecue sauce. Heat the sauce gently until it is hot. Pour the sauce over the chicken.

Serves 4

Indian Chicken

5 ml./1 teaspoon ground
    turmeric
5 ml./1 teaspoon ground
    cumin
10 ml./2 teaspoons ground
    coriander
1.25 ml./¼ teaspoon chilli
    powder
1 garlic clove, crushed
350 ml./12 fl. oz. plain
    yogurt
4 large chicken breasts,
    skinned, boned and cut
    into small pieces
50 g./2 oz. butter
1 onion, chopped
1.25 ml./¼ teaspoon ground
    cloves
5 ml./1 teaspoon ground
    cinnamon

Mix the turmeric, cumin, coriander, chilli powder and garlic together, then stir in the yogurt. Add the chicken and set aside to marinate for 1 hour.

Melt the butter in a flameproof casserole. Add the onion and fry for 5 minutes. Stir in the cloves and cinnamon and fry for 2 minutes. Stir in the chicken and marinade. Transfer to the oven pre-heated to warm (170°C/325°F or Gas Mark 3). Cook for 1½ hours or until the chicken is cooked through.

Serves 4

Chicken with Tarragon

4 boned chicken breasts
50 g./2 oz. seasoned flour
75 g./3 oz. butter
30 ml./2 tablespoons flour
225 ml./8 fl. oz. chicken
    stock
10 ml./2 teaspoons chopped
    fresh tarragon
2.5 ml./½ teaspoon finely
    grated lemon rind
salt and pepper
125 ml./4 fl. oz. single cream

Roll the chicken breasts in the seasoned flour. Melt the butter in a frying-pan. Add the chicken pieces and brown on all sides. Transfer to a plate. Stir the flour into the butter in the pan to form a smooth paste. Gradually add the stock, stirring constantly. Bring to the boil. Stir in the tarragon, lemon rind and salt and pepper, and cook the sauce for 2 minutes.

Return the chicken breasts to the sauce and simmer for 25 to 30 minutes, or until the chicken is cooked through. Transfer the chicken breasts to a warmed serving dish. Stir the cream into the sauce and heat gently for 2 minutes, without bringing to the boil. Pour the sauce over the chicken.

Serves 4

Devilled Chicken

45 ml./3 tablespoons chutney
15 ml./1 tablespoon tomato
  purée
1.25 ml./¼ teaspoon Tabasco
  sauce
1.25 ml./¼ teaspoon prepared
  mustard
salt and pepper
4 chicken joints, skinned

Mix the chutney, tomato purée, Tabasco sauce, mustard, salt and pepper together. Make two or three deep slits in each chicken joint and fill them with the chutney mixture. Put the joints in a roasting pan and cover. Put into the oven preheated to moderately hot (200°C/400°F or Gas Mark 6) and roast for 35 minutes. Uncover and continue to roast for 10 minutes, or until the chicken is cooked through.

Serves 4

Chicken Kiev

4 boned chicken breasts,
  skinned
75 g./3 oz. butter
1 garlic clove, crushed
10 ml./2 teaspoons chopped
  fresh chives
5 ml./1 teaspoon paprika
salt and pepper
50 g./2 oz. seasoned flour
2 eggs, beaten
125 g./4 oz. dry breadcrumbs
oil for deep frying

Put the chicken breasts on a flat surface and beat with a mallet until they are thin. Mix the butter, garlic, chives, paprika and salt and pepper together. Divide into four and put one piece in the centre of each chicken breast. Roll up the breasts, like parcels, to enclose the butter mixture completely. Dip the chicken parcels in the seasoned flour, then in the eggs and finally in the breadcrumbs. Chill in the refrigerator for 1 hour.

Deep-fry the chicken for 6 to 8 minutes or until golden brown. Drain on kitchen paper towels.

Serves 4

Chicken Maryland

1 × 1½ kg./3 lb. chicken, cut
  into serving pieces
50 g./2 oz. seasoned flour
2 eggs, beaten
125 g./4 oz. dry breadcrumbs
50 g./2 oz. butter
50 ml./2 fl. oz. cooking oil

Dip the chicken pieces in the seasoned flour, then in the beaten eggs and finally in the breadcrumbs. Set aside for 10 minutes.

Heat the butter and oil in a flameproof casserole. Add the chicken pieces and brown on all sides. Transfer to the oven preheated to moderate (180°C/350°F or Gas Mark 4) and cook for 40 minutes, or until the chicken is cooked through.
Note: Chicken Maryland is usually served with a garnish of fried bananas and pineapple rings.

Serves 4

Spiced Chicken

150 ml./5 fl. oz. plain yogurt
5 ml./1 teaspoon ground
 cumin
5 ml./1 teaspoon ground
 coriander
2.5 ml./½ teaspoon ground
 cardamom
1 garlic clove, crushed
salt and pepper
1 × 1½ kg./3 lb. chicken, cut
 into 4 serving pieces

Mix the yogurt, cumin, coriander, cardamom, garlic and salt and pepper together. Add the chicken pieces and leave to marinate at room temperature for 3 hours. Line the grill pan with foil and put the chicken pieces on the rack. Grill for 20 minutes or until the chicken is cooked through.

Serves 4

Chicken Tandoori

225 ml./8 fl. oz. plain yogurt
2 garlic cloves, crushed
7.5 ml./1½ teaspoons finely
 chopped fresh ginger
5 ml./1 teaspoon garam
 masala
10 ml./2 teaspoons coriander
 seeds
1 dried red chilli, finely
 chopped
1 × 1½ kg./3 lb. chicken, cut
 into serving pieces
50 g./2 oz. butter

Mix the yogurt, garlic, ginger, garam masala, coriander seeds and chilli together in a large, shallow dish. Add the chicken pieces and leave to marinate at room temperature for 12 hours, or overnight.

Melt the butter in a roasting pan. Add the chicken pieces, then spoon over the marinating mixture. Put the pan into the oven preheated to moderate (180°C/350°F or Gas Mark 4) and bake for 45 minutes, or until the chicken is cooked through. Baste the chicken frequently with the marinade during the cooking period.

Serves 4

Chicken Hash

350 g./12 oz. cooked
 chicken, diced
½ kg./1 lb. cooked potatoes,
 mashed
1 onion, chopped
2 carrots, cooked and
 chopped
salt and pepper
30 ml./2 tablespoons tomato
 ketchup
5 ml./1 teaspoon dry mustard
50 ml./2 fl. oz. cooking oil

Mix all the ingredients, except the oil, together. Heat the oil in a frying-pan. Add the chicken mixture and fry for 20 minutes, stirring occasionally.

Serves 4

Chicken with Celery and Pineapple Sauce

1 × 2 kg./4 lb. boiling
chicken
15 ml./1 tablespoon
cornflour
15 ml./1 tablespoon soy
sauce
5 ml./1 teaspoon finely
chopped fresh ginger
1 × 225 g./8 oz. can
pineapple rings, chopped
60 ml./4 tablespoons brown
sugar
60 ml./4 tablespoons vinegar
3 celery stalks, diagonally
sliced
2 carrots, diagonally sliced
2 eggs, beaten
50 g./2 oz. flour or cornflour
oil for deep frying

Put the chicken in a saucepan and add enough water to cover. Cover the pan, bring to the boil and simmer for 2 hours or until the chicken is cooked through. Drain and set aside to cool.

Mix the cornflour, soy sauce, ginger, 60 ml./4 tablespoons of pineapple syrup from the can and sugar in a saucepan and bring to the boil, stirring. Pour in the vinegar and cook for 2 minutes. Stir in the celery, carrots and pineapple and set the sauce aside. Joint the cooled chicken, then halve each joint. Dip the pieces in the beaten egg then in the flour or cornflour. Deep-fry the chicken pieces for 5 minutes or until they are deep golden brown. Drain on kitchen towels, then transfer them to a warmed serving dish.

Meanwhile, reheat the sauce for 3 to 5 minutes or until it is very hot. Pour over the chicken.

Serves 4-6

Chicken Pie

50 g./2 oz. butter
125 g./4 oz. mushrooms,
sliced
25 g./1 oz. flour
300 ml./10 fl. oz. milk
275 g./10 oz. cooked
chicken, chopped
175 g./6 oz. cooked ham,
chopped
2.5 ml./½ teaspoon ground
mace
5 ml./1 teaspoon dried mixed
herbs
salt and pepper
juice of ½ lemon
225 g./8 oz. rough puff
pastry*
1 egg, beaten with a little
milk

Melt half of the butter in a saucepan. Add the mushrooms and fry for 3 minutes. Transfer to a plate. Melt the remaining butter in the pan. Stir in the flour to form a smooth paste. Gradually add the milk and bring to the boil, stirring constantly. Add the chicken, ham, mace, herbs, salt and pepper, lemon juice and mushrooms. Cook for 3 to 5 minutes or until the meat is heated through. Transfer to a deep, medium pie dish.

Roll out the dough until it is about .75 cm./¼ in. thick. Cover the pie dish with the dough, trimming off the ends to fit. Brush the dough with the egg mixture. Put into the oven preheated to fairly hot (190°C/375°F or Gas Mark 5) and bake for 30 to 35 minutes or until the pastry is deep golden brown.

Serves 4-6

Chicken Tetrazzini

1 × 2 kg./4 lb. boiling
  chicken
1 onion, chopped
1 bay leaf
1.25 ml./¼ teaspoon dried
  thyme
salt and pepper
350 g./12 oz. spaghetti
50 g./2 oz. butter
45 ml./3 tablespoons flour
175 g./6 oz. mushrooms,
  sliced
150 ml./5 fl. oz. double
  cream
15 ml./1 tablespoon sherry
  (optional)

Put the chicken, onion, bay leaf, thyme and salt and pepper in a saucepan, and add enough water to cover. Cover the pan, bring to the boil and simmer for 2 hours, or until the chicken is cooked through. Drain and reserve 350 ml./12 fl. oz. of the stock. Set the chicken aside until it is cool enough to handle, then remove the meat from the bones and cut it into bite-sized pieces.

Cook the spaghetti in boiling, salted water for 10 to 12 minutes or until it is 'al dente'.

Meanwhile, melt three-quarters of the butter in a saucepan. Stir in the flour to form a smooth paste. Gradually add the reserved stock, stirring constantly. Cook the sauce for 2 to 3 minutes, or until it has thickened and is smooth.

Melt the remaining butter in a small pan. Add the mushrooms and fry for 3 minutes. Add the mushrooms and chicken meat to the sauce, then return to the heat. Cook for 3 minutes, or until hot but not boiling. Stir in the cream and sherry if you are using it and heat gently. Drain the spaghetti and top with the chicken mixture.

Serves 4-6

Hindle Wakes

1 × 3 kg./6 lb. boiling
  chicken
125 ml./4 fl. oz. vinegar
15 ml./1 tablespoon sugar
Stuffing
275 g./10 oz. prunes,
  chopped
50 g./2 oz. shredded suet
50 g./2 oz. fresh
  breadcrumbs
5 ml./1 teaspoon grated
  lemon rind
10 ml./2 teaspoons chopped
  fresh parsley
salt and pepper

Mix the stuffing ingredients together and fill the cavity of the chicken with the mixture. Secure the cavity with string or skewers. Put the chicken in a large saucepan and pour in enough water to cover. Add the vinegar and sugar and bring to the boil. Cover and simmer for 2½ hours, or until the chicken is cooked through.

Cool the chicken in the liquid, then carve with the stuffing and serve cold.

Serves 8

Chicken Mousse

50 g./2 oz. butter, melted
450 g./1 lb. cooked chicken,
  finely minced
425 ml./15 fl. oz. mornay
  sauce *
15 ml./1 tablespoon gelatine,
  dissolved in 30 ml./2
  tablespoons hot water
salt and pepper
5 ml./1 teaspoon paprika
75 ml./3 fl. oz. double cream,
  lightly whipped

Beat the butter and chicken together until they are thoroughly blended. Gradually beat in the sauce. Fold in the remaining ingredients. Spoon into a rinsed mould or soufflé dish. Chill in the refrigerator for 3 hours, or until set.

Serves 6

Leftover Chicken with Sherry

2 egg yolks, beaten
225 ml./8 fl. oz. single cream
50 ml./2 fl. oz. sherry
10 ml./2 teaspoons finely
  grated lemon rind
675 g./1½ lb. cooked chicken,
  cut into small pieces

Put the egg yolks in a heatproof bowl. Beat in the cream, sherry and lemon rind. Put the bowl over a pan of water and cook, stirring constantly, for 3 minutes or until the sauce thickens slightly.

Arrange the chicken pieces in a serving dish and pour the sauce over them. Chill in the refrigerator for 30 minutes before serving.

Serves 4

Chicken Vol-Au-Vents

4 vol-au-vent cases
50 g./2 oz. butter
50 g./2 oz. flour
25 ml./1½ tablespoons curry
  powder
425 ml./15 fl. oz. chicken
  stock
15 ml./1 tablespoon lemon
  juice
15 ml./1 tablespoon
  redcurrant jelly
salt and pepper
450 g./1 lb. cooked chicken,
  chopped

Put the vol-au-vent cases on a baking sheet and put into the oven preheated to moderate (180°C/350°F or Gas Mark 4). Heat the cases for 15 minutes.

Meanwhile, melt the butter in a saucepan. Stir in the flour and curry powder to form a smooth paste. Gradually stir in the chicken stock, lemon juice, redcurrant jelly, salt and pepper. Bring to the boil and simmer the sauce, stirring constantly, for 2 to 3 minutes, or until it is very thick and smooth.

Add the chicken pieces to the sauce and stir to mix. Simmer gently for 5 minutes, or until the chicken is heated through. Spoon into the vol-au-vent cases.

Serves 4

Chicken Chop Suey

50 ml./2 fl. oz. cooking oil
450 g./1 lb. cooked chicken,
  chopped
4 Chinese dried mushrooms,
  soaked in water for 20
  minutes, drained and
  thinly sliced
1 × 150 g./5 oz. can bamboo
  shoot, sliced
1 onion, sliced
1 green pepper, pith and
  seeds removed and sliced
1 × 450 g./1 lb. can bean
  sprouts, drained
300 ml./10 fl. oz. chicken
  stock
2.5 ml./½ teaspoon sugar
5 ml./1 teaspoon soy sauce
salt and pepper
5 ml./1 teaspoon cornflour
15 ml./1 tablespoon dry
  sherry

Heat the oil in a saucepan. Add the chicken and vegetables and stir-fry for 4 minutes. Stir in the stock, sugar, soy sauce and salt and pepper. Bring to the boil and simmer for 5 minutes, stirring constantly.

Mix the cornflour and sherry together, then add to the pan. Simmer for 3 minutes.

Serves 4-6

Honey Chicken

75 g./3 oz. butter
1 × 1½ kg./3 lb. chicken
Sauce
4 spring onions, chopped
5 ml./1 teaspoon finely
  chopped fresh ginger
15 ml./1 tablespoon honey
15 ml./1 tablespoon soy
  sauce
2.5 ml./½ teaspoon salt
150 ml./5 fl. oz. sherry

Melt the butter in a roasting pan. Add the chicken and baste it thoroughly with the butter. Put into the oven preheated to moderate (180°C/350°F or Gas Mark 4) and roast for 45 minutes. Baste frequently with the melted butter during the cooking time.

Mix all the sauce ingredients together and pour over the chicken. Return to the oven and continue to roast for 30 to 40 minutes, or until the chicken is cooked through. Baste frequently with the sauce during the cooking time. Serve with the cooking juices.

Serves 4

Duck With Orange

1 × 2½ kg./5 lb. duck
salt and black pepper
1 orange, cut into segments
300 ml./10 fl. oz. duck stock
  (made with the duck
  giblets)
30 ml./2 tablespoons clear
  honey
50 g./2 oz. butter
25 g./1 oz. flour
150 ml./5 fl. oz. fresh orange
  juice
125 ml./4 fl. oz. red wine
15 ml./1 tablespoon finely
  grated orange rind
15 ml./1 tablespoon
  redcurrant jelly
Garnish
1 orange, thinly sliced
watercress sprigs

Rub the duck inside and out with the salt and pepper. Fill the cavity with the orange segments, then secure the cavity with string or skewers. Put the duck on a rack in a roasting pan and put into the oven preheated to warm (170°C/325°F or Gas Mark 3). Roast for 2 hours.

Mix 60 ml./4 tablespoons of the stock and the honey together. Prick the duck's skin and brush it all over with the honey mixture. Return to the oven and roast for a further 30 minutes, or until the duck is cooked through. Meanwhile, melt the butter in a saucepan. Stir in the flour to form a smooth paste. Gradually stir in the remaining stock, orange juice and wine, and bring to the boil. Stir in the orange rind and simmer the sauce until it is thick and smooth. Stir in the redcurrant jelly. Garnish the duck with the orange slices and watercress and serve with the sauce.

Serves 4

Duck with Cider

1 × 2½ kg./5 lb. duck
salt and pepper
2 apples, cored and sliced
350 ml./12 fl. oz. cider
25 g./1 oz. butter
25 g./1 oz. flour
150 ml./5 fl. oz. single cream
salt and pepper

Rub the duck inside and out with the salt and pepper. Fill the cavity with the apple slices, then secure the cavity with string or skewers. Put the duck on a rack in a roasting pan and pour over the cider. Put into the oven preheated to warm (170°C/325°F or Gas Mark 3) and roast for 2½ hours, or until the duck is cooked through. Baste the duck with the cooking liquid every 15 minutes during the cooking time. Transfer the duck to a carving board and keep hot. Strain the cooking liquid into a jug.

Melt the butter in a saucepan. Stir in the flour to form a smooth paste. Gradually add the strained cooking liquid and bring to the boil. Cook the sauce, stirring constantly, for 2 to 3 minutes or until it is smooth and thick. Stir in the cream, salt and pepper and heat gently. Pour into a sauceboat and serve with the duck.

Serves 4

Duck with Pineapple and Ginger

45 ml./3 tablespoons lemon juice
30 ml./2 tablespoons treacle
30 ml./2 tablespoons soy sauce
15 ml./1 tablespoon sherry
2 spring onions, chopped
1 × 2½ kg./5 lb. duck
30 ml./2 tablespoons preserved ginger
30 ml./2 tablespoons syrup from preserved ginger
2 canned pineapple rings, chopped
150 ml./5 fl. oz. syrup from pineapple can
10 ml./2 teaspoons cornflour

Mix the lemon juice, treacle, soy sauce and sherry together in a saucepan. Heat until the treacle dissolves. Mix 15 ml./1 tablespoon of the mixture and the spring onions together. Fill the cavity of the duck with the spring onion mixture, then secure the cavity with string or skewers. Put the duck on a rack in a roasting pan and spoon some of the remaining treacle mixture over the top. Put into the oven preheated to moderate (180°C/350°F or Gas Mark 4) and roast the duck for 2¼ hours, or until it is cooked through. Baste frequently with the treacle mixture during the cooking period.

Mix all the remaining ingredients together in a saucepan and bring to the boil. Simmer the sauce for 3 minutes or until it is hot. Serve the duck with the sauce.

Serves 4

Duck Casserole

1 × 2½ kg./5 lb. duck
175-225 g./6-8 oz. sage and onion stuffing*
12 pickling onions
2 garlic cloves, halved
5 carrots, quartered
425 ml./15 fl. oz. duck stock (made with the duck giblets)
25 g./1 oz. flour
salt and pepper
4 potatoes, quartered
2 parsley sprigs to garnish

Fill the cavity of the duck with the sage and onion stuffing, then secure the cavity with string or skewers. Put the duck on a rack in a roasting pan and put into the oven preheated to hot (220°C/425°F or Gas Mark 7). Roast for 35 minutes or until the duck is crisp and brown and a lot of the fat has run out.

Meanwhile, simmer the onions, garlic and carrots in 300 ml./10 fl. oz. of the stock for 30 minutes. Mix the remaining stock and flour together and stir into the pan. Season to taste with salt and pepper, bring to the boil and simmer for 3 minutes or until the sauce has thickened and is smooth. Pour into a large ovenproof casserole and add the potatoes. Place the duck on top of the vegetables. Cover the casserole and put it into the oven preheated to warm (170°C/325°F or Gas Mark 3). Cook for 1½ hours or until the duck is cooked through. Garnish with the parsley.

Serves 4

Duck with Sweet and Pungent Sauce

1 × 2½ kg./5 lb. duck
10 ml./2 teaspoons salt
1 garlic clove, crushed
3 spring onions, chopped
45 ml./3 tablespoons soy
  sauce
30 ml./2 tablespoons sherry
30 ml./2 tablespoons honey

Sauce
30 ml./2 tablespoons oil
5 ml./1 teaspoon finely
  chopped fresh ginger
1 garlic clove, crushed
1 small green pepper, pith
  and seeds removed and
  chopped
1 × 150 g./5 oz. can bamboo
  shoot, cut into strips
2 dried Chinese mushrooms,
  soaked in water for 20
  minutes, drained and
  chopped
150 ml./5 fl. oz. duck stock
  (made with the giblets)
30 ml./2 tablespoons clear
  honey
150 ml./5 fl. oz. syrup from
  pineapple can
30 ml./2 tablespoons vinegar
5 ml./1 teaspoon tomato
  purée
15 ml./1 tablespoon sherry
15 ml./1 tablespoon soy
  sauce
salt and pepper
30 ml./2 tablespoons
  cornflour
1 × 300 g./11 oz. can
  mandarin oranges,
  drained
4 canned pineapple rings,
  chopped

Rub the duck inside and out with the salt. Mix the garlic, spring onions, soy sauce and sherry together. Divide the mixture into two, and stir the honey into one half. Prick the duck's skin and brush it all over with the honey mixture. Allow to dry. Put the duck on a rack in a roasting pan and pour over the soy sauce mixture. Pour about 5 cm./2 in. of water into the roasting pan and put into the oven preheated to moderate (180°C/350°F or Gas Mark 4). Roast for 2¼ hours, or until the duck is cooked through. Dilute the remaining honey-soy sauce mixture with a little water and baste the duck with this every 20 minutes during the cooking period.

Meanwhile to make the sauce, heat the oil in a large saucepan. Add the ginger, garlic, green pepper, bamboo shoot and mushrooms and fry for 5 minutes. Add the stock and bring to the boil. Add the honey, pineapple syrup and vinegar and return to the boil, stirring. Stir in the tomato purée, sherry, soy sauce and salt and pepper. Mix the cornflour with a little water and stir into the pan. Cook, stirring constantly, for 3 minutes or until the sauce has thickened and become translucent. Garnish the duck with the mandarin oranges and pineapple and serve with the sauce.

Serves 4

Duck in Honey and Chestnut Sauce

1 × 2½ kg./5 lb. duck, cut into
   serving pieces
50 g./2 oz. seasoned flour
75 g./3 oz. butter
Sauce
425 ml./15 fl. oz. duck stock
   (made with the duck
   giblets)
25 g./1 oz. flour
salt and pepper
10 ml./2 teaspoons finely
   grated orange rind
45 ml./3 tablespoons clear
   honey
350 g./12 oz. whole
   chestnuts, peeled

Roll the duck pieces in the seasoned flour. Melt the butter in a flameproof casserole. Add the duck pieces and brown on all sides.

Heat 300 ml./10 fl. oz. of the stock in a saucepan. Mix the remaining stock and flour together and stir into the pan. Season to taste with salt and pepper, bring to the boil and simmer for 3 minutes or until the sauce has thickened and is smooth. Stir in the orange rind and honey. Pour over the duck pieces and stir in the chestnuts. Put the casserole into the oven preheated to warm (170°C/325°F or Gas Mark 3) and braise for 2 hours, or until the duck pieces are cooked through.

Serves 4

Creamed Turkey with Duchess Potatoes

675 g./1½ lb. cooked
   potatoes, mashed
2 eggs
50 g./2 oz. butter
salt and pepper
125 g./4 oz. button
   mushrooms, halved
1 green pepper, pith and
   seeds removed and
   chopped
300 ml./10 fl. oz. turkey
   stock (made from the
   carcass or giblets)
25 g./1 oz. flour
150 ml./5 fl. oz. milk
dash of Tabasco sauce
½ kg./1 lb. cooked turkey,
   chopped
45 ml./3 tablespoons single
   cream
15 ml./1 tablespoon chopped
   fresh parsley

Mix the potatoes, 1 egg and half the butter together until well blended. Season to taste. Pipe into a decorative border around the edge of an ovenproof dish. Brush with the remaining egg and put into the oven preheated to moderate (180°C/350°F or Gas Mark 4). Bake for 20 minutes or until the potatoes are golden brown.

Meanwhile, simmer the mushrooms and green pepper in the turkey stock for 10 minutes. Strain the stock and reserve both the stock and vegetables. Melt the remaining butter in a saucepan. Stir in the flour to form a smooth paste. Gradually stir in the milk, then the stock. Cook the sauce for 3 minutes, stirring constantly. Flavour with the Tabasco sauce, then add the chopped turkey meat and reserved vegetables. Heat gently for 5 minutes. Stir in the cream.

Remove the potato ring from the oven. Pile the turkey mixture into the centre and garnish with the parsley.

Note: Cooked pheasant, goose or duck may be substituted for the turkey.

Serves 4-6

Roast Turkey with Chestnut Stuffing

1 × 6 kg./12 lb. turkey
salt and pepper
675 g./1½ lb. chestnut
stuffing*
125 g./4 oz. butter, melted

Rub the turkey inside and out with the salt and pepper. Fill the cavities with the stuffing, then secure with string or skewers. Put the turkey in a large roasting pan and brush all over with the melted butter. Put into the oven preheated to very hot (230°C/450°F or Gas Mark 8) and roast for 10 minutes. Reduce the oven temperature to warm (170°C/325°F or Gas Mark 3) and continue to roast for 3 to 4 hours, or until the turkey is cooked through. Baste frequently with the fat in the pan during the cooking period.

Serves 12-14

Turkey Escalopes with Herb Butter

4 large turkey escalopes
50 g./2 oz. seasoned flour
1 egg, beaten
50 g./2 oz. fine breadcrumbs
50 g./2 oz. butter
Herb Butter
75 g./3 oz. butter, softened
10 ml./2 teaspoons lemon
juice
10 ml./2 teaspoons chopped
fresh parsley
5 ml./1 teaspoon chopped
fresh tarragon

To make the herb butter, beat all the ingredients together until they are thoroughly blended. Form into a sausage shape, wrap in foil and chill in the refrigerator for 30 minutes.

Coat the escalopes in the flour, then in the egg and finally in the breadcrumbs. Melt the butter in a frying-pan. Add the escalopes and fry for 4 to 6 minutes, or until they are evenly browned and cooked through. Top each escalope with a lump of herb butter.

Serves 4

Turkey Croquettes

300 ml./10 fl. oz. milk
2.5 ml./½ teaspoon crushed
  black peppercorns
1 onion, sliced
1 carrot, sliced
40 g./1½ oz. butter
50 g./2 oz. flour
450 g./1 lb. cooked turkey,
  finely chopped
2 egg yolks
225 g./8 oz. mushrooms,
  sliced
1.25 ml./¼ teaspoon ground
  allspice
salt and pepper
2 eggs, beaten
150 g./5 oz. dry breadcrumbs
oil for deep frying

Put the milk, peppercorns, onion and carrot in a saucepan. Bring to the boil, then simmer for 5 minutes. Strain the milk. Melt the butter in a saucepan. Stir in the flour to form a smooth paste. Gradually stir in the strained milk. Bring to the boil, stirring constantly. Add the turkey meat, egg yolks, mushrooms, allspice, salt and pepper, and stir to mix. Simmer for 3 minutes, or until very thick. Spoon into a shallow dish, cover and chill in the refrigerator for 1 hour, or until set and firm.

Divide the mixture into sausage shapes, about 8 cm./3 in. long. Dip in the beaten eggs, then in the breadcrumbs. Chill in the refrigerator for 1 hour, then deep-fry for 4 to 6 minutes or until evenly browned. Drain the croquettes on kitchen towels.

Serves 4

Turkey à la King

75 g./3 oz. butter
1 green pepper, pith and
  seeds removed and
  chopped
1 onion, chopped
175 g./6 oz. mushrooms,
  sliced
30 ml./2 tablespoons flour
300 ml./10 fl. oz. single
  cream
150 ml./5 fl. oz. milk
675 g./1½ lb. cooked turkey,
  chopped
salt and pepper
10 ml./2 teaspoons paprika
1 tablespoon chopped fresh
  parsley

Melt the butter in a saucepan. Add the green pepper and onion and fry for 5 minutes. Stir in the mushrooms and cook for 3 minutes. Stir in the flour to form a smooth paste. Gradually stir in the cream and milk. Bring to the boil. Stir in all the remaining ingredients and cook for 10 to 15 minutes, or until the turkey is heated through.

Serves 4

Turkey Suprême

25 g./1 oz. butter
75 g./3 oz. mushrooms,
  sliced
1 small onion, chopped
25 g./1 oz. flour
300 ml./10 fl. oz. chicken
  stock
10 ml./2 teaspoons lemon
  juice
450 g./1 lb. cooked turkey,
  chopped
225 g./8 oz. long-grain rice
1 egg yolk
50 ml./2 fl. oz. double cream
salt and pepper
30 ml./2 tablespoons
  chopped fresh parsley

Melt the butter in a saucepan. Add the mushrooms and onion and fry for 5 minutes. Stir in the flour to form a smooth paste. Gradually stir in the chicken stock. Bring to the boil, then simmer for 2 minutes, stirring constantly. Stir in the lemon juice and turkey and cook the sauce for 30 minutes.

Meanwhile, cook the rice in boiling, salted water for 15 to 20 minutes, or until the rice is tender and the liquid is absorbed. Transfer the rice to a warmed serving dish and keep hot.

Mix the egg yolk, cream, salt and pepper together, then stir in 45 ml./3 tablespoons of the sauce. Gradually stir into the sauce and cook gently for 2 minutes without bringing to the boil. Spoon the sauce over the rice and garnish with the parsley.

Serves 4

Rabbit Stew

1 rabbit, cut into serving
  pieces
25 g./1 oz. butter
2 bacon slices, chopped
1 celery stalk, chopped
4 tomatoes, skinned and
  chopped
1 garlic clove, crushed
5 ml./1 teaspoon dried thyme
salt and pepper
1 green pepper, pith and
  seeds removed and
  chopped
1 aubergine, chopped and
  dégorged
Marinade
225 ml./8 fl. oz. white wine
50 ml./2 fl. oz. olive oil
45 ml./3 tablespoons water
1 garlic clove, crushed
1 bay leaf
1 thyme sprig

Mix all the marinade ingredients together in a large, shallow dish. Add the rabbit pieces and marinate them at room temperature for 6 hours. Remove the rabbit pieces from the marinade and dry. Strain the marinade and reserve.

Melt the butter in a saucepan. Add the bacon, celery and rabbit pieces and fry until the rabbit pieces are browned on all sides. Stir in the tomatoes, garlic, thyme, salt and pepper and mix well. Pour over the reserved marinade and bring to the boil. Simmer for 1 hour.

Stir in the green pepper and aubergine and simmer for a further 20 minutes or until the rabbit is cooked.

Serves 4-6

Rabbit with Prunes

1¼ l./2 pints water
45 ml./3 tablespoons vinegar
1 rabbit, cut into serving
    pieces
50 g./2 oz. seasoned flour
50 ml./2 fl. oz. cooking oil
1 onion, chopped
175 g./6 oz. prunes, chopped
5 ml./1 teaspoon grated
    lemon rind
salt and pepper
15 ml./1 tablespoon sugar
300 ml./10 fl. oz. red wine
150 ml./5 fl. oz. chicken
    stock
25 ml./1½ tablespoons
    cornflour dissolved in 15
    ml./1 tablespoon water

Mix the water and 15 ml./1 tablespoon of vinegar together in a large bowl. Add the rabbit pieces and marinate them at room temperature for 6 hours. Drain the rabbit and dry. Roll them in the seasoned flour.

Heat the oil in a saucepan. Add the rabbit pieces and brown on all sides. Transfer to a plate. Add the onion and 125 g./4 oz. of the prunes to the pan and fry for 5 minutes. Stir in the lemon rind, salt and pepper, sugar, red wine, stock and remaining vinegar. Bring to the boil. Return the rabbit pieces to the pan, cover and simmer for 1¼ hours, or until the rabbit is cooked.

Transfer the rabbit pieces to a warmed serving dish and keep hot. Add the remaining prunes to the sauce and boil rapidly for 3 minutes or until it has reduced a little. Stir in the cornflour mixture and cook the sauce, stirring constantly, for 2 minutes or until it has thickened. Pour the sauce over the rabbit.

Serves 4-6

Rabbit with Mustard Sauce

1 rabbit, cut into serving
    pieces
50 ml./2 fl. oz. cooking oil
50 g./2 oz. butter
40 g./1½ oz. flour
300 ml./10 fl. oz. single
    cream
15 ml./1 tablespoon mustard
salt and pepper
Marinade
225 ml./8 fl. oz. white wine
125 ml./4 fl. oz. cooking oil
1 garlic clove, crushed
1 onion, chopped
10 ml./2 teaspoons dried
    rosemary

Mix all the marinade ingredients together in a large shallow dish. Put the rabbit pieces in the marinade and set aside for 6 hours.

Drain the rabbit pieces and dry. Reserve the marinade. Heat the oil in a saucepan. Add the rabbit pieces and brown on all sides. Add the marinade to the pan, cover and simmer for 1¼ hours, or until the rabbit is cooked. Transfer the rabbit pieces to a warmed serving dish and keep hot. Strain the cooking liquid and reserve 150 ml./5 fl. oz.

Melt the butter in a saucepan. Stir in the flour to form a smooth paste. Gradually stir in the reserved cooking juices and bring to the boil. Stir in the cream, mustard and salt and pepper to taste, and cook the sauce, stirring constantly, for 2 to 3 minutes or until it is thick and smooth. Pour over the rabbit pieces.

Serves 4-6

Rabbit Pie

675 g./1½ lb. boned rabbit
  pieces
50 g./2 oz. seasoned flour
50 ml./2 fl. oz. cooking oil
300 ml./10 fl. oz. chicken
  stock
125 g./4 oz. cooked ham,
  finely chopped
2 carrots, chopped
2 onions, chopped
5 ml./1 teaspoon dried thyme
salt and pepper
225 g./8 oz. shortcrust pastry*
1 tablespoon milk
Marinade
225 ml./8 fl. oz. white wine
50 ml./2 fl. oz. cooking oil
2 garlic cloves, crushed
5 ml./1 teaspoon grated
  lemon rind
15 ml./1 tablespoon chopped
  fresh parsley

Mix all the marinade ingredients together in a large, shallow dish. Add the rabbit pieces and marinate them at room temperature for 6 hours.

Remove the rabbit pieces from the marinade and dry. Strain the marinade and reserve. Roll the rabbit pieces in the seasoned flour. Heat the oil in a saucepan. Add the rabbit pieces and brown on all sides. Add the reserved marinade, stock, ham, carrots, onions, thyme and salt and pepper, and stir to mix. Bring to the boil. Simmer for 1¼ hours, or until the rabbit is cooked through. Transfer to a deep pie dish and leave until cold.

Roll out the pastry dough until it is as large as the pie dish. Cover the pie dish with the dough, trimming off the ends to fit. Brush with the milk. Put into the oven preheated to fairly hot (190°C/375°F or Gas Mark 5) and bake for 30 to 35 minutes, or until the pastry is deep golden brown.

Serves 6

Jugged Hare

75 g./3 oz. bacon fat
1 hare, cut into serving pieces
2 onions, sliced
2 carrots, sliced
grated rind of 1 lemon
1 bay leaf
2 parsley sprigs
pinch of cayenne pepper
10 ml./2 teaspoons crushed
  black peppercorns
salt and pepper
1 l./1¾ pints beef stock
75 g./3 oz. beurre manié*
150 ml./5 fl. oz. port
25 ml./1½ tablespoons
  redcurrant jelly
30 ml./2 tablespoons
  chopped fresh parsley

Melt the bacon fat in a flameproof casserole. Add the hare pieces and brown on all sides. Add the vegetables, lemon rind, bay leaf, parsley, cayenne, peppercorns, seasoning and stock and stir to mix. Bring to the boil. Cover the casserole and put it into the oven preheated to warm (170°C/325°F or Gas Mark 3). Braise for 3 hours or until the hare pieces are very tender.

Transfer the hare pieces and vegetables to a warmed serving dish and keep hot. Strain the cooking liquid into a saucepan. Bring to the boil. Add the beurre manié, a little at a time, stirring until the sauce has thickened and is smooth. Add the port and redcurrant jelly and cook the sauce, stirring constantly, for 2 minutes or until the jelly has dissolved. Pour the sauce over the hare and vegetables and garnish with the parsley.

Serves 6

Hare Casserole

75 g./3 oz. butter
1 hare, cut into serving pieces
18 pickling onions
Sauce
50 g./2 oz. butter
50 g./2 oz. flour
425 ml./15 fl. oz. hare stock
   (made with the hare
   giblets)
30 ml./2 tablespoons
   redcurrant jelly
150 ml./5 fl. oz. red wine
salt and pepper

To make the sauce, melt the butter in a saucepan. Stir in the flour to form a smooth paste, then gradually stir in the stock. Simmer the sauce for 3 minutes, stirring constantly. Stir in the redcurrant jelly, wine and salt and pepper to taste. Bring to the boil, then set aside.

Melt the butter in a flameproof casserole. Add the hare pieces and brown on all sides. Add the onions and fry for 5 minutes. Pour over the sauce and stir to mix. Put into the oven preheated to warm (170°C/325°F or Gas Mark 3) and braise for 3 hours or until the hare pieces are very tender.

Serves 6

Hare in Madeira Sauce

50 g./2 oz. seasoned flour
15 ml./1 teaspoon dried sage
1 hare, cut into serving pieces
75 g./3 oz. butter
15 ml./1 tablespoon cooking
   oil
175 g./6 oz. button
   mushrooms, sliced
300 ml./10 fl. oz. Madeira
5 ml./1 teaspoon dried mixed
   herbs
salt and pepper

Mix the flour and sage together then roll the hare pieces in the mixture. Heat half the butter and the oil in a saucepan. Add the hare pieces and brown on all sides. Transfer to an ovenproof casserole.

Melt the remaining butter in the saucepan. Add the mushrooms and fry for 3 minutes. Stir in the Madeira, herbs and salt and pepper to taste, then bring to the boil. Pour into the casserole and put it into the oven preheated to fairly hot (190°C/375°F or Gas Mark 5). Braise for 1½ hours or until the hare pieces are tender.

Serves 6

Grouse Casserole

50 g./2 oz. bacon fat
3 mature grouse, halved
2 onions, chopped
3 celery stalks, chopped
1 turnip, chopped
4 bacon slices, chopped
425 ml./15 fl. oz. beef stock
grated rind of ½ orange
30 ml./2 tablespoons
   damson jelly
2.5 ml./½ teaspoon ground
   mace
salt and pepper

Melt the bacon fat in a frying-pan. Add the grouse and brown on both sides. Transfer to an ovenproof casserole. Add the vegetables and bacon to the pan and fry until the bacon is crisp. Add all the remaining ingredients to the pan and stir to mix. Bring to the boil and add to the casserole. Cover and put into the oven preheated to cool (150°C/300°F or Gas Mark 2). Braise for 2½ hours or until the grouse are very tender.

Serves 6

Roast Goose with Sage and Onion Stuffing

1 × 4 kg./8 lb. goose
salt and pepper
1 lemon, quartered
450 g./1 lb. sage and onion
stuffing*

Rub the goose inside and out with the salt and pepper. Squeeze the lemon juice all over the skin, then rub it in. Fill the cavity with the stuffing, then secure the cavity with string, or skewers. Put the goose on a rack in a roasting pan and prick the skin with a fork. Put into the oven preheated to very hot (230°C/450°F or Gas Mark 8) and roast for 15 minutes. Reduce the oven temperature to moderate (180°C/350°F or Gas Mark 4) and continue to roast the goose for 2½ to 3 hours, or until it is cooked through. Baste occasionally with the cooking fat and remove any excess fat with a bulb or spoon during the cooking period.

Serves 6-8

Goose Casserole

1 × 4 kg./8 lb. goose, cut into
serving pieces
salt, pepper and paprika
125 g./4 fl. oz. cooking oil
2 onions, sliced
1 garlic clove, crushed
4 carrots, sliced
2 turnips, chopped
600 ml./1 pint stock
2 bouquets garnis

Rub the goose pieces with the salt, pepper and paprika. Heat the oil in a large flameproof casserole. Add the goose pieces and brown on all sides. Transfer to a plate. Add the onions, garlic, carrots and turnips to the casserole and fry for 5 minutes. Pour in the stock and add the bouquets garnis. Bring to the boil. Return the goose pieces to the casserole and put it into the oven preheated to warm (170°C/325°F or Gas Mark 3). Braise for 4½ hours, or until the goose is cooked through.

Transfer the goose and vegetables to a warmed serving dish and keep hot. Strain the cooking juice into a saucepan and boil rapidly for 15 to 20 minutes, or until reduced by about half. Skim any scum from the surface of the liquid and pour over the goose and vegetables.

Serves 6-8

Roast Pheasant with Red Wine Sauce

2 young pheasants
salt and pepper
50 g./2 oz. butter
4 streaky bacon slices
425 ml./15 fl. oz. red wine
1 bouquet garni
5 ml./1 teaspoon dried thyme
30 ml./2 tablespoons flour
125 ml./4 fl. oz. single cream

Rub the pheasants with the salt and pepper. Melt half of the butter in a roasting pan. Add the pheasants and brown on all sides. Put the bacon slices over the pheasant breasts, pour over the wine and add the bouquet garni and thyme. Bring to the boil. Put into the oven preheated to moderate (180°C/350°F or Gas Mark 4) and roast the pheasants for 1 to 1¼ hours, or until they are cooked through. Transfer the pheasants to a carving board and keep hot. Strain the cooking juices into a jug.

Melt the remaining butter in a saucepan. Stir in the flour to form a smooth paste. Gradually stir in the reserved cooking juices. Bring to the boil and simmer the sauce for 2 minutes, or until it has thickened and is smooth. Stir in the cream and heat gently. Serve the sauce with the pheasant.

Serves 4

Pigeons with Chestnuts

350 g./12 oz. chestnuts, slit
    at the pointed ends
50 ml./2 fl. oz. cooking oil
3 pigeons, halved
30 ml./2 tablespoons flour
425 ml./15 fl. oz. chicken
    stock
12 pickling onions
peeled rind and juice of 1
    orange
10 ml./2 teaspoons
    redcurrant jelly
salt and pepper
5 ml./1 teaspoon dried thyme
15 ml./1 tablespoon chopped
    fresh parsley

Blanch the chestnuts in boiling water for 2 minutes. Drain, then peel, removing the inner skin as well.

Heat the oil in a flameproof casserole. Add the pigeons and brown on both sides. Transfer to a plate. Add the chestnuts to the casserole and fry for 5 minutes. Transfer to the plate.

Stir the flour into the oil in the casserole to form a smooth paste. Gradually add the stock and bring to the boil, stirring constantly. Add all the remaining ingredients. Return the pigeons and chestnuts to the casserole and mix well. Put into the oven preheated to warm (170°C/325°F or Gas Mark 3) and cook for 1¾ to 2 hours, or until the pigeons are cooked.

Serves 6

Fish & Shellfish

Bream in Egg Butter

6 bream fillets, skinned
75 g./3 oz. seasoned flour
50 g./2 oz. butter
Egg Butter
75 g./3 oz. butter
10 ml./2 teaspoons lemon
    juice
2 hard-boiled eggs, chopped
15 ml./1 tablespoon chopped
    fresh parsley

Roll the fish in the seasoned flour. Melt the butter in a frying-pan. Add the fish and fry for 8 to 10 minutes, or until it is cooked and flakes easily.

Meanwhile to make the egg butter, melt the butter in a small pan. Stir in the remaining ingredients and heat for 2 minutes. Pour over the fish.

Serves 6

Norwegian Fish

675 g./1½ lb. cod fillets,
    skinned and cut into about
    12 pieces
2 egg whites, beaten until
    frothy
50 g./2 oz. dry breadcrumbs
75 g./3 oz. butter
25 g./1 oz. flour
425 ml./15 fl. oz. fish stock *
60 ml./4 tablespoons double
    cream
30 ml./2 tablespoons sherry
2 lemons, thinly sliced
15 ml./1 tablespoon chopped
    fresh dill

Coat the fillets in the egg whites, then in the breadcrumbs. Melt half the butter in a frying-pan. Add the fish and brown on all sides. Set aside.

Melt the remaining butter in a saucepan. Stir in the flour to form a smooth paste, then gradually stir in the stock. Bring to the boil and simmer for 2 to 3 minutes, stirring constantly, or until the sauce thickens. Stir in the cream and sherry.

Arrange half the fillets in an ovenproof dish. Cover with a layer of lemon slices and half the sauce. Continue making layers in this way until all the ingredients are used. Put into the oven pre-heated to moderate (180°C/350°F or Gas Mark 4) and bake for 15 to 20 minutes, or until the fish is cooked and flakes easily. Garnish with the dill.

Serves 4-6

Cod Escabeche

1 kg./2 lb. cod fillets, skinned
   and cut into 5 cm./2 in.
   pieces
75 g./3 oz. seasoned flour
2 eggs, beaten
50 ml./2 fl. oz. milk
oil for deep frying
Pickle
2 carrots, cut into 5 cm./2 in.
   lengths
1 small turnip, cut into 5
   cm./2 in. pieces
2 celery stalks, cut into 5
   cm./2 in. pieces
1 green pepper, pith and
   seeds removed and cut
   into 5 cm./2 in. pieces
1 red pepper, pith and seeds
   removed and cut into 5
   cm./2 in. pieces
175 g./6 oz. pickling onions
900 ml./1½ pints distilled
   vinegar
50 g./2 oz. sugar
5 ml./1 teaspoon celery seeds
Dressing
60 ml./4 tablespoons salad
   oil
30 ml./2 tablespoons wine
   vinegar
30 ml./2 tablespoons white
   wine
2.5 ml./½ teaspoon dry
   mustard
salt and pepper

First make the pickle. Put the vegetables and vinegar into a saucepan and bring to the boil. Stir in the sugar until it has dissolved, then add the celery seeds. Simmer for 15 minutes or until the vegetables are cooked but firm. Drain and discard the vinegar.

Meanwhile, roll the fish pieces in half the seasoned flour. Dip them in the eggs, the milk and then in the remaining flour. Deep-fry for 3 to 5 minutes, or until deep golden brown. Drain on kitchen towels, then transfer to a warmed serving dish.

To make the dressing, mix all the ingredients together until they are thoroughly blended. Pour over the pickled vegetables and toss well to blend. Arrange over the fish.

Serves 6

Devilled Cod

6 cod steaks
50 g./2 oz. butter
10 ml./2 teaspoons curry
   powder
5 ml./1 teaspoon
   Worcestershire sauce
30 ml./2 tablespoons
   sultanas
15 ml./1 tablespoon sweet
   chutney
salt and pepper
45 ml./3 tablespoons fresh
   breadcrumbs

Arrange the cod steaks in a shallow ovenproof dish. Mix all the remaining ingredients together and spread over the fish. Put into the oven pre-heated to moderately hot (190°C/375°F or Gas Mark 5) and bake for 20 to 25 minutes, or until the fish is cooked and flakes easily.

Serves 6

Cod Au Poivre

4 cod steaks
25 g./1 oz. black
   peppercorns, crushed
125 g./4 oz. butter
150 ml./5 fl. oz. double
   cream
15 ml./1 tablespoon chopped
   fresh parsley

Coat the steaks with the peppercorns. Melt the butter in a frying-pan. Add the steaks and fry for 10 to 15 minutes or until the fish is cooked and flakes easily. Stir in the cream and heat gently for 2 minutes. Garnish with the chopped parsley.

Serves 4

Sweet and Sour Cod

300 ml./10 fl. oz. chicken
   stock
15 ml./1 tablespoon tomato
   purée
15 ml./1 tablespoon soy
   sauce
45 ml./3 tablespoons white
   wine or water
5 ml./1 teaspoon ground
   ginger
1 kg./2 lb. cod fillets, skinned
   and cut into bite-sized
   pieces
225 g./8 oz. shelled prawns
75 g./3 oz. cornflour
75 ml./3 fl. oz. cooking oil
2 onions, sliced
4 celery stalks, sliced
1 red pepper, pith and seeds
   removed and sliced
15 ml./1 tablespoon chopped
   fresh chives
salt and pepper

Mix half the stock, the tomato purée, soy sauce, wine or water and ginger together. Add the fish pieces and prawns and marinate at room temperature for 1 hour.

Drain and reserve the marinade. Roll the fish pieces and prawns in the cornflour, reserving 15 ml./1 tablespoon. Heat the oil in a frying-pan. Add the fish and prawns and fry for 8 to 12 minutes, or until the fish is cooked and flakes easily. Transfer to a plate and keep hot.

Add the vegetables, chives and seasoning to taste to the pan and fry for 3 minutes. Add to the fish.

Mix the remaining cornflour with the remaining stock and add to the pan. Bring to the boil, stirring constantly. Gradually stir in the reserved marinade and simmer for 3 minutes or until the sauce becomes translucent. Stir the fish and vegetables into the sauce and reheat gently.

Serves 6

Cod Sauté

25 g./1 oz. butter
4 cod steaks
1 onion, chopped
1 garlic clove, crushed
175 g./6 oz. mushrooms,
   sliced
2 tomatoes, skinned and
   chopped
75 ml./3 fl. oz. white wine or
   fish stock *
salt and pepper
15 ml./1 tablespoon toasted
   breadcrumbs
15 ml./1 tablespoon chopped
   fresh parsley

Melt the butter in a frying-pan. Add the fish and fry for 10 to 15 minutes, or until it is cooked and flakes easily. Transfer to a warmed serving dish and keep hot.

Add the onion and garlic to the pan and fry for 5 minutes. Stir in the mushrooms and tomatoes and fry for 3 minutes. Pour over the wine or stock and bring to the boil. Simmer for 5 minutes, then season to taste. Pour the sauce over the fish and garnish with the breadcrumbs and parsley.

Serves 4

Haddock Kebabs

675 g./1½ lb. haddock fillets,
  skinned and cut into 4
  cm./1½ in. cubes
24 small mushrooms
1 red pepper, pith and seeds
  removed and cut into
  squares
1 green pepper, pith and
  seeds removed and cut
  into squares
125 g./4 oz. butter, melted
30 ml./2 tablespoons lemon
  juice
dash of chilli sauce
salt and pepper
15 ml./1 tablespoon chopped
  fresh parsley

Thread the fish, mushrooms and peppers on to skewers. Mix the melted butter, lemon juice, chilli sauce and salt and pepper to taste together. Brush the mixture generously over the kebabs and grill for 8 to 12 minutes, or until the fish is cooked and flakes easily. Brush the kebabs with the butter mixture frequently during the cooking period.

Stir the parsley into the remaining melted butter and pour over the kebabs.

Serves 6

Haddock with Capers

4 large haddock fillets,
  skinned
salt and pepper
30 ml./2 tablespoons lemon
  juice
50 g./2 oz. seasoned flour
75 g./3 oz. butter
10 ml./2 teaspoons finely
  grated lemon rind
30 ml./2 tablespoons capers
15 ml./1 tablespoon chopped
  fresh parsley

Rub the fillets with the salt and pepper, then sprinkle over half the lemon juice. Roll the fillets in the seasoned flour. Melt half the butter in a frying-pan. Add the fillets and fry for 8 to 12 minutes, or until they are cooked and flake easily. Transfer to a warmed serving dish.

Add the remaining butter to the pan, then stir in the remaining lemon juice and remaining ingredients. Heat gently and pour over the fish.

Serves 4

Finnan Haddie

675 g./1½ lb. smoked
  haddock, cut into small
  pieces
300 ml./10 fl. oz. milk
150 ml./5 fl. oz. single cream
25 g./1 oz. butter
pepper
6 hot poached eggs

Arrange the fish pieces in an ovenproof dish. Heat the milk, cream and butter together until the butter has melted, then stir in pepper to taste. Pour over the fish and put into the oven preheated to moderate (180°C/350°F or Gas Mark 4). Cook for 20 minutes, or until the fish is cooked and flakes easily. Top with the poached eggs.

Serves 6

Haddock Charlotte

575 g./1¼ lb. haddock,
  minced or very finely
  flaked
1 egg, beaten
150 ml./5 fl. oz. milk
salt and pepper
5 ml./1 teaspoon finely
  grated lemon rind
10 ml./2 teaspoons finely
  chopped fresh parsley
5 large slices of buttered
  bread, crusts removed and
  cut into fingers

Mix the fish, egg, milk, salt and pepper to taste, lemon rind and parsley together. Line the bottom of a 1¼ l./2 pint pie dish with bread fingers, buttered side down. Spoon in the fish mixture and top with the remaining fingers, buttered sides up. Put into the oven preheated to moderate (180°C/350°F or Gas Mark 4) and bake for 40 to 45 minutes, or until the topping is crisp and golden brown.

Serves 4-6

Haddock Pie

1 kg./2 lb. haddock fillets,
  skinned and cut into 5
  cm./2 in. pieces
50 g./2 oz. seasoned flour
50 ml./2 fl. oz. cooking oil
675 g./1½ lb. cooked
  potatoes, mashed
45 ml./3 tablespoons cream
salt and pepper
25 g./1 oz. Cheddar cheese,
  grated

Roll the haddock pieces in the seasoned flour. Heat the oil in a frying-pan. Add the fish and brown on all sides. Transfer to an ovenproof dish and flake slightly.

Mix the potatoes, cream and salt and pepper to taste together, then spread over the fish. Sprinkle over the grated cheese and put into the oven preheated to moderate (180°C/350°F or Gas Mark 4). Bake for 15 to 20 minutes or until the top is brown.

Serves 6

Haddock Soufflé

300 ml./10 fl. oz. thick
  béchamel sauce*
225 g./8 oz. cooked fresh or
  smoked haddock, flaked
4 eggs, separated

Heat the béchamel sauce until it is hot, then stir in the fish. Beat in the egg yolks, one at a time.

Beat the egg whites until they are stiff. (You should be able to turn the bowl upside-down without the mixture falling out.) Quickly fold the egg whites into the fish mixture. Spoon into a well-greased soufflé dish and put into the oven preheated to fairly hot (190°C/375°F or Gas Mark 5). Bake for 35 minutes or until the soufflé has risen and is golden brown.

Serves 3-4

Haddock Mornay

4 large haddock fillets,
  skinned
175 ml./6 fl. oz. milk
175 ml./6 fl. oz. water
1 bouquet garni
25 g./1 oz. butter
125 g./4 oz. mushrooms,
  sliced
350 ml./12 fl. oz. mornay
  sauce*
15 ml./1 tablespoon dry
  breadcrumbs
25 g./1 oz. Parmesan cheese,
  grated

Put the fillets in a well-greased ovenproof dish and pour over the milk and water. Add the bouquet garni, cover and put into the oven preheated to warm (170°C/325°F or Gas Mark 3). Cook the fish for 20 to 25 minutes, or until it is cooked and flakes easily. Drain and discard the cooking liquid. Transfer the fish to a warmed flameproof dish and keep hot.

Melt the butter in a saucepan. Add the mushrooms and fry for 3 minutes. Stir in the mornay sauce and simmer until it is reheated. Pour over the fish and sprinkle over the breadcrumbs and grated cheese. Grill for 5 minutes or until the top is brown.

Serves 4

Smoked Haddock Cakes

675 g./1½ lb. smoked
  haddock
300 ml./10 fl. oz. water
150 ml./5 fl. oz. milk
675 g./1½ lb. cooked
  potatoes, mashed
30 ml./2 tablespoons
  chopped fresh parsley
salt and pepper
5 ml./1 teaspoon mustard
25 g./1 oz. flour
2 eggs, beaten
50 g./2 oz. dry breadcrumbs
oil for deep frying
Sauce
15 ml./1 tablespoon butter
15 ml./1 tablespoon flour

Put the fish into a saucepan and pour over the water and milk. Cover and simmer gently for 12 to 15 minutes, or until the fish is cooked and flakes easily. Drain, reserving the cooking liquid, and remove the skin and bones. Put the fish into a bowl and stir in the potatoes, parsley, salt and pepper and mustard.

To make the sauce, boil the reserved cooking liquid until it has reduced to about 150 ml./5 fl. oz. Melt the butter in a saucepan and stir in the flour to form a smooth paste. Gradually stir in the cooking liquid. Bring to the boil, then simmer for 2 minutes, stirring constantly, or until it has thickened. Add just enough sauce to the fish mixture to bind it stiffly. Divide the mixture into about 12 patties. Dip in flour, then in beaten eggs and finally in breadcrumbs.

Chill for 15 minutes, then deep-fry for 3 to 5 minutes, or until deep golden brown. Drain on kitchen towels. Reheat the remaining sauce and serve with the fish cakes.

Serves 4

American Haddock Pie

3 streaky bacon slices,
   chopped
1 large onion, chopped
3 large tomatoes, skinned
   and chopped
25 g./1 oz. flour
425 ml./15 fl. oz. chicken or
   fish stock *
675 g./1½ lb. cooked
   haddock, skinned and
   flaked
½ kg./1 lb. cooked potatoes,
   mashed
25 g./1 oz. butter, cut into
   small pieces

Fry the bacon in a frying-pan for 3 minutes. Add the onion and fry for 5 minutes. Stir in the tomatoes and fry for 3 minutes. Stir in the flour to form a smooth paste, then gradually stir in the stock. Bring to the boil and simmer for 2 to 3 minutes, stirring constantly, or until the sauce thickens. Stir in the fish and simmer for 3 minutes, or until it is heated.

Spoon the mixture into a deep ovenproof dish and spread over the mashed potatoes. Dot over the butter pieces and put into the oven preheated to fairly hot (190°C/375°F or Gas Mark 5). Bake for 15 to 20 minutes, or until the top is brown.

Serves 6

Baked Haddock

1 × 1½ kg./3 lb. haddock,
   cleaned
25 g./1 oz. butter, melted
Stuffing
40 g./1½ oz. butter
30 ml./2 tablespoons
   chopped onion
60 ml./4 tablespoons soft
   white breadcrumbs
30 ml./2 tablespoons
   chopped fresh parsley
finely grated rind and juice
   of 1 orange
salt and pepper
1 egg, beaten

To make the stuffing, melt the butter in a small pan. Add the onion and fry for 2 minutes. Remove from the heat and stir in all the remaining ingredients. Add a little extra orange juice if the mixture is too dry. Put the fish on a flat surface and spoon the stuffing into the cavity. Secure the cavity with string or skewers. Put the fish into a well-greased ovenproof dish and brush generously with the melted butter. Put into the oven preheated to moderate (180°C/350°F or Gas Mark 4) and bake for 35 to 40 minutes, or until the fish is cooked and flakes easily.

Serves 4

Grilled Hake Cutlets

4 hake cutlets
salt and pepper
50 g./2 oz. butter, melted
25 g./1 oz. Parmesan cheese,
  grated
25 g./1 oz. butter
125 g./4 oz. mushrooms,
  sliced
75 g./3 oz. blanched
  almonds

Rub the cutlets with salt and pepper. Put the cutlets on the grill rack. Generously brush with the melted butter and sprinkle over half the grated cheese. Grill for 5 to 8 minutes or until the top is golden brown. Turn and brush the other side with the remaining melted butter and sprinkle with the remaining grated cheese. Grill for a further 5 to 8 minutes, or until the fish is cooked and flakes easily.

Meanwhile, melt the 25 g./1 oz. butter in a frying-pan. Add the mushrooms and almonds and fry for 3 minutes. Spoon over the fish.

Serves 4

Halibut Portuguese

2 large halibut steaks,
  halved
40 g./1½ oz. seasoned flour
75 g./3 oz. butter
Sauce
15 ml./1 tablespoon cooking
  oil
1 onion, finely chopped
1 small green pepper, pith
  and seeds removed and
  chopped
4 tomatoes, skinned and
  roughly chopped
75 ml./3 fl. oz. white wine or
  stock
12 stuffed olives

First make the sauce. Heat the oil in a saucepan. Add the onion and pepper and fry for 5 minutes. Add the remaining ingredients, bring to the boil and simmer for 20 minutes.

Meanwhile, roll the fish steaks in the seasoned flour. Melt the butter in a frying-pan. Add the fish steaks and fry for 10 to 12 minutes, or until they are cooked and flake easily.

Pour half the sauce into a serving dish and arrange the fish on top. Cover with the remaining sauce.

Serves 4

Herrings in Oatmeal

4 large herrings, cleaned and
  head and backbone
  removed
75 g./3 oz. rolled oats
salt and pepper
50 g./2 oz. butter
1 lemon, thinly sliced

Roll the herrings in the oats, seasoned to taste with the salt and pepper. Melt the butter in a frying-pan. Add the herrings and fry for 6 to 8 minutes, or until they are cooked and flake easily. Garnish with the lemon slices.

Serves 4

Herring Fillets with Mustard Sauce

4 large herrings, filleted
salt and pepper
30 ml./2 tablespoons lemon
  juice
75 g./3 oz. butter
25 g./1 oz. flour
300 ml./10 fl. oz. milk
15 ml./1 tablespoon dry
  mustard
5 ml./1 teaspoon sugar
5 ml./1 teaspoon vinegar

Rub the herrings with the salt and pepper and sprinkle over the lemon juice. Set aside for 10 minutes.

Melt 50 g./2 oz. of butter in a frying-pan. Add the herrings and fry for 6 to 8 minutes or until the fish is cooked and flakes easily.

Meanwhile melt the remaining butter in a saucepan. Stir in the flour to form a smooth paste, then gradually stir in the milk. Bring to the boil and simmer, stirring constantly, for 2 minutes or until the sauce thickens. Stir in the remaining ingredients and simmer for a further minute. Pour the sauce over the herrings.

Serves 4

Normandy Herrings

4 large herrings, cleaned and
  head and backbone
  removed
50 g./2 oz. seasoned flour
75 g./3 oz. butter
1 large onion, chopped
2 dessert apples, cored and
  sliced
15 ml./1 tablespoon lemon
  juice

Roll the herrings in the seasoned flour. Melt half the butter in a frying-pan. Add the herrings and fry for 6 to 8 minutes, or until they are cooked and flake easily. Transfer to a warmed serving plate and keep hot.

Add the remaining butter to the pan with the onion and 1 apple and fry for 5 minutes. Stir in the lemon juice and arrange the mixture around the fish. Garnish with the remaining apple slices.

Serves 4

Spiced Herrings

4 large herrings, filleted
1 large onion, chopped
1 large dessert apple, cored
  and sliced
10 ml./2 teaspoons ground
  mixed spice
300 ml./10 fl. oz. apple juice
15 ml./1 tablespoon chopped
  fresh parsley
3 gherkins, chopped

Roll up the fillets and secure with a wooden tooth-pick. Arrange in a well-greased baking dish and sprinkle over the onion and apple. Mix the mixed spice and apple juice together and pour over the fish. Cover and put into the oven preheated to warm (170°C/325°F or Gas Mark 3). Bake for 45 minutes, or until the fish is cooked and flakes easily. Garnish with the chopped parsley and gherkins.

Serves 4

Flounder Florentine

675 g./1½ lb. cooked spinach,
    chopped
675 g./1½ lb. flounder fillets
salt, pepper and grated
    nutmeg
30 ml./2 tablespoons lemon
    juice
1 lemon, thinly sliced
chopped parsley to garnish
Sauce
25 g./1 oz. butter
30 ml./2 tablespoons flour
300 ml./10 fl. oz. milk
40 g./1½ oz. Cheddar cheese,
    grated
25 g./1 oz. Parmesan cheese,
    grated
salt and pepper
2.5 ml./½ teaspoon grated
    nutmeg

Arrange the spinach in a well-greased, shallow ovenproof dish. Arrange the fillets on top and sprinkle over salt, pepper and nutmeg to taste. Pour over the lemon juice. Cover and put into the oven preheated to moderate (180°C/350°F or Gas Mark 4). Cook for 15 to 20 minutes, or until the fish is cooked and flakes easily.

Meanwhile to make the sauce, melt the butter in a saucepan. Stir in the flour to form a smooth paste. Gradually add the milk, stirring constantly. Bring to the boil, then stir in the cheeses, seasoning to taste and nutmeg. Simmer for 2 to 3 minutes, stirring constantly, or until thick and smooth. Pour the sauce over the fish and garnish with the lemon slices and parsley.

Serves 4-6

Stuffed Plaice in Cream

450 g./1 lb. cooked potatoes,
    mashed
salt and pepper
50 g./2 oz. butter
75 g./3 oz. mushrooms,
    chopped
3 lean bacon slices, chopped
4 plaice fillets, skinned
150 ml./5 fl. oz. double
    cream

Mix the potatoes, salt and pepper to taste and half the butter together. Spoon into a piping bag with a plain nozzle and pipe a decorative border around a well-greased baking dish.

Melt the remaining butter in a frying-pan. Add the mushrooms and bacon and fry until the bacon is crisp. Lay the fish fillets out flat and spoon a little of the bacon mixture on to the centre of each one. Roll up and secure with a wooden toothpick. Arrange the rolls in the baking dish and pour over the cream. Cover loosely with foil (taking care not to disturb the potato border) and put into the oven preheated to moderate (180°C/350°F or Gas Mark 4). Bake for 15 to 20 minutes or until the fish is cooked and flakes easily. Remove the foil and bake for 5 minutes longer to lightly brown the potato border.

Serves 4

Plaice Milanaise

4 plaice fillets, skinned
salt and pepper
45 ml./3 tablespoons white
  wine
50 g./2 oz. butter
175 g./6 oz. ribbon noodles
125 g./4 oz. button
  mushrooms, sliced
75 g./3 oz. cooked peas
5 ml./1 teaspoon paprika

Arrange the fillets on a well-greased ovenproof plate. Sprinkle over salt and pepper to taste, wine and about 15 ml./1 tablespoon of butter, cut into small pieces. Put the plate over a pan of boiling water and cover with foil or a saucepan lid. Steam for 12 to 15 minutes, or until the fish is cooked and flakes easily.

Meanwhile, cook the noodles in boiling, salted water for 6 to 8 minutes, or until 'al dente'. Drain.

Melt the remaining butter in a frying-pan. Add the mushrooms and fry for 3 minutes. Stir in the peas and paprika and fry for 2 minutes. Stir the mixture into the noodles, then transfer to a warmed serving dish. Arrange the fish on top of the noodles and sprinkle over any cooking liquid.

Serves 4

Stuffed Plaice Fillets

4 plaice fillets, skinned
salt and pepper
30 ml./2 tablespoons lemon
  juice
50 g./2 oz. parsley and
  thyme stuffing*
50 g./2 oz. seasoned flour
2 eggs, beaten
50 g./2 oz. dry breadcrumbs
125 g./4 oz. butter

Rub the fillets with the salt and pepper and sprinkle over the lemon juice. Divide the stuffing between the fillets. Roll up into parcels, to enclose the stuffing. Dip the parcels in the seasoned flour, then in the beaten eggs and finally in the bread-crumbs. Set aside for 10 minutes.

Melt the butter in a frying-pan. Add the fish parcels and fry for 8 to 12 minutes, or until the fish is cooked and flakes easily.

Serves 4

Mackerel with Cider Sauce

4 mackerel, cleaned and
  backbone removed
150 ml./5 fl. oz. dry cider
30 ml./2 tablespoons
  tarragon vinegar
1 bay leaf
juice of 1 lemon
1 bouquet garni
salt and pepper
lemon or orange slices to
  garnish

Put the fish into an ovenproof dish. Pour over the cider and vinegar and add the bay leaf, lemon juice, bouquet garni and salt and pepper to taste. Put into the oven preheated to moderate (180°C/350°F or Gas Mark 4) and cook the fish for 20 to 25 minutes, or until it is cooked and the flesh flakes easily. Garnish with lemon or orange slices.

Serves 4

Mullet with Bacon

4 red mullets, cleaned
8 streaky bacon slices
25 g./1 oz. butter
25 g./1 oz. flour
300 ml./10 fl. oz. chicken
  stock
125 g./4 oz. mushrooms,
  sliced
125 g./4 oz. peas
15 ml./1 tablespoon brown
  sugar
salt and pepper

Wrap two bacon slices round each fish and secure with a wooden toothpick. Arrange the fish in a well-greased baking dish.

Melt the butter in a saucepan. Stir in the flour to form a smooth paste. Gradually stir in the stock and bring to the boil. Cook for 2 minutes, stirring constantly, or until the sauce thickens. Stir in the remaining ingredients. Pour over the fish and put into the oven preheated to moderate (180°C/350°F or Gas Mark 4). Bake the fish for 20 to 25 minutes, or until it is cooked and the flesh flakes easily.

Serves 4

Grilled Mullet

4 mullets, cleaned
salt and pepper
30 ml./2 tablespoons lemon
  juice
2 lemons, sliced
125 g./4 oz. butter, melted

Rub the mullets with salt and pepper. Make slits along the side of each fish, then rub with lemon juice. Halve the slices of 1 lemon and insert them into the slits. Put the fish on the grill rack. Generously brush the fish with the melted butter and grill for 8 to 12 minutes, or until the fish is cooked and the flesh flakes easily. Baste with the melted butter once or twice during the cooking period. Garnish with the remaining lemon slices.

Serves 4

Salmon Bake

1 × 225 g./8 oz. can salmon,
  drained and flaked
225 ml./8 fl. oz. tomato
  sauce*
2.5 ml./½ teaspoon Tabasco
  sauce
45 ml./3 tablespoons
  mayonnaise
45 ml./3 tablespoons cream
salt and pepper
1 large tomato, thinly sliced
25 g./1 oz. Cheddar cheese,
  grated

Put the flaked salmon in a shallow, ovenproof dish, Mix the tomato sauce, Tabasco, mayonnaise, cream and salt and pepper together, then pour over the salmon. Arrange the tomato slices on top and sprinkle over the grated cheese. Put into the oven preheated to moderate (180°C/350°F or Gas Mark 4) and bake for 15 to 20 minutes or until the top is brown.

Serves 4

Fresh Salmon with Prawns

1 × 1¼ kg./2½ lb. tail piece of
   salmon
300 ml./10 fl. oz. water
175 ml./6 fl. oz. white wine
1 bay leaf
2 parsley sprigs
6 peppercorns
Garnish
7.5 ml./1½ teaspoons gelatine
1 × 425 g./15 oz. can
   consommé
½ cucumber, thinly sliced
175 g./6 oz. cooked shelled
   prawns

Put the salmon in a large ovenproof dish. Add the remaining ingredients. Cover and put into the oven preheated to warm (170°C/325°F or Gas Mark 3). Bake for about 45 minutes, or until the salmon is cooked and flakes easily. Baste the salmon from time to time during the cooking period. Leave to cool in the dish.

When the fish is cold, remove the skin. Divide it in half by cutting along both sides of the flat backbone. Arrange on a large serving dish, with a tail at each end of the dish. Chill.

To make the garnish, dissolve the gelatine in the consommé over low heat, stirring constantly. Cool until the consommé has thickened. Arrange the cucumber in overlapping slices around the salmon, put the prawns in the centre of the plate and spoon the consommé over the top. Chill until the consommé has set.

Serves 6

Salmon Pie

50 g./2 oz. butter
25 g./1 oz. flour
300 ml./10 fl. oz. fish stock *
150 ml./5 fl. oz. double
   cream
3 cooked carrots, sliced
50 g./2 oz. cooked peas
2 hard-boiled eggs, chopped
25 g./1 oz. Cheddar cheese,
   grated
450 g./1 lb. cooked salmon,
   flaked
450 g./1 lb. puff pastry *

Melt the butter in a saucepan. Stir in the flour to form a smooth paste, then gradually stir in the stock. Bring to the boil and simmer for 2 to 3 minutes, stirring constantly, or until the sauce is thick. Stir in the cream, carrots, peas, eggs, cheese and salmon and heat gently for 3 minutes.

Meanwhile, divide the dough into two uneven pieces. Roll out the smaller piece into a rectangle about .75 cm./¼ in. thick. Transfer it to a baking sheet. Spoon the salmon mixture on to the dough, leaving a 1.25 cm./½ in. margin all round the edge. Roll out the other piece of dough into a rectangle large enough to cover the filling. Arrange the dough over the filling, wet the edges and crimp to seal. Make a slit in the centre and brush with a little milk or beaten egg.

Put into the oven preheated to fairly hot (190°C/375°F or Gas Mark 5) and bake for 25 to 35 minutes, or until the pastry is deep golden brown.

Serves 4-6

Salmon Croquettes

1 × 225 g./8 oz. can salmon, drained and flaked
275 g./10 oz. cooked potatoes, mashed
5 ml./1 teaspoon curry powder
1 small onion, finely chopped
10 ml./2 teaspoons chopped fresh parsley
10 ml./2 teaspoons lemon juice
salt and pepper
3 eggs
50 g./2 oz. dry breadcrumbs
50 ml./2 fl. oz. cooking oil

Mix the salmon, potatoes, curry powder, onion, parsley, lemon juice and seasoning together. Beat in one egg to bind, then chill for 1 hour, or until firm.

Divide the mixture into sausage shapes about 8 cm./3 in. long. Beat the remaining eggs, then dip the croquettes first in the eggs, then in the breadcrumbs. Chill for 1 hour.

Heat the oil in a frying-pan. Add the croquettes and fry for 8 to 10 minutes or until they are golden brown.

Serves 4

Salmon Mousse

6 hard-boiled eggs, sliced
4 gherkins, sliced
225 ml./8 fl. oz. white wine
10 ml./2 teaspoons white vinegar
125 ml./4 fl. oz. lemon juice
25 ml./1½ tablespoons gelatine dissolved in 225 ml./8 fl. oz. hot water
1 × 425 g./15 oz. can salmon, drained and flaked
salt and pepper
4 large lettuce leaves
2 tomatoes, thinly sliced

Decorate the bottom of a rinsed mould with some of the slices of egg and gherkin. Mix the wine, vinegar, lemon juice and gelatine mixture together. Pour a little over the egg decoration and chill until set.

Mix the salmon, remaining eggs and gherkins and seasoning together. Stir in the remaining gelatine mixture. Pour into the mould and chill for at least 3 hours, or until set.

Line a serving plate with lettuce leaves. Turn out the mousse on to the lettuce and garnish with tomato slices.

Serves 8

Trout Woolpack

150 g./5 oz. butter
4 trout, cleaned
125 g./4 oz. mushrooms, sliced
125 g./4 oz. small shelled shrimps
30 ml./2 tablespoons lemon juice

Melt the butter in a frying-pan. Add the trout and fry for 8 to 10 minutes or until they are cooked and the flesh flakes easily. Transfer to a warmed serving dish. Add the mushrooms and shrimps to the pan and fry for 5 minutes. Stir in the lemon juice, then pour over the fish.

Serves 4

Trout Nansen

4 trout, cleaned and
    backbone removed
300 ml./10 fl. oz. white wine
    or water
150 ml./5 fl. oz. fish stock *
1 bouquet garni
15 g./½ oz. aspic powder
45 ml./3 tablespoons
    mayonnaise
10 ml./2 teaspoons chopped
    fresh parsley
15 ml./3 teaspoons chopped
    capers
15 ml./1 tablespoon chopped
    gherkins
Garnish
2 lemons, thinly sliced
125 g./4 oz. cooked shelled
    shrimps or prawns
2 tomatoes, skinned and cut
    into wedges
1 × 225 g./8 oz. can
    asparagus tips, drained
4 parsley sprigs

Put the fish into a large saucepan and pour over the wine or water and stock. Add the bouquet garni and simmer for 8 to 10 minutes, or until the trout are cooked and the flesh flakes easily. Transfer to a serving dish. Strain the liquid and reserve about 300 ml./10 fl. oz. Mix the aspic powder with a little of the liquid and bring the remaining liquid to the boil. Gradually stir into the aspic mixture until it has dissolved. Cool until the mixture stiffens and thickens slightly.

Mix the mayonnaise, parsley, capers and gherkins together and spoon a little inside each fish. Arrange the lemon slices around the fish and separate them with the shrimps. Put clusters of tomato wedges and asparagus tips at the tails and a sprig of parsley at the head. Carefully coat the mixture with the cooled aspic and chill until firm and set.

Serves 4

Trout with Almonds

75 g./3 oz. butter
50 g./2 oz. flaked almonds
4 trout, cleaned
salt and pepper
4 black olives
parsley sprigs to garnish

Melt half the butter in a frying-pan. Add the almonds and fry until they are golden brown. Transfer to a plate.

Add the remaining butter to the pan. Add the trout and fry for 8 to 10 minutes or until they are cooked and the flesh flakes easily. Season to taste with the salt and pepper. Transfer to a warmed serving plate and put an olive in each mouth. Pour over the butter remaining in the pan, scatter over the almonds and garnish with the parsley.

Serves 4

Sole Bonne Femme

8 sole fillets, skinned
300 ml./10 fl. oz. fish stock*
150 ml./5 fl. oz. white wine
   or water
150 ml./5 fl. oz. water
15 ml./1 tablespoon lemon
   juice
salt and pepper
Sauce
40 g./1½ oz. butter
25 g./1 oz. flour
125 g./4 oz. button
   mushrooms, sliced
salt and pepper
2.5 ml./½ teaspoon grated
   nutmeg
50 ml./2 fl. oz. double cream

Fold the fillets in half and arrange in a well-greased ovenproof dish. Pour over the stock, wine, water and lemon juice and season to taste. Put into the oven preheated to warm (170°C/325°F or Gas Mark 3) and bake the fish for 20 to 25 minutes, or until it is cooked and flakes easily. Transfer to a warmed serving dish and keep hot. Strain the cooking liquid and reserve about 225 ml./8 fl. oz.

To make the sauce, melt the butter in a saucepan. Stir in the flour to form a smooth paste, then gradually stir in the reserved cooking liquid. Bring to the boil, then simmer, stirring constantly, for 2 minutes or until it thickens. Stir in the mushrooms, salt and pepper and nutmeg and simmer for a further 2 minutes. Stir in the cream then pour the sauce over the fish.

Serves 4

Sole Bercy

8 sole fillets, skinned
300 ml./10 fl. oz. fish stock*
75 g./3 oz. butter
2 shallots or spring onions,
   chopped
300 ml./10 fl. oz. white wine
salt and pepper
juice of ½ lemon
30 ml./2 tablespoons
   chopped fresh parsley
75 ml./3 fl. oz. double cream
30 ml./2 tablespoons dry
   breadcrumbs

Fold the fillets in half and arrange in a well-greased ovenproof dish. Pour over the stock. Cover and put into the oven preheated to moderate (180°C/350°F or Gas Mark 4). Bake the fish for 15 to 20 minutes, or until it is cooked and flakes easily. Transfer to a flameproof dish and keep hot. Strain the cooking liquid and reserve about 225 ml./8 fl. oz.

Melt 25 g./1 oz. of butter in a saucepan. Add the shallots or spring onions and fry for 3 minutes. Pour in the wine and bring to the boil. Boil for about 10 minutes, or until the liquid has reduced by half. Pour in the reserved cooking liquid, add salt and pepper to taste, lemon juice and parsley. Return to the boil, add the remaining butter and stir until it melts. Remove from the heat and stir in the cream. Pour over the fish. Sprinkle over the breadcrumbs and grill for 3 to 5 minutes or until the top is lightly brown.

Serves 4

Sole and Asparagus with White Wine

8 sole fillets, skinned
300 ml./10 fl. oz. white wine
1 × 225 g./8 oz. can
 asparagus tips
Sauce
40 g./1½ oz. butter
30 ml./2 tablespoons flour
175 ml./6 fl. oz. milk
salt and pepper

Fold the fillets in half and arrange in a well-greased ovenproof dish. Pour over the wine. Put into the oven preheated to warm (170°C/325°F or Gas Mark 3) and bake for 20 to 25 minutes, or until the fish is cooked and flakes easily. Transfer to a warmed serving dish and keep hot. Strain the cooking liquid and reserve about 50 ml./2 fl. oz.

Heat the asparagus tips in the can liquid until they are hot. Drain and arrange over the fish.

To make the sauce, melt the butter in a saucepan. Stir in the flour to form a smooth paste. Gradually add the milk and reserved cooking liquid, stirring constantly. Bring to the boil, then simmer for 2 to 3 minutes, stirring constantly, or until the sauce thickens. Stir in salt and pepper to taste and pour over the fish.

Serves 4

Sole Veronique

8 sole fillets, skinned
1 onion, thinly sliced
2 bay leaves
8 peppercorns
15 ml./1 tablespoon lemon
 juice
50 g./2 oz. butter
30 ml./2 tablespoons flour
300 ml./10 fl. oz. milk
salt and pepper
125 g./4 oz. seedless grapes,
 peeled

Roll up the fillets and secure with wooden toothpicks. Stand upright in a well-greased ovenproof dish. Add the onion, seasonings and lemon juice, then pour in enough water to come halfway up the sides of the fish. Cover and put into the oven preheated to warm (170°C/325°F or Gas Mark 3). Bake the fish for 20 to 25 minutes, or until it is cooked and flakes easily. Transfer to a serving dish and keep hot. Strain the cooking liquid and reserve about 225 ml./8 fl. oz.

Melt the butter in a saucepan. Stir in the flour to form a smooth paste. Gradually stir in the milk and reserved cooking liquid. Bring to the boil, then simmer for 2 to 3 minutes, stirring constantly, or until the sauce thickens. Stir in salt and pepper to taste and the grapes. Pour over the fish.

Serves 4

Sole and Cucumber Sauce

12 sole fillets, skinned
25 g./1 oz. butter, cut into
    small pieces
juice of ½ lemon
1.25 ml./¼ teaspoon black
    pepper
5 ml./1 teaspoon chopped
    fresh parsley
Sauce
150 ml./5 fl. oz. mayonnaise
150 ml./5 fl. oz. double
    cream, lightly whipped
juice of ½ lemon
salt and pepper
½ cucumber, diced

Fold the fillets in half and arrange in a well-greased ovenproof dish. Dot over the butter and add the lemon juice, pepper and parsley. Cover and put into the oven preheated to warm (170°C/325°F or Gas Mark 3). Bake the fish for 20 to 25 minutes, or until it is cooked and flakes easily. Transfer the fish to a warmed serving dish and keep hot.

Mix the mayonnaise, cream, lemon juice and salt and pepper together, then stir in the cucumber dice. Serve with the fish.

Serves 6

Sole in Red Wine

8 sole fillets, skinned
300 ml./10 fl. oz. red wine
5 ml./1 teaspoon grated
    lemon rind
1 small onion, thinly sliced
    into rings
salt and pepper
25 ml./1½ tablespoons beurre
    manié *

Fold the fillets in half and arrange in a well-greased ovenproof dish. Pour over the wine and scatter over the lemon rind and onion rings. Season to taste with salt and pepper. Put into the oven preheated to warm (170°C/325°F or Gas Mark 3) and bake the fish for 20 to 25 minutes, or until it is cooked and flakes easily. Transfer to a warmed serving dish and strain the liquid into a small saucepan. Bring to the boil. Stir in the beurre manié, a little at a time, until the mixture thickens somewhat. Pour over the fish.

Serves 4

Sardine Bake

675 g./1½ lb. fresh sardines,
    boned and heads removed
salt and pepper
5 ml./1 teaspoon grated
    nutmeg
3 tomatoes, skinned and
    sliced
1 onion, grated
25 g./1 oz. dry breadcrumbs
50 g./2 oz. butter, melted

Arrange the sardines in a well-greased baking dish. Sprinkle over salt and pepper to taste and the nutmeg. Cover with a layer of tomato slices, then sprinkle over the onion and breadcrumbs. Pour over the melted butter. Put into the oven preheated to moderate (180°C/350°F or Gas Mark 4) and bake for 15 to 20 minutes or until the fish is cooked and flakes easily.

Serves 4

Baked Minted Whitefish

4 medium whitefish
salt and pepper
2 lemons, thinly sliced
8 mint sprigs
30 ml./2 tablespoons lemon
    juice
10 ml./2 teaspoons finely
    grated lemon rind
40 g./1½ oz. butter, cut into
    small pieces

Rub the whitefish with the salt and pepper. Make slits along the side of each fish, then insert a halved lemon slice. Rub the cavity with a lemon slice and insert the mint sprigs. Put into a well-greased, shallow ovenproof dish. Sprinkle over the lemon juice and rind and dot over the butter pieces. Cover and put into the oven preheated to moderate (180°C/350°F or Gas Mark 4). Bake the fish for 20 to 25 minutes, or until it is cooked and flakes easily. Garnish with the remaining lemon slices.

Serves 4

Whiting and Bacon Whirls

6 small whiting fillets,
    skinned
2 eggs, beaten
75 g./3 oz. dry breadcrumbs
75 g./3 oz. butter
12 streaky bacon slices
3 tomatoes, thinly sliced

Dip the fillets in the beaten eggs, then in the breadcrumbs. Melt the butter in a frying-pan. Add the fillets and brown on all sides. Remove from the pan and carefully wrap two bacon slices round each fillet, securing with a wooden toothpick. Return the fillets to the pan, with the sliced tomatoes, and fry for a further 5 to 8 minutes, or until the bacon is cooked.

Serves 3

Whiting with Noodles

4 large whiting fillets,
    skinned
salt and pepper
125 g./4 oz. cream cheese,
    softened
10 ml./2 teaspoons lemon
    juice
175 g./6 oz. ribbon noodles
25 g./1 oz. butter
125 g./4 oz. mushrooms,
    sliced
125 g./4 oz. cooked peas
50 g./2 oz. cooked shelled
    shrimps

Place the fillets on the grill rack. Season to taste with salt and pepper, then spread over the cream cheese and lemon juice. Grill for 10 to 15 minutes, or until the fish is cooked and flakes easily.

Meanwhile, cook the noodles in boiling, salted water for 6 to 8 minutes or until they are 'al dente'. Drain.

Melt the butter in a saucepan. Add the mushrooms and fry for 3 minutes. Stir in the peas, shrimps, noodles and salt and pepper to taste and heat gently. Top with the fish.

Serves 4

Whiting with Parsley Sauce

4 large whiting fillets,
  skinned
300 ml./10 fl. oz. fish stock*
1 bouquet garni
salt and pepper
Sauce
25 g./1 oz. butter
30 ml./2 tablespoons flour
75 ml./3 fl. oz. milk or single
  cream
30 ml./2 tablespoons
  chopped fresh parsley

Fold the fillets in half and arrange in a well-greased ovenproof dish. Pour over the stock and add the bouquet garni and salt and pepper to taste. Put into the oven preheated to warm (170°C/325°F or Gas Mark 3) and bake the fish for 20 to 25 minutes or until it is cooked and flakes easily. Transfer to a warmed serving dish and keep hot. Strain the cooking liquid and reserve about 150 ml./5 fl. oz.

Melt the butter in a saucepan. Stir in the flour to form a smooth paste, then gradually stir in the reserved cooking liquid. Bring to the boil and simmer for 2 to 3 minutes, stirring constantly, or until thick. Stir in the milk or cream and parsley and heat gently for a further 2 minutes. Pour over the fish.

Serves 4

Piquant Fish Casserole

4 white fish fillets, skinned
salt and pepper
25 g./1 oz. butter
175 g./6 oz. mushrooms,
  sliced
30 ml./2 tablespoons
  chopped spring onions
5 ml./1 teaspoon chopped
  fresh parsley
150 ml./5 fl. oz. single cream
10 ml./2 teaspoons
  Angostura bitters

Arrange the fillets in a well-greased shallow oven-proof dish and sprinkle over the salt and pepper to taste. Melt the butter in a saucepan. Add the mushrooms and spring onions and fry for 3 minutes. Stir in the remaining ingredients and heat for 2 minutes. Pour over the fish and put into the oven preheated to warm (170°C/325°F or Gas Mark 3). Bake for 20 to 25 minutes, or until the fish is cooked and flakes easily.

Serves 4

Whiting Madeira

4 large whiting fillets,
  skinned
25 g./1 oz. flour
very finely grated rind and
  juice of 1 lemon
50 g./2 oz. butter
150 ml./5 fl. oz. Madeira
225 g./8 oz. cockles

Roll the fillets in the flour, then sprinkle over the lemon rind and juice. Melt the butter in a frying-pan. Add the fish and fry for 8 to 12 minutes, or until it is cooked and flakes easily. Stir in the wine and cockles and simmer gently until they are heated through.

Serves 4

194

Batter-Fried White Fish

8 small white fish fillets,
  skinned
75 g./3 oz. seasoned flour
oil for deep frying
1 lemon, cut into wedges
Batter
125 g./4 oz. flour
pinch of salt
1 egg
175 ml./6 fl. oz. milk

To make the batter, sift the flour and salt into a bowl. Gradually beat in the egg, then the milk to form a smooth batter. Roll up the fillets and secure them with wooden toothpicks. Dip them in the seasoned flour, then in the batter. Deep-fry for 4 to 5 minutes, or until crisp and golden brown. Drain on kitchen towels and garnish with lemon wedges.

Serves 4-6

Savoury Turbot Steaks

4 turbot steaks
salt and pepper
75 g./3 oz. butter
15 ml./1 tablespoon lemon
  juice
5 ml./1 teaspoon paprika
1 lemon, cut into wedges

Rub the steaks with salt and pepper. Put on the grill rack. Melt the butter in a saucepan and cook until it is a rich golden brown. Remove from the heat and stir in the lemon juice and paprika. Generously brush the mixture over the steaks and grill for 10 to 15 minutes, or until the fish is cooked and flakes easily. Baste with the butter occasionally during the cooking period. Garnish with the lemon wedges.

Serves 4

Tuna Mornay Scallops

1 × 225 g./8 oz. can tuna,
  drained and flaked
finely grated rind and juice
  of 1 lemon
15 ml./1 tablespoon chopped
  fresh parsley
350 ml./12 fl. oz. béchamel
  sauce*
50 g./2 oz. Cheddar cheese,
  grated
salt and pepper
1.25 ml./¼ teaspoon cayenne
  pepper
50 g./2 oz. toasted
  breadcrumbs
lemon segments to garnish

Arrange the flaked tuna in six or eight individual moulds or scallop shells. Sprinkle over the lemon rind and juice and parsley. Mix the béchamel sauce, cheese and seasonings together over low heat until the cheese has melted, then pour over the tuna. Sprinkle over the breadcrumbs.

Put the moulds or shells on a baking sheet and put into the oven preheated to moderate (180°C/350°F or Gas Mark 4). Cook for 15 to 20 minutes or until the sauce is browned and bubbly. Garnish with the lemon segments.

Serves 3-4

Tuna Fingers

350 g./12 oz. puff pastry*
4 tomatoes, thinly sliced
salt and pepper
15 ml./1 tablespoon dried
  basil
3 hard-boiled eggs, sliced
1 × 350 g./12 oz. can tuna,
  drained and flaked
grated rind and juice of 1
  lemon
1 egg, beaten

Divide the dough into two equal pieces. Roll out both pieces to oblongs about .75 cm./¼ in. thick. Transfer one piece to a baking sheet. Arrange the tomato slices over the dough, leaving a 1.25 cm./½ in. border all round. Sprinkle over salt and pepper to taste and the basil. Cover with a layer of egg slices, then the tuna. Sprinkle over the lemon rind and juice. Brush the dough edges with water, then cover with the remaining dough piece, crimping the edges to seal. Brush the beaten egg over the top and put into the oven preheated to very hot (230°C/450°F or Gas Mark 8). Bake for 15 minutes. Reduce the oven-temperature to warm (170°C/325°F or Gas Mark 3) and continue to bake for 10 to 15 minutes, or until golden brown and puffed up. Cut into fingers to serve.

Serves 4

Chiopino

75 ml./3 fl. oz. cooking oil
3 garlic cloves, crushed
1 green pepper, pith and
  seeds removed and
  chopped
1 × 400 g./14 oz. can
  tomatoes
30 ml./2 tablespoons tomato
  purée
salt and pepper
225 ml./8 fl. oz. chicken
  stock
1 kg./2 lb. white fish fillets,
  skinned and chopped
½ kg./1 lb. shelled shrimps
24 mussels
6 rounds toasted French
  bread

Heat the oil in a saucepan. Add 2 garlic cloves and the pepper and fry for 5 minutes. Stir in the tomatoes and can juice, tomato purée, salt and pepper to taste and stock. Bring to the boil, then simmer for 15 minutes. Stir in the fish fillets and shrimps and continue to simmer for a further 10 minutes.

Meanwhile fill a large saucepan with about 2.5 cm./1 in. of salted water. Add the mussels, cover and steam for 6 to 8 minutes or until the shells open (discard any that do not open).

Rub the remaining garlic over the toasted bread and put one round in each of six serving bowls. Pour over the chiopino and top with the steamed mussels.

Serves 6

Fish Chaudfroid

15 g./½ oz. aspic powder
5 ml./1 teaspoon gelatine
300 ml./10 fl. oz. water
300 ml./10 fl. oz. thick
    béchamel sauce*
6-8 portions of cooked fish,
    such as salmon, salmon
    trout or plaice
Garnish
1 lemon, thinly sliced
¼ cucumber, thinly sliced
1 small red pepper, pith and
    seeds removed and cut
    into thin strips

Mix the aspic and gelatine together, then add 15 ml./1 tablespoon of water. Bring the remaining water to the boil, then gradually stir into the aspic mixture until both the aspic and gelatine are dissolved. Cool, then stir in the béchamel sauce. Chill until the sauce stiffens and thickens slightly.

Arrange the fish on a serving dish and coat with the sauce. Arrange the garnish ingredients over the top and sides attractively, and chill until the sauce is firm and set.

Serves 6-8

Curried Fish

1 kg./2 lb. white fish fillets,
    skinned and halved
salt and pepper
juice of 2 lemons
5 ml./1 teaspoon turmeric
15 ml./1 tablespoon curry
    powder
oil for deep frying

Rub the fish pieces with the salt and pepper, then sprinkle over half the lemon juice. Set aside for 5 minutes, then sprinkle over the remaining lemon juice and rub generously with the turmeric and curry powder. Deep-fry for 5 to 8 minutes, or until golden brown. Drain on kitchen towels.

Serves 6

Fritto Misto

675 g./1½ lb. mixed fish (such
    as white fish fillets,
    shrimps, scallops etc.)
50 g./2 oz. seasoned flour
oil for deep frying
300 ml./10 fl. oz. tartare
    sauce*
Batter
125 g./4 oz. flour
pinch of salt
2 eggs, separated
150 ml./5 fl. oz. milk
30 ml./2 tablespoons water

To make the batter, sift the flour and salt into a bowl. Beat in the egg yolks, one at a time, then gradually beat in the milk and water to form a smooth batter. Beat the egg whites until they are stiff, then fold them into the batter.

Roll the fish in the seasoned flour, then dip in the batter. Deep-fry for 4 to 5 minutes, or until deep golden brown. Drain on kitchen towels and serve with the tartare sauce.

Serves 4-6

Devilled White Fish

10 ml./2 teaspoons
  Worcestershire sauce
2.5 ml./½ teaspoon curry
  powder
pinch of cayenne pepper
2.5 ml./½ teaspoon celery salt
25 g./1 oz. butter, melted
4 white fish fillets, skinned

Mix the Worcestershire sauce, curry powder, cayenne, celery salt and melted butter together. Put the fillets on the grill rack. Generously brush the butter mixture over the fillets and grill for 8 to 12 minutes, or until they are cooked and flake easily. Baste with the butter frequently during the cooking period.

Serves 4

Soused Fish

1 onion, sliced
6 herrings or mullets,
  cleaned and backbone
  removed
900 ml./1½ pints vinegar
300 ml./10 fl. oz. water
4 bay leaves
2 cloves
12 allspice berries
salt and pepper

Put a slice of onion in the centre of each fish. Roll up and secure with a wooden toothpick. Place in an ovenproof dish. Add all the remaining ingredients and put into the oven preheated to cool (150°C/300°F or Gas Mark 2). Bake for 3 hours, or until the fish is cooked and flakes easily. Transfer to a serving dish and strain over the cooking liquid. Cool, then chill until the cooking liquid has set into a soft jelly.

Serves 3-6

Mediterranean Fish Stew

50 ml./2 fl. oz. olive oil
1 kg./2 lb. firm fish (such as
  mullet, herring or
  mackerel), cleaned,
  heads, fins and tails
  removed, and cut into 5
  cm./2 in. pieces
1 onion, chopped
2 garlic cloves, crushed
1 × 675 g./1½ lb. can
  tomatoes
60 ml./4 tablespoons
  chopped fresh parsley
2 lemons, thinly sliced
450 g./1 lb. hot cooked long-
  grain rice

Heat the oil in a saucepan. Add the fish pieces, onion and garlic and fry until the fish is browned on all sides. Add the tomatoes and can juice, parsley and half the lemon slices and bring to the boil. Simmer for 15 minutes, or until the fish is cooked and flakes easily. Arrange the rice on a serving dish. Pour over the stew and garnish with the remaining lemon slices.

Serves 4-6

Fish Meunière

675 g./1½ lb. white fish fillets
  (such as whiting, sole,
  plaice, haddock, etc.),
  skinned
50 g./2 oz. seasoned flour
125 g./4 oz. butter
25 ml./1½ tablespoons lemon
  juice
chopped parsley to garnish

Roll the fillets in the seasoned flour. Melt the butter in a frying-pan. Add the fillets and fry for 8 to 12 minutes, or until they are cooked and flake easily. Transfer to a warmed serving dish.

Stir the lemon juice into the butter in the pan, then pour over the fish. Garnish with the parsley.

Serves 4

Clam Bake

1 × 225 g./8 oz. can
  sweetcorn, drained
125 g./4 oz. shelled shrimps
1 × 450 g./1 lb. can clams,
  drained
2 tomatoes, skinned and
  chopped
salt and pepper
15 ml./1 tablespoon chopped
  fresh parsley
225 ml./8 fl. oz. single cream
4 eggs, beaten
25 g./1 oz. Parmesan cheese,
  grated

Mix the sweetcorn, shrimps and clams together in a well-greased baking dish. Cover with the tomatoes, salt and pepper to taste and parsley.

Beat the remaining ingredients together and season to taste. Pour over the fish and stir to mix. Put into the oven preheated to moderate (180°C/350°F or Gas Mark 4) and bake for 20 to 30 minutes, or until the mixture has set.

Serves 4

Steamed Clams with Melted Butter

3 l./6 pints clams
salt and pepper
125 g./4 oz. butter, melted
15 ml./1 tablespoon finely
  chopped fresh parsley

Discard any clams that are open or have holes in them. Scrub and remove any surface blemishes, then wash in cold running water until the water is clear.

Fill a large saucepan with about 1.25 cm./½in. of salted water. Add the clams, cover and steam for 6 to 10 minutes, or until the shells open. (Discard any that do not open.) Transfer the clams to a warmed serving bowl and pour over the melted butter. Strain the cooking liquid into a jug and stir in the parsley. Serve with the clams.

Serves 4-6

Mussels in Mustard Brandy Sauce

3 l./6 pints mussels
50 g./2 oz. butter
2 onions, chopped
1 garlic clove, crushed
150 ml./5 fl. oz. water
salt and pepper
1 bouquet garni
25 g./1 oz. flour
150 ml./5 fl. oz. dry white
wine
10 ml./2 teaspoons prepared
mustard
75 ml./3 fl. oz. brandy
150 ml./5 fl. oz. single cream

Discard any mussels that are open or have holes in them. Scrub and remove any surface blemishes, then wash in cold running water until the water is clear.

Melt half the butter in a saucepan. Add the onions and garlic and fry for 5 minutes. Stir in the mussels, water, salt and pepper to taste and bouquet garni. Bring to the boil and simmer for 5 to 7 minutes or until the mussel shells open. (Discard any that do not open.) Strain and reserve the cooking liquid and onions. Remove the mussels from the shells and keep warm.

Melt the remaining butter in a saucepan. Stir in the flour to form a smooth paste. Gradually stir in the reserved cooking liquid and onions and wine and bring to the boil. Cook for 2 minutes, stirring constantly, or until the sauce thickens. Stir in the mustard, then the mussels, brandy and cream. Heat gently for 2 minutes.

Serves 4

Sautéed Prawns

125 g./4 oz. butter
675 g./1½ lb. large prawns
salt and pepper
15 ml./1 tablespoon chopped
fresh parsley
15 ml./1 tablespoon chopped
fresh fennel
juice of 2 lemons

Melt the butter in a frying-pan. Add the prawns and fry for 8 to 10 minutes, or until they turn pink all over. Shell the prawns and transfer to a large, warmed serving bowl. Sprinkle over salt and pepper to taste, parsley, fennel and lemon juice.

Serves 4

Prawns in Cream Sauce

½ kg./1 lb. shelled prawns
salt and pepper
125 g./4 oz. butter
50 ml./2 fl. oz. brandy,
warmed
300 ml./10 fl. oz. double
cream
10 ml./2 teaspoons finely
chopped fresh parsley
1 lemon, cut into wedges

Rub the prawns with the salt and pepper. Melt the butter in a frying-pan. Add the prawns and fry for 3 to 5 minutes, or until they are cooked through. Pour in the brandy and ignite. When the flames have died away, simmer for 2 minutes then stir in the cream. Cook for 2 minutes, then stir in the parsley. Garnish with the lemon wedges.

Serves 4

Curried Prawns

600 ml./1 pint chicken stock
125 g./4 oz. grated or
    desiccated coconut
50 ml./2 fl. oz. cooking oil
3 onions, chopped
4 celery stalks, chopped
1 apple, cored and chopped
3 large tomatoes, skinned
    and chopped
15 ml./1 tablespoon curry
    powder
2.5 ml./½ teaspoon ground
    ginger
2.5 ml./½ teaspoon turmeric
1.25 ml./¼ teaspoon cayenne
    pepper
pinch of cinnamon
salt and pepper
300 ml./10 fl. oz. white wine
juice of ½ lemon
15 ml./1 tablespoon
    redcurrant jelly
15 ml./1 tablespoon
    cornflour dissolved in 30
    ml./2 tablespoons water
½ kg./1 lb. shelled prawns

Put the stock in a saucepan and bring to the boil. Pour over the coconut, cover and set aside for 15 minutes. Strain and reserve the liquid.

Heat the oil in a saucepan. Add the onions and fry for 5 minutes. Add the celery, apple and tomatoes and fry for 3 minutes. Stir in the spices and seasoning, then add the strained coconut liquid and wine. Bring to the boil, cover and simmer for 45 minutes.

Strain, pressing as much of the vegetables through as possible. Stir in the lemon juice and jelly. Stir the cornflour mixture into the sauce and bring to the boil. Simmer for 2 minutes, stirring constantly, or until it thickens. Stir in the prawns and heat gently for 5 minutes.

Serves 4

Lobster Newburg

2 × 675 g./1½ lb. lobsters
50 g./2 oz. butter
50 ml./2 fl. oz. brandy
150 ml./5 fl. oz. Madeira
150 ml./5 fl. oz. double
    cream
salt and pepper
2 egg yolks

Put the lobsters in a large saucepan and just cover with water. Bring slowly to the boil, then simmer for 25 minutes. Drain and cool, then halve the lobsters and remove the meat. Reserve the shells.

Melt the butter in a frying-pan. Add the lobster meat and fry for 2 minutes. Pour over the brandy and ignite. When the flames have died away, stir in the Madeira and simmer for 5 minutes. Stir in 125 ml./4 fl. oz. of the cream and salt and pepper to taste and heat for 1 minute. Remove from the heat. Mix the egg yolks with the remaining cream and stir into the pan. Return to the heat and heat gently, without boiling, until the mixture thickens a little. Pour into the reserved shells.

Serves 4

Lobster Thermidor

2 × 675 g./1½ lb. lobsters
300 ml./10 fl. oz. milk
1 onion, sliced
3 cloves
1 bay leaf
25 g./1 oz. butter
30 ml./2 tablespoons flour
2 spring onions, chopped
150 ml./5 fl. oz. white wine
150 ml./5 fl. oz. double
   cream
salt and pepper
2.5 ml./½ teaspoon dry
   mustard
125 g./4 oz. Gruyère cheese,
   grated

Put the lobsters in a large saucepan and just cover with water. Bring slowly to the boil, then simmer for 25 minutes. Drain and cool, then halve the lobsters and remove the meat. Reserve the shells.

Put the milk, onion, cloves and bay leaf into a saucepan. Bring to the boil, cover and set aside for 10 minutes. Strain the milk.

Melt half the butter in a saucepan. Stir in the flour to form a smooth paste. Gradually stir in the milk and bring to the boil. Set the sauce aside.

Melt the remaining butter in another saucepan. Add the spring onions and fry for 3 minutes. Pour over the wine and boil until it has reduced by about half. Add the reserved sauce, cream, salt and pepper to taste and mustard to the pan and stir to mix. Add three-quarters of the grated cheese and the lobster meat and stir until the cheese melts. Spoon the mixture into the reserved lobster shells and sprinkle over the remaining grated cheese. Grill for 3 to 5 minutes or until the tops are brown and bubbly.

Serves 4

Dressed Crab

2 × 1 kg./2 lb. crabs
salt and pepper
5 ml./1 teaspoon dry mustard
2 hard-boiled eggs, separated
lettuce leaves to garnish

Put the crabs in a large saucepan and just cover with salted water. Bring slowly to the boil, then simmer for 30 minutes. Drain and cool.

Remove the large claws, then twist off the small ones and remove the undershells. Take out the small sacs from the crabs' shells, any green matter and the spongy lungs from around the large shell. Scrape the brown creamy part into a bowl. Remove the white meat and reserve the shells.

Crack the large claws, remove the meat and shred it. Mix all the white meat together. Mix the brown creamy part with salt and pepper to taste and the mustard. Place the brown mixture across the centre of the shells, with the white meat on either side. Chop the egg whites and yolks separately and garnish. Serve on a bed of lettuce leaves.

Serves 4

Crab Cakes

½ kg./1 lb. crabmeat, flaked
50 g./2 oz. fresh
   breadcrumbs
15 ml./1 tablespoon lemon
   juice
1 egg, beaten
salt and pepper
5 ml./1 teaspoon dried thyme
1.25 ml./¼ teaspoon cayenne
   pepper
1 hard-boiled egg, chopped
50 g./2 oz. seasoned flour
125 ml./4 fl. oz. cooking oil

Mix the crabmeat, breadcrumbs, lemon juice, egg, salt and pepper to taste, thyme, cayenne and chopped egg together. Shape into patties, then coat in the seasoned flour. Heat the oil in a frying-pan. Add the patties and fry for 6 to 12 minutes or until they are cooked through and browned.

Serves 4

Moules Marinières

3 l./6 pints mussels
150 ml./5 fl. oz. white wine
1 large onion, chopped
1 garlic clove, crushed
1 celery stalk, sliced
15 ml./1 tablespoon chopped
   fresh parsley

Discard any mussels that are open or have holes in them. Scrub and remove any surface blemishes, then wash in cold running water until the water is clear. Put the mussels in a large, wide saucepan and add all the remaining ingredients. Bring to the boil and simmer for 5 to 7 minutes or until the mussel shells open. (Discard any that do not open.) Remove the empty shell halves and transfer the mussels and liquid to a warmed serving bowl.

Serves 4

Fried Scallops

60 ml./4 tablespoons lemon
   juice
15 ml./1 tablespoon cooking
   oil
5 ml./1 teaspoon salt
2.5 ml./½ teaspoon paprika
30 ml./2 tablespoons
   chopped fresh parsley
8 scallops, shelled
2 eggs, beaten
50 g./2 oz. dry breadcrumbs
30 ml./2 tablespoons grated
   cheese
oil for deep frying
1 lemon, cut into wedges

Mix the lemon juice, oil, salt, paprika and parsley together. Add the scallops and marinate at room temperature for 1 hour.

Drain the scallops and dry on kitchen towels. Dip in the beaten eggs. Mix the breadcrumbs with the grated cheese, then dip the scallops into the mixture. Deep-fry for 3 to 5 minutes, or until deep golden brown. Drain on kitchen towels and garnish with lemon.

Serves 4

Scallops in Cream Sauce

300 ml./10 fl. oz. white wine
8 scallops, shelled
50 g./2 oz. butter
50 g./2 oz. mushrooms, sliced
30 ml./2 tablespoons chopped fresh chives
10 ml./2 teaspoons chopped fresh parsley
salt and pepper
5 ml./1 teaspoon curry powder
30 ml./2 tablespoons flour
75 ml./3 fl. oz. single cream
50 g./2 oz. toasted breadcrumbs

Put the wine in a saucepan and bring to the boil. Add the scallops and simmer for 3 minutes. Drain and reserve the liquid.

Melt the butter in a saucepan. Add the mushrooms and chives and fry for 3 minutes. Stir in the parsley, salt and pepper to taste, curry powder and flour to form a smooth paste. Gradually stir in the reserved cooking liquid and bring to the boil. Simmer for 2 minutes, stirring constantly, or until the sauce thickens.

Stir in the scallops and cream. Spoon the mixture into greased scallop or individual flameproof dishes. Sprinkle over the breadcrumbs and grill for 5 minutes, or until the tops are brown.

Serves 4

Barbecued Scallops

1 kg./2 lb. scallops, shelled
1 garlic clove, crushed
5 ml./1 teaspoon finely chopped fresh root ginger
15 ml./1 tablespoon sugar
125 ml./4 fl. oz. soy sauce
125 ml./4 fl. oz. dry sherry or sake
1 green pepper, pith and seeds removed and cut into 2.5 cm./1 in. pieces
125 g./4 oz. small mushrooms

Put the scallops into a wide shallow bowl and stir in the garlic, ginger, sugar, soy sauce and sherry or sake. Marinate at room temperature for 2 hours. Drain and thread on to six skewers with the pepper and mushrooms. Put the skewers on the grill rack. Brush with the reserved marinade and grill for 5 minutes. Reduce the heat to moderate and continue to grill for 5 to 8 minutes, or until the scallops are cooked through. Baste with the marinade occasionally during the cooking period.

Serves 6

Scampi with Tartare Sauce

24 frozen scampi (large shrimps), thawed
50 g./2 oz. seasoned flour
2 eggs, beaten
50 g./2 oz. dry breadcrumbs
oil for deep frying
300 ml./10 fl. oz. tartare sauce*

Roll the scampi in the seasoned flour, then the eggs and finally in the breadcrumbs. Set aside for 10 minutes. Deep-fry for 3 to 5 minutes, or until crisp and golden brown. Drain on kitchen towels and serve with tartare sauce.

Serves 4

Shrimps Creole

50 ml./2 fl. oz. cooking oil
2 onions, chopped
1 garlic clove, crushed
1 large green pepper, pith
  and seeds removed and
  chopped
1 small red pepper, pith and
  seeds removed and
  chopped
1 × 400 g./14 oz. can
  tomatoes
125 ml./4 fl. oz. chicken
  stock
15 ml./1 tablespoon vinegar
15 ml./1 tablespoon brown
  sugar
salt and pepper
5 ml./1 teaspoon chilli
  seasoning
½ kg./1 lb. shelled shrimps

Heat the oil in a saucepan. Add the onions, garlic
and peppers and fry for 5 minutes. Stir in the
tomatoes and can juice, stock, vinegar, sugar, salt
and pepper to taste and chilli seasoning. Bring to
the boil, then simmer for 15 minutes.

Stir in the shrimps and simmer for 5 to 6 minutes
or until they are cooked through.

Serves 4

Shrimps Provençal

50 ml./2 tablespoons cooking
  oil
1 onion, finely chopped
1 garlic clove, crushed
1 red pepper, pith and seeds
  removed and chopped
2 celery stalks, chopped
6 tomatoes, skinned and
  chopped
5 ml./1 teaspoon grated
  lemon rind
salt and pepper
125 ml./4 fl. oz. chicken
  stock
6 black olives, chopped
½ kg./1 lb. shelled shrimps

Heat the oil in a saucepan. Add the onion, garlic,
pepper and celery and fry for 5 minutes. Add the
tomatoes, lemon rind, salt and pepper to taste and
stock and bring to the boil. Simmer for 20 minutes.

Stir in the olives and shrimps and continue to
simmer for 5 to 6 minutes, or until the shrimps are
cooked through.

Serves 4

Vegetable Dishes

Baked Artichokes

2 garlic cloves, crushed
30 ml./2 tablespoons
    chopped fresh parsley
25 g./1 oz. butter
salt and pepper
4 globe artichokes, stalks
    removed and the tips of the
    leaves trimmed
300 ml./10 fl. oz. hot water
oil
50 g./2 oz. butter, melted

Put the garlic, parsley, butter and a little salt and
pepper in a mortar and pound until the mixture is
smooth. Put little dabs of this mixture between the
leaves of the artichokes. Arrange them in a shallow
ovenproof dish, pour in the hot water and sprinkle
each artichoke with a little oil. Cover and put into
the oven preheated to moderate (180°C/350°F or
Gas Mark 4). Bake for 40 minutes, or tender. Pour
over the melted butter.

Serves 4

Stuffed Artichokes

4 globe artichokes, stalks
    and outer leaves removed
25 g./1 oz. butter
½ small onion, finely chopped
1 garlic clove, crushed
4 mushrooms, sliced
30 ml./2 tablespoons fresh
    breadcrumbs
15 ml./1 tablespoon chopped
    fresh parsley
salt and pepper
30 ml./2 tablespoons oil
125 ml./4 fl. oz. white wine

Cut off about 2.5 cm./1 in. from the tops of the
artichokes. Pull the leaves apart and carefully
remove the chokes. Melt the butter in a saucepan.
Add the onion, garlic and mushrooms and fry for 5
minutes. Stir in the breadcrumbs and parsley and
season to taste with salt and pepper. Use this mixture to stuff the artichokes.

Heat the oil in a saucepan large enough to hold
all the artichokes. Put them in the pan and add the
wine. Cover and simmer for 1 hour.

Serves 4

Artichokes in Vinaigrette

4 globe artichokes
½ lemon
salt
125 ml./4 fl. oz. French dressing*

Remove and discard the coarse outer leaves of the artichokes. Slice off the stems and rub the base with the lemon half. Cook in boiling, salted water, to which a squeeze of lemon juice has been added, for 40 minutes or until the artichokes are tender. Test by pulling off a leaf; if it comes away easily the artichokes are cooked. Remove from the pan, drain upside down and cool. Carefully remove the chokes and serve the artichokes with the French dressing.

Serves 4

Asparagus with Hollandaise Sauce

1 bunch asparagus spears
salt
150 ml./5 fl. oz. Hollandaise sauce*

Cut off the tough ends of the asparagus spears so that they are all about the same length. Scrape off the skin at the cut end for about 2.5 cm./1 in. Wash the spears and tie them into a bundle. Bring a saucepan of salted water to the boil and stand the asparagus in it so that the tips are above the water. Cover with foil and simmer for 12 to 15 minutes or until the asparagus is tender. Carefully lift out, drain and untie the spears.
Serve hot with Hollandaise sauce.

Serves 3

Aubergines with Cheese and Tomatoes

1 kg./2 lb. aubergines, peeled, sliced lengthways and dégorged
flour
75 ml./3 fl. oz. oil
225 g./8 oz. Mozzarella cheese, sliced
150 ml./5 fl. oz. tomato sauce*
50 g./2 oz. Parmesan cheese, grated

Sprinkle the aubergines lightly with flour. Heat the oil in a large frying-pan. Add the aubergine slices and fry for 5 minutes or until they are evenly browned. Arrange a layer of aubergine slices on the bottom of a well-greased ovenproof dish. Cover with a thin layer of cheese and then a little tomato sauce. Continue making layers until all the ingredients are used up. Top with grated Parmesan and sprinkle over a little oil. Put into the oven pre-heated to moderate (180°C/350°F or Gas Mark 4) and bake for 25 minutes.

Serves 6

Aubergines Gratinées

30 ml./2 tablespoons oil
2 large aubergines, halved
   lengthways and dégorged
225 g./8 oz. cooked ham,
   finely chopped
30 ml./2 tablespoons
   chopped spring onions
50 g./2 oz. fresh
   breadcrumbs
30 ml./2 tablespoons
   chopped fresh parsley
2 eggs, beaten
salt and pepper
50 g./2 oz. dry breadcrumbs
50 g./2 oz. Parmesan cheese,
  grated
40 g./1½ oz. butter

Heat the oil in a frying-pan. Add the aubergine halves and fry for 5 minutes or until they are evenly browned. Arrange in a shallow ovenproof dish, cut side uppermost. Mix together the ham, spring onions, fresh breadcrumbs, parsley and eggs. Season well and spread this mixture over the aubergines. Sprinkle over the dry breadcrumbs and cheese and dot with pieces of butter. Put into the oven preheated to moderate (180°C/350°F or Gas Mark 4) and bake for 25 minutes.

Serves 4

Beans Niçoise

30 ml./2 tablespoons oil
1 small onion, chopped
1 garlic clove, crushed
½ kg./1 lb. tomatoes, skinned
   and chopped
½ kg./1 lb. runner beans,
   sliced, cooked and
   cooking liquid reserved
salt and pepper
30 ml./2 tablespoons
   chopped fresh parsley

Heat the oil in a saucepan. Add the onion and garlic and fry for 5 minutes. Add the tomatoes and cook for 2 minutes. Add the beans with 150 ml./5 fl. oz. of the reserved cooking liquid and season to taste. Simmer for 5 minutes or until the beans are heated through. Garnish with the parsley.

Serves 4

French Beans Almondine

50 g./2 oz. butter
25 g./1 oz. almonds, slivered
pinch of salt
10 ml./2 teaspoons lemon
   juice
½ kg./1 lb. hot cooked French
   beans, drained

Melt the butter in a saucepan. Add the almonds and sauté for 2 to 3 minutes or until they are lightly browned. Stir in the salt and lemon juice and pour over the beans.

Serves 4

Stuffed Aubergines

3 large aubergines, halved
 lengthways
90 ml./6 tablespoons fresh
 breadcrumbs
15 ml./1 tablespoon chopped
 fresh parsley
2.5 ml./½ teaspoon dried
 oregano
6 anchovy fillets, finely
 chopped
12 large black olives, stoned
 and chopped
3 tomatoes, skinned and
 chopped
50 ml./2 fl. oz. oil

Scoop out most of the aubergine flesh, put it in a basin and mash well. Add the breadcrumbs, parsley, oregano, anchovy fillets, olives and tomatoes and mix well. Fill the aubergine halves with this mixture. Arrange them in a shallow, greased ovenproof dish and pour over the oil. Cover and put into the oven preheated to moderate (180°C/350°F or Gas Mark 4). Bake for 1 hour.

Serves 6

Runner Beans with Carrots

225 g./8 oz. carrots, thinly
 sliced
salt and pepper
½ kg./1 lb. runner beans,
 thinly sliced
30 ml./2 tablespoons oil

Put the carrots in a saucepan and cover with 2.5 cm./1 in. of water. Season with salt and pepper, cover and cook for 10 minutes. Add the beans and oil and continue cooking for a further 20 minutes or until the vegetables are very tender and most of the water has evaporated. Drain off any remaining water.

Serves 4

Beans with Sweet Peppers

4 streaky bacon slices, cut
 into strips
½ kg./1 lb. hot cooked French
 beans, drained
45 ml./3 tablespoons diced
 red peppers
45 ml./3 tablespoons red
 wine vinegar
2.5 ml./½ teaspoon sugar
1.25 ml./¼ teaspoon dry
 mustard
3-4 drops of Tabasco sauce

Fry the bacon in a frying-pan until crisp. Drain on kitchen towels and mix with the beans. Keep hot. Add the peppers, vinegar, sugar and mustard to the fat in the pan and bring to the boil. Stir in the Tabasco sauce and pour over the beans and bacon.

Serves 4

Boston Baked Beans

½ kg./1 lb. dried haricot
   beans, soaked in cold
   water for 12 hours
2 large tomatoes, skinned
   and chopped
30 ml./2 tablespoons black
   treacle
10 ml./2 teaspoons mustard
salt and pepper
350 g./12 oz. fat salt pork,
   diced
2 onions, thinly sliced

Simmer the beans in the soaking water for 15
minutes. Drain, reserving 300 ml./10 fl. oz. of the
cooking liquid. Pour the liquid into a saucepan,
add the tomatoes and simmer for 10 minutes.
Strain the liquid and return it to the pan. Add the
treacle, mustard and a generous amount of seasoning.

Put the beans, pork and onions into a deep ovenproof dish. Pour over the tomato sauce and stir
well. Allow plenty of space for the beans to swell
during cooking. Cover and put into the oven preheated to very cool (140°C/275°F or Gas Mark 1).
Cook for 5 hours. After 2½ hours, examine the
beans. If they are still very hard, raise the oven
temperature a little; if they are becoming too dry,
add a little boiling water.

Serves 8

Russian Cabbage

50 g./2 oz. butter
1 large onion, chopped
2 dessert apples, peeled and
   sliced
1 small red cabbage,
   shredded, cooked and
   drained

Melt the butter in a saucepan. Add the onion and
apples and fry for 5 minutes. Stir in the cabbage
and mix well. Continue cooking for 3 minutes or
until the cabbage is heated through.

Serves 4-6

Sweet and Sour Cabbage

½ small red cabbage,
   shredded
1 tart apple, peeled, cored
   and sliced
1 onion, thinly sliced
salt and pepper
15 ml./1 tablespoon sugar
1 bay leaf
pinch of thyme
15 ml./1 tablespoon port
15 ml./1 tablespoon wine
   vinegar

Put the cabbage in a large ovenproof dish in alter-
nate layers with the apple and onion. Season each
layer with salt, pepper and sugar. Put the herbs in
the middle layer. Pour over the port and vinegar.
Cover and put into the oven preheated to cool
(150°C/300°F or Gas Mark 2). Bake for 2 hours or
until the cabbage is tender.

Serves 4

Curried Cabbage

1 medium cabbage,
   shredded
75 g./3 oz. butter
10 ml./2 teaspoons chutney
2.5 ml./½ teaspoon curry
   powder
grated rind and juice of 1
   lemon

Blanch the cabbage in boiling salted water for 4 minutes. Drain well and keep hot. Melt the butter in a small saucepan. Add the chutney, curry powder, lemon rind and juice. Pour over the cabbage and leave in a warm place for 10 minutes before serving.

Serves 4

Cabbage with Bacon and Fennel

4 streaky bacon slices,
   chopped
1 small, firm cabbage,
   shredded
600 ml./1 pint water
15 ml./1 tablespoon vinegar
salt and pepper
5 ml./1 teaspoon fennel seeds

Fry the bacon in a large saucepan until the fat begins to run. Add the cabbage, water, vinegar, salt and pepper to taste and fennel seeds. Cook gently for 10-15 minutes or until the cabbage is tender and most of the liquid has evaporated.

Serves 6-8

Cauliflower Basket

1 hot cooked cauliflower,
   drained and 150 ml./5 fl.
   oz. cooking liquid reserved
Sauce
25 g./1 oz. butter
25 g./1 oz. flour
150 ml./5 fl. oz. milk
salt and pepper
125 g./4 oz. Cheddar cheese,
   grated
2 hard-boiled eggs, chopped
15 ml./1 tablespoon chopped
   gherkins
15 ml./1 tablespoon chopped
   fresh parsley
15 ml./1 tablespoon chopped
   chives

Melt the butter in a saucepan. Stir in the flour to form a smooth paste. Gradually add the milk and reserved cooking liquid and bring to the boil, stirring constantly. Season with salt and pepper to taste and stir in nearly all the cheese.

Mix together the eggs, gherkins, parsley and chives. Scoop out the centre of the cauliflower and chop coarsely. Add this to the egg mixture and stir it all into the sauce. Stand the cauliflower in a heated flameproof serving dish and pile the cheese sauce mixture into the centre. Top with the remainder of the cheese and grill for 2 to 3 minutes or until the top is lightly browned.

Serves 4

Cauliflower Fritters

1 cauliflower, cooked and
    separated into flowerets
oil for deep frying
Batter
125 g./4 oz. flour
pinch of salt
2 eggs, separated
150 ml./5 fl. oz. water
60 ml./4 tablespoons milk

To make the batter, sift the flour and salt into a bowl. Add the egg yolks, water and milk and mix well. Beat the egg whites until they are stiff and carefully fold into the mixture. Dip the flowerets into the batter and deep fry, a few at a time for 1 to 2 minutes or until they are golden brown. Drain on kitchen towels and serve hot.

Serves 4-6

Cauliflour with Brown Sauce Topping

1 cauliflower, divided into
    flowerets
salt
tomato juice
25 g./1 oz. butter
25 g./1 oz. flour
yeast extract
chopped parsley to garnish

Cook the cauliflower in boiling salted water for 15 to 20 minutes or until tender. Drain and reserve the cooking liquid. Keep the cauliflower hot while you make the sauce. Measure the cooking liquid and add enough tomato juice to make just over 300 ml./10 fl. oz.

Melt the butter in a saucepan. Stir in the flour to form a smooth paste. Gradually add the cooking liquid mixture and bring to the boil, stirring constantly. Cook for 2 to 3 minutes, or until the sauce thickens. Stir in yeast extract to taste. Spoon the sauce over the cauliflower and garnish with the parsley.

Serves 4

Carrots Vichy

350 g./12 oz. small new
    carrots, sliced
25 g./1 oz. butter
salt
10 ml./2 teaspoons sugar
425 ml./15 fl. oz. water
chopped parsley to garnish

Put the carrots, 15 g./½ oz. of the butter, salt to taste, sugar and water in a saucepan. Cook for 8 to 10 minutes or until the carrots are tender and most of the water has evaporated. If there is any water left, drain it off. Add the rest of the butter and allow to melt, shaking the pan to prevent the carrots sticking. Garnish with the parsley.

Serves 4

Courgettes with Ham

½ kg./1 lb. courgettes, sliced
50 g./2 oz. seasoned flour
50 ml./2 fl. oz. oil
2 onions, chopped
1 garlic clove, crushed
225 g./8 oz. ham, cut into
    four slices
50 g./2 oz. Parmesan cheese,
    grated

Roll the courgette slices in the seasoned flour. Heat the oil in a large frying-pan. Add the onions and garlic and fry for 5 minutes. Add the ham and fry for 5 minutes or until browned. Transfer the ham and onions to two plates. Add the courgette slices to the pan, adding more oil if necessary, and fry for 4 to 6 minutes or until they are lightly browned.

Arrange three quarters of the courgette slices in a well-greased, ovenproof dish. Sprinkle with half of the onions and half of the grated cheese. Put the ham slices on top, sprinkle with the remaining onion and cheese and top with the remaining courgettes. Put the dish into the oven preheated to fairly hot (190°C/375°F or Gas Mark 5) and bake for 15 minutes.

Serves 4

Stuffed Courgettes

1 large slice of bread, crusts
    removed
milk
½ kg./1 lb. courgettes
4 mushrooms, chopped
2 anchovy fillets, chopped
2 bacon slices, chopped
45 ml./3 tablespoons grated
    Parmesan cheese
5 ml./1 teaspoon chopped
    fresh basil
salt and pepper
1 egg yolk
10 ml./2 teaspoons fresh
    breadcrumbs
oil

Soak the bread for 10 minutes in a little milk, then squeeze dry. Blanch the courgettes in boiling salted water for 3 minutes and drain. Cut the courgettes in half lengthways and scoop out the flesh with a teaspoon. Mix together the mushrooms, anchovy fillets, bacon, 30 ml./2 tablespoons of the cheese, basil, soaked bread and courgette flesh. Season with salt and pepper to taste and bind together with the egg yolk. Fill the courgette halves with this mixture and arrange them in a lightly-oiled ovenproof dish. Mix the remaining cheese with the breadcrumbs and sprinkle over the top. Sprinkle with a little oil and put into the oven preheated to moderate (180°C/350°F or Gas Mark 4). Bake for 40 minutes, or until the courgettes are tender.

Serves 4

Braised Celery

2 small heads of celery,
  trimmed, blanched for 10
  minutes in boiling water
  and drained
300 ml./10 fl. oz. chicken
  stock
15 g./½ oz. butter
1 small onion, chopped
15 ml./1 tablespoon flour
salt and pepper
paprika

Tie up the blanched celery heads and put in a saucepan with the stock. Cover and bring to the boil. Simmer for 20 minutes or until tender. Drain, remove the string and keep the celery hot. Reserve 300 ml./10 fl. oz. of the cooking liquid making up this amount with water if necessary.

Melt the butter in a saucepan. Add the onion and fry for 5 minutes. Stir in the flour to form a smooth paste, then gradually stir in the reserved stock. Bring to the boil, stirring constantly. Cook for 2 to 3 minutes, or until the sauce thickens. Season to taste with the salt and pepper, pour over the celery and sprinkle with paprika.

Serves 4

Braised Chicory

675 g./1½ lb. chicory
25 g./1 oz. butter
50 ml./2 fl. oz. water
5 ml./1 teaspoon lemon juice
5 ml./1 teaspoon sugar
salt and pepper

Blanch the chicory in boiling water for 2 minutes. Drain and rinse with cold water. Use half the butter to grease a shallow ovenproof dish. Arrange the chicory in the dish. Mix together the remaining ingredients and add to the chicory. Dot with the remaining butter and cover with foil. Put the dish into the oven preheated to cool (150°C/300°F or Gas Mark 2) and cook for 1 to 1¼ hours, or until the chicory is tender. Serve with the cooking juices.

Serves 4

Chicory au Gratin

675 g./1½ lb. chicory,
  quartered lengthways
juice of 1 lemon
25 g./1 oz. butter, cut into
  small pieces
5 ml./1 teaspoon sugar
salt and pepper
Topping
50 g./2 oz. Parmesan cheese,
  grated
25 g./1 oz. dry breadcrumbs

Arrange the chicory in a greased, shallow ovenproof dish. Add the lemon juice and turn the chicory in it until it is well coated. Dot with the butter and sprinkle over the sugar. Season with salt and pepper to taste. Cover tightly and put into the oven preheated to moderate (180°C/350°F or Gas Mark 4). Cook for 45 minutes, or until just tender. Uncover and sprinkle over the cheese and breadcrumbs. Return to the oven and cook for a further 5 to 10 minutes or until the top is golden brown.

Serves 4

Chicory Soufflé

8 heads of chicory
300 ml./10 fl. oz. béchamel
    sauce *
3 egg yolks, beaten
salt and pepper
pinch of grated nutmeg
3 egg whites, stiffly beaten

Cook the chicory in boiling salted water for 20 minutes. Drain and chop finely. Add to the sauce with the egg yolks, salt and pepper to taste and nutmeg. Fold in the egg whites and spoon into a buttered soufflé dish. Put into the oven preheated to fairly hot (190°C/375°F or Gas Mark 5) and bake for 20 minutes, or until the soufflé has risen and is golden brown.

Serves 4

Corn on the Cob with Lemon Butter Sauce

4 ears of corn, leaves and silk
    removed
Sauce
125 g./4 oz. butter
salt and pepper
25 ml./1 fl. oz. lemon juice
pinch of grated nutmeg

Put the corn in a large saucepan of boiling water. Simmer for 5 to 8 minutes or until tender. Meanwhile, put all the sauce ingredients in a small saucepan and heat gently. Toss the drained corn in the sauce and serve hot, with the remaining sauce.

Serves 4

Buttered Cucumbers

2 medium cucumbers, peeled
    and thickly sliced
50 g./2 oz. butter
salt and pepper
lemon juice
chopped fresh parsley to
    garnish

Blanch the cucumber slices in boiling salted water for 2 minutes. Drain well. Melt the butter in a frying-pan. Add the cucumber and salt and pepper to taste and fry for 3 to 5 minutes or until lightly browned. Do not overcook. Add a good squeeze of lemon juice and stir well. Garnish with the parsley.

Serves 4

French-Fried Fennel

1 fennel root, sliced
50 g./2 oz. flour
1 egg
125 ml./4 fl. oz. milk
salt and pepper
oil for deep frying

Push the fennel slices out into rings. Beat the flour, egg and milk to a smooth batter and season to taste with salt and pepper. Dip the fennel rings into the batter and deep fry, a few at a time for 2 to 3 minutes, or until crisp and golden brown. Drain on kitchen towels and serve hot.

Serves 4

Leeks in Cheese Sauce

25 g./1 oz. butter
25 g./1 oz. flour
300 ml./10 fl. oz. milk
125 g./4 oz. cheese, grated
salt and pepper
4 hot cooked leeks, drained

Melt the butter in a saucepan and stir in the flour to form a smooth paste. Gradually add the milk and bring to the boil, stirring constantly. Cook for 2 to 3 minutes, or until the sauce thickens. Add most of the cheese and season to taste. Stir well until the cheese has melted.

Arrange the leeks in a shallow flameproof dish and pour over the sauce. Sprinkle over the remaining cheese. Grill for 5 minutes, or until the top is golden brown.

Serves 4

Marrow with Tomatoes

50 ml./2 fl. oz. oil
1 large onion, chopped
4 tomatoes, skinned and
    chopped
125 ml./4 fl. oz. tomato juice
salt and pepper
2.5 ml./$\frac{1}{2}$ teaspoon dried
    mixed herbs
1 kg./2 lb. marrow, peeled,
    seeded and cubed
50 g./2 oz. Parmesan cheese,
    grated

Heat the oil in a saucepan. Add the onion and fry for 5 minutes. Add the tomatoes and fry for 1 minute. Stir in the tomato juice, salt and pepper to taste and herbs, and cook for 3 minutes. Add the marrow cubes. Cover and simmer for 30 minutes, or until the marrow is tender. Sprinkle over the cheese.

Serves 6-8

Mushrooms in Cream Sauce

25 g./1 oz. butter
15 ml./1 tablespoon oil
225 g./8 oz. mushrooms,
    thinly sliced
salt and pepper
pinch of grated nutmeg
15 ml./1 tablespoon chopped
    fresh parsley
$\frac{1}{2}$ shallot, finely chopped
50 ml./2 fl. oz. double cream

Heat the butter and oil in a frying-pan. Add the mushrooms and cook for 1 minute. Add salt and pepper to taste, nutmeg, parsley and shallot and continue to cook for 5 minutes. Stir in the cream and cook for a further 3 minutes, or until the cream is heated through.

Serves 4

Herb-Stuffed Mushrooms

½ kg./1 lb. large cup-shaped
    mushrooms
50 g./2 oz. cooked ham,
    diced
2.5 ml./½ teaspoon dried
    oregano
pinch of dried thyme
5 ml./1 teaspoon chopped
    fresh parsley
30 ml./2 tablespoons grated
    Parmesan cheese
30 ml./2 tablespoons fresh
    breadcrumbs
salt and pepper
oil

Remove the stalks from the mushrooms and chop them finely. Mix the chopped stalks with the ham, herbs, cheese and breadcrumbs. Season to taste. Put the mushroom caps in a shallow ovenproof dish and fill each cap with some of the ham mixture. Pour a little oil over each mushroom. Cover and put the dish into the oven preheated to moderate (180°C/350°F or Gas Mark 4). Bake for 20 to 25 minutes, or until the mushrooms are tender. Add a little extra oil, if necessary, while the mushrooms are cooking so that they do not become too dry.

Serves 4

Creamed Mushrooms

3 large slices white bread,
    crusts removed and diced
50 ml./2 fl. oz. oil
½ kg./1 lb. mushrooms, sliced
juice of 1 lemon
3 egg yolks, beaten
300 ml./10 fl. oz. double
    cream
salt and pepper
4 hot grilled bacon slices,
    diced

Fry the diced bread in the oil until golden brown. Drain on kitchen towels.

Put the mushrooms in a saucepan with the lemon juice and sufficient water to cover. Bring to the boil and simmer for 2 minutes. Drain thoroughly. Beat the egg yolks with the cream in a heatproof bowl set over a pan of simmering water until thick. Add the mushrooms and season to taste with salt and pepper. Turn into a shallow warmed serving dish and top with the fried bread and bacon.

Serves 4

Baked Onions

8 large onions
50 g./2 oz. butter, cut into
    small pieces
salt and pepper

Dot the onions with the butter and season with salt and pepper to taste. Wrap each onion in foil and place on a baking sheet. Put into the oven preheated to moderate (180°C/350°F or Gas Mark 4) and bake for about 1½ hours, or until tender.

Serves 4

Green Peas with Ham

50 g./2 oz. butter
1 small onion, finely
  chopped
½ kg./1 lb. shelled small peas
50 ml./2 fl. oz. water
salt
50 g./2 oz. cooked ham, cut
  into thin strips

Melt the butter in a saucepan. Add the onion and fry for 5 minutes. Add the peas, water and salt to taste, and cook for 5 minutes. Add the ham and continue to cook very gently for a further 10 to 15 minutes or until the peas are tender.

Serves 4

Peas Cooked with Lettuce

½ small lettuce
½ kg./1 lb. shelled fresh peas
4 spring onions, chopped
1 mint sprig
30 ml./2 tablespoons water
50 g./2 oz. butter
2.5 ml./½ teaspoon salt
5 ml./1 teaspoon sugar

Put the lettuce in a saucepan and add the remaining ingredients. Cover tightly and simmer for 20 minutes, or until the peas are tender. Remove the lettuce and mint and turn the peas into a warmed serving dish.

Serves 4

Stuffed Onions

350 g./12 oz. cooked beef,
  minced
75 g./3 oz. butter, melted
75 g./3 oz. fresh
  breadcrumbs
pinch of dried sage
15 ml./1 tablespoon chopped
  fresh parsley
salt and pepper
4 large onions

Mix the meat with half of the butter, the bread-crumbs and herbs. Season with salt and pepper to taste.

Boil the onions in salted water for 30 minutes, or until the outsides are tender. Drain and cool. Remove the centre of each onion, chop coarsely and add to the meat mixture. Brush the bottom of an ovenproof dish with some of the remaining melted butter and put the onion shells in the dish. Spoon the meat mixture into the onions, piling it quite high. Pour the remaining butter over the top. Put the dish into the oven preheated to moderate (180°C/350°F or Gas Mark 4) and bake for 1 hour. If the stuffing is becoming too brown, cover the dish with foil.

Serves 4

218

Onions à la King

about 24 small pickling or
    pearl onions
salt and pepper
1 green pepper, pith and
    seeds removed and cut
    into thin strips
4 eggs
40 g./1½ oz. butter
40 g./1½ oz. flour
425 ml./15 fl. oz. milk
60 ml./4 tablespoons canned
    sweetcorn

Cook the onions in boiling salted water for 20 minutes or until just tender. Add the pepper strips for the last 5 minutes. Drain and keep warm.

Meanwhile, boil the eggs until just firm. Shell and slice, and set aside. Melt the butter in a saucepan and stir in the flour to form a smooth paste. Gradually add the milk and bring to the boil, stirring constantly. Cook for 2 to 3 minutes or until the sauce thickens. Add the sweetcorn, sliced eggs, drained onions and peppers to the sauce and season well. Heat for 2 minutes.

Serves 4

Parsnip Croquettes

½ kg./1 lb. parsnips, diced
125 ml./4 fl. oz. milk
25 g./1 oz. butter
30 ml./2 tablespoons
    chopped chives
1 egg
30 ml./2 tablespoons flour
2 bacon slices, grilled and
    chopped
salt and pepper
50 g./2 oz. seasoned flour
2 eggs, beaten
125 g./4 oz. dry breadcrumbs
oil for deep frying

Put the parsnips in a saucepan with the milk. Cover and simmer for 25 minutes, or until they are tender and most of the liquid is absorbed. Mash well and add the butter, chives, egg, flour and bacon. Season with salt and pepper and mix well. Cool. Roll spoonfuls of the parsnip mixture in the seasoned flour, then shape into croquettes. Roll first in the beaten eggs and then in the breadcrumbs. Chill for 1 hour to firm, then deep fry for 2 to 3 minutes or until golden brown. Drain on kitchen towels.

Serves 4

Red Peppers with Tomatoes

75 ml./3 fl. oz. oil
15 g./½ oz. butter
1 small onion, finely
    chopped
½ garlic clove, crushed
4 red peppers, pith and seeds
    removed and cut into strips
salt and pepper
4 large tomatoes, skinned
    and quartered
chopped parsley to garnish

Heat the oil and butter in a saucepan. Add the onion and garlic and fry for 5 minutes. Add the peppers and salt and pepper to taste, cover and cook for 15 minutes. Add the tomatoes and simmer for 30 minutes or until the mixture is fairly thick and dry. Sprinkle with chopped parsley.

Serves 4

Stuffed Green Peppers

4 green peppers
150 ml./5 fl. oz. oil
1 small onion, finely
   chopped
175 g./6 oz. bacon, chopped
1 × 200 g./7 oz can tomatoes
salt and pepper
175 g./6 oz. cooked rice

Slice off the tops of the stalk end of the peppers and remove the seeds and pith. Blanch in boiling water for 5 minutes and drain well.

Heat about 30 ml./2 tablespoons of the oil in a frying-pan. Add the onion and fry for 5 minutes. Add the bacon, fry for 3 minutes, then add the tomatoes and can juice and salt and pepper to taste. Simmer for 4 minutes, then stir in the rice.

Arrange the peppers in a deep ovenproof dish and spoon an equal amount of the rice mixture into each one. Pour over the rest of the oil. Cover and put into the oven preheated to moderate (180°C/350°F or Gas Mark 4). Cook for 40 minutes.

Serves 4

Potatoes Anna

1 kg./2 lb. potatoes, very
   thinly sliced
125 g./4 oz. butter, softened
salt and pepper
chopped parsley to garnish

Chill the potato slices in iced water for 30 minutes. Drain and dry well. Place a layer of potato over the base of a generously buttered baking dish. Spread over some of the softened butter. Season lightly with salt and pepper. Repeat layers of potato, butter and seasoning, ending with a layer of butter. Put the dish into the oven preheated to hot (220°C/425°F or Gas Mark 7) and bake for 45 to 55 minutes, or until the potatoes are soft. Turn out on to a warmed serving dish and garnish with parsley.

Serves 4

Cheese and Potato Bake

½ kg./1 lb. potatoes, cooked
   and mashed
90 ml./6 tablespoons milk
25 g./1 oz. butter
175 g./6 oz. grated cheese
1 egg

Mix the ingredients together, except 50 g./2 oz. of the cheese for garnish, and spoon into a well-greased baking dish. Top with the reserved grated cheese and put into the oven preheated to fairly hot (190°C/375°F or Gas Mark 5). Bake for about 25 minutes, or until golden brown on top.

Serves 4

Roast Potatoes

1 kg./2 lb. potatoes
salt
75 g./3 oz. lard

Cut the potatoes up, if they are too large, and put into a pan of salted water. Bring to the boil, cook for 8 minutes and drain.

Melt the lard in a roasting pan and add the potatoes. Turn in the hot fat until they are evenly coated. Put the pan into the oven preheated to moderate (180°C/350°F or Gas Mark 4) if you are cooking them on their own, otherwise put them above the meat. Roast for about 1 hour, or until crisp and golden.

Serves 6-8

Potato Pancakes

½ kg./1 lb. potatoes, cooked
and mashed
15 g./½ oz. butter, melted
salt and pepper
10 ml./2 teaspoons chopped
fresh parsley
1 shallot, finely chopped
25 g./1 oz. Parmesan cheese,
grated
2 tomatoes, skinned and
finely chopped
50 g./2 oz. flour
50 ml./2 fl. oz. oil

Press the potatoes through a coarse strainer and mix with the butter, salt and pepper to taste, parsley, shallot, cheese, tomatoes and flour. Mix well together. Roll out on a lightly floured board to 1 cm./½ in. thick and cut into circles about 10 cm./4 in. diameter. Heat the oil in a frying-pan. When it is hot add the cakes and fry for 5 to 8 minutes or until evenly browned. Drain on kitchen towels.

Serves 4

Potatoes Dauphinois

1 garlic clove, halved
675 g./1½ lb. potatoes, thinly
sliced
salt and pepper
300 ml./10 fl. oz. single
cream
25 g./1 oz. butter, cut into
small pieces

Rub a shallow, ovenproof dish with the garlic halves and discard the garlic. Arrange the potato slices in the dish and season to taste with salt and pepper. Pour over the cream and dot with the butter. Put the dish into the oven preheated to cool (150°C/300°F or Gas Mark 2) and bake for 1½ hours. Increase the oven temperature to hot (220°C/425°F or Gas Mark 7) for the last 10 minutes to obtain a crust on the top of the potatoes.

Serves 6

Potato Nests

½ kg./1 lb. potatoes, cooked
   and mashed
50 g./2 oz. butter
2 egg yolks
Filling
300 ml./10 fl. oz. natural
   yogurt
45 ml./3 tablespoons canned
   sweetcorn
225 g./8 oz. cooked chicken,
   chopped
1 red pepper, seeds and pith
   removed and chopped
salt and pepper

Mix the mashed potatoes with the butter and egg yolks. Form into six flan shapes or nests. Put the nests on a well-greased baking sheet and put into the oven preheated to fairly hot (200°C/400°F or Gas Mark 6). Bake for about 10 minutes, or until golden brown.

Meanwhile, put the yogurt, sweetcorn and chicken into the top of a double boiler, or a heat-proof bowl set over simmering water. Heat through. Add the red pepper and seasoning to taste. Spoon into the centres of the nests.

Serves 6

Potatoes au Gratin

½ kg./1 lb. potatoes, cooked
   and sliced
double cream
salt and pepper
125 g./4 oz. Cheddar cheese,
   grated
25 g./1 oz. dry breadcrumbs
25 g./1 oz. butter, cut into
   small pieces

Put one-third of the potato slices on the bottom of a shallow, ovenproof dish. Top with a little cream, salt and pepper to taste and one-third of the cheese. Make layers in the same way until the ingredients are finished, then sprinkle over the breadcrumbs.

Dot over the butter and put the dish into the oven preheated to fairly hot (200°C/400°F or Gas Mark 6). Bake for 20 minutes or until the top is golden brown.

Serves 4

Stuffed Potatoes

4 potatoes, baked and
   halved
25 g./1 oz. butter
3 eggs, separated
50 g./2 oz. cooked ham,
   diced
salt and pepper
50 g./2 oz. Parmesan cheese,
   grated

Scoop the pulp out of the potatoes and mash well. Mix in the butter, egg yolks and ham. Press the mixture back into the potato halves. Beat the egg whites until they are stiff, and fold in seasoning to taste and cheese. Put the potatoes on a baking sheet and pile the mixture on top. Put the sheet into the oven preheated to warm (170°C/325°F or Gas Mark 3) and bake for 10 minutes.

Serves 4

Potato and Almond Balls

225 g./8 oz. potatoes, cooked
    and mashed
75 g./3 oz. blanched
    almonds, finely chopped
1 egg, beaten
oil for deep-frying

Mix the potato with about one-third of the nuts. Form into small balls. Coat with the beaten egg and the remaining nuts. Deep fry until crisp and golden brown. Drain on kitchen towels.

Serves 2-3

Caramellized Potatoes

30 ml./2 tablespoons sugar
50 g./2 oz. butter
675 g./1½ lb. hot cooked new
    potatoes

Put the sugar into a frying-pan and cook over gentle heat until it melts. Add the butter and mix with the sugar. Toss the cooked potatoes in the sugar and butter and heat gently until they are golden brown.

Serves 6

Duchess Potatoes

½ kg./1 lb. potatoes, cooked
    and mashed
1 egg yolk
25 g./1 oz. butter
salt and pepper
1 egg, beaten for glazing

Mix together the mashed potatoes, egg yolk and butter. Season with salt and pepper to taste. Pipe in large rosettes on to a greased baking sheet and brush with the beaten egg. Put the sheet into the oven preheated to hot (220°C/425°F or Gas Mark 7) and bake for 10 minutes or until the potatoes are golden brown.

Serves 4

Potato and Cheese Fritters

2 large potatoes, grated
225 g./8 oz. cream cheese
50 g./2 oz. flour
1 egg
salt and pepper
little milk
75 ml./3 fl. oz. oil

Mix together the potatoes, cheese, flour, egg, salt and pepper to taste and just enough milk to make a smooth batter. Heat the oil in a frying-pan. Drop in spoonfuls of the batter and fry for 3 to 5 minutes or until the fritters are evenly browned. Drain on kitchen towels.

Serves 4

Scalloped Potatoes with Onions

1½ kg./3 lb. potatoes, peeled
   and sliced
salt and pepper
½ kg./1 lb. onions, thinly
   sliced into rings
300 ml./10 fl. oz. milk
25 g./1 oz. butter, cut into
   small pieces

Put a layer of potatoes on the bottom of a large, well-greased ovenproof dish. Season lightly with salt and pepper and cover with a layer of onions. Repeat these layers, ending with a layer of potatoes, seasoning each layer with salt and pepper. Pour over the milk. Dot the top with the butter and cover with a lid or piece of foil. Put the dish into the oven preheated to fairly hot (190°C/375°F or Gas Mark 5) and bake for 1½ hours. Remove the lid for the last 20 minutes of cooking so that the potatoes can brown on top.

Serves 8

Egg-Stuffed Tomatoes

4 large tomatoes
salt and pepper
20 ml./4 teaspoons cooked
   ham, chopped
4 eggs
60 ml./4 tablespoons double
   cream, warmed
pinch of dried basil
25 g./1 oz. Parmesan cheese,
   grated

Slice off the tops of the tomatoes and scoop out the pulp. Turn upside down to drain. When dry, put upright on a greased baking sheet and season inside with salt and pepper. Put 5 ml./1 teaspoon of chopped ham inside each tomato and then gently break an egg into each tomato shell. Pour in a little cream and sprinkle with the basil and Parmesan. Put the sheet into the oven preheated to moderate (180°C/350°F or Gas Mark 4) and bake for 15 to 20 minutes or until the eggs are set.

Serves 4

Tomatoes with Olives

4 large tomatoes, halved
45 ml./3 tablespoons
   chopped green olives
175 g./6 oz. cooked ham,
   finely chopped
45 ml./3 tablespoons finely
   chopped fresh parsley
2.5 ml./½ teaspoon chopped
   basil
mayonnaise*

Place the tomatoes, cut side up, in a well-greased flameproof baking dish. Put the dish into the oven preheated to moderate (180°C/350°F or Gas Mark 4) and cook for 8 minutes. Be careful not to over-cook. Mix together the olives, ham, parsley and basil and add just enough mayonnaise to bind. Spoon the mixture on top of the tomatoes and grill for 3 to 4 minutes, or until the top is lightly browned.

Serves 4

Stuffed Turnips

4 medium turnips
salt and pepper
50 g./2 oz. butter
225 g./8 oz. cooked peas
15 ml./1 tablespoon chopped
  fresh parsley

Cook the turnips in boiling salted water for 30 minutes. Drain well and scoop out the centres, leaving shells about 1 cm./½ in. thick. Keep warm while you make the stuffing. Melt the butter in a saucepan. Stir in the peas, parsley and salt and pepper to taste. Fill the turnip cases with the mixture.

Serves 4

Ratatouille

60 ml./4 tablespoons oil
2 large onions, chopped
2 garlic cloves, crushed
½ kg./1 lb. tomatoes, skinned
  and chopped
1 large aubergine, diced and
  dégorged
225 g./8 oz. courgettes, sliced
2 red or green peppers, pith
  and seeds removed and
  chopped
salt and pepper

Heat the oil in a saucepan. Add the onions, garlic and tomatoes and fry for 5 minutes. Add the aubergine, courgettes and peppers, stir well and cover. Simmer gently for 30 to 45 minutes or until the vegetables are tender. Season to taste. Serve hot or cold.

Serves 6-8

Spinach Niçoise

75 g./3 oz. butter
1 kg./2 lb. spinach, cooked
  and finely chopped
30 ml./2 tablespoons double
  cream
salt and pepper
4 large tomatoes, skinned
  and chopped
2 onions, chopped
125 g./4 oz. cheese, grated

Melt half the butter in a saucepan. Add the chopped spinach and cream and heat gently. Season to taste with salt and pepper. Meanwhile, melt the remaining butter in a saucepan. Add the tomatoes and onions and fry for 5 minutes. Stir in the cheese and seasoning and remove from the heat.

Put the spinach mixture into a shallow flame-proof dish and top with the tomato and cheese mixture. Grill for 3 to 5 minutes or until the topping is golden brown.

Serves 4

Salads

American Salad

125 g./4 oz. cooked green
   beans, cut into lengths
1 × 125 g./4 oz. can
   sweetcorn, drained
1 red pepper, pith and seeds
   removed and chopped
125 g./4 oz. mushrooms,
   sliced
3 tomatoes, sliced
12 black olives, halved
50 ml./2 fl. oz. French
   dressing*

Mix all the ingredients, except the dressing, together in a salad bowl. Pour over the dressing and toss well.

Serves 6

Bean Salad

1 × 400 g./14 oz. can red
   kidney beans, drained
1 × 400 g./14 oz. can white
   haricot beans, drained
1 green pepper, pith and
   seeds removed and
   chopped
2 spring onions, chopped
50 ml./2 fl. oz. French
   dressing*

Mix all the vegetables together in a salad bowl. Pour over the dressing and toss well to coat. Chill for 15 minutes.

Serves 4

Beetroot Salad

½ kg./1 lb. cooked beetroot,
   diced
1 Spanish onion, thinly
   sliced in rings
15 ml./1 tablespoon chopped
   fresh parsley
50 ml./2 fl. oz. French
   dressing*

Put the beetroot into a shallow salad dish, then arrange the onion rings over the top. Sprinkle over the parsley, then dribble over the dressing. Chill for 15 minutes.

Serves 4-6

Bean Sprout Salad

½ kg./1 lb. bean sprouts
1 carrot, grated
4 water chestnuts, sliced
25 g./1 oz. flaked almonds,
    toasted
15 ml./1 tablespoon soy
    sauce
50 ml./2 fl. oz. French
    dressing*

Mix the bean sprouts, carrot, water chestnuts and almonds together in a salad bowl. Stir in the soy sauce and chill in the refrigerator for 15 minutes. Pour over the dressing and toss well to coat.

Serves 4-6

Belgian Salad

2 heads of chicory, thinly
    sliced
1 red pepper, pith and seeds
    removed and chopped
1 onion, thinly sliced into
    rings
125 ml./4 fl. oz.
    mayonnaise*
1.25 ml./¼ teaspoon cayenne
    pepper

Put the chicory and red pepper into a salad bowl and top with the onion rings. Mix the mayonnaise and cayenne together and pour over the vegetables. Toss well to coat.

Serves 4

Burghul Salad

225 g./8 oz. burghul or
    cracked wheat
45 ml./3 tablespoons spring
    onions, finely chopped
salt and pepper
50 g./2 oz. finely chopped
    fresh parsley
75 g./3 oz. finely chopped
    fresh mint
30 ml./2 tablespoons olive oil
30 ml./2 tablespoons lemon
    juice
Garnish
12 black olives, halved
4 tomatoes, thinly sliced
½ cucumber, thinly sliced
4 parsley sprigs

Soak the burghul or cracked wheat in water for 30 minutes; it will expand enormously. Drain, then wring in a tea towel. Spread out to dry.

Mix the burghul with the spring onions, salt and pepper to taste, parsley, mint, oil and lemon juice and toss well to coat. Garnish with the olives, tomatoes, cucumber and parsley sprigs.

Serves 4

Caesar Salad

60 ml./4 tablespoons olive oil
1 garlic clove, crushed
4 × .75 cm./¼ in. slices of
   white bread, crusts
   removed and cut into
   small cubes
1 egg
1 Romaine lettuce, shredded
1 × 50 g./2 oz. can
   anchovies, drained and
   chopped
50 ml./2 fl. oz. French
   dressing*
15 ml./1 tablespoon lemon
   juice
45 ml./3 tablespoons grated
   Parmesan cheese

Heat the oil in a frying-pan. Add the garlic and bread cubes and fry until crisp and golden brown. Drain on kitchen towels.

Put the egg in a heatproof bowl, cover with boiling water and 'coddle' for 2 minutes. Put the lettuce in a salad bowl with the anchovies and bread cubes. Pour over the dressing and lemon juice and toss well to coat. Break the egg into the mixture, add the grated cheese and toss again.

Serves 6

Carrot Salad

25 g./1 oz. butter
50 g./2 oz. soft breadcrumbs
50 g./2 oz. unsalted peanuts
6 medium carrots, grated
30 ml./2 tablespoons salad
   oil
15 ml./1 tablespoon wine
   vinegar
salt and pepper

Melt the butter in a saucepan. Add the breadcrumbs and fry until they are crisp and golden brown. Stir in the peanuts and cool.

Put the remaining ingredients into a salad bowl, then add the breadcrumb mixture. Toss well to coat. Chill for 30 minutes.

Serves 6

Cauliflower Salad

1 cooked cauliflower, broken
   into flowerets
125 ml./4 fl. oz.
   mayonnaise*
salt and pepper
30 ml./2 tablespoons tomato
   purée
5 ml./1 teaspoon paprika
2 hard-boiled eggs, finely
   chopped

Put the cauliflower into a salad bowl. Mix the mayonnaise, salt and pepper to taste, tomato purée and paprika together, then pour over the cauliflower. Toss well to coat. Sprinkle over the chopped eggs.

Serves 4-6

Celery Salad

4 celery stalks, sliced
1 large dessert apple, cored
  and diced
50 g./2 oz. raisins
25 g./1 oz. chopped walnuts
125 ml./4 fl. oz.
  mayonnaise*

Put the celery, fruit and nuts into a salad bowl. Add the mayonnaise and toss well to coat.

Serves 4

Celery, Apple and Almond Salad

4 celery stalks, sliced
2 red apples, cored and
  chopped
50 g./2 oz. blanched
  almonds
25 ml./1 fl. oz. French
  dressing*

Mix the celery, apples and almonds together in a salad bowl. Pour over the dressing and toss well to coat.

Serves 4

Chicory and Endive Salad

2 small heads of chicory,
  sliced
1 endive, shredded
1 dessert apple, peeled, cored
  and sliced
15 ml./1 tablespoon lemon
  juice
3 celery stalks, chopped
2 spring onions, chopped
30 ml./2 tablespoons
  chopped walnuts
125 ml./4 fl. oz. French
  dressing*

Soak the chicory and endive in cold water for 10 minutes. Drain, then transfer to a large salad bowl. Add the remaining ingredients and toss well to coat.

Serves 4

Citrus Green Salad

1 lettuce, shredded
1 bunch of watercress,
  chopped
2 grapefruit, cut into sections
2 oranges, cut into sections
50 ml./2 fl. oz. French
  dressing*

Put the lettuce into a salad bowl, then stir in the watercress, grapefruit and oranges. Pour over the dressing and toss well to coat.

Serves 6-8

Coleslaw

450 g./1 lb. white cabbage,
  finely shredded
1 red apple, cored and finely
  chopped
1 carrot, grated
25 g./1 oz. raisins
45 ml./3 tablespoons olive oil
25 ml./1½ tablespoons wine
  vinegar
5 ml./1 teaspoon sugar
125 ml./4 fl. oz. coleslaw
  dressing*

Put the cabbage, apple, carrot and raisins in a salad bowl and mix well. Mix the oil, vinegar and sugar together and pour over the salad ingredients. Toss well to coat. Stir in the dressing, then chill for 15 minutes. Stir just before serving.

Serves 4-6

Pasta Slaw

125 g./4 oz. macaroni rings
½ medium cabbage, finely
  shredded
1 green pepper, pith and
  seeds removed and
  chopped
2 celery stalks, thinly sliced
2 carrots, grated
125 ml./4 fl. oz. coleslaw
  dressing*

Cook the macaroni rings in boiling, salted water for 8 to 10 minutes, or until they are 'al dente'. Drain, then rinse in cold water. Put the rings in a salad bowl with the cabbage, pepper, celery and carrots and mix well. Pour over the dressing and toss well to coat. Chill for 1 hour.

Serves 4-6

Lentil Salad

225 g./8 oz. yellow lentils,
  soaked overnight in salted
  water
salt and pepper
50 ml./2 fl. oz. olive oil
1 onion, finely chopped

Drain the lentils and set them aside. Put the soaking liquid in a saucepan and bring to the boil. Cool. When cold, add the lentils and bring back to the boil. Simmer for 30 minutes. Drain the lentils and discard the cooking liquid. Return the lentils to the saucepan and cover with boiling, salted water. Cover the pan and simmer for 1 hour, or until the lentils are tender. Drain, and transfer the lentils to a salad bowl. Stir in the remaining ingredients and toss well to coat. Cool completely.

Serves 4-6

Almond Coleslaw

½ medium cabbage, finely
    shredded
2 celery stalks, sliced
½ cucumber, sliced
1 green pepper, pith and
    seeds removed and finely
    chopped
1 onion, grated
150 ml./5 fl. oz.
    mayonnaise*
15 ml./1 tablespoon vinegar
25 g./1 oz. flaked almonds,
    toasted

Mix the cabbage, celery, cucumber, pepper and onion together in a salad bowl. Pour over the mayonnaise and vinegar and toss well to coat. Scatter over the almonds.

Serves 4

Rice Coleslaw

½ medium white cabbage,
    shredded
175 g./6 oz. cooked rice
½ red pepper, pith and seeds
    removed and chopped
½ green pepper, pith and seeds
    removed and chopped
6 radishes, sliced
1 onion, grated
1 × 275 g./10 oz. can
    sweetcorn kernels, drained
150 ml./5 fl. oz. French
    dressing*
salt and pepper
2.5 ml./½ teaspoon dry
    mustard
10 ml./2 teaspoons sugar
1 garlic clove, crushed

Put the cabbage, rice and other vegetables in a large salad bowl. Mix the remaining ingredients together in a screw-top jar, then pour over the salad ingredients. Toss well to coat.

Serves 6

Corn Salad

2 hard-boiled eggs
2 cooked potatoes, diced
½ kg./1 lb. cooked sweetcorn
150 ml./5 fl. oz.
    mayonnaise*
1.25 ml./¼ teaspoon cayenne
    pepper
6 lettuce leaves

Finely chop one of the eggs and mix with the potatoes and corn. Mix the mayonnaise and cayenne together, then add to the corn mixture. Toss well to coat. Line a salad bowl with the lettuce leaves. Spoon the sweetcorn mixture into the centre. Slice the remaining egg and garnish.

Serves 4

Cucumber Salad

2 medium cucumbers, thinly
  sliced
1 small onion, chopped
45 ml./3 tablespoons white
  vinegar
15 ml./1 tablespoon water
5 ml./1 teaspoon sugar
1.25 ml./¼ teaspoon white
  pepper

Arrange the cucumbers in a shallow salad bowl.
Add all the remaining ingredients and toss well to
coat. Chill for 30 minutes. Drain off the liquid
before serving.

Serves 4

Greek Salad

½ small red cabbage,
  shredded
125 g./4 oz. cooked beetroot,
  cut into strips
125 g./4 oz. cooked green
  beans, sliced
15 ml./1 tablespoon capers
30 ml./2 tablespoons
  chopped black olives
50 ml./2 fl. oz. French
  dressing*

Put the cabbage, beetroot, beans, capers and olives
in a salad bowl. Pour over the dressing and toss
well to coat. Chill for 30 minutes.

Serves 6-8

Cucumber and Yogurt Salad

1 cucumber, thinly sliced
300 ml./10 fl. oz. plain
  yogurt
salt and pepper
5 ml./1 teaspoon paprika
10 ml./2 teaspoons lemon
  juice

Put the cucumber in a salad bowl. Mix all the
remaining ingredients together, then stir into the
cucumber. Chill for 1 hour.

Serves 4-6

Mixed Green Salad

1 lettuce, shredded
½ cucumber, sliced
1 green pepper, pith and
  seeds removed and cut
  into strips
1 celery stalk, sliced
50 ml./2 fl. oz. French
  dressing*

Put the lettuce, cucumber, pepper and celery in a
salad bowl. Pour over the dressing and toss well to
coat.

Serves 6

Green Bean Salad

½ kg./1 lb. green beans, cut
   into 5 cm./2 in. slices
1 garlic clove, halved
·50 ml./2 fl. oz. olive oil
25 ml./5 teaspoons lemon
   juice
salt and pepper
1 spring onion, chopped

Cook the beans in boiling, salted water for 5 to 15
minutes, or until they are tender. Drain and cool
slightly. Rub the insides of a salad bowl with the
garlic halves, then discard them. Transfer the
beans to the bowl, and add the oil, lemon juice, salt
and pepper to taste. Toss well to coat. Garnish with
the spring onion and chill for 15 minutes.

Serves 4

Mushroom and Bean Salad

1 × 275 g./10 oz. can lima or
   broad beans, drained
175 g./6 oz. button
   mushrooms, sliced
1 spring onion, chopped
2.5 ml./½ teaspoon grated
   nutmeg
50 ml./2 fl. oz. French
   dressing*

Put the beans, mushrooms, spring onion and
nutmeg in a salad bowl. Pour over the dressing and
toss well to coat. Chill for 30 minutes.

Serves 4

Green Lychee Salad

1 lettuce, shredded
1 bunch of watercress,
   chopped
1 × 450 g./1 lb. can lychees,
   drained
50 ml./2 fl. oz. French
   dressing*

Mix the lettuce, watercress and lychees together in
a salad bowl. Pour over the dressing and toss well
to coat.

Serves 6

Orange Mint Salad

4 navel oranges, thinly sliced
15 ml./1 tablespoon chopped
   fresh mint
75 ml./3 fl. oz. olive oil
25 ml./1½ tablespoons lemon
   juice
25 ml./1½ tablespoons
   brandy

Arrange the orange slices in overlapping circles,
then sprinkle with mint. Mix all the remaining
ingredients together and dribble over the oranges.

Serves 4

Pea Salad

½ kg./1 lb. cooked peas
125 g./4 oz. mushrooms,
   thinly sliced
2 celery stalks, thinly sliced
30 ml./2 tablespoons
   sultanas
30 ml./2 tablespoons olive oil
30 ml./2 tablespoons wine
   vinegar
salt and pepper
2.5 ml./½ teaspoon dry
   mustard
5 ml./1 teaspoon sugar
1 garlic clove, crushed

Mix the peas, mushrooms, celery and sultanas together in a salad bowl. Mix the remaining ingredients together, then pour over the vegetables and toss well to coat. Chill for 1 hour.

Serves 6

Potato and Celery Salad

½ kg./1 lb. cooked potatoes,
   sliced
75 ml./3 fl. oz. French
   dressing*
4 celery stalks, chopped
1 small leek, finely chopped
2 sweet gherkins, sliced
150 ml./5 fl. oz.
   mayonnaise*
salt and pepper
15 ml./1 tablespoon chopped
   fresh chives

Put the potato slices in a large salad bowl and pour over the dressing. Toss well to coat. Add the remaining ingredients, except the chives, and toss well to coat. Sprinkle over the chives.

Serves 4

Red Cabbage Salad

225 ml./8 fl. oz. vinegar
50 g./2 oz. sugar
1 garlic clove, crushed
2 bay leaves
10 ml./2 teaspoons
   peppercorns
10 ml./2 teaspoons salt
1 red cabbage, shredded
2 large apples, cored and
   chopped
2 spring onions, chopped

Put the vinegar, sugar, garlic, bay leaves, peppercorns and salt in a saucepan. Bring to the boil, stirring constantly. Boil for 2 minutes. Strain.

Put all the remaining ingredients in a salad bowl. Pour over the flavoured vinegar and toss well to coat. Chill for 1 hour. Toss before serving.

Serves 8-10

Orange and Chicory Salad

2 small heads of chicory,
  sliced
1 small apple, peeled, cored
  and sliced
2 oranges, peeled and
  chopped
30 ml./2 tablespoons French
  dressing*
1 small onion, thinly sliced
  into rings

Mix the chicory, apple and oranges together in a shallow salad bowl. Pour over the dressing and toss well to coat. Garnish with the onion rings.

Serves 4

Potato Salad

½ kg./1 lb. cooked potatoes,
  sliced
2 spring onions, chopped
15 ml./1 tablespoon chopped
  fresh parsley
2.5 ml./½ teaspoon finely
  grated lemon rind
salt, pepper and paprika
125 ml./4 fl. oz.
  mayonnaise*

Put the potatoes, spring onions, parsley and lemon rind into a salad bowl and season to taste with the salt, pepper and paprika. Add the mayonnaise and toss well to coat. Cover and chill for 20 minutes.

Serves 4

Radish and Cucumber Salad

1 bunch of radishes, thinly
  sliced
½ cucumber, thinly sliced
300 ml./10 fl. oz. sour cream
juice of 1 lemon
salt and pepper

Mix all the ingredients together until the vegetables are well coated with the sour cream. Chill for 1 hour.

Serves 6

Tomato Rice Salad

175 g./6 oz. long-grain rice
60 ml./4 tablespoons olive oil
30 ml./2 tablespoons
  tarragon vinegar
1.25 ml./¼ teaspoon grated
  nutmeg
4 tomatoes, skinned and
  sliced

Cook the rice in boiling, salted water for 15 to 20 minutes, or until it is tender and the liquid has been absorbed. Stir in the oil, vinegar and nutmeg and cool.

Top with the tomatoes and chill for 1 hour.

Serves 4

Blue Cheese and Pear Salad

1 lettuce, shredded
1 × 675 g./1½ lb. can pear
  halves, drained
125 g./4 oz. black grapes,
  halved
Dressing
175 g./6 oz. blue cheese,
  crumbled
125 ml./4 fl. oz.
  mayonnaise*
125 ml./4 fl. oz. sour cream
25 g./1 oz. chopped nuts
salt and pepper
pinch of cayenne pepper

Line a salad bowl with the lettuce and arrange the
pear halves on it. Mix all the dressing ingredients
together. Spoon over the pear halves to cover them
completely. Garnish with the grapes.

Serves 4-6

Spring Salad

175 g./6 oz. cooked green
  beans, sliced
2 cooked potatoes, thinly
  sliced
2 spring onions, finely
  chopped
30 ml./2 tablespoons olive oil
15 ml./1 tablespoon vinegar
salt and pepper
150 ml./5 fl. oz. plain yogurt
10 ml./2 teaspoons chopped
  fresh parsley
5 ml./1 teaspoon chopped
  fresh mint

Put the green beans, potatoes and spring onions
into a salad bowl. Add the oil, vinegar and salt and
pepper to taste. Toss well to coat. Stir in the
yogurt, parsley and mint and toss well.

Serves 4

Tomato and Cucumber Salad

350 g./12 oz. tomatoes,
  thinly sliced
1 medium cucumber, thinly
  sliced
1 spring onion, very finely
  chopped
25 ml./1½ tablespoons finely
  chopped fresh parsley
50 ml./2 fl. oz. French
  dressing*

Arrange the tomatoes and cucumber slices decoratively in a shallow dish. Sprinkle over the spring
onion and parsley, then dribble over the dressing.
Chill for 15 minutes.

Serves 4

Spinach and Bacon Salad

350 g./12 oz. cookeJ
  spinach, chopped
1 large cooked potato, cubed
50 g./2 oz. Gruyère cheese,
  cubed
4 bacon slices, grilled until
  crisp and chopped
15 ml./1 tablespoon chopped
  fresh parsley
50 ml./2 fl. oz. French
  dressing*

Put the spinach, potato, cheese and bacon into a salad bowl. Pour over the dressing and toss well to coat. Sprinkle over the parsley.

Serves 4

Spinach and Mushroom Salad

½ kg./1 lb. spinach, washed
  and shaken dry
350 g./12 oz. button
  mushrooms, finely
  chopped
2 spring onions, finely
  chopped
15 ml./1 tablespoon finely
  chopped fresh parsley
Dressing
60 ml./4 tablespoons olive oil
15 ml./1 tablespoon tarragon
  vinegar
15 ml./1 tablespoon lemon
  juice
1 garlic clove, crushed
salt and pepper

Tear the spinach leaves and put them in a salad bowl. Add the mushrooms and spring onions and mix well. Mix all the dressing ingredients together. Pour over the spinach and toss well to coat. Sprinkle over the chopped parsley.

Serves 4

Tomato Salad

½ kg./1 lb. tomatoes, thinly
  sliced
15 ml./1 tablespoon chopped
  fresh basil
2.5 ml./½ teaspoon finely
  grated lemon rind
50 ml./2 fl. oz. French
  dressing*

Arrange the tomato slices decoratively in a shallow dish. Sprinkle over the basil and lemon rind, then dribble over the dressing. Chill for 15 minutes.

Serves 4

Avocado Bowl

1 lettuce, shredded

1 avocado, peeled and
  chopped

1 × 450 g./1 lb. can
  asparagus tips, drained

1 × 400 g./14 oz. can
  artichoke hearts, drained

15 ml./1 tablespoon chopped
  green olives

50 ml./2 fl. oz. French
  dressing*

Mix all the ingredients, except the dressing, together in a salad bowl. Pour over the dressing and toss well to coat.

Serves 6

Walnut and Avocado Salad

2 ripe avocados, halved

7.5 ml./1½ teaspoons lemon
  juice

2 small apples, peeled, cored
  and finely chopped

50 g./2 oz. walnuts, finely
  chopped

50 ml./2 fl. oz. French
  dressing*

8 walnut halves

Carefully remove the avocado flesh from the skins without breaking the skins. Put the flesh in a bowl and stir in the lemon juice, apples and walnuts. Beat with a fork until smooth and well blended. Stir in dressing to taste. Spoon back into the avocado shells and garnish with the walnut halves.

Serves 4

Beef Salad

350 g./12 oz. cooked beef,
  chopped

2 cooked potatoes, chopped

125 g./4 oz. cooked green
  beans, sliced

125 g./4 oz. cooked
  sweetcorn

4 tomatoes, cut into wedges

8 stuffed olives, halved

50 ml./2 fl. oz. mayonnaise*

125 ml./4 fl. oz. sour cream

5 ml./1 teaspoon prepared
  horseradish

salt and pepper

15 ml./1 tablespoon chopped
  fresh chives

Put the beef, potatoes, beans, sweetcorn, tomatoes and olives into a salad bowl. Mix the mayonnaise, sour cream, horseradish and salt and pepper to taste together, then pour over the salad. Toss well to coat. Cover and chill for 20 minutes, then garnish with the chives.

Serves 4

Scandinavian Chicken Salad

450 g./1 lb. cooked chicken,
   cut into bite-sized pieces
2 apples, peeled, cored and
   chopped
2 celery stalks, chopped
30 ml./2 tablespoons
   chopped walnuts
1 green pepper, pith and
   seeds removed and
   chopped
125 ml./4 fl. oz.
   mayonnaise*
125 ml./4 fl. oz. sour cream
2.5 ml./½ teaspoon cayenne
   pepper
15 ml./1 tablespoon chopped
   fresh dill

Put the chicken, apples, celery, walnuts and pepper together in a salad bowl. Mix the mayonnaise, sour cream and cayenne together. Pour over the chicken mixture and toss well to coat. Garnish with the chopped dill.

Serves 4

Chicken and Celery Salad

1 × 1½ kg./3 lb. cooked
   chicken, cut into small
   pieces
1 head of celery, finely
   chopped
50 g./2 oz. smoked ham, cut
   into thin strips
Dressing
1 hard-boiled egg, separated
1 egg yolk
salt and pepper
2.5 ml./½ teaspoon prepared
   mustard
15 ml./1 tablespoon olive oil
15 ml./1 tablespoon white
   wine vinegar

Put the chicken pieces and celery in a salad bowl. Cover and chill for 1 hour.

Mash the hard-boiled egg yolk into the raw egg yolk then add salt and pepper to taste and mustard. Beat until the mixture is smooth, then gradually beat in the oil and vinegar. Pour over the chicken mixture and toss well to coat. Garnish with chopped egg white and smoked ham.

Serves 4

Waldorf Salad

6 red apples, cored and diced
juice of 2 lemons
6 celery stalks, chopped
50 g./2 oz. walnut halves
125 ml./4 fl. oz.
  mayonnaise*
125 ml./4 fl. oz. sour cream
salt and pepper
6-8 lettuce leaves

Put the apples into a bowl and sprinkle over the lemon juice. Add the celery and walnuts. Mix the mayonnaise and sour cream together and add salt and pepper to taste. Pour over the apple mixture and toss well to coat.

Line a salad bowl with the lettuce leaves. Spoon the apple and celery mixture into the centre.

Serves 4-6

Watercress and Gruyère Salad

1 bunch of watercress,
  chopped
125 g./4 oz. Gruyère cheese,
  cubed
3 tomatoes, cut into wedges
50 g./2 oz. small button
  mushrooms, halved
50 ml./2 fl. oz. French
  dressing*

Mix all the vegetables together in a salad bowl. Pour over the dressing and toss well to coat. Chill for 15 minutes.

Serves 6

Chicken and Pasta Salad

225 g./8 oz. pasta
  (preferably small shells)
75 ml./3 fl. oz. olive oil
30 ml./2 tablespoons wine
  vinegar
15 ml./1 tablespoon lemon
  juice
1 garlic clove, crushed
salt and pepper
350 g./12 oz. cooked
  chicken, chopped
175 g./6 oz. cooked peas
1 red pepper, pith and seeds
  removed and cut into strips
2 celery stalks, sliced
125 g./4 oz. mushrooms,
  sliced
4 lettuce leaves
2.5 ml./½ teaspoon grated
  nutmeg

Cook the pasta in boiling, salted water for 5 to 8 minutes, or until it is 'al dente'. Drain, then place in a salad bowl. Add the oil, vinegar, lemon juice, garlic and salt and pepper to taste. Toss well to coat. Cool completely.

Add the remaining ingredients, except the lettuce and nutmeg, and toss well to coat. Line a salad bowl with the lettuce leaves and spoon the chicken mixture into the centre. Sprinkle over the nutmeg.
Note: Cooked turkey may be substituted for the chicken.

Serves 4

Chinese Chicken Salad

10 ml./2 teaspoons cooking oil
5 ml./1 teaspoon sesame seeds
5 ml./1 teaspoon finely chopped fresh root ginger
30 ml./2 tablespoons soy sauce
1 garlic clove, crushed
45 ml./3 tablespoons sugar
2.5 ml./½ teaspoon 5-spice powder
1 × 1½ kg./3 lb. chicken, jointed
oil for deep frying
4 spring onions, sliced
2 celery stalks, sliced
6 water chestnuts, sliced
1 × 150 g./5 oz. can bamboo shoot, cut into strips
salt and pepper
6-8 lettuce leaves

Heat the oil in a frying-pan. Add the sesame seeds and fry until they are golden brown. Drain on kitchen towels.

Mix the ginger, soy sauce, garlic, sugar and half the 5-spice powder together. Pour over the chicken pieces and set aside for 20 minutes. Drain the chicken pieces, then deep-fry for 5 to 8 minutes, or until they are cooked through and tender. Drain on kitchen towels and set aside until they are cool enough to handle. Remove the meat from the bones and cut it into strips. Chill for 15 minutes.

Add the spring onions, celery, water chestnuts and bamboo shoot to the chicken strips. Season with the remaining 5-spice powder and salt and pepper to taste. Line a salad bowl with the lettuce leaves and spoon the chicken mixture into the centre. Sprinkle over a little oil and the sesame seeds.

Serves 4

Chef's Salad

125 g./4 oz. cooked turkey, chopped
125 g./4 oz. cooked ham, chopped
50 g./2 oz. Gruyère cheese, chopped
1 hard-boiled egg, thinly sliced
1 spring onion, chopped
2 tomatoes, cut into wedges
75 ml./3 fl. oz. French dressing*
6-8 lettuce leaves

Put the turkey, ham, cheese, egg, spring onion and tomatoes in a bowl. Pour over the dressing and toss well to coat. Line a salad bowl with the lettuce leaves and spoon the mixture into the centre. Chill for 10 minutes.

Serves 4

Cottage Cheese and Nut Salad

350 g./12 oz. cottage cheese
25 g./1 oz. chopped nuts
1 dessert apple, cored and
   diced
30 ml./2 tablespoons
   chopped pineapple
6 lettuce leaves

Mix the cheese, nuts and fruit together. Line a salad bowl with the lettuce leaves and spoon the cheese mixture into the centre.

Serves 4

Devilled Potato Salad with Frankfurters

½ kg./1 lb. potatoes
75 ml./3 fl. oz. French
   dressing*
1 garlic clove, crushed
10 ml./2 teaspoons French
   mustard
1.25 ml./¼ teaspoon
   Worcestershire sauce
pinch of cayenne pepper
3 tomatoes, skinned and
   chopped
1 small green pepper, pith
   and seeds removed and
   chopped
5 spring onions, chopped
salt and pepper
5 ml./1 teaspoon paprika
8 cooked frankfurters

Cook the potatoes in boiling, salted water for 15 minutes, or until they are cooked. Drain and chop roughly. Mix the dressing, garlic, mustard, Worcestershire sauce and cayenne together and stir into the potatoes. Cool completely.

When the potatoes are cold, add the tomatoes, pepper, spring onions and salt and pepper to taste. Spoon into a salad dish and sprinkle over the paprika. Arrange the frankfurters around the sides.

Serves 4

Lobster Mayonnaise

2 × 675 g./1½ lb. cooked
   lobsters, halved
300 ml./10 fl. oz.
   mayonnaise*
45 ml./3 tablespoons double
   cream
salt and pepper
30 ml./2 tablespoons
   chopped fresh parsley
juice of ½ lemon
1 lemon, cut into wedges

Remove the meat from the lobsters and cut it into bite-sized pieces. Reserve the shells. Mix together the remaining ingredients, except the lemon. Fold in the lobster meat, then spoon into the shells. Garnish with the lemon wedges.

Serves 4

Egg and Bacon Salad

150 g./5 oz. lean bacon
1 lettuce, shredded
3 spring onions, chopped
3 celery stalks, chopped
1 garlic clove, crushed
2 tomatoes, cut into wedges
4 hard-boiled eggs,
    quartered
50 ml./2 fl. oz. French
    dressing*

Grill the bacon until it is crisp. Drain on kitchen towels and chop. Add half the bacon pieces to a salad bowl with the lettuce, spring onions, celery, garlic, tomatoes and eggs. Pour over the dressing and toss well to coat. Garnish with the remaining bacon pieces.

Serves 4

Garlic Sausage Salad

225 g./8 oz. long-grain rice
75 ml./3 fl. oz. French
    dressing*
175 g./6 oz. garlic sausage,
    chopped
75 g./3 oz. cooked peas
1 red pepper, pith and seeds
    removed and chopped
2 tomatoes, cut into wedges
6 black olives

Cook the rice in boiling, salted water for 15 to 20 minutes, or until it is tender and the liquid has been absorbed. Stir in half the dressing and cool. Chill for 1 hour, or until it is very cold.

Mix the sausage, peas and pepper together and pour over the remaining dressing. Toss well to coat, then stir into the rice. Arrange the tomato wedges and olives attractively over the top.

Serves 4

Ham and Pasta Salad

225 g./8 oz. macaroni
350 g./12 oz. cooked ham,
    chopped
225 g./8 oz. Bel Paese
    cheese, chopped
4 celery stalks, chopped
5 spring onions, chopped
15 ml./1 tablespoon prepared
    mustard
225 ml./8 fl. oz.
    mayonnaise*
salt and pepper
2 hard-boiled eggs, chopped
2 tomatoes, cut into wedges

Cook the macaroni in boiling, salted water for 8 to 10 minutes, or until it is 'al dente'. Drain, then cool.

Put the ham, cheese, celery and spring onions into a salad bowl. Stir in the macaroni. Stir the mustard into the mayonnaise and season to taste. Stir into the salad and toss well to coat. Garnish with the chopped eggs and tomato wedges.

Serves 4

Salade Marguerite

1 small cauliflower, broken
    into flowerets
225 g./8 oz. green beans,
    sliced
225 g./8 oz. potatoes
1 × 275 g./10 oz. can
    asparagus tips, drained
175 ml./6 fl. oz.
    mayonnaise*
salt and pepper
1.25 ml./¼ teaspoon cayenne
    pepper
1 lettuce, shredded
4 hard-boiled eggs, thinly
    sliced

Cook the cauliflower and beans in boiling, salted water for 8 to 10 minutes, or until they are tender. Meanwhile, cook the potatoes in boiling, salted water for 15 minutes, or until they are cooked. Drain the vegetables. Slice the potatoes and put into a bowl with the cauliflower and beans. Stir in the asparagus tips.

Mix the mayonnaise, salt and pepper to taste and cayenne together, then pour over the vegetables. Toss well to coat. Line a salad bowl with the lettuce and spoon the vegetable mixture into the centre. Arrange the egg whites over the salad to look like flower petals. Finely chop the yolks and add to the centre of the petals to resemble the stamens.

Serves 4-6

Maryland Salad

125 g./4 oz. macaroni shells
125 g./4 oz. cooked
    sweetcorn
1 red pepper, pith and seeds
    removed and chopped
2 spring onions, chopped
75 ml./3 fl. oz. thousand
    island dressing*

Cook the macaroni shells in boiling, salted water for 8 to 10 minutes or until they are 'al dente'. Drain; then rinse in cold water. Put the shells into a salad bowl with the sweetcorn, pepper and spring onions and mix well. Pour over the dressing and toss well to coat.

Serves 4-6

Sweet and Sour Pork Salad

675 g./1½ lb. cooked pork, cut
  into bite-sized pieces
8 small pickled gherkins,
  sliced
4 pineapple rings, chopped
30 ml./2 tablespoons
  sultanas
45 ml./3 tablespoons flaked
  almonds
Marinade
10 ml./2 teaspoons French
  mustard
60 ml./4 tablespoons white
  wine vinegar
90 ml./6 tablespoons olive oil
2 garlic cloves, crushed
5 ml./1 teaspoon soy sauce
15 ml./1 tablespoon honey
Garnish
1 cooked beetroot, sliced
2 cooked potatoes, sliced

Mix all the marinade ingredients together. Add the pork, gherkins, pineapple chunks and sultanas and marinate at room temperature for 15 minutes. Reserve any marinade not absorbed and stir in the nuts. Pile the pork mixture on to a serving dish and garnish with the beetroot and potato slices. Spoon any reserved marinade over the top.

Serves 6

Rice Salad

175 g./6 oz. long-grain rice
50 ml./2 fl. oz. olive oil
15 ml./1 tablespoon tarragon
  vinegar
salt and pepper
1 red pepper, pith and seeds
  removed and cut into strips
30 ml./2 tablespoons flaked
  almonds
½ fennel root, chopped
30 ml./2 tablespoons
  sultanas
125 g./4 oz. cooked green
  beans
125 g./4 oz. cooked ham,
  chopped
15 ml./1 tablespoon chopped
  fresh parsley
6 lettuce leaves

Cook the rice in boiling, salted water for 15 to 20 minutes, or until it is tender and the liquid has been absorbed. Mix the oil, vinegar, salt and pepper to taste into the rice. Add the remaining ingredients, except the lettuce, and toss well to blend. Cool completely.

Arrange the lettuce leaves in a salad bowl, then pile the rice mixture on top.

Serves 4

Cheese, Shrimp and Apple Salad

350 g./12 oz. ricotta or
cottage cheese
125 g./4 oz. chopped nuts
½ lettuce, shredded
2 dessert apples, cored, sliced
and brushed with lemon
juice
20 shelled shrimps
Dressing
50 ml./2 fl. oz. olive oil
15 ml./1 tablespoon white
wine vinegar
5 ml./1 teaspoon lemon juice
salt and pepper
½ avocado, mashed
15 ml./1 tablespoon cream

Mix the cheese and nuts together, then roll into small, walnut-sized balls. Chill for 10 minutes.

Arrange the lettuce in a shallow salad dish. Arrange the cheese balls, apple slices and shrimps on the lettuce. Mix all the dressing ingredients together and pour over the salad.

Serves 4

Salade Niçoise

225 g./8 oz. cooked potatoes,
diced
1 × 200 g./7 oz. tuna,
drained and flaked
275 g./10 oz. cooked green
beans
4 tomatoes, cut into wedges
15 ml./1 tablespoon chopped
fresh parsley
75 ml./3 fl. oz. French
dressing*
Garnish
1 × 50 g./2 oz. can
anchovies, drained
6-12 black olives

Put the potatoes into a large salad bowl, then cover with the tuna. Add a layer of beans, then tomatoes. Sprinkle over the parsley and carefully pour over the dressing. Garnish with the anchovies and olives.

Serves 4-6

246

Tongue and Chutney Salad

350 g./12 oz. cooked tongue,
   cut into strips
1 lettuce, shredded
2 hard-boiled eggs, sliced
Dressing
5 ml./1 teaspoon curry
   powder
45 ml./3 tablespoons chutney
30 ml./2 tablespoons
   mustard pickle
75 ml./5 tablespoons
   mayonnaise*

Mix all the dressing ingredients together. Stir in the tongue strips and toss well to coat. Line a salad bowl with the lettuce and spoon the tongue mixture into the centre. Garnish with the egg slices.

Serves 4

Rollmop Salad

6 rollmops, chopped
225 g./8 oz. cooked beetroot,
   diced
350 g./12 oz. cooked potato,
   diced
1 onion, chopped
1 large apple, cored and
   chopped
1 pickled cucumber, chopped
125 ml./4 fl. oz. sour cream
125 ml./4 fl. oz.
   mayonnaise*
2.5 ml./½ teaspoon dried dill
6 lettuce leaves
2 hard-boiled eggs, chopped

Put the rollmops, beetroot, potato, onion, apple and cucumber into a bowl. Mix the sour cream, mayonnaise and dill together and spoon over the salad. Toss well to coat. Line a salad bowl with the lettuce leaves and pile the rollmop mixture in the centre. Garnish with the chopped egg.

Serves 4

Rollmop and Potato Salad

4 rollmops, chopped
3 cooked potatoes, diced
1 large cooked beetroot,
   chopped
2 spring onions, chopped
50 ml./2 fl. oz. French
   dressing*
1 hard-boiled egg, finely
   chopped

Mix the rollmops, potatoes, beetroot and spring onions together in a salad bowl. Pour over the dressing and toss well to coat. Garnish with the chopped egg.

Serves 4

Tomato and Scampi Salad

4 large firm tomatoes
60 ml./4 tablespoons cold
   cooked rice
30 ml./2 tablespoons capers
2 pickled gherkins, finely
   chopped
15 ml./1 tablespoon chopped
   fresh parsley
½ green pepper, pith and seeds
   removed and chopped
225 g./8 oz. scampi (frozen
   or canned)
150 ml./5 fl. oz.
   mayonnaise*
salt and pepper
4 black olives

Cut a slice from the top of each tomato. Carefully remove the pulp from each one, leaving the shells intact. Set the shells upside-down on kitchen towels to drain, and transfer the pulp to a bowl. Add the rice, capers, gherkins, parsley, pepper and scampi to the bowl, reserving a few scampi for decoration. Stir in the mayonnaise and salt and pepper to taste and toss well to coat. Spoon into the tomato shells and garnish with the olives and reserved scampi.

Serves 4

Seafood Salad

1 lettuce, separated into
   leaves
225 g./8 oz. shelled prawns
225 g./8 oz. cooked
   crabmeat, flaked
225 g./8 oz. cooked clams or
   scallops, chopped
225 g./8 oz. cooked white
   fish, cut into small pieces
4 tomatoes, cut into wedges
8 black olives
Dressing
350 ml./12 fl. oz.
   mayonnaise*
juice of 1 lemon
15 ml./1 tablespoon finely
   chopped spring onion
2.5 ml./½ teaspoon dry
   mustard
1.25 ml./¼ teaspoon saffron
   threads soaked in 30 ml./2
   tablespoons water
salt and pepper

Line a salad bowl with the lettuce leaves, then arrange the prawns, crabmeat, clams or scallops and fish in the centre. Garnish with the tomatoes and olives.

Mix the mayonnaise, lemon juice, spring onion and mustard together. Stir in the saffron mixture and salt and pepper to taste. Chill for 5 minutes. Serve the salad, accompanied by the dressing.

Serves 6

Smoked Oyster Salad

225 g./8 oz. long-grain rice
150 ml./5 fl. oz. French
  dressing*
5 ml./1 teaspoon curry
  powder
6 spring onions, finely
  chopped
1 red pepper, pith and seeds
  removed and chopped
2 × 200 g./7 oz. cans
  smoked oysters, drained

Cook the rice in boiling, salted water for 15 to 20 minutes, or until it is tender and the liquid has been absorbed. Stir in the dressing and cool. Stir in the remaining ingredients and toss well to coat.

Serves 4-6

Smoked Salmon and Egg Salad

4 hard-boiled eggs,
  separated
30 ml./2 tablespoons
  mayonnaise*
125 g./4 oz. smoked salmon,
  finely chopped
juice of 1 lemon
pinch of cayenne pepper
6-8 lettuce leaves
2 tomatoes, cut into wedges

Mix the egg yolks and mayonnaise together until soft and creamy. Divide the smoked salmon among the egg whites and sprinkle over the lemon juice and cayenne. Spoon the egg yolk mixture into a piping bag with a rosette nozzle and pipe decoratively over the salmon. Arrange the lettuce leaves in a shallow salad dish and top with the filled egg whites. Garnish with the tomato wedges.

Serves 4

Tuna Fish Salad

1 × 275 g./10 oz. can tuna,
  drained and flaked
3 hard-boiled eggs, chopped
2 gherkins, finely chopped
4 tomatoes, cut into wedges
4 black olives, chopped
50 ml./2 fl. oz. French
  dressing*
15 ml./1 tablespoon chopped
  fresh parsley

Mix the tuna, eggs, gherkins, tomatoes and olives in a salad bowl. Pour over the dressing and toss well to coat. Chill for 30 minutes, then garnish with the chopped parsley.

Serves 4

Potato and Tuna Salad

4 potatoes
50 ml./2 fl. oz. French
    dressing*
1 onion, thinly sliced in rings
2.5 ml./½ teaspoon paprika
1 × 200 g./7 oz. can tuna,
    drained and flaked
15 ml./1 tablespoon chopped
    fresh parsley
10 ml./2 teaspoons capers

Cook the potatoes in boiling, salted water for 15 to 20 minutes, or until they are tender. Drain and slice. Put the slices in a salad bowl and, while they are warm, add the dressing. Toss well to coat. Cool to room temperature. Add the onion, paprika and tuna and gently toss well to coat. Garnish with the parsley and capers.

Serves 4

Salami Salad

225 g./8 oz. salami, chopped
125 g./4 oz. Gruyère cheese,
    cubed
1 celery stalk, sliced
225 g./8 oz. cooked potato,
    cubed
3 spring onions, chopped
225 ml./8 fl. oz.
    mayonnaise*
salt and pepper
2.5 ml./½ teaspoon paprika

Put the salami, cheese, celery, potato and spring onions into a salad bowl. Mix the mayonnaise, salt and pepper to taste and paprika together, then pour over the salad. Toss well to coat.

Serves 2

Russian Salad

350 g./12 oz. cooked
    potatoes, diced
225 g./8 oz. cooked carrots,
    diced
225 g./8 oz. cooked green
    beans, sliced
125 g./4 oz. cooked peas
125 g./4 oz. cooked
    sweetcorn
125 ml./4 fl. oz.
    mayonnaise*
Garnish
2 hard-boiled eggs, thinly
    sliced
1 cooked beetroot, chopped
6 green olives, chopped

Put the potatoes, carrots, green beans, peas and sweetcorn into a salad bowl. Add the mayonnaise and toss well to coat. Cover and chill for 20 minutes. Garnish with the eggs, beetroot and olives.

Note: You can make Russian Salad a filling main dish by adding 125 g./4 oz. of cold cooked, shredded chicken and 125 g./4 oz. of chopped garlic sausage to the mixture.

Serves 4

Prawn Salad

1 garlic clove, halved
1 lettuce, shredded
3 tomatoes, cut into wedges
675 g./1½ lb. shelled prawns
1 celery stalk, sliced
1 green pepper, pith and
   seeds removed and cut
   into strips
30 ml./2 tablespoons
   sultanas
50 g./2 oz. unsalted cashew
   nuts
Dressing
90 ml./6 tablespoons olive oil
30 ml./2 tablespoons lemon
   juice
salt and pepper

Rub the garlic halves around the inside of a salad bowl, then discard them. Add the remaining salad ingredients and toss well. Mix the dressing ingredients together. Pour over the prawn mixture and toss well to coat.

Serves 4

Curried Salad

150 ml./5 fl. oz. French
   dressing*
2.5 ml./½ teaspoon
   Worcestershire sauce
salt and pepper
7.5 ml./1½ teaspoons curry
   powder
½ cauliflower, broken into
   flowerets
125 g./4 oz. cooked long-
   grain rice
1 kg./2 lb. prawns, shelled
1 green pepper, pith and
   seeds removed and sliced
3 celery stalks, sliced
2 small onions, chopped

Mix the dressing, Worcestershire sauce, salt and pepper and curry powder together in a large salad bowl. Add the cauliflower flowerets and cooked rice and toss well to coat. Marinate the mixture, stirring occasionally, for 1½ hours.

Stir the prawns and remaining vegetables into the mixture. Chill for 15 minutes.

Serves 6-8

Pasta & Pizzas

Cannelloni with Cheese Sauce

8 cannelloni tubes
Filling
50 ml./2 fl. oz. cooking oil
1 onion, chopped
1 garlic clove, crushed
1 streaky bacon slice,
   chopped
225 g./8 oz. minced beef
1 × 225 g./8 oz. can
   tomatoes
5 ml./1 teaspoon dried basil
salt and pepper
Sauce
25 g./1 oz. butter
25 g./1 oz. flour
300 ml./10 fl. oz. milk
75 g./3 oz. Cheddar cheese,
   grated
2.5 ml./½ teaspoon dry
   mustard
salt and pepper

To make the filling, heat the oil in a saucepan. Add the onion, garlic and bacon and fry for 5 minutes. Stir in the beef and fry until it loses its pinkness. Stir in the tomatoes and can juice, basil, salt and pepper. Bring to the boil, then simmer for 30 minutes, or until very thick.

Meanwhile, cook the cannelloni tubes, a few at a time, in boiling, salted water for 8 to 10 minutes or until they are 'al dente'. Drain. Carefully spoon the filling mixture into the cannelloni tubes, then lay them in a large, shallow ovenproof dish.

To make the sauce, melt the butter in a saucepan. Stir in the flour to form a smooth paste. Gradually stir in the milk. Bring to the boil, then cook for 2 minutes. Stir in the grated cheese, mustard, salt and pepper. Pour the sauce over the filled tubes, then put the dish in the oven preheated to fairly hot (190°C/375°F or Gas Mark 5). Bake for 30 minutes, or until the sauce is brown and bubbling.

Serves 4

Fettuccine with Tuna Fish Sauce

30 ml./2 tablespoons cooking
  oil
1 × 275 g./10 oz. can tuna
  fish, drained and flaked
1 small onion, finely
  chopped
15 ml./1 tablespoon chopped
  fresh parsley
25 g./1 oz. black olives,
  stoned and chopped
150 ml./5 fl. oz. chicken
  stock
½ kg./1 lb. fettuccine
25 g./1 oz. butter, cut into
  small pieces

Heat the oil in a saucepan. Add the tuna, onion and parsley and fry for 5 minutes. Stir in the olives and stock and bring to the boil. Cover and simmer for 10 minutes.

Meanwhile, cook the fettuccine in boiling, salted water for 5 to 8 minutes or until it is 'al dente'. Drain in a colander, then toss in the butter. Pour over the tuna sauce.

Serves 4

Lasagne I

350 g./12 oz. lasagne
2 × 175 g./6 oz. Mozzarella
  cheese, thinly sliced
175 g./6 oz. Italian sausage,
  thinly sliced
2 hard-boiled eggs
125 g./4 oz. Parmesan
  cheese, grated
225 g./8 oz. ricotta cheese
Sauce
1½ kg./3 lb. tomatoes,
  skinned and chopped
45 ml./3 tablespoons tomato
  purée
2 carrots, chopped
1 onion, chopped
2 garlic cloves, crushed
2 celery stalks, chopped
15 ml./1 tablespoon chopped
  fresh parsley
2.5 ml./½ teaspoon grated
  lemon rind
30 ml./2 tablespoons olive oil
15 g./½ oz. butter

Put all the sauce ingredients, except the oil and butter, into a large saucepan. Cover and simmer for 45 minutes. Purée the mixture in a blender, then return it to the pan. Continue to simmer for 30 minutes or until thick.

Meanwhile, cook the lasagne sheets, a few at a time, in boiling salted water for 15 minutes or until they are 'al dente'. Drain. Line the bottom of a well-greased baking dish with about one-third of the lasagne. Cover with half the Mozzarella, half the sausage and half the eggs. Sprinkle with one-third of the Parmesan, then spread over half the ricotta and half the sauce. Continue making layers, finishing with a thick covering of Parmesan cheese. Put into the oven preheated to moderate (180°C/350°F or Gas Mark 4) and bake for 40 minutes.

Serves 6

Lasagne II

350 g./12 oz. lasagne

1½ kg./3 lb. cooked spinach, drained

2 × 175 g./6 oz. Mozzarella cheese, thinly sliced

125 g./4 oz. Parmesan cheese, grated

Sauce

45 ml./3 tablespoons cooking oil

1 onion, finely chopped

1 garlic clove, crushed

1 green pepper, pith and seeds removed and chopped

225 g./8 oz. minced beef

5 ml./1 teaspoon paprika

60 ml./4 tablespoons tomato purée

1 × 675 g./1½ lb. can tomatoes

salt and pepper

To make the sauce, heat the oil in a saucepan. Add the onion, garlic and green pepper and fry for 5 minutes. Stir in the beef and fry until it loses its pinkness. Add all the remaining sauce ingredients and bring to the boil. Cover and simmer for 30 minutes or until thick.

Meanwhile, cook the lasagne sheets, a few at a time, in boiling, salted water for 15 minutes or until they are 'al dente'. Drain. Line the bottom of a well-greased baking dish with about one-third of the lasagne. Cover with half of the cooked spinach, half of the Mozzarella, then half of the sauce. Sprinkle over about one third of the grated Parmesan. Continue making layers, finishing with a thick covering of Parmesan cheese. Put into the oven preheated to moderate (180°C/350°F or Gas Mark 4) and bake for 40 minutes.

Serves 6

Macaroni and Cheese

½ kg./1 lb. macaroni

50 g./2 oz. butter

40 g./1½ oz. flour

425 ml./15 fl. oz. milk

225 g./8 oz. Cheddar cheese, grated

10 ml./2 teaspoons dry mustard

salt and pepper

2 tomatoes, sliced

Cook the macaroni in boiling, salted water for 8 to 10 minutes, or until it is 'al dente'. Meanwhile, melt the butter in a saucepan. Stir in the flour to form a smooth paste. Gradually add the milk, stirring constantly. Bring the sauce to the boil, then cook for 2 minutes, stirring constantly. Stir in 175 g./6 oz. of the grated cheese, the mustard, salt and pepper and cook until the cheese has melted and the sauce is thick and smooth.

Drain the macaroni, then transfer it to an oven-proof dish. Pour over the sauce and stir to mix. Arrange the tomato slices on top, sprinkle over the remaining grated cheese and put the dish into the oven preheated to moderate (180°C/350°F or Gas Mark 4). Bake for 15 to 20 minutes, or until the top is brown and bubbling.

Serves 4

Macaroni with Mussels

45 ml./3 tablespoons cooking
  oil
1 onion, chopped
2 garlic cloves, crushed
6 tomatoes, skinned and
  chopped
75 ml./3 fl. oz. red wine
15 ml./1 tablespoon chopped
  fresh parsley
salt and pepper
1½ l./2½ pints mussels,
  steamed until they open
50 g./2 oz. Parmesan cheese,
  grated
275 g./10 oz. macaroni
  shells
45 ml./3 tablespoons dry
  breadcrumbs

Heat the oil in a saucepan. Add the onion and garlic and fry for 5 minutes. Stir in the tomatoes, wine, parsley, salt and pepper to taste and bring to the boil. Cover and simmer for 10 minutes. Remove the mussels from the shells and stir into the sauce with half the cheese. Simmer for a further 10 minutes.

Meanwhile, cook the macaroni in boiling, salted water for 8 to 10 minutes or until it is 'al dente'. Drain. Stir the macaroni into the sauce, then pour into an ovenproof dish. Sprinkle over the remaining cheese and breadcrumbs and put the dish into the oven preheated to moderate (180°C/350°F or Gas Mark 4). Bake for 15 to 20 minutes, or until the top is brown and bubbly.

Serves 4

Noodle Bake

30 ml./2 tablespoons cooking
  oil
1 onion, chopped
1 garlic clove, crushed
1 green pepper, pith and
  seeds removed and
  chopped
½ kg./1 lb. minced pork
1 × 400 g./14 oz. can
  tomatoes
10 ml./2 teaspoons chopped
  fresh oregano
salt and pepper
350 g./12 oz. noodles
15 g./½ oz. butter, cut into
  small pieces
25 g./1 oz. Cheddar cheese,
  grated

Heat the oil in a saucepan. Add the onion, garlic and pepper and fry for 5 minutes. Add the pork and fry until it loses its pinkness. Stir in the tomatoes and can juice, oregano and salt and pepper to taste. Bring to the boil, cover and simmer for 20 minutes.

Meanwhile, cook the noodles in boiling, salted water for 6 to 8 minutes or until they are 'al dente'. Drain. Spoon one-third of the meat mixture into an ovenproof dish and top with half of the noodles. Continue making layers until all the ingredients are finished. Sprinkle over the butter and grated cheese and put the dish into the oven preheated to moderate (180°C/350°F or Gas Mark 4). Cook for 30 minutes, or until the top is brown and bubbly.

Serves 4-6

Chow Mein

½ kg./1 lb. Chinese egg
  noodles
45 ml./3 tablespoons cooking
  oil
1 onion, finely sliced
250 ml./9 fl. oz. chicken
  stock
3 celery stalks, chopped
2 carrots, chopped
125 g./4 oz. button
  mushrooms, sliced
8 water chestnuts, sliced
450 g./1 lb. bean sprouts
1 × 150 g./5 oz. can bamboo
  shoot, sliced
15 ml./1 tablespoon
  cornflour
30 ml./2 tablespoons soy
  sauce
2.5 ml./½ teaspoon white
  pepper

Cook the noodles in boiling, salted water for 15 to 20 minutes, or until they are soft. Heat the oil in a saucepan. Add the onion and fry for 5 minutes. Add 225 ml./8 fl. oz. of stock and bring to the boil. Stir in the celery, carrots, mushrooms, water chestnuts, bean sprouts and bamboo shoot. Fry for 3 minutes.

Mix the cornflour, soy sauce, remaining stock and pepper together and add to the pan. Bring to the boil, then cook for 3 minutes, stirring constantly. Drain the noodles and top with the sauce.

Serves 4

Noodle Ring with Meat Sauce

30 ml./2 tablespoons cooking
  oil
1 onion, chopped
1 garlic clove, crushed
350 g./12 oz. minced beef
30 ml./2 tablespoons tomato
  purée
1 small apple, cored and
  chopped
2.5 ml./½ teaspoon sugar
salt and pepper
1.25 ml./¼ teaspoon dried
  basil
1 × 400 g./14 oz. can
  tomatoes
½ kg./1 lb. noodles
30 ml./2 tablespoons
  chopped fresh parsley

Heat the oil in a saucepan. Add the onion and garlic and fry for 5 minutes. Add the beef and fry until it loses its pinkness. Stir in the tomato purée, apple, sugar, salt and pepper to taste, basil and tomatoes and can juice. Simmer for 30 minutes.

Meanwhile, cook the noodles in boiling, salted water for 6 to 8 minutes or until they are 'al dente'. Drain, then pack into a well-greased ring mould. Keep the mould hot for 5 minutes.

Turn the noodle ring out on to a warmed serving dish and spoon the sauce into the centre. Sprinkle over the parsley.

Serves 4

256

Crispy Noodles with Chicken and Vegetables

½ kg./1 lb. Chinese dried egg
noodles
45 ml./3 tablespoons cooking
oil
25 ml./1½ tablespoons soy
sauce
2.5 ml./½ teaspoon sugar
225 g./8 oz. cooked chicken,
cut into strips
3 spring onions, chopped
2.5 cm./1 in. slice fresh root
ginger, thinly sliced
1 × 65 g./2¼ oz. can bamboo
shoot, cut into thin strips
2 celery stalks, sliced
diagonally
1 large carrot, sliced
diagonally
2 Chinese dried mushrooms,
soaked in water for 20
minutes, drained and
chopped
5 ml./1 teaspoon cornflour
dissolved in 45 ml./3
tablespoons chicken stock
oil for deep frying

Cook the noodles in boiling, salted water for 10 minutes. Drain, then stir in 15 ml./1 tablespoon of oil.

Mix the soy sauce and sugar together in a bowl. Stir in the chicken and spring onions and set aside for 20 minutes.

Heat the remaining oil in a large frying-pan. Add the ginger and fry for 2 minutes. Add the vegetables and fry for 5 minutes. Stir in the cornflour mixture and chicken mixture. Fry for a further 3 to 5 minutes, or until it is thoroughly heated. Set aside and keep hot.

Deep fry the noodles in the oil for 2 to 3 minutes, or until they are crisp and golden brown. Drain on kitchen towels, then use to garnish the chicken mixture.

Serves 4

Noodles with Mushrooms

50 g./2 oz. butter
175 g./6 oz. mushrooms,
sliced
30 ml./2 tablespoons flour
225 ml./8 fl. oz. chicken
stock
5 ml./1 teaspoon grated
nutmeg
½ kg./1 lb. noodles
150 ml./5 fl. oz. sour cream
5 ml./1 teaspoon caraway
seeds

Melt the butter in a saucepan. Add the mushrooms and fry for 3 minutes. Stir in the flour to form a smooth paste. Gradually add the stock and nutmeg, stirring constantly. Simmer the sauce for 3 minutes or until it thickens.

Meanwhile, cook the noodles in boiling salted water for 6 to 8 minutes, or until they are 'al dente'. Drain. Stir the sour cream and caraway into the sauce. Heat gently and pour over the noodles.

Serves 4

Chinese Prawns and Ham with Noodles

275 g./10 oz. Chinese dried
  egg noodles
125 g./4 oz. prawns, shelled
  and chopped
40 g./1½ oz. cooked ham,
  shredded
1 celery stalk, chopped
1.25 cm./½ in. slice fresh root
  ginger, thinly sliced
75 g./3 oz. minced pork
45 ml./3 tablespoons cooking
  oil
2.5 ml./½ teaspoon hot chilli
  sauce
15 ml./1 tablespoon tomato
  sauce
15 ml./1 tablespoon soy
  sauce
15 ml./1 tablespoon
  cornflour dissolved in 55
  ml./3½ tablespoons
  chicken stock
salt and pepper

Cook the noodles in boiling, salted water for 15 to
20 minutes, or until they are soft. Meanwhile, mix
the prawns, ham, celery, ginger and pork together.
Heat the oil in a frying-pan. Add the prawn mixture and fry, stirring constantly, for 4 minutes. Add
the chilli sauce, tomato and soy sauces, cornflour,
salt and pepper. Continue frying and stirring for a
further 8 minutes. Drain the noodles and top with
the prawn mixture.

Serves 4

Noodles with Cream

½ kg./1 lb. green ribbon
  noodles
50 g./2 oz. butter, cut into
  small pieces
2 egg yolks
125 g./4 oz. Parmesan
  cheese, grated
75 ml./3 fl. oz. double cream
2.5 ml./½ teaspoon black
  pepper
grated cheese

Cook the noodles in boiling, salted water for 6 to 8
minutes, or until they are 'al dente'. Drain, then
toss in the butter, egg yolks, Parmesan cheese and
cream. Toss the mixture until the egg yolks are
'cooked' and the butter has melted. Stir in the
pepper and garnish with the grated cheese.

Serves 4

Baked Rigatoni

225 g./8 oz. rigatoni
600 ml./1 pint tomato sauce*
50 g./2 oz. Parmesan cheese,
  grated
Filling
15 ml./1 tablespoon cooking
  oil
2 onions, chopped
1 garlic clove, crushed
675 g./1½ lb. minced beef
75 g./3 oz. fresh
  breadcrumbs
1 egg, beaten
salt and pepper

To make the filling, heat the oil in a saucepan. Add the onions and garlic and fry for 5 minutes. Stir in the minced beef and fry until it loses its pinkness. Stir in the remaining ingredients and simmer for 10 minutes, stirring occasionally.

Meanwhile, cook the rigatoni in boiling, salted water for 5 to 8 minutes or until it is 'al dente'. Drain, then rinse quickly in cold water so that it is cool enough to handle. Stuff the filling into the rigatoni, then arrange the pasta in an ovenproof dish. Heat the sauce, then pour it over the pasta. Sprinkle over the grated cheese and put into the oven preheated to moderate (180°C/350°F or Gas Mark 4). Bake for 30 minutes, or until the top is bubbly and brown.

Serves 4

Spaghetti Bolognese I

15 ml./1 tablespoon cooking
  oil
125 g./4 oz. bacon, chopped
1 onion, chopped
1 garlic clove, crushed
1 carrot, chopped
1 celery stalk, chopped
350 g./12 oz. minced beef
175 g./6 oz. chicken livers,
  chopped
45 ml./3 tablespoons tomato
  purée
150 ml./5 fl. oz. red wine
300 ml./10 fl. oz. beef stock
salt and pepper
1.25 ml./¼ teaspoon grated
  nutmeg
½ kg./1 lb. spaghetti
25 g./1 oz. butter, cut into
  small pieces
50 ml./2 fl. oz. double cream

Heat the oil in a saucepan. Add the bacon, onion, garlic, carrot and celery and fry for 10 minutes. Add the beef and chicken livers and fry until the beef loses its pinkness. Add the tomato purée, wine, stock, salt and pepper and nutmeg and stir to mix. Simmer the sauce for 30 minutes.

Meanwhile, cook the spaghetti in boiling, salted water for 10 to 12 minutes, or until it is 'al dente'. Drain, then toss in the butter until it has melted. Stir the cream into the sauce and heat for 1 minute. Pour the sauce over the spaghetti.

Serves 4

Spaghetti Bolognese II

50 ml./2 fl. oz. cooking oil
2 onions, chopped
1 garlic clove, crushed
1 green pepper, pith and
   seeds removed and
   chopped
125 g./4 oz. mushrooms,
   thinly sliced
½ kg./1 lb. minced beef
50 g./2 oz. tomato purée
1 × 675 g./1½ lb. can
   tomatoes
5 ml./1 teaspoon dried thyme
5 ml./1 teaspoon dried basil
salt and pepper
½ kg./1 lb. spaghetti
50 g./2 oz. Parmesan cheese,
   grated
15 ml./1 tablespoon chopped
   fresh parsley

Heat the oil in a saucepan. Add the onions, garlic and pepper and fry for 5 minutes. Add the mushrooms and beef and fry until the beef loses its pinkness. Add the tomato purée, tomatoes and can juice, thyme, basil, salt and pepper. Stir to mix, then bring to the boil. Cover and simmer for 35 to 40 minutes, or until thick.

Meanwhile, cook the spaghetti in boiling, salted water for 10 to 12 minutes, or until it is 'al dente'. Drain. Stir the grated Parmesan into the sauce and simmer until it has melted. Pour the sauce over the spaghetti and garnish with the parsley.

Serves 4

Spaghetti Milanaise

40 g./1½ oz. butter
125 g./4 oz. mushrooms,
   sliced
125 g./4 oz. cooked ham,
   chopped
125 g./4 oz. cooked tongue,
   chopped
1 × 65 g./2½ oz. can tomato
   purée
150 ml./5 fl. oz. stock
5 ml./1 teaspoon dried mixed
   herbs
15 ml./1 tablespoon chopped
   fresh parsley
salt and pepper
½ kg./1 lb. spaghetti
grated cheese

Melt the butter in a saucepan. Add the mushrooms and fry for 3 minutes. Stir in the ham, tongue, tomato purée, stock, herbs, parsley, salt and pepper. Bring to the boil, cover and simmer for 15 minutes.

Meanwhile, cook the spaghetti in boiling, salted water for 10 to 12 minutes, or until it is 'al dente'. Drain, then add it to the meat mixture, stirring to mix. Simmer for 5 minutes. Garnish with the grated cheese.

Serves 4

Spaghetti Carbonara

½ kg./1 lb. spaghetti
15 ml./1 tablespoon cooking
  oil
175 g./6 oz. lean bacon,
  chopped
50 ml./2 fl. oz. double cream
2 eggs, beaten
125 g./4 oz. Parmesan
  cheese, grated
salt and pepper
pinch of cayenne pepper
25 g./1 oz. butter, cut into
  small pieces

Cook the spaghetti in boiling, salted water for 10 to 12 minutes, or until it is 'al dente'. Meanwhile, heat the oil in a small frying-pan. Add the bacon and fry until it is crisp. Stir in the cream and set aside.

Mix the eggs, cheese, salt, pepper and cayenne together. Drain the spaghetti, then toss in the butter until it has melted. Stir in the bacon and cream mixture, then the egg mixture and toss and stir until the eggs are 'cooked' and the spaghetti is thoroughly coated.

Serves 4

Spaghetti with Clam Sauce

15 ml./1 tablespoon olive oil
1 onion, chopped
1 × 400 g./14 oz. can
  tomatoes
2.5 ml./½ teaspoon dried
  marjoram
salt and pepper
1 × 450 g./1 lb. can clams
½ kg./1 lb. spaghetti
25 g./1 oz. butter, cut into
  small pieces
grated Parmesan cheese

Heat the oil in a saucepan. Add the onion and fry for 5 minutes. Stir in the tomatoes and can juice, marjoram, salt and pepper. Cover and simmer for 15 minutes. Add the clams and can juice and stir. Simmer for 12 minutes.

Meanwhile, cook the spaghetti in boiling, salted water for 10 to 12 minutes, or until it is 'al dente'. Drain, then toss in the butter until it has melted. Pour the sauce over the spaghetti and garnish with the grated cheese.

Serves 4

Spaghetti Marinara

½ kg./1 lb. spaghetti
25 g./1 oz. butter, cut into
  small pieces
Sauce
50 g./2 oz. butter
1 garlic clove, crushed
30 ml./2 tablespoons finely
  chopped fresh parsley
6 large tomatoes, skinned
  and chopped
1 × 225 g./8 oz. can oysters
225 g./8 oz. shelled shrimps
salt and pepper

Cook the spaghetti in boiling, salted water for 10 to 12 minutes or until it is 'al dente'. Meanwhile to make the sauce, melt the butter in a saucepan. Add the garlic and parsley and fry for 1 minute. Stir in the tomatoes and simmer for 5 minutes. Add all the remaining ingredients and simmer, stirring occasionally, for 5 minutes.

Drain the spaghetti, then toss in the butter until it has melted. Stir in the sauce.

Serves 4

261

Spaghetti with Chicken Liver Sauce

50 ml./2 fl. oz. cooking oil
1 onion, chopped
1 garlic clove, crushed
10 ml./2 teaspoons dried
  mixed herbs
1 × 675 g./1½ lb. can
  tomatoes
salt and pepper
25 g./1 oz. butter
½ kg./1 lb. chicken livers,
  chopped
½ kg./1 lb. spaghetti

Heat the oil in a saucepan. Add the onion and garlic and fry for 5 minutes. Stir in the herbs, tomatoes and can juice, salt and pepper. Bring to the boil, then simmer for 30 minutes.

Meanwhile, melt the butter in a frying-pan. Add the chicken livers and fry until they are lightly browned. Transfer the livers to the tomato sauce and continue to simmer for a further 15 minutes.

Meanwhile, cook the spaghetti in boiling, salted water for 10 to 12 minutes, or until it is 'al dente'. Drain and top with the sauce.

Serves 4

Spaghetti with Tomatoes and Olives

60 ml./4 tablespoons cooking
  oil
1 onion, chopped
1 garlic clove, crushed
1 × 400 g./14 oz. can
  tomatoes
salt and pepper
5 ml./1 teaspoon dried basil
1.25 ml./¼ teaspoon sugar
30 ml./2 tablespoons tomato
  purée
½ kg./1 lb. spaghetti
12 black olives, stoned and
  chopped
25 g./1 oz. butter, cut into
  small pieces
grated Parmesan cheese

Heat 45 ml./3 tablespoons of the oil in a saucepan. Add the onion and garlic and fry for 5 minutes. Stir in the tomatoes and can juice, salt and pepper, basil, sugar and tomato purée. Cover and simmer for 25 minutes.

Meanwhile, cook the spaghetti in boiling, salted water for 10 to 12 minutes or until it is 'al dente'.

Heat the remaining oil in a small pan and sauté the olives for 2 minutes. Transfer to the sauce and simmer for a further 5 minutes.

Drain the spaghetti, then toss in the butter until it has melted. Pour over the sauce and garnish with the cheese.

Serves 4

Spaghetti with Meatballs

½ kg./1 lb. minced beef
1 garlic clove, crushed
15 ml./1 tablespoon finely
    chopped fresh parsley
5 ml./1 teaspoon grated
    lemon rind
1 large slice of white bread,
    soaked in a little milk
1 egg
salt and pepper
50 ml./2 fl. oz. cooking oil
425 ml./15 fl. oz. tomato
    sauce *
½ kg./1 lb. spaghetti
25 g./1 oz. butter, cut into
    small pieces
grated Parmesan cheese

Mix together the beef, garlic, parsley, lemon rind, bread mixture, egg, salt and pepper. Roll into small balls with floured hands, then roll the balls lightly in flour. Heat the oil in a frying-pan. Add the meatballs and fry until they are evenly browned.

Heat the tomato sauce in a saucepan and add the meatballs. Simmer for 30 minutes.

Meanwhile, cook the spaghetti in boiling, salted water for 10 to 12 minutes or until it is 'al dente'. Drain, then toss in the butter until it has melted. Arrange the meatballs and sauce over the spaghetti and garnish with the grated Parmesan.

Serves 4

Tagliatelle with Bacon and Tomato Sauce

75 g./3 oz. butter
225 g./8 oz. lean bacon,
    chopped
1 carrot, diced
4 celery stalks, diced
1 garlic clove, crushed
1 × 65 g./2½ oz. can tomato
    purée
225 ml./8 fl. oz. chicken
    stock
salt and pepper
½ kg./1 lb. tagliatelle
grated cheese

Melt 50g./2 oz. of the butter in a saucepan. Add the bacon, carrot, celery and garlic and fry until the bacon is crisp. Stir in the tomato purée, stock, salt and pepper. Bring to the boil, then simmer for 15 minutes.

Meanwhile, cook the tagliatelle in boiling, salted water for 8 to 10 minutes, or until it is 'al dente'. Drain, then toss in the remaining butter, cut into small pieces, until it has melted. Pour the sauce over the tagliatelle and garnish with the grated cheese.

Serves 4

Basic Pizza Dough

2.5 ml/½ teaspoon sugar
25g./1 oz. yeast
150 ml./5 fl. oz. tepid water
450 g./1 lb. flour
5 ml./1 teaspoon salt
1 tablespoon olive oil

Mix the sugar, yeast and 30 ml./2 tablespoons of the tepid water to a paste. Set aside in a warm place for 15 minutes or until the mixture is frothy.

Meanwhile, sift the flour and salt into a large, warmed bowl. Add the yeast mixture, the remaining tepid water and oil, and mix to a smooth dough. Knead for about 8 minutes or until smooth and elastic. Set aside in a warm place for 45 minutes or until the dough has doubled in size. The dough is now ready to use.

Makes 4 individual pizza bases or 1 large base for 4 people

Pizza with Olives and Anchovies

450 g./1 lb. basic pizza
  dough*
Filling
1 × 150 g./5 oz. can tomato
  purée
6 tomatoes, skinned and
  sliced
12 anchovy fillets
125 g./4 oz. black olives,
  stoned and chopped
2.5 ml./½ teaspoon dried
  oregano
125 g./4 oz. Cheddar cheese,
  grated
10 ml./2 teaspoons olive oil

Roll out the pizza dough, either to one large round or four individual rounds, about .75 cm./¼ in. thick. Spread the tomato purée over the base or bases, then arrange the tomato slices, anchovy fillets and chopped olives over it. Sprinkle over the oregano, then the grated cheese, then the olive oil. Put the pizza or pizzas into the oven preheated to very hot (230°C/450°F or Gas Mark 8) and bake for 20 minutes.

Serves 4

Pizza with Mushrooms and Onions

450 g./1 lb. basic pizza
  dough*
Filling
45 ml./3 tablespoons olive oil
1 onion, chopped
175 g./6 oz. button
  mushrooms, sliced
1 × 450 g./1 lb. can tomatoes
salt and pepper
1.25 ml./¼ teaspoon grated
  nutmeg
75 g./3 oz. Cheddar cheese,
  grated
1 large onion, thinly sliced in
  rings
5 ml./1 teaspoon dried
  oregano

Heat 30 ml./2 tablespoons of oil in a saucepan. Add the onion and fry for 5 minutes. Add the mushrooms and fry for 3 minutes. Stir in the tomatoes and can juice, salt and pepper and nutmeg. Simmer for 25 minutes or until very thick.

Meanwhile, roll out the pizza dough, either to one large round or four individual rounds about .75 cm./¼ in. thick. Carefully spoon the sauce filling over the base or bases. Sprinkle over the grated cheese, then arrange the onion rings over the cheese. Sprinkle over the oregano and remaining oil. Put the pizza or pizzas into the oven preheated to very hot (230°C/450°F or Gas Mark 8) and bake for 20 minutes.

Serves 4

Pizza with Sausage and Cheese

450 g./1 lb. basic pizza
  dough*
Filling
60 ml./4 tablespoons olive oil
1 onion, chopped
1 × 450 g./1 lb. can tomatoes
5 ml./1 teaspoon dried basil
salt and pepper
225 g./8 oz. Italian hot
  sausage, sliced
125 g./4 oz. Cheddar or
  Parmesan cheese, grated

Heat 30 ml./2 tablespoons of oil in a saucepan. Add the onion and fry for 5 minutes. Stir in the tomatoes and can juice, basil, salt and pepper. Simmer for 25 minutes or until very thick.

Meanwhile, fry the sausage slices in another tablespoon of oil in a small frying-pan for 5 minutes.

Roll out the pizza dough, either to one large round or four individual rounds about .75 cm./¼ in. thick. Carefully spoon the sauce filling over the base or bases. Arrange the sausage slices over the sauce, then sprinkle over the grated cheese and remaining olive oil. Put the pizza or pizzas into the oven preheated to very hot (230°C/450°F or Gas Mark 8) and bake for 20 minutes.

Serves 4

Pizza with Tomatoes and Cheese

450 g./1 lb. basic pizza
dough*
Filling
45 ml./3 tablespoons olive oil
1 onion, chopped
1 garlic clove, crushed
1 × 450 g./1 lb. can tomatoes
5 ml./1 teaspoon dried
oregano
salt and pepper
1 × 175 g./6 oz. Mozzarella
cheese, thinly sliced

Heat 30 ml./2 tablespoons of oil in a saucepan. Add the onion and garlic and fry for 5 minutes. Stir in the tomatoes and can juice, half the oregano, salt and pepper. Simmer for 25 minutes or until very thick.

Meanwhile, roll out the pizza dough, either to one large round or four individual rounds about .75 cm./¼ in. thick. Carefully spoon the sauce filling over the base or bases. Arrange the Mozzarella slices over the sauce, then dribble over the remaining oil and oregano. Put the pizza or pizzas into the oven preheated to very hot (230°C/450°F or Gas Mark 8) and bake for 20 minutes.

Serves 4

Pizza with Tuna and Pears

450 g./1 lb. basic pizza
dough*
Filling
1 × 200 g./7 oz. can tuna
1 large onion, chopped
2 dessert pears, peeled, cored
and chopped
1 × 400 g./14 oz. can
tomatoes
2.5 ml./½ teaspoon dried
oregano
salt and pepper
12 black olives, stoned and
chopped
10 ml./2 teaspoons olive oil

Drain the oil from the tuna and pour it into a saucepan. When it is hot, add the onion and pears and cook for 3 minutes. Flake the tuna and stir it into the pan, then add the tomatoes and can juice, oregano, salt and pepper. Simmer for 20 minutes. Stir in the olives and continue to simmer for 5 to 8 minutes or until very thick.

Meanwhile, roll out the pizza dough, either to one large round or four individual rounds about .75 cm./¼ in. thick. Carefully spoon the sauce filling over the base or bases, then dribble over the olive oil. Put the pizza or pizzas into the oven preheated to very hot (230°C/450°F or Gas Mark 8) and bake for 20 minutes.

Serves 4

Gnocchi

600 ml./1 pint milk
1 onion, finely chopped
pinch of salt
150 g./5 oz. semolina
2 eggs, beaten
75 g./3 oz. Parmesan cheese,
grated
40 g./1½ oz. butter, melted

Put the milk, onion and salt into a saucepan and bring slowly to the boil. Cover and set aside for 20 minutes. Strain the milk and put into a saucepan with the semolina. Bring to the boil, stirring constantly. Cook until smooth and thick. Remove from the heat and stir in the eggs and half the cheese. Spoon into a well-greased shallow ovenproof dish. Sprinkle over the remaining grated cheese and melted butter. Set aside for 15 minutes. Put the dish into the oven preheated to moderate (180°C/350°F or Gas Mark 4) and bake the gnocchi for 30 minutes or until it is golden brown. Cut into squares to serve.

Serves 4

Spinach Gnocchi

50 ml./2 fl. oz. cooking oil
675 g./1½ lb. cooked spinach,
chopped
225 g./8 oz. cottage cheese
salt and pepper
1 egg, beaten
50 g./2 oz. Parmesan cheese,
grated
125 g./4 oz. flour
50 g./2 oz. butter, melted

Heat the oil in a frying-pan. Add the spinach, cottage cheese and salt and pepper to taste. Simmer for 5 minutes, stirring occasionally. Remove from the heat and beat in the egg, half the grated cheese and the flour. Chill in the refrigerator for 1½ hours or until very firm.

Roll the mixture into small balls. Cook the balls in boiling, salted water until they rise to the surface, then drain on kitchen towels. Transfer the balls to a flameproof dish and pour over the melted butter and remaining cheese. Grill for 3 to 4 minutes or until the top is brown and bubbly.

Serves 4

Rice Dishes

Cheese Rice

225 ml./8 fl. oz. milk
225 ml./8 fl. oz. water
225 g./8 oz. long-grain rice
salt and pepper
125 g./4 oz. Cheddar cheese,
  grated
15 ml./1 tablespoon chopped
  fresh parsley
15 ml./1 tablespoon chopped
  fresh mint

Put the milk and water in a saucepan and bring to
the boil. Add the rice and salt and pepper to taste
and return to the boil. Cover and simmer for 15 to
20 minutes, or until the rice is cooked and tender
and the liquid has been absorbed. Stir in the
remaining ingredients and continue to simmer for
a further 3 to 4 minutes, or until the cheese has
melted.

Serves 4

Chinese Fried Rice

15 ml./1 tablespoon cooking
  oil
125 g./4 oz. cooked pork, cut
  into thin strips
225 g./8 oz. cooked long-
  grain rice
salt and pepper
175 g./6 oz. shelled shrimps
1 egg
5 ml./1 teaspoon soy sauce,
  blended with 5 ml./1
  teaspoon water
2 spring onions, chopped
50 g./2 oz. cooked ham,
  finely chopped

Heat the oil in a saucepan. Add the pork. Fry for 1
minute, then stir in the rice and salt and pepper to
taste. Fry for 10 minutes, stirring constantly. Stir in
the shrimps. Make a hollow in the mixture and
pour in the egg. When it is nearly cooked, stir it
through the rice. Add all the remaining ingredients
and simmer for a further 2 minutes.

Serves 4

Coconut Rice

30 ml./2 tablespoons cooking
   oil
1 onion, chopped
225 g./8 oz. long-grain rice
125 g./4 oz. creamed
   coconut, blended with 450
   ml./16 fl. oz. water
salt and pepper
40 g./1½ oz. sultanas
½ fresh coconut, flaked and
   toasted for 10 minutes

Heat the oil in a saucepan. Add the onion and fry for 5 minutes. Stir in the rice and cook for 2 minutes. Pour over the coconut liquid and bring to the boil. Stir in salt and pepper to taste and the sultanas. Cover and simmer for 15 to 20 minutes, or until the rice is cooked and tender and the liquid has been absorbed. Stir in half the toasted coconut flakes. Garnish with the remaining flakes.

Serves 4

Orange Rice

425 ml./15 fl. oz. chicken
   stock
150 ml./5 fl. oz. fresh orange
   juice
250 g./9 oz. long-grain rice
15 ml./1 tablespoon finely
   grated orange rind
salt and pepper
15 ml./1 tablespoon olive oil
10 ml./2 teaspoons white
   wine vinegar

Put the stock and orange juice in a saucepan and bring to the boil. Add the rice, orange rind and salt and pepper to taste and return to the boil. Cover and simmer for 15 to 20 minutes, or until the rice is cooked and tender and the liquid has been absorbed. Stir in the remaining ingredients.

Serves 4

Spanish Rice

50 g./2 oz. butter
1 garlic clove, crushed
2 onions, chopped
125 g./4 oz. mushrooms,
   sliced
3 tomatoes, skinned and
   chopped
225 g./8 oz. long-grain rice
150 ml./5 fl. oz. dry sherry
425 ml./15 fl. oz. chicken
   stock
350 g./12 oz. cooked
   chicken, chopped
25 g./1 oz. olives, chopped

Melt the butter in a saucepan. Add the garlic, onions, mushrooms and tomatoes and fry for 5 minutes. Stir in the rice and fry for 2 minutes. Pour in the sherry and stock and bring to the boil. Simmer for 15 minutes. Stir in the remaining ingredients and cook for 5 minutes, or until the rice is cooked and tender and the liquid has been absorbed.

Serves 4

Raisin Yellow Rice

15 g./½ oz. butter
250 g./9 oz. long-grain rice
600 ml./1 pint chicken stock
30 ml./2 tablespoons sugar
7.5 ml./1½ teaspoons
    turmeric
75 g./3 oz. raisins
salt and pepper

Melt the butter in a saucepan. Add the rice and fry for 2 minutes. Pour in the stock and bring to the boil. Add all the remaining ingredients and simmer for 15 to 20 minutes, or until the rice is cooked and tender and the liquid has been absorbed.

Serves 6

Tomato Rice

45 ml./3 tablespoons cooking
    oil
1 onion, chopped
1 garlic clove, crushed
15 ml./1 tablespoon finely
    chopped fresh root ginger
½ kg./1 lb. tomatoes, skinned
    and chopped
225 g./8 oz. long-grain rice
425 ml./15 fl. oz. chicken
    stock
salt and pepper
15 ml./1 tablespoon chopped
    fresh coriander leaves

Heat the oil in a saucepan. Add the onion, garlic, ginger and tomatoes and fry for 5 minutes. Stir in the rice and cook for 2 minutes. Pour over the stock and bring to the boil. Stir in salt and pepper to taste, cover and simmer for 15 to 20 minutes, or until the rice is cooked and tender and the liquid has been absorbed. Garnish with the coriander leaves.

Serves 4

Arroz con Pollo

45 ml./3 tablespoons cooking
    oil
4 lean bacon slices, chopped
1 large onion, chopped
2 garlic cloves, crushed
4 chicken pieces, skinned
1 × 400 g./14 oz. can
    tomatoes
2.5 ml./½ teaspoon saffron
    threads soaked in 30 ml./2
    tablespoons water
225 g./8 oz. long-grain rice
600 ml./1 pint chicken stock
175 g./6 oz. peas

Heat the oil in a saucepan. Add the bacon, onion and garlic and fry for 5 minutes. Transfer to a casserole. Add the chicken to the pan and brown on all sides. Transfer to the casserole. Add the tomatoes and can juice, saffron mixture and rice to the pan and cook for 2 minutes. Pour over the stock and bring to the boil. Transfer to the casserole.

Cover the casserole and put into the oven preheated to moderate (180°C/350°F or Gas Mark 4). Cook for 35 minutes. Stir in the peas and continue to cook for a further 10 to 15 minutes, or until the rice and chicken are cooked.

Serves 4

Rice Cacciatori

45 ml./3 tablespoons cooking
 oil
3 streaky bacon slices,
 chopped
2 onions, chopped
2 garlic cloves, crushed
½ kg./1 lb. minced beef
1 × 400 g./14 oz. can
 tomatoes
5 ml./1 teaspoon dried mixed
 herbs
25 g./1 oz. Parmesan cheese,
 grated
Rice
30 ml./2 tablespoons cooking
 oil
1 onion, chopped
1 green pepper, pith and
 seeds removed and
 chopped
225 g./8 oz. long-grain rice
425 ml./15 fl. oz. chicken
 stock
50 g./2 oz. salted peanuts
salt and pepper

Heat the oil in a saucepan. Add the bacon, onions and garlic and fry for 5 minutes. Stir in the beef and fry until it loses its pinkness. Stir in the tomatoes and can juice and mixed herbs and bring to the boil. Simmer for 45 minutes, or until thick and rich.

Meanwhile to make the rice, heat the oil in another saucepan. Add the onion and pepper and fry for 5 minutes. Stir in the rice and fry for 2 minutes. Pour over the stock and bring to the boil. Cover and simmer for 15 minutes. Stir in the peanuts and salt and pepper to taste and simmer for a further 5 minutes, or until the rice is cooked and tender and the stock has been absorbed. Serve the beef mixture on the rice, sprinkled with the grated cheese.

Serves 4

Jambalaya

50 ml./2 fl. oz. cooking oil
1 onion, chopped
1 garlic clove, crushed
1 green pepper, pith and
 seeds removed and
 chopped
350 g./12 oz. long-grain rice
600 ml./1 pint water
salt and pepper
10 ml./2 teaspoons mild
 chilli seasoning
1 × 400 g./14 oz. can
 tomatoes
175 g./6 oz. cooked ham,
 chopped
275 g./10 oz. cooked shrimps

Heat the oil in a saucepan. Add the onion, garlic and pepper and fry for 5 minutes. Stir in the rice and fry for 2 minutes. Pour in the water and bring to the boil. Simmer for 5 minutes. Add all the remaining ingredients and bring back to the boil. Simmer for 15 minutes, or until the rice is cooked and tender and the liquid has been absorbed.

Serves 4-6

Kedgeree

275 g./10 oz. long-grain rice
600 ml./1 pint chicken stock
275 g./10 oz. smoked
  haddock or cod
125 g./4 oz. butter
125 g./4 oz. mushrooms,
  sliced
2 hard-boiled eggs, chopped
salt and pepper
50 ml./2 fl. oz. single cream

Cook the rice in the boiling stock for 15 to 20 minutes or until it is cooked and tender and the liquid has been absorbed.

Meanwhile, pour boiling water over the smoked fish and set aside for 10 to 15 minutes or until it is cooked. Skin, bone and flake the fish. Melt the butter in a saucepan. Add the mushrooms and fry for 3 minutes. Stir in the cooked fish, rice, eggs, salt and pepper and cook for 5 minutes. Stir in the cream and serve.

Serves 4

Lamb Pilaff

50 g./2 oz. butter
1 kg./2 lb. lean lamb, cubed
1 onion, chopped
1 garlic clove, crushed
600 ml./1 pint chicken stock
1 × 400 g./14 oz. can
  tomatoes
salt and pepper
10 ml./2 teaspoons ground
  saffron
275 g./10 oz. long-grain rice
25 g./1 oz. flaked almonds

Melt the butter in a saucepan. Add the lamb, onion and garlic and fry until the lamb is evenly browned. Add half the stock and bring to the boil. Simmer for 30 minutes. Stir in all the remaining ingredients, except the almonds but including the remaining stock. Bring to the boil and simmer for a further 20 to 30 minutes or until the rice is cooked and tender and the lamb is cooked through. Stir in the almonds and simmer for 5 minutes.

Serves 4-6

Pineapple and Almond Pilaff

30 ml./2 tablespoons cooking
  oil
1 onion, chopped
1 garlic clove, crushed
15 ml./1 tablespoon finely
  chopped fresh root ginger
2 celery stalks, sliced
1 × 225 g./8 oz. can
  pineapple chunks
225 g./8 oz. long-grain rice
425 ml./15 fl. oz. water
salt and pepper
50 g./2 oz. chopped almonds

Heat the oil in a saucepan. Add the onion, garlic, ginger, celery and pineapple chunks. Fry for 5 minutes, then stir in the rice and fry for 2 minutes. Pour over the pineapple can juice and water and bring to the boil. Stir in salt and pepper to taste, cover and simmer for 10 minutes. Stir in the nuts, re-cover and continue to simmer for 5 to 10 minutes, or until the rice is cooked and tender and the liquid has been absorbed.

Serves 4

Nasi Goreng

225 g./8 oz. long-grain rice
75 g./3 oz. butter
225 g./8 oz. shelled shrimps
1 onion, chopped
4 spring onions, chopped
2 garlic cloves, crushed
½ kg./1 lb. rump beef, cut into
    thin strips
salt and pepper
30 ml./2 tablespoons soy
    sauce
125 g./4 oz. bean sprouts
Omelet
5 eggs
45 ml./3 tablespoons milk
15 g./½ oz. butter

Cook the rice in boiling, salted water for 15 to 20 minutes or until it is cooked and tender and the liquid is absorbed. Melt 25 g./1 oz. of the butter in a frying-pan. Add the shrimps and sauté for 2 minutes. Set aside. Melt the remaining butter in the pan. Add the onion, spring onions and garlic and fry for 5 minutes. Stir in the meat and salt and pepper and fry, stirring constantly, for 5 minutes or until the meat is cooked through. Set aside.

To make the omelet, beat together the eggs, milk and salt and pepper to taste. Melt the butter in another frying-pan. Add the mixture and cook until the top is creamy and the underside brown. Remove from the pan and cut into thin strips.

Return the pan with the meat to low heat. Stir in the rice, shrimps, omelet strips, soy sauce and bean sprouts and cook for 5 minutes or until the mixture is hot.

Serves 4

Paella

50 g./2 oz. butter
4 small chicken joints,
    skinned
1 onion, chopped
1 garlic clove, crushed
1¼ l./2 pints water
2 tomatoes, skinned and
    chopped
125 g./4 oz. long-grain rice
1 chicken stock cube,
    crumbled
2.5 ml./½ teaspoon ground
    saffron
2 scallops, chopped
8 large shrimps or prawns,
    shelled
8 mussels
225 g./8 oz. peas
1 red pepper, pith and seeds
    removed and chopped

Melt the butter in a saucepan. Add the chicken, onion and garlic and fry until the chicken is evenly browned. Stir in half the water and bring to the boil. Simmer for 15 minutes. Add the tomatoes, rice, stock cube, saffron and remaining water. Simmer for 5 minutes. Add all the remaining ingredients, bring to the boil and simmer for a further 10 to 15 minutes or until the rice is cooked and tender and the liquid has been absorbed.

Serves 4

Biryani

50 ml./2 fl. oz. cooking oil
1 onion, chopped
1 garlic clove, crushed
1 kg./2 lb. lean lamb, cubed
5 ml./1 teaspoon ground
  cinnamon
10 ml./2 teaspoons ground
  cloves
5 ml./1 teaspoon ground
  cardamom
300 ml./10 fl. oz. plain
  yogurt
600 ml./1 pint water
275 g./10 oz. long-grain rice
5 ml./1 teaspoon ground
  saffron
25 g./1 oz. almonds, toasted
  and chopped

Heat the oil in a saucepan. Add the onion, garlic and lamb and fry until the lamb is evenly browned. Stir in the spices and yogurt and bring to the boil. Simmer for 40 minutes.

Meanwhile boil the water, then add the rice and saffron. Simmer for 15 to 20 minutes or until the rice is cooked and tender and the liquid has been absorbed. Transfer about one-third of the rice to an ovenproof casserole. Spoon over half the lamb mixture. Continue making layers until all the ingredients have been used up. Put the dish into the oven preheated to moderate (180°C/350°F or Gas Mark 4) and cook for 30 minutes. Garnish with the toasted almonds.

Serves 6

Curried Rice and Prawns

50 g./2 oz. butter
1 large onion, chopped
1 dessert apple, cored and
  chopped
15 ml./1 tablespoon curry
  powder
225 g./8 oz. long-grain rice
15 ml./1 tablespoon tomato
  purée
425 ml./15 fl. oz. chicken
  stock
salt and pepper
1 carrot, chopped
275 g./10 oz. shelled prawns
1 green pepper, pith and
  seeds removed and sliced
  in rings
1 lemon, thinly sliced

Melt the butter in a saucepan. Add the onion and apple and fry for 5 minutes. Stir in the curry powder and rice and fry for 2 minutes, then add the tomato purée, stock and salt and pepper to taste. Bring to the boil and simmer for 15 to 20 minutes, stirring occasionally. Stir in the carrot and prawns and cook for a further 5 minutes, or until the rice is cooked and tender and the liquid has been absorbed. Garnish with the pepper and lemon.

Serves 4

Dry Chicken Curry with Yellow Rice

40 g./1½ oz. butter
1 onion, chopped
1 green pepper, pith and
    seeds removed and
    chopped
15 ml./1 tablespoon hot curry
    powder
5 ml./1 teaspoon chilli
    powder
4 chicken joints, skinned
50 ml./2 fl. oz. chicken stock
4 tomatoes, skinned and
    chopped
50 ml./2 fl. oz. plain yogurt
Rice
25 g./1 oz. butter
225 g./8 oz. long-grain rice
10 ml./2 teaspoons turmeric
2.5 ml./½ teaspoon ground
    cloves
5 ml./1 teaspoon ground
    cumin
600 ml./1 pint chicken stock

Melt the butter in a flameproof casserole. Add the onion and pepper and fry for 5 minutes. Stir in the curry and chilli powders, then add the chicken joints and brown on all sides. Stir in the stock and tomatoes and bring to the boil. Cover and simmer for 1 hour, or until the chicken is cooked and tender.

Meanwhile to make the rice, melt the butter in a saucepan. Add the rice and fry for 5 minutes. Add all the remaining ingredients and bring to the boil. Cover and simmer for 15 to 20 minutes or until the rice is cooked and tender and the liquid has been absorbed.

Stir the yogurt into the chicken mixture, then pour over the rice.

Serves 4

Chicken Pilaff

30 ml./2 tablespoons cooking
    oil
2 onions, chopped
1 garlic clove, crushed
225 g/8 oz. long-grain rice
600 ml./1 pint chicken stock
50 g./2 oz. sultanas
25 g./1 oz. chopped almonds
350 g./12 oz. cooked
    chicken, chopped
5 ml./1 teaspoon dried thyme
salt and pepper

Heat the oil in a saucepan. Add the onions and garlic and fry for 5 minutes. Stir in the rice and fry for 2 minutes. Pour in the stock and bring to the boil. Simmer for 10 minutes. Stir in all the remaining ingredients, cover and continue to simmer for a further 5 to 10 minutes or until the rice is cooked and tender and the liquid has been absorbed.

Serves 4

Beef Risotto Milanaise

50 ml./2 fl. oz. cooking oil
2 onions, chopped
2 garlic cloves, crushed
½ kg./1 lb. minced beef
1 × 400 g./14 oz. can
   tomatoes
4 carrots, chopped
salt and pepper
5 ml./1 teaspoon dried thyme
50 g./2 oz. tomato purée
225 g./8 oz. long-grain rice
600 ml./1 pint chicken stock

Heat the oil in a saucepan. Add the onions and garlic and fry for 5 minutes. Stir in the beef and fry until it loses its pinkness. Stir in the tomatoes and can juice, carrots, salt and pepper to taste, thyme and tomato purée. Bring to the boil, then simmer for 45 minutes, or until thick and rich.

Meanwhile put the rice and stock into a saucepan and bring to the boil. Cover and simmer for 15 to 20 minutes or until the rice is cooked and tender and the stock has been absorbed. Serve the beef mixture on the cooked rice.

Serves 4

Chicken Liver Risotto

125 g./4 oz. butter
2 onions, finely chopped
3 celery stalks, chopped
½ kg./1 lb. chicken livers,
   chopped
225 g./8 oz. long-grain rice
600 ml./1 pint chicken stock
50 g./2 oz. Parmesan cheese,
   grated
salt and pepper

Melt half the butter in a saucepan. Add the onions and celery and fry for 5 minutes. Stir in the chicken livers and fry for 5 minutes. Add the rice and remaining butter and fry, stirring constantly, for 3 minutes. Pour in the stock and bring to the boil. Simmer for 15 to 20 minutes, or until the rice is cooked and tender and the liquid has been absorbed. Stir in the cheese and salt and pepper to taste.

Serves 4

Corn Risotto

45 ml./3 tablespoons cooking
   oil
1 onion, chopped
1 green pepper, pith and
   seeds removed and
   chopped
1 red pepper, pith and seeds
   removed and chopped
225 g./8 oz. long-grain rice
600 ml./1 pint water
salt and pepper
2.5 ml./½ teaspoon cayenne
   pepper
275 g./10 oz. sweetcorn
50 ml./2 fl. oz. double cream

Heat the oil in a saucepan. Add the onion and peppers and fry for 5 minutes. Stir in the rice and cook for 2 minutes. Pour in the water and bring to the boil. Stir in the salt and pepper to taste and cayenne, cover and simmer for 10 minutes. Stir in the sweetcorn, re-cover and continue to simmer for 5 to 10 minutes, or until the rice is cooked and tender and the liquid has been absorbed. Stir in the cream and heat gently for 2 minutes.

Serves 4

Fish Risotto

45 ml./3 tablespoons cooking
  oil
1 onion, chopped
1 garlic clove, crushed
225 g./8 oz. long-grain rice
600 ml./1 pint fish stock *
5 ml./1 teaspoon lemon
  thyme
10 ml./2 teaspoons finely
  grated lemon rind
30 ml./2 tablespoons lemon
  juice
½ kg./1 lb. white fish fillets,
  skinned and chopped
15 ml./1 tablespoon chopped
  fresh parsley

Heat the oil in a saucepan. Add the onion and garlic and fry for 5 minutes. Stir in the rice and fry for 2 minutes. Pour over the stock and bring to the boil. Stir in the lemon thyme, lemon rind and juice. Cover and simmer for 5 minutes. Stir in the fish, re-cover and continue to simmer for 10 to 15 minutes, or until the rice is cooked and tender and the liquid has been absorbed. Garnish with the parsley.

Serves 4

Oven-Baked Risotto

45 ml./3 tablespoons cooking
  oil
2 onions, sliced
1 garlic clove, crushed
1 green pepper, pith and
  seeds removed and
  chopped
125 g./4 oz. mushrooms,
  thinly sliced
225 g./8 oz. long-grain rice
900 ml./1½ pints chicken
  stock
salt and pepper
75 g./3 oz. sultanas
175 g./6 oz. chicken livers,
  chopped
25 g./1 oz. Cheddar cheese,
  grated

Heat the oil in a flameproof casserole. Add the onions, garlic, pepper and mushrooms and fry for 5 minutes. Stir in the rice and fry for 2 minutes. Pour over the stock and bring to the boil. Stir in salt and pepper to taste, the sultanas and livers. Cover the casserole and put into the oven preheated to moderate (180°C/350°F or Gas Mark 4). Bake for 1 hour, or until the rice is cooked and tender and the liquid has been absorbed. Sprinkle over the cheese.

Serves 4

Risotto

25 g./1 oz. butter
1 onion, finely chopped
450 g./1 lb. Italian rice
1¼ l./2 pints chicken stock
25 g./1 oz. Parmesan cheese,
  grated

Melt half the butter in a saucepan. Add the onion and fry for 5 minutes. Add the rice and stir to mix well. Pour in about one-third of the stock and simmer until it has been absorbed. Add another one-third, and continue the process until all the stock has been used and the rice is cooked and tender. Stir in the remaining butter and the grated cheese until they melt.

Serves 6

Risotto Milanese

50 g./2 oz. butter
1 onion, chopped
30 ml./2 tablespoons beef
  marrow
450 g./1 lb. Italian rice
1¼ l./2 pints chicken stock
5 ml./1 teaspoon ground
  saffron
25 g./1 oz. Parmesan cheese,
  grated

Melt the butter in a saucepan. Add the onion and marrow and fry for 5 minutes. Add the rice and stir to mix well. Pour in about one-third of the stock and saffron. Simmer until it has been absorbed. Add another one-third and continue the process until all the stock has been used and the rice is cooked and tender. Stir in the grated cheese until it melts.

Serves 6

Vegetable Risotto I

125 g./4 oz. butter
3 onions, chopped
2 green peppers, pith and
  seeds removed and
  chopped
1 red pepper, pith and seeds
  removed and chopped
175 g./6 oz. mushrooms,
  thinly sliced
225 g./8 oz. long-grain rice
425 ml./15 fl. oz. water
salt and pepper
2.5 ml./½ teaspon saffron
  threads soaked in 30 ml./2
  tablespoons water
50 g./2 oz. Cheddar cheese,
  grated

Melt the butter in a saucepan. Add the onions, peppers and mushrooms and fry for 5 minutes. Stir in the rice and fry for 2 minutes. Pour over the water and bring to the boil. Stir in salt and pepper to taste and the saffron mixture. Cover and simmer for 15 to 20 minutes, or until the rice is cooked and tender and the liquid has been absorbed. Stir in half the cheese and heat for 2 minutes, or until it has melted. Sprinkle over the remaining cheese.

Serves 4

Vegetable Risotto II

50 ml./2 fl. oz. cooking oil
1 large leek, chopped
3 carrots, chopped
225 g./8 oz. mushrooms,
   sliced
½ kg./1 lb. tomatoes, skinned
   and chopped
125 g./4 oz. peas
225 g./8 oz. long-grain rice
425 ml./15 fl. oz. chicken
   stock
30 ml./2 tablespoons
   chopped fresh parsley
175 g./6 oz. Cheddar cheese,
   grated

Heat the oil in a saucepan. Add the leek, carrots, mushrooms and tomatoes and fry for 5 minutes. Stir in the peas and rice and fry for 2 minutes. Pour in the stock and bring to the boil. Cover and simmer for 15 to 20 minutes, or until the rice is cooked and tender and the liquid has been absorbed. Stir in the parsley and half the cheese and heat for 3 to 4 minutes, or until the cheese has melted. Sprinkle over the remaining cheese.

Serves 4

Mushroom Risotto

50 g./2 oz. butter
1 onion, chopped
1 garlic clove, crushed
225 g./8 oz. mushrooms,
   sliced
450 g./1 lb. Italian rice
1¼ l./2 pints chicken stock
5 ml./1 teaspoon grated
   nutmeg
25 g./1 oz. Parmesan cheese,
   grated

Melt the butter in a saucepan. Add the onion and garlic and fry for 5 minutes. Add the mushrooms and fry for 3 minutes. Add the rice and stir to mix well. Pour in about one-third of the stock and the nutmeg. Simmer until it has been absorbed. Add another one-third and continue the process until all the stock has been used and the rice is cooked and tender. Stir in the grated cheese until it melts.

Serves 6

Risi e Bisi

50 g./2 oz. butter
1 onion, chopped
3 streaky bacon slices,
   chopped
450 g./1 lb. Italian rice
1¼ l./2 pints chicken stock
175 g./6 oz. peas
25 g./1 oz. Parmesan cheese,
   grated

Melt the butter in a saucepan. Add the onion and bacon and fry for 5 minutes. Add the rice and stir to mix well. Pour in about one-third of the stock and simmer until it has been absorbed. Add another one-third and the peas and continue the process until all the stock has been used and the rice is cooked and tender. Stir in the grated cheese until it melts.

Serves 6

Cheese & Egg Dishes

Scrambled Eggs

25 g./1 oz. butter
4 eggs, lightly beaten
salt and pepper
2 slices hot buttered toast

Melt half of the butter in a saucepan. Add the eggs, salt and pepper to taste and cook over low heat until the eggs start to thicken. Add the remaining butter and cook, stirring, for a further 30 seconds. Remove from the heat and serve on hot buttered toast.

Serves 2

Welsh Rarebit

25 g./1 oz. butter
5 ml./1 teaspoon mustard
salt and pepper
pinch of cayenne pepper
15 ml./1 tablespoon beer
175 g./6 oz. Cheddar cheese,
*   grated*
4 slices buttered toast

Mix together the butter, mustard, salt and pepper to taste, cayenne, beer and cheese in a saucepan. Heat gently until the cheese begins to melt. Spread over the toast and brown under the grill for 3 minutes.

Serves 4

Cheese Fritters

50 g./2 oz. cooked macaroni,
  or other pasta, finely
  chopped
2 eggs, lightly beaten
50 g./2 oz. Cheddar cheese,
  grated
salt and pepper
pinch of dried mixed herbs
50 ml./2 fl. oz. oil

Mix together the pasta, eggs, cheese, salt and pepper to taste and herbs. Heat the oil in a frying-pan. When it is hot, drop in spoonfuls of the cheese mixture and fry for 2 to 4 minutes or until they are evenly browned. Drain on kitchen towels.

Serves 2

Yorkshire Pudding

125 g./4 oz. flour
salt
1 large egg
300 ml./10 fl. oz. milk
15 ml./1 tablespoon oil

Sift together the flour and salt. Mix in the egg with half of the milk. Beat for 10 minutes or until the batter is bubbly. Stir in the remaining milk. Cover and set aside for 30 minutes.

Heat the oil in a flameproof baking dish and pour in the batter. Put into the oven preheated to hot (220°C/425°F or Gas Mark 7) and bake for 1 hour, or until risen and golden brown.

Serves 4

Omelet

3 eggs
salt and pepper
15 g./½ oz. butter

Beat the eggs and seasoning to taste with a fork until lightly mixed. Slowly heat a heavy, 18 cm./7 in. omelet pan. Add the butter and, as soon as it has melted, pour in the eggs. Using the fork, keep drawing some of the mixture to the middle from the sides of the pan so the uncooked egg may set. Cook for 1½ to 2 minutes or until the omelet is soft but not runny. At this point, the filling, if required, should be added. Remove the pan from the heat and fold the omelet in half.

Note: A 2-egg omelet should ideally be cooked in a 15 cm./6 in. omelet pan for the best results.

Serves 1-2

Bread and Cheese Pie

8 slices of bread, crusts
removed
200 ml./7 fl. oz. milk
1 thick slice of bread, crusts
removed and cubed
50 g./2 oz. butter
3 eggs, separated
50 g./2 oz. flour, sifted
225 g./8 oz. cheese, grated
salt
pinch of cayenne pepper
125 ml./4 fl. oz. single cream

Put the bread slices in a dish and pour over half of the milk. Put the bread cubes in another dish and pour over the remaining milk. Cream the butter and mix in the egg yolks. Stir in the flour, soaked bread cubes, cheese, salt, cayenne and cream. Beat the egg whites until they are stiff and fold into the cheese mixture.

Line a greased, straight-sided ovenproof dish with the soaked bread slices and pour in the cheese mixture. Put into the oven preheated to moderate (180°C/350°F or Gas Mark 4) and bake for 40 minutes, or until the filling is firm and golden brown.

Serves 4

Eggs Florentine

675 g./1½ lb. spinach, cooked
and puréed
350 ml./12 fl. oz. hot
béchamel sauce*
pinch of grated nutmeg
8 hot poached eggs
50 g./2 oz. cheese, grated

Put the spinach in a saucepan and stir in about one-quarter of the béchamel sauce and the nutmeg. Cook for 3 minutes or until hot and smooth. Pour into a flameproof serving dish and carefully place the eggs on top. Pour over the remaining béchamel sauce and sprinkle over the cheese. Grill for 3 minutes or until the cheese is golden brown and bubbling.

Serves 4

Cheese Soufflé

25 g./1 oz. butter
25 g./1 oz. flour
150 ml./5 fl. oz. milk
salt and pepper
3 egg yolks
75 g./3 oz. cheese, grated
3 egg whites, stiffly beaten

Melt the butter in a saucepan and stir in the flour to form a smooth paste. Gradually stir in the milk and bring to the boil. Cook for 2 to 3 minutes, stirring constantly, or until the mixture thickens. Season with salt and pepper to taste. Remove from the heat and stir in the egg yolks and cheese. Fold in the egg whites and spoon into a greased soufflé dish. Put into the oven preheated to fairly hot (200°C/400°F or Gas Mark 6) and bake for 30 minutes, or until the soufflé has risen and is golden brown.

Serves 4

Pipérade

50 g./2 oz. butter
2 red or green peppers, pith
    and seeds removed and
    chopped
1 onion, chopped
2 tomatoes, skinned and
    chopped
1 garlic clove, crushed
6 eggs
salt and pepper

Melt the butter in a saucepan. Add the peppers, onion, tomatoes and garlic and cook gently for 10 to 15 minutes or until the vegetables are tender. Beat the eggs with salt and pepper to taste and stir into the vegetable mixture. Leave for 1 minute, then cook, stirring gently, until the eggs have scrambled and are lightly set.

Serves 3

Fried Eggs Turque

50 g./2 oz. butter
6 chicken livers, sliced
10 ml./2 teaspoons chopped
    fresh parsley
4 large tomatoes, skinned
    and chopped
salt and pepper
4 eggs

Melt half of the butter in a frying-pan. Add the chicken livers and fry for 8 to 12 minutes or until they are tender. Stir in the parsley, then spoon into the centre of a warmed serving dish. Keep hot.

Put the tomatoes and salt and pepper to taste in a small saucepan and cook until they form a thick purée. Spoon the tomatoes over the chicken livers. Melt the remaining butter in a frying-pan. Break in the eggs and fry until they are done to taste. Arrange around the tomato and liver mixture.

Serves 4

Eggs in Curry Sauce

6 hard-boiled eggs, halved
   lengthways
½ lettuce, shredded
300 ml./10 fl. oz.
   mayonnaise
10 ml./2 teaspoons lemon
   juice
5 ml./1 teaspoon curry
   powder
15 ml./1 tablespoon chutney
pinch of chilli powder
salt and pepper

Arrange the eggs, cut sides down, on six small plates with the lettuce. Blend together the remaining ingredients and spoon over the eggs.

Serves 6

Eggs Ragoût-in-a-pan

125 g./4 oz. streaky bacon,
   diced
1 large onion, thinly sliced
1 medium can baked beans
salt and pepper
50 g./2 oz. butter, cut into
   pieces
4–6 eggs

Cook the bacon in a frying-pan until it has rendered most of its fat. Add the onion and fry for 5 minutes. Add the beans, season with salt and pepper to taste and stir well. Make four or six 'wells' in the mixture. Put a small knob of butter into each well. When the butter has melted, drop in an egg and cook for 3 to 5 minutes or until the egg whites have set.

Serves 4-6

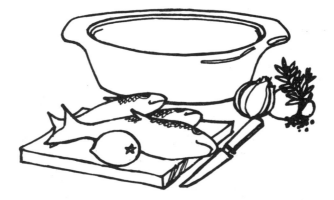

Eggs Au Gratin

4 hard-boiled eggs, halved
25 g./1 oz. butter
25 g./1 oz. flour
300 ml./10 fl. oz. milk
salt and pepper
125 g./4 oz. Cheddar cheese,
    grated
Topping
30 ml./2 tablespoons grated
    Cheddar cheese
30 ml./2 tablespoons
    breadcrumbs

Arrange the eggs, cut sides down, in a flameproof serving dish and keep warm. Melt the butter in a saucepan and stir in the flour to form a smooth paste. Gradually stir in the milk and bring to the boil. Cook for 2 to 3 minutes, stirring constantly, or until the sauce thickens. Season well and stir in the grated cheese. When the cheese has melted, pour the sauce over the eggs. Sprinkle over the cheese and breadcrumbs for the topping and grill for 3 minutes or until golden brown.

Serves 2

Fish Ramekins

1 × 200 g./7 oz. can tuna,
    drained and flaked
salt and pepper
150 ml./5 fl. oz. double
    cream
4 eggs
50 g./2 oz. Cheddar cheese,
    grated

Mix together the tuna, salt and pepper to taste and 45 ml./3 tablespoons of the cream. Put an equal amount of the mixture into four individual oven-proof ramekin dishes. Carefully break one egg into each of the dishes. Top with the rest of the cream, then sprinkle over the grated cheese.

Put into the oven preheated to hot (220°C/425°F or Gas Mark 7) and bake for 15 minutes, or until the eggs have set and the cheese is golden brown.

Serves 4

Flans & Quiches

German Onion Flan

23 cm./9 in. shortcrust pastry
  flan case*
25 g./1 oz. butter
3 medium onions, thinly
  sliced
3 eggs
150 ml./5 fl. oz. single cream
5 ml./1 teaspoon caraway
  seeds
salt and pepper

Put the flan case on a baking sheet. Melt the butter in a frying-pan. Add the onions and fry for 5 minutes. Mix together the eggs, cream, caraway seeds and salt and pepper to taste. Add to the onions and stir well. Pour into the flan case. Put into the oven preheated to fairly hot (200°C/400°F or Gas Mark 6) and bake for 40 minutes, or until the filling is firm and golden brown. Serve hot or cold.

Serves 4-6

Sardine and Tomato Flan

23 cm./9 in. shortcrust pastry
  flan case*
1 onion, blanched for 5
  minutes in boiling water,
  drained and chopped
1 × 275 g./10 oz. can
  sardines, drained
3 tomatoes, thinly sliced
6 anchovies
6 black olives
3 eggs
175 ml./6 fl. oz. single cream
salt and pepper

Put the flan case on a baking sheet. Arrange the onion over the base of the flan case and lay the sardines and tomatoes on top. Put the anchovies and olives in a decorative pattern over the tomatoes. Mix together the eggs, cream and salt and pepper to taste. Pour into the flan case very carefully. Put into the oven preheated to fairly hot (200°C/400°F or Gas Mark 6) and bake for 40 minutes, or until the filling is firm and golden brown. Serve hot or cold.

Serves 4-6

Cauliflower and Walnut Flan

23 cm./9 in. shortcrust pastry
  flan case*
1 small cauliflower, cooked
  and divided into sprigs
15 g./½ oz. butter
1 onion, finely chopped
3 eggs
150 ml./5 fl. oz. single cream
75 g./3 oz. walnuts, chopped
salt and pepper
pinch of of grated nutmeg
50 g./2 oz. cheese, grated

Put the flan case on a baking sheet and arrange the cauliflower sprigs over the base. Melt the butter in a frying-pan. Add the onion and fry for 5 minutes. Mix together the eggs, cream, walnuts, salt and pepper to taste and nutmeg. Stir in the grated cheese and add to the onion. Mix well and pour into the flan case. Put into the oven preheated to fairly hot (200°C/400°F or Gas Mark 6) and bake for 40 minutes, or until the filling is firm and golden brown. Serve hot or cold.

Serves 4-6

Cod and Leek Flan

23 cm./9 in. shortcrust pastry
  flan case*
25 g./1 oz. butter
½ kg./1 lb. leeks, sliced
½ kg./1 lb. cod, skinned,
  boned and flaked
salt and pepper
15 ml./1 tablespoon chopped
  fresh parsley
300 ml./10 fl. oz. hot
  béchamel sauce*

Put the flan case on a baking sheet. Melt the butter in a saucepan. Add the leeks and fry for 5 minutes. Stir in the fish, salt and pepper to taste, parsley and béchamel sauce. Pour the mixture into the flan case and put into the oven preheated to fairly hot (200°C/400°F or Gas Mark 6). Bake for 30 minutes, or until the filling is firm and golden brown. Serve hot.

Serves 4-6

Cream Cheese Flan

23 cm./9 in. shortcrust pastry
  flan case*
250 g./9 oz. cream cheese
125 ml./4 fl. oz. double
  cream
6 eggs
30 ml./2 tablespoons
  chopped spring onions
salt and pepper
15 ml./1 tablespoon chopped
  fresh parsley

Put the flan case on a baking sheet. Beat the cream cheese and cream together until smooth. Beat in the eggs, spring onions, salt and pepper to taste and parsley. Spoon into the flan case and put into the oven preheated to fairly hot (200°C/400°F or Gas Mark 6). Bake for 40 minutes, or until the filling is firm and golden brown. Serve hot or cold.

Serves 4-6

Carrot Flan

23 cm./9 in. shortcrust pastry
  flan case*
½ kg./1 lb. carrots, sliced
10 ml./2 teaspoons sugar
50 ml./2 fl. oz. water
50 ml./2 oz. butter
1 onion, chopped
5 ml./1 teaspoon cornflour
150 ml./5 fl. oz. double
  cream
salt and pepper

Put the flan case on a baking sheet. Put the carrots, sugar and water in a saucepan and bring to the boil. Cover and simmer for 20 minutes or until the carrots are just tender. Drain and reserve the cooking liquid.

Melt the butter in a frying-pan. Add the onion and fry for 5 minutes. Add the carrots. Mix the cornflour with the reserved carrot cooking liquid to form a smooth paste and add to the onion and carrots. Cook, stirring constantly, for 2 to 3 minutes or until the mixture thickens. Stir in the cream and salt and pepper to taste. Pour into the flan case. Put into the oven preheated to fairly hot (200°C/400°F or Gas Mark 6) and bake for 20 minutes, or until the filling is firm and golden brown. Serve hot or cold.

Serves 4-6

Vegetable Flan

23 cm./9 in. shortcrust pastry
  flan case, baked blind*
25 g./1 oz. butter
1 onion, finely chopped
25 g./1 oz. flour
300 ml./10 fl. oz. milk
1 large potato, cooked and
  sliced
1 large carrot, cooked and
  sliced
30 ml./2 tablespoons frozen
  peas
salt and pepper
4 hard-boiled eggs, sliced
50 g./2 oz. cheese, grated

Put the flan case on a baking sheet. Melt the butter in a frying-pan. Add the onion and fry for 5 minutes. Stir in the flour to form a smooth paste. Gradually stir in the milk and bring to the boil. Cook for 2 to 3 minutes, stirring constantly, or until the liquid thickens. Add the potato, carrot, peas and salt and pepper. Arrange the eggs in the flan case and pour in the vegetable mixture. Sprinkle over the cheese and grill for 4 minutes or until the cheese has melted and is golden brown. Serve hot.

Serves 4-6

Leek and Mushroom Flan

23 cm./9 in. shortcrust pastry
   flan case*
25 g./1 oz. butter
2 medium leeks, sliced into
   thin rings
125 g./4 oz. mushrooms,
   sliced
150 ml./5 fl. oz. single cream
3 eggs
175 g./6 oz. cheese, grated
salt and pepper

Put the flan case on a baking sheet. Melt the butter in a frying-pan. Add the leeks and cook gently for 10 minutes. Add the mushrooms and cook for 5 minutes. Transfer the leeks and mushrooms to the flan case.

Mix together the cream, eggs, cheese, salt and pepper to taste and pour into the flan case. Put into the oven preheated to fairly hot (200°C/400°F or Gas Mark 6) and bake for 40 minutes, or until the filling is firm and golden brown. Serve hot or cold.

Serves 4-6

Chicken Flan

23 cm./9 in. shortcrust pastry
   flan case*
225 g./8 oz. cooked chicken,
   chopped
50 g./2 oz. cooked bacon,
   chopped
150 ml./5 fl. oz. single cream
3 eggs
50 g./2 oz. Gruyère cheese,
   grated
15 ml./1 tablespoon chopped
   chives
salt and pepper

Put the flan case on a baking sheet. Put the chicken and bacon on the base of the flan case. Mix together the cream, eggs, cheese, chives and salt and pepper to taste. Pour into the flan case. Put into the oven preheated to fairly hot (200°C/400°F or Gas Mark 6) and bake for 40 minutes, or until the filling is firm and golden brown. Serve hot or cold.

Serves 4-6

Pissaladière

23 cm./9 in. rich shortcrust
   pastry flan case*
15 ml./1 tablespoon oil
25 g./1 oz. butter
675 g./1½ lb. onions, finely
   sliced
salt and pepper
pinch of grated nutmeg
3 egg yolks
45 ml./3 tablespoons milk
125 g./4 oz. cream cheese,
   softened
Topping
about 16 anchovy fillets and
   16 black olives

Put the flan case on a baking sheet. Heat the oil
and butter in a frying-pan. Add the onions, cover
and cook gently for 30 minutes or until they are
soft and pale gold. Stir in salt, pepper and nutmeg
and put on one side.

Mix together the egg yolks, milk and cheese.
Add to the onion mixture and stir well. Pour into
the flan case and put into the oven preheated to
moderate (180°C/350°F or Gas Mark 4). Bake for
20 minutes, or until the filling is set. Arrange the
anchovy fillets in a lattice on top of the filling with
the black olives. Bake for a further 10 minutes.
Serve hot or cold.

Serves 4-6

Sausagemeat Flan

23 cm./9 in. shortcrust pastry
   flan case,* dough
   trimmings reserved
50 g./2 oz. butter
2 onions, finely chopped
225 g./8 oz. sausagemeat
225 g./8 oz. cooked beef,
   minced
30 ml./2 tablespoons tomato
   ketchup
salt and pepper
2.5 ml./½ teaspoon dried sage
1 egg, beaten

Put the flan case on a baking sheet. Melt the butter
in a frying-pan. Add the onions and fry for 5
minutes. Add the sausagemeat and fry until it loses
its pinkness. Stir in the beef, tomato ketchup, salt
and pepper to taste and sage and cook for a further
2 minutes. Cool, then spoon into the flan case.

Roll out the reserved dough trimmings and cut
into thin strips. Arrange the strips over the flan to
form a lattice. Brush the dough with the beaten egg
and put into the oven preheated to moderate
(180°C/350°F or Gas Mark 4) Bake for 40
minutes, or until the pastry is golden brown. Serve
hot or cold.

Serves 4-6

Smoked Haddock Quiche

23 cm./9 in. shortcrust pastry
    flan case*
225 g./8 oz. smoked
    haddock fillets
30 ml./2 tablespoons frozen
    peas
25 g./1 oz. butter
1 onion, chopped
15 ml./1 tablespoon chopped
    fresh parsley
pepper
pinch of cayenne pepper
150 ml./5 fl. oz. single cream
3 eggs
50 g./2 oz. Cheddar cheese,
    grated

Put the flan case on a baking sheet. Put the haddock and peas in a heatproof bowl and pour over enough boiling water to cover. When the water has cooled, drain the haddock and peas. Flake and skin the haddock and set aside.

Melt the butter in a frying-pan. Add the onion and fry for 5 minutes. Stir in the flaked haddock, peas, parsley, pepper and cayenne. Mix together the cream, eggs and cheese and stir into the haddock mixture. Pour into the flan case. Put into the oven preheated to fairly hot (200°C/400°F or Gas Mark 6) and bake for 40 minutes, or until the filling is firm and golden brown. Serve hot or cold.

Serves 4-6

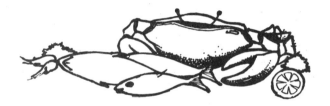

Salmon Quiche

23 cm./9 in. shortcrust pastry
    flan case*
25 g./1 oz. butter
1 large onion, finely chopped
30 ml./2 tablespoons
    chopped green pepper
1 × 200 g./7 oz. can salmon,
    drained and flaked
salt and pepper
pinch of cayenne pepper
150 ml./5 fl. oz. single cream
3 eggs
50 g./2 oz. Cheddar cheese,
    grated
50 g./2 oz. green olives,
    chopped

Put the flan case on a baking sheet. Melt the butter in a frying-pan. Add the onion and fry for 5 minutes. Stir in the green pepper, salmon, salt, pepper and cayenne. Cook for 2 minutes and cool.

Mix together the cream, eggs, cheese and olives. Stir into the salmon and pepper mixture and pour into the flan case. Put into the oven preheated to fairly hot (200°C/400°F or Gas Mark 6) and bake for 40 minutes, or until the filling is firm and golden brown. Serve hot or cold.

Serves 4-6

Quiche Lorraine

23 cm./9 in. shortcrust pastry
flan case*
125 g./4 oz. Gruyère cheese,
thinly sliced
225 g./8 oz. bacon, fried and
chopped
125 ml./5 fl. oz. single cream
3 eggs
salt and pepper

Put the flan case on a baking sheet. Arrange the cheese slices over the base of the flan. Sprinkle over the chopped bacon. Mix together the cream, eggs and salt and pepper to taste and pour into the flan case. Put into the oven preheated to fairly hot (200°C/400°F or Gas Mark 6) and bake for 40 minutes, or until the filling is firm and golden. Serve hot or cold.

Serves 4-6

Tomato and Basil Quiche

23 cm./9 in. shortcrust pastry
flan case*
25 g./1 oz. butter
1 onion, thinly sliced
5 large tomatoes, skinned
and thinly sliced
150 ml./5 fl. oz. single cream
3 eggs
50 g./2 oz. Cheddar cheese,
grated
30 ml./2 tablespoons
chopped fresh basil
salt and pepper

Put the flan case on a baking sheet. Melt the butter in a frying-pan. Add the onion and fry for 5 minutes. Spread the onion over the base of the flan case. Arrange the tomatoes in circles over the onion. Mix together the cream, eggs and cheese. Stir in the basil, salt and pepper to taste. Pour over the tomatoes. Put into the oven preheated to fairly hot (200°C/400°F or Gas Mark 6) and bake for 40 minutes, or until the filling is firm and golden brown. Serve hot or cold.

Serves 4-6

Prawn and Courgette Quiche

23 cm./9 in. shortcrust pastry
flan case*
50 g./2 oz. butter
1 onion, finely chopped
4 courgettes, sliced
275 g./10 oz. shelled prawns
salt and pepper
pinch of grated nutmeg
150 ml./5 fl. oz. single cream
3 eggs
50 g./2 oz. Cheddar cheese,
grated

Put the flan case on a baking sheet. Melt the butter in a saucepan. Add the onion and fry for 5 minutes. Add the courgettes and fry for 10 minutes, or until they are lightly browned. Stir in the prawns and cook for 3 minutes. Stir in the salt, pepper and nutmeg and cool.

Mix together the cream, eggs and cheese, then add to the prawns and courgettes. Pour into the flan case. Put into the oven preheated to fairly hot (200°C/400°F or Gas Mark 6) and bake for about 40 minutes, or until the filling is firm and golden brown. Serve hot or cold.

Serves 4-6

Spinach Quiche

23 cm./9 in. shortcrust pastry
   flan case*
50 g./2 oz. butter
1 onion, chopped
675 g./1½ lb. spinach
150 ml./5 fl. oz. single cream
3 eggs
50 g./2 oz. Cheddar cheese,
   grated
1.25 ml./¼ teaspoon grated
   nutmeg
salt and pepper

Put the flan case on a baking sheet. Melt the butter in a frying-pan. Add the onion and fry for 5 minutes. Add the spinach and cook gently for a further 5 minutes. Mix together the cream, eggs, cheese, nutmeg and salt and pepper to taste. Add to the spinach and onion and stir well. Spoon into the flan case. Put into the oven preheated to fairly hot (200°C/400°F or Gas Mark 6) and bake for 40 minutes, or until the filling is firm and golden brown. Serve hot or cold.

Serves 4-6

Mushroom Quiche

23 cm./9 in. shortcrust pastry
   flan case*
50 g./2 oz. butter
1 small onion, thinly sliced
½ kg./1 lb. mushrooms, thinly
   sliced
salt and pepper
15 ml./1 tablespoon chopped
   fresh parsley
150 ml./5 fl. oz. single cream
3 eggs
50 g./2 oz. Cheddar cheese,
   grated

Put the flan case on a baking sheet. Melt the butter in a saucepan. Add the onion and mushrooms and fry for 5 minutes. Stir in the salt, pepper and parsley. Mix together the cream, eggs and cheese and stir into the mushrooms and onions. Pour into the flan case. Put into the oven preheated to fairly hot (200°C/400°F or Gas Mark 6) and bake for about 40 minutes, or until the filling is firm and golden brown. Serve hot or cold.

Serves 4-6

Asparagus Quiche

23 cm./9 in. shortcrust pastry
   flan case*
15 g./½ oz. butter
1 onion, thinly sliced
12 asparagus spears, cooked
   and drained
125 ml./4 fl. oz. double
   cream
75 ml./3 fl. oz. milk
3 eggs
50 g./2 oz. Cheddar cheese,
   grated
salt and pepper

Put the flan case on a baking sheet. Melt the butter in a saucepan. Add the onion and fry for 5 minutes. Spread the onion over the bottom of the flan case. Arrange the asparagus spears over the onions. Mix together the cream, milk, eggs, cheese, salt and pepper and pour over the asparagus. Put into the oven preheated to fairly hot (200°C/400°F or Gas Mark 6) and bake for 40 minutes, or until the filling is firm and golden brown. Serve hot or cold.

Serves 4-6

Desserts & Puddings

Almond Junket

75 g./3 oz. sugar
15 ml./1 tablespoon gelatine
  dissolved in 150 ml./5 fl.
  oz. hot water
150 ml./5 fl. oz. boiling
  water
425 ml./15 fl. oz. milk
1.25 ml./¼ teaspoon almond
  essence

Beat the sugar and gelatine mixture together, then pour over the water, stirring until the sugar has dissolved. Stir in the milk and almond essence. Pour into four serving glasses, cool, then chill until set.

Serves 4

Caramel Rice

1 × 450 g./1 lb. can creamed
  rice
150 ml./5 fl. oz. double
  cream, stiffly whipped
45 ml./3 tablespoons brown
  sugar
30 ml./2 tablespoons flaked
  almonds

Mix the rice and cream together in a flameproof dish. Sprinkle over the sugar and nuts. Grill for 3 to 5 minutes, or until the topping has caramelized.

Serves 4

Chestnut Cream

1 × 225 g./8 oz. can
  unsweetened chestnut
  purée
300 ml./10 fl. oz. double
  cream, stiffly whipped
50 g./2 oz. marrons glacés
2 egg whites, stiffly beaten
50 g./2 oz. strawberries,
  hulled

Mix the chestnut purée and cream together. Chop half the marrons glacés and stir into the mixture. Fold in the egg whites. Spoon into a glass serving bowl and chill for 1 hour, or until set. Decorate with the remaining marrons glacés and strawberries.

Serves 4

Biscuit Tortini

2 egg whites
125 g./4 oz. castor sugar
125 g./4 oz. blanched
  almonds, toasted and
  chopped
300 ml./10 fl. oz. double
  cream, stiffly whipped
30 ml./2 tablespoons sherry
  or Marsala

Beat the egg whites until they are frothy. Gradually beat in the sugar until the mixture is stiff and glossy. Reserve about 30 ml./2 tablespoons of almonds for decoration, then fold the remainder, with the cream, and sherry or Marsala into the egg whites. Spoon into six small moulds and sprinkle over the reserved almonds. Put the moulds in the freezing compartment of the refrigerator and freeze until set.

Serves 6

Charlotte Malakov

8 sponge finger biscuits
30 ml./2 tablespoons sweet
  sherry or orange juice
125 g./4 oz. butter
175 g./6 oz. castor sugar
3 egg yolks
1.25 ml./¼ teaspoon almond
  essence
175 g./6 oz. ground almonds
300 ml./10 fl. oz. double
  cream, lightly whipped

Line a charlotte mould or 15 cm./6 in. cake tin with a double thickness of greased greaseproof paper. Arrange the biscuits around the sides of the mould and pour the sherry or juice over them.

Cream the butter and sugar together until fluffy. Gradually beat in the egg yolks, then the almond essence and ground almonds. Fold in 175 ml./6 fl. oz. of the cream. Spoon into the lined mould, then trim the biscuits to the same height. Cover and chill overnight or until set.

Turn the malakov out on to a serving dish. Beat the remaining cream until stiff and use to decorate the top.

Serves 8

Chestnut Sundae

75 g./3 oz. unsweetened
  chestnut purée
30 ml./2 tablespoons plain
  yogurt
600 ml./1 pint vanilla ice-
  cream
2 meringues, crushed

Mix the chestnut purée and yogurt together. Put the ice-cream in four serving glasses and sprinkle over the crushed meringue. Top with the chestnut mixture.

Serves 4

Crème Caramel

125 g./4 oz. sugar
125 ml./4 fl. oz. water
Custard
3 eggs
2 egg yolks
2.5 ml./½ teaspoon vanilla
  essence
50 g./2 oz. castor sugar
300 ml./10 fl. oz. milk
300 ml./10 fl. oz. double
  cream

Put the sugar and water in a saucepan and stir to dissolve the sugar. Bring to the boil and boil, without stirring, until it turns a caramel colour. Pour into the bottom of a baking dish. Swirl the caramel around to cover the bottom completely.

Beat the eggs, egg yolks, vanilla and sugar together. Heat the milk and cream to scalding point, then cool slightly. Stir into the egg mixture. Strain into the dish and put the dish into a deep baking tin, half-filled with hot water. Put the tin into the oven preheated to cool (150°C/300°F or Gas Mark 2) and bake for 30 minutes, or until set. Cool, then chill for 2 or 3 hours. To turn out, dip quickly in hot water.

Serves 4-6

Chocolate Ice-Box Cake

1 × 18 cm./7 in. sponge
  cake, cut into thin slices
4 egg yolks
75 g./3 oz. sugar
125 g./4 oz. plain chocolate,
  melted-
60 ml./4 tablespoons milk
5 ml./1 tablespoon vanilla
  essence
300 ml./10 fl. oz. double
  cream, stiffly whipped
grated chocolate to decorate

Line a 15 cm./6 in. cake tin with a double thickness of greased greaseproof paper. Cover the bottom and sides with some of the cake slices.

Put the egg yolks and sugar in a heatproof bowl. Put the bowl over a pan of hot water over low heat and beat until the mixture thickens. Mix the chocolate and milk together, then beat into the egg yolk mixture. Stir in the vanilla. Pour about one-third of the chocolate mixture into the cake tin, then cover with about half the remaining cake slices. Continue to make layers until the chocolate and cake are finished.

Cover and chill overnight, or until the mixture is firm and set. Turn out on to a plate. Spread whipped cream on top and decorate with grated chocolate.

Serves 8

Chocolate Crumble

45 ml./3 tablespoons
    cornflour
45 ml./3 tablespoons
    chocolate powder
10 ml./2 tablespoons finely
    grated orange rind
425 ml./15 fl. oz. milk
30 ml./2 tablespoons orange
    juice
125 g./4 oz. sugar
175 g./6 oz. rolled oats
75 g./3 oz. butter, softened

Mix the cornflour, chocolate powder and orange rind to a paste with a little of the milk. Bring the remaining milk and juice to the boil, then gradually stir in the cornflour mixture. Simmer for 2 to 3 minutes, stirring constantly, or until very thick. Stir in half the sugar until it has dissolved. Transfer to an ovenproof dish.

Mix the oats and butter together, then stir in the remaining sugar until the mixture is crumbly, Spread over the chocolate mixture and put into the oven preheated to moderate (180°C/350°F or Gas Mark 4). Bake for 10 to 15 minutes, or until the top is crisp. Cool, then chill until very cold.

Serves 4

Chocolate Mould

175 g./6 oz. plain chocolate,
    cut into small pieces
425 ml./15 fl. oz. milk
75 g./3 oz. digestive biscuits,
    crushed
1 egg, separated
50 g./2 oz. chopped nuts

Melt the chocolate over low heat. Cool slightly, then stir in the milk and biscuits. Beat in the egg yolk and cook gently for 3 minutes, stirring constantly.

Beat the egg white until it is stiff, then fold it into the chocolate mixture. Spoon into an oiled 600 ml./1 pint mould and put the mould in a deep baking tin, half-filled with hot water. Put the tin into the oven preheated to moderate (180°C/350°F or Gas Mark 4) and bake for 45 minutes or until set.

Cool in the mould, then turn out on to a plate. Scatter over the chopped nuts.

Serves 4

Diplomat Pudding

600 ml./1 pint thick custard
3 macaroons, finely chopped
2 bananas, sliced
125 g./4 oz. redcurrant jelly
225 ml./8 fl. oz. double
    cream, stiffly whipped

Mix the custard, macaroons and bananas together in a serving dish. Spread over the jelly and top with the whipped cream, bringing it up into decorative peaks.

Serves 4-6

Creamy Chocolate Mousse

125 g./4 oz. plain chocolate,
  cut into small pieces
15 ml./1 tablespoon brandy
4 eggs, separated
300 ml./10 fl. oz. double
  cream, stiffly whipped

Melt the chocolate with the brandy over low heat. Cool slightly, then beat in the egg yolks, one at a time. Continue beating until the mixture is rich and thick. Fold in the cream.

Beat the egg whites until they are stiff, then quickly fold into the chocolate mixture. Spoon into a large mould or individual serving dishes and chill for at least 2 hours.

Serves 4-6

Chocolate Sundae

600 ml./1 pint vanilla ice-
  cream
125 ml./4 fl. oz. double
  cream, whipped
Sauce
175 g./6 oz. plain chocolate,
  cut into small pieces
25 g./1 oz. butter
5 ml./1 teaspoon vanilla
  essence

To make the sauce, put the chocolate in a heat-proof bowl over a pan of hot water over low heat and melt gently. Stir in the butter and vanilla until the butter melts.

Put a portion of ice-cream into each of four chilled serving bowls. Top with some whipped cream, then pour over the sauce.

Serves 4

Floating Islands

900 ml./1½ pints milk
5 ml./1 teaspoon vanilla
  essence
3 eggs, separated
150 g./5 oz. castor sugar
50 g./2 oz. strawberries,
  hulled

Bring the milk to the boil, then stir in the vanilla. Beat two egg whites until they are frothy. Beat in 125 g./4 oz. sugar until the mixture is stiff and glossy. Spoon tablespoons of the meringue mixture on top of the milk and poach for 10 minutes, or until set. Remove the meringues from the milk and set aside.

Strain the milk and reserve 600 ml./1 pint. Beat the egg yolks, remaining egg white and sugar together. Pour over the milk, return to the pan and simmer gently, stirring constantly, until the custard has thickened. Strain into a shallow dish. Arrange the meringue islands on top and decorate with the strawberries.

Serves 4

Dried Fruit Compôte

125 g./4 oz. dried apples
125 g./4 oz. dried apricots
125 g./4 oz. dried prunes,
stoned
50 g./2 oz. dried bananas
50 g./2 oz. sultanas or raisins
300 ml./10 fl. oz. water
125 ml./4 fl. oz. red wine
finely grated rind and juice
of 1 large lemon
150 g./5 oz. sugar
5 ml./1 teaspoon ground
allspice

Soak all the dried fruit in cold water for at least 12 hours. Drain. Put all the remaining ingredients in a saucepan and stir to dissolve the sugar. Stir in the fruit and simmer for 20 to 30 minutes, or until it is very tender. Transfer the fruit to a serving dish.

Boil the liquid rapidly until it reduces by about one-third. Pour over the fruit, cover and chill for 1 hour.

Serves 4-6

Ginger Cream Roll

150 ml./5 fl. oz. double
cream
150 ml./5 fl. oz. single cream
45 ml./3 tablespoons brandy
or whisky
15 ml./1 tablespoon castor
sugar
350 g./12 oz. gingernut
biscuits
6 slices of crystallized ginger

Beat the creams together until stiff, then beat in the brandy or whisky and sugar. Put one heaped teaspoonful of cream on each biscuit, then sandwich the biscuits together to make a long roll or two smaller rolls. Transfer to a serving plate. Spread the remaining cream over the top and sides of the roll. Chill for 2 hours, or until the roll is solid. Decorate with crystallized ginger slices.

Serves 4-6

Iced Cream Cheese

225 g./8 oz. full-fat cream
cheese
225 ml./8 fl. oz. double
cream, stiffly whipped
finely grated rind of 1 lemon
30 ml./2 tablespoons castor
sugar

Strain the cheese, then beat in the cream until the mixture is smooth. Beat in the remaining ingredients. Line a small soufflé dish with a double thickness of cheesecloth, and spoon in the cheese mixture. Cover with foil and chill in the freezing compartment of the refrigerator for 2 hours, or until very firm.

Note: This dessert is usually served with fresh berry fruits, such as wild strawberries, raspberries or blackberries.

Serves 6

Jellied Fruit Snow

300 ml./10 fl. oz. thick apple
    purée
5 ml./1 teaspoon gelatine
    dissolved in 15 ml./1
    tablespoon hot water
30 ml./2 tablespoons
    warmed cider
150 ml./5 fl. oz. double
    cream, lightly whipped
3 egg whites

Put the purée into a saucepan and simmer gently until it is hot. Mix the gelatine and cider together and stir into the purée. Cool, then fold in half the cream.

Beat two of the egg whites until they are stiff and fold them into the purée mixture. Spoon into individual serving dishes and chill for 30 minutes, or until lightly set.

Beat the remaining cream until it is stiff. In a separate bowl, beat the remaining egg white until it is stiff. Fold the egg white into the cream and arrange on top of the purée.

Serves 4

Iced Lemon Soufflé

juice and finely grated rind
    of 3 lemons
3 large eggs, separated
150 g./5 oz. castor sugar
15 ml./1 tablespoon gelatine,
    dissolved in 45 ml./3
    tablespoons hot water
150 ml./5 fl. oz. double
    cream, lightly whipped

Put the lemon juice and rind, egg yolks and sugar in a heatproof basin over a pan of hot water over low heat and beat until the mixture thickens. Remove the bowl from the pan and stir in the gelatine. Cool, stirring ocasionally, until beginning to thicken.

Beat the egg whites until stiff. Fold the cream into the lemon mixture, then the egg whites. Put a greaseproof collar, about 2.5 cm./1 in. higher than the dish, around a medium soufflé dish. Spoon the mixture into the dish and chill for at least 1 hour, or until set.

Serves 6

Lemon Syllabub

juice and finely grated rind
    of 1 large lemon
50 ml./2 fl. oz. medium
    sherry
30 ml./2 tablespoons brandy
50 g./2 oz. castor sugar
300 ml./10 fl. oz. double
    cream, lightly whipped

Put the lemon juice and rind in a bowl with the sherry, brandy and sugar. Stir until the sugar has dissolved. Gradually add the cream, beating constantly until the mixture is thick and creamy. Spoon into individual serving dishes and chill for at least 30 minutes.

Serves 4

Queen of Puddings

75 g./3 oz. jam
50 g./2 oz. fresh
* breadcrumbs*
2 eggs, separated
75 g./3 oz. castor sugar
425 ml./15 fl. oz. milk,
* warmed*
50 g./2 oz. chopped fresh
* fruit*

Spread half the jam over the bottom of an oven-proof dish. Add the crumbs. Beat the egg yolks and sugar together until pale. Gradually beat into the milk and strain over the crumbs. Put the dish into the oven preheated to cool (150°C/300°F or Gas Mark 2) and bake for 1 hour, or until the custard is firm.

Meanwhile, beat the egg whites until very stiff. Spread the custard with the remaining jam and chopped fruit and top with the egg whites. Return to the oven preheated to fairly hot (190°C/375°F or Gas Mark 5) and bake for 15 minutes, or until the meringue is pale brown.

Serves 4

Summer Pudding

10 slices of white bread,
* crusts removed*
225 g./8 oz. rhubarb, cut into
* lengths*
125 g./4 oz. blackberries,
* hulled*
225 g./8 oz. blackcurrants
350 g./12 oz. sugar
50 ml./2 fl. oz. water
½ kg./1 lb. strawberries,
* hulled and sliced*
125 g./4 oz. raspberries

Cut about 4 large slices of bread to fit the bottom and sides of a large pudding bowl or soufflé dish. Cut the remaining slices into fingers. Put the rhubarb, blackberries, blackcurrants, sugar and water into a saucepan and simmer for 15 minutes or until the fruit is soft. Stir in the remaining ingredients and simmer for a further 3 minutes. Spoon into the prepared bowl or dish and top with the remaining bread, pressing down firmly. Cover the bowl or dish with a plate and press down with weights. Leave to soak overnight.

Serves 8

Yogurt Whip

300 ml./10 fl. oz. sweetened
* thick fruit purée*
150 ml./5 fl. oz. plain yogurt,
* chilled*
1 egg white, stiffly whipped

Put the fruit purée into a bowl. Beat in the yogurt, then fold in the egg white. Spoon into serving bowls and serve.

Serves 4

301

Eugenie's Rice

1¼ l./2 pints milk
150 g./5 oz. sugar
pinch of salt
75 g./3 oz. rice
5 ml./1 teaspoon vanilla
  essence
300 ml./10 fl. oz. thick
  custard
150 ml./5 fl. oz. double
  cream, stiffly whipped
30 ml./2 tablespoons
  gelatine, dissolved in 30
  ml./2 tablespoons hot
  water
50 g./2 oz. flaked almonds
25 g./1 oz. sultanas
30 ml./2 tablespoons
  chopped glacé cherries

Put the milk, sugar and salt in a saucepan and bring to the boil. Gradually add the rice and simmer, stirring occasionally, for 45 minutes to 1 hour, or until most of the liquid is absorbed and the rice is tender. Stir in the vanilla and cool, then chill until completely cold.

Beat in the custard and cream, then stir in the gelatine, nuts and fruit. Spoon into a rinsed decorative ring or other mould and chill for 3 to 5 hours, or until completely set.

Serves 6

Zabaglione

5 egg yolks
40 g./1½ oz. sugar
150 ml./5 fl. oz. Marsala

Put the egg yolks and sugar in a heatproof bowl over a pan of hot water over low heat and beat until the mixture thickens. Gradually beat in the Marsala and continue to beat until the mixture is thick and foamy. Spoon into individual serving glasses and serve warm.

Serves 4-6

Banana Cream Posset

3 ripe bananas, mashed
30 ml./2 tablespoons lemon
  juice
30 ml./2 tablespoons dry
  white wine
15 ml./1 tablespoon brandy
45 ml./3 tablespoons castor
  sugar
300 ml./10 fl. oz. double
  cream, stiffly whipped
1 egg white, stiffly beaten

Mix together the bananas, lemon juice, wine, brandy and castor sugar. Fold in the cream, then the egg white. Spoon into serving bowls and chill for 30 minutes.

Serves 4

Apple Charlotte

125 g./4 oz. flour
50 g./2 oz. self-raising flour
25 g./1 oz. custard powder
25 g./1 oz. cornflour
30 ml./2 tablespoons icing
    sugar
125 g./4 oz. butter
60 ml./4 tablespoons water
Filling
1 kg./2 lb. sweet thick apple
    purée
15 ml./1 tablespoon lemon
    juice
5 ml./1 teaspoon ground
    cinnamon
Icing
175 g./6 oz. icing sugar,
    sifted
milk
few drops of green food
    colouring
25 g./1 oz. chopped angelica

Sift all the dry ingredients together. Rub in the butter until the mixture resembles fine breadcrumbs. Add the water and mix to a firm dough. Roll out two-thirds of the dough to a circle large enough to line a well-greased 18 cm./7 in. springform tin.

Mix all the filling ingredients together and spoon into the tin. Roll out the remaining dough to a circle large enough to cover the filling and place over the tin. Wet and crimp the edges to seal. Make a cross in the centre and brush with a little milk. Put into the oven preheated to hot (220°C/425°F or Gas Mark 7) and bake for 25 to 30 minutes, or until the pastry is golden brown. Remove from the tin and cool on a wire rack.

To make the icing, beat the icing sugar with enough milk to make a thick, spreading consistency. Add a few drops of green food colouring until the mixture is very pale green, then fold in the angelica. Spread the icing over the pastry and set aside until it is set.

Serves 6

Banana Rum Mousse

1 packet lemon jelly
2 large bananas, mashed
225 ml./8 fl. oz. double
    cream, stiffly whipped
30 ml./2 tablespoons rum

Make the jelly according to packet instructions and chill until it is half set. Beat in all the remaining ingredients and chill until set.

Serves 6

Danish Berry Dessert

275 g./10 oz. redcurrants
275 g./10 oz. raspberries
600 ml./1 pint water
75 g./3 oz. castor sugar
50 g./2 oz. cornflour,
    blended with 50 ml./2 fl.
    oz. water
225 ml./8 fl. oz. double
    cream, stiffly whipped

Put the fruit, water and sugar into a saucepan. Simmer for 8 to 12 minutes, or until the mixture forms a purée. Stir in the cornflour and bring to the boil. Simmer for 2 to 3 minutes, stirring constantly, or until the mixture is very thick. Cool, then chill until cold and set. Top with the cream.

Serves 4-6

Rich Apricot Cheesecake

225 g./8 oz. digestive
  biscuits, crushed
125 g./4 oz. butter, melted
5 ml./1 teaspoon ground
  cinnamon
675 g./1½ lb. cream or cottage
  cheese
15 ml./1 tablespoon finely
  grated orange rind
15 ml./1 tablespoon orange
  juice
2 eggs, beaten
175 g./6 oz. castor sugar
1 × 675 g./1½ lb. can apricot
  halves, drained

Mix the biscuits, melted butter and cinnamon together. Line the bottom and sides of an 18 cm./7 in. springform tin with the mixture. Chill for 1 hour.

Meanwhile, beat the cheese, orange rind and juice, eggs and sugar together. Cut half the apricot halves into slices. Arrange the slices over the bottom of the biscuit case, then spoon over the cheese mixture. Put into the oven preheated to slow (150°C/300°F or Gas Mark 2) and bake for 30 to 40 minutes, or until set. Turn off the heat and leave in the oven to cool, then chill overnight. Decorate with the remaining apricot halves.

Serves 8-10

Honey Banana Cream

3 large bananas, mashed
30 ml./2 tablespoons lemon
  juice
45 ml./3 tablespoons clear
  honey
300 ml./10 fl. oz. milk
150 ml./5 fl. oz. water
10 ml./2 teaspoons very
  finely chopped lemon rind
15 ml./1 tablespoon gelatine,
  dissolved in 30 ml./2
  tablespoons hot water
300 ml./10 fl. oz. double
  cream, stiffly whipped

Mix the bananas and lemon juice together. Put the honey and milk in a saucepan and heat, stirring, until they are blended. Beat into the bananas, with the water and lemon rind. Stir in the gelatine. Pour into a serving bowl and leave until the mixture stiffens slightly, then fold in the cream.

Serves 4

Gooseberry Fool

½ kg./1 lb. gooseberries
45 ml./3 tablespoons sugar
45 ml./3 tablespoons water
300 ml./10 fl. oz. double
  cream, stiffly whipped

Put the gooseberries, sugar and water into a saucepan and simmer for 10 to 15 minutes, or until the gooseberries are tender. Mash to a purée, or blend in a blender and cool, then fold in the cream. Chill for 15 minutes.

Serves 6

Apricot and Orange Cream

½ kg./1 lb. apricots, stoned
125 g./4 oz. sugar
150 ml./5 fl. oz. water
finely grated rind and juice
    of 2 large oranges
15 ml./1 tablespoon gelatine
300 ml./10 fl. oz. double
    cream, lightly whipped
15 ml./1 tablespoon brown
    sugar

Put the apricots, sugar and water in a saucepan and simmer for 10 to 15 minutes, or until the apricots are tender. Mash to a purée, or blend in a blender, then stir in all the orange rind and the juice of one orange.

Pour the remaining orange juice into a cup and stir in the gelatine. Put the cup in a pan of hot water and simmer, stirring constantly, until the gelatine has dissolved. Stir the gelatine into the apricot mixture and cool.

When the mixture begins to thicken, fold in the cream. Pour into a 1 l./1¾ pint dish and chill in the refrigerator until completely set. Sprinkle over the brown sugar.

Serves 6

Blackcurrant Flummery

1 packet lemon jelly
300 ml./10 fl. oz. boiling
    water
60 ml./4 tablespoons
    blackcurrant syrup
150 ml./5 fl. oz. evaporated
    milk
150 ml./5 fl. oz. plain yogurt
8 slices crystallized lemon

Dissolve the jelly in the water, stirring constantly. Set aside until it begins to stiffen. Divide between two bowls. Beat the evaporated milk into one, and the yogurt into the other. Spoon a little of each mixture into four serving glasses and chill until set. Decorate with the crystallized lemon.

Serves 4

Grapefruit Mousse

2 eggs, separated
125 g./4 oz. castor sugar
finely grated rind and juice
    of 1 large grapefruit
15 ml./1 tablespoon gelatine,
    dissolved in 45 ml./3
    tablespoons hot water
300 ml./10 fl. oz. double
    cream, stiffly whipped
grapefruit segments to
    decorate

Put the egg yolks, sugar, grapefruit rind and juice in a heatproof bowl over a pan of hot water over low heat and beat until the mixture thickens. Cool to lukewarm, then stir in the gelatine.

Beat the egg whites until they are stiff, then fold into the egg yolk mixture with the cream. Chill for at least 3 hours or until set. Decorate with grapefruit segments.

Cherry Compôte

125 ml./4 fl. oz. red wine
45 ml./3 tablespoons
  redcurrant jelly
15 ml./1 tablespoon sugar
grated rind and juice of 1
  orange
1.25 ml./¼ teaspoon ground
  cinnamon
675 g./1½ lb. black cherries,
  stoned
15 ml./1 tablespoon
  arrowroot, blended with
  30 ml./2 tablespoons water

Put the wine, redcurrant jelly, sugar, orange rind and juice and cinnamon in a saucepan. Cover and simmer until the jelly has dissolved. Stir in the cherries, cover and simmer for 5 minutes. Stir in the arrowroot and bring to the boil, stirring constantly. Cool to room temperature.

Serves 6

Cherries Jubilee

1 × 450 g./1 lb. can black
  cherries, stoned
15 ml./1 tablespoon finely
  grated lemon rind
10 ml./2 teaspoons cornflour,
  dissolved in 15 ml./1
  tablespoon cherry can
  liquid
50 ml./2 fl. oz. brandy
600 ml./1 pint vanilla ice-
  cream

Put the cherries and can juice into a saucepan. Add the lemon rind and bring to the boil. Stir in the cornflour and simmer, stirring, until the mixture thickens. Warm the brandy and add to the pan. Ignite, then wait until the flames have died away. Put a portion of ice-cream into chilled serving bowls. Pour over the cherry mixture.

Serves 4

Melon Ambrosia

350 g./12 oz. melon balls
1 orange, cut into sections
1 banana, sliced
125 g./4 oz. strawberries,
  hulled and sliced
50 g./2 oz. seedless grapes
75 g./3 oz. peaches, sliced
juice of 1 lemon
30 ml./2 tablespoons sugar
25 g./1 oz. desiccated
  coconut

Arrange the fruit decoratively in a serving bowl. Sprinkle over the lemon juice and sugar and chill for 15 minutes. Top with the coconut.

Serves 4-6

Melon and Grape Salad

1 melon, seeds removed and
   cut into chunks
15 ml./1 tablespoon castor
   sugar
juice of 1 lemon
225 g./8 oz. seedless grapes
300 ml./10 fl. oz. double
   cream, stiffly whipped

Put the melon chunks in a bowl. Sprinkle over the sugar and lemon, then scatter over the grapes. Spoon over the cream.

Serves 4

Oranges in Liqueur

8 oranges, peeled and cut
   into thin slices
45 ml./3 tablespoons finely
   grated orange rind
125 g./4 oz. castor sugar
75 ml./3 fl. oz. orange
   liqueur

Arrange the orange slices in a shallow dish. Sprinkle over the orange rind and sugar and chill for 15 minutes. Pour over the liqueur.

Serves 6-8

Mandarin Surprise

1 × 450 g./1 lb. can
   mandarin oranges,
   drained
50 g./2 oz. flaked almonds
225 ml./8 fl. oz. sour cream
30 ml./2 tablespoons
   chopped crystallized
   ginger

Mix the oranges, almonds and sour cream together. Sprinkle over the crystallized ginger and chill for 15 minutes.

Serves 4

Peaches in Brandy

125 g./4 oz. sugar
300 ml./10 fl. oz. water
4 large ripe peaches,
   skinned, stoned and
   halved
75 ml./3 fl. oz. brandy

Put the sugar and water into a saucepan and stir to dissolve the sugar. Add the peach halves and simmer gently for 15 minutes, or until they are tender but retain their shape. Transfer to a serving dish.

Boil the syrup until it has reduced by about two-thirds. Stir in the brandy and pour over the peaches.

Serves 4

Peaches with Cherry Sauce

1 × 675 g./1½ lb. can peach
  slices
1 × 225 g./8 oz. can cherries
30 ml./2 tablespoons lemon
  juice
10 ml./2 teaspoons cornflour,
  blended with 15 ml./1
  tablespoon water

Pour the peach can liquid into a saucepan and arrange the slices in a serving dish. Pour the cherry liquid into the pan and reserve the cherries. Add the lemon juice to the pan and bring to the boil. Stir in the cornflour mixture and simmer, stirring, until the mixture thickens. Stir in the cherries and heat gently. Pour over the peaches.

Serves 4-6

Peach Tipsy Cake

50 g./2 oz. butter
50 g./2 oz. sugar
1 egg, beaten
few drops of vanilla essence
23 ml./1½ tablespoons milk
75 g./3 oz. self-raising flour,
  sifted
1 × 450 g./1 lb. can peach
  halves
50 ml./2 fl. oz. sherry
75 g./3 oz. raspberry jam,
  warmed
150 ml./5 fl. oz. double
  cream, stiffly whipped

Cream the butter and sugar together until fluffy. Gradually beat in the egg, then the vanilla and milk. Fold in the flour to form a smooth batter. Pour into a well-greased 18 cm./7 in. sandwich tin and put into the oven preheated to moderate (180°C/350°F or Gas Mark 4). Bake for 20 minutes, or until it springs back when lightly pressed in the centre. Cool in the tin.

Drain the peach halves and reserve. Mix 50 ml./2 fl. oz. of the can liquid with the sherry and pour over the cake. Leave until all the liquid has been absorbed. Transfer to a plate and arrange the peach halves over the top. Brush with the warmed jam. Spoon the cream into a piping bag with a star nozzle and pipe around and between the peaches.

Serves 6

Pears Helene

600 ml./1 pint vanilla ice-
  cream
4 large ripe pears, peeled,
  cored and halved
Sauce
125 g./4 oz. plain chocolate,
  cut into small pieces
45 ml./3 tablespoons water
15 g./½ oz. butter

To make the sauce, put the chocolate and water in a heatproof bowl over a pan of hot water over low heat and melt the chocolate. Stir in the butter until it melts.

Put a portion of ice-cream into four chilled serving bowls. Top with two pear halves, then pour over the chocolate sauce.

Serves 4

Pineapple in Kirsch

1 pineapple, peeled, cored
    and cut into rings
50 ml./2 fl. oz. pineapple
    juice
50 ml./2 fl. oz. kirsch
15 ml./1 tablespoon brown
    sugar

Arrange the pineapple rings in a shallow dish. Pour over the juice and kirsch and sprinkle over the sugar. Chill for 15 minutes.

Serves 4-6

Pineapple in Sour Cream

225 ml./8 fl. oz. pineapple
    juice
15 ml./1 tablespoon gelatine,
    dissolved in 45 ml./3
    tablespoons hot water
175 g./6 oz. chopped
    pineapple
225 ml./8 fl. oz. sour cream
125 ml./4 fl. oz. double
    cream, stiffly whipped

Mix together the pineapple juice and gelatine. Chill until the mixture is on the point of setting. Fold in the pineapple and sour cream. Return to the refrigerator and chill until completely set. Serve topped with whipped cream.

Serves 6

Danish Plum Crumble

125 g./4 oz. butter
125 g./4 oz. wholemeal
    breadcrumbs
175 g./6 oz. macaroons,
    crushed
1 × 1 kg./2 lb. can plums,
    drained and juice reserved
15 ml./1 tablespoon
    arrowroot
150 ml./5 fl. oz. double
    cream, stiffly whipped

Melt the butter in a saucepan and stir in the bread-crumbs and crushed macaroons. Press half the mixture over the bottom of a well-greased serving bowl and chill for 10 minutes. Arrange the plums on top of the crumb mixture and top with the remaining crumb mixture. Return to the refrigerator and chill for 15 minutes or until firm.

Blend the arrowroot with a little of the reserved plum can juice. Pour 300 ml./10 fl. oz. of the juice into a saucepan and stir in the arrowroot mixture. Bring to the boil, stirring until the mixture thickens. Cool.

Spoon the cream into a piping bag with a plain nozzle and pipe around the top edge of the crumble. Serve with the plum sauce.

Serves 6

Raspberry Chantilly

3 egg whites
175 g./6 oz. castor sugar
Filling
225 g./8 oz. raspberries
300 ml./10 fl. oz. double
cream, stiffly whipped
25 g./1 oz. castor sugar
15 ml./1 tablespoon orange
liqueur or juice

Line two baking sheets with non-stick silicone or greased greaseproof paper. Draw a circle, about 15 cm./6 in. in diameter on each sheet.

Beat the egg whites until they are frothy. Gradually beat in the sugar until the mixture is stiff and glossy. (You should be able to turn the bowl upside-down without the mixture falling out.) Spoon the meringue into a piping bag with a plain nozzle and pipe half the mixture into each circle on the baking sheets. Using two teaspoons, bring the edges of the circle up to make a case. Put into the oven preheated to very cool (130°C/250°F or Gas Mark ½) and bake for 1½ hours, or until pale cream and slightly crisp on the outside. Remove the paper, then return the meringues, upside-down, to the oven to dry out completely for a further 20 minutes.

To make the filling, mix all the ingredients together. Spoon into the meringue cases.

Serves 6

Italian Lemon Ice

400 g./14 oz. sugar
60 ml./4 tablespoons lemon
juice
1½ l./2½ pints water
grated rind of 1 lemon
300 ml./10 fl. oz. double
cream, stiffly whipped

Put the sugar, lemon juice, water and lemon rind in a saucepan and bring slowly to the boil, stirring until the sugar has dissolved. Boil for 15 minutes, strain and cool.

When cold, fold in the cream, then spoon into ice-cube or freezer trays. Put in the freezing compartment of the refrigerator and freeze for 2 to 4 hours, or until set. Stir frequently during the freezing period.
Note: Don't worry if the cream and lemon mixture don't combine when you first stir in the cream. If you stir frequently during the freezing period, the two mixtures will be blended by the time you serve the ice.

Serves 6

Rhubarb Velvet

1 kg./2 lb. rhubarb, cut into
    lengths
15 ml./1 tablespoon finely
    grated orange rind
150 g./5 oz. brown sugar
50 ml./2 fl. oz. water
350 ml./12 fl. oz. double
    cream, stiffly whipped
15 ml./1 tablespoon gelatine,
    dissolved in 30 ml./2
    tablespoons hot water
2 egg whites, stiffly beaten

Put the rhubarb, orange rind, sugar and water into a saucepan. Simmer for 15 minutes, or until the rhubarb forms a purée. Cool, then chill.

Beat the cream and gelatine into the rhubarb mixture, then fold in the egg whites. Spoon into a rinsed decorative ring or other mould. Chill for 3 hours, or until set.

Serves 6

Strawberry Fruit Whip

1 packet strawberry jelly
300 ml./10 fl. oz. boiling
    water
2 eggs, separated
25 g./1 oz. sugar
150 ml./5 fl. oz. double
    cream, lightly beaten

Dissolve the jelly in the water, stirring constantly. Cool.

Beat the egg yolks and sugar together until pale. Add the warm jelly and stir to mix. Leave until the mixture begins to stiffen.

Meanwhile, beat the egg whites until they are stiff. Fold the cream and beaten egg whites into the jelly mixture and chill for 1 hour, or until set.

Serves 4

Blackcurrant Sorbet

1 × 450 g./1 lb. can
    blackcurrants, drained
    and juice reserved
175 g./6 oz. sugar
finely grated rind and juice
    of 1 lemon
5 ml./1 teaspoon gelatine,
    dissolved in 15 ml./1
    tablespoon hot water
2 egg whites, softly whipped

Measure the blackcurrant juice and make up to 400 ml./15 fl. oz. with water. Pour into a saucepan and add the sugar. Stir until the sugar has dissolved. Simmer for 2 minutes, then remove from the heat and beat in the lemon rind and juice.

Purée the blackcurrants, then stir them into the syrup with the gelatine. Pour into ice-cube or freezer trays. Cover and put in the freezing compartment of the refrigerator. Freeze until almost on the point of setting. Spoon into a bowl and beat until smooth and creamy. Fold in the egg whites. Return to the trays and continue to freeze for at least 1 hour, or until set.

Serves 6

Strawberry Mousse

2 egg whites
75 g./3 oz. castor sugar
300 ml./10 fl. oz. double
 cream, stiffly whipped
½ kg./1 lb. strawberries,
 puréed
15 ml./1 tablespoon lemon
 juice
15 ml./1 tablespoon gelatine,
 dissolved in 15 ml./1
 tablespoon hot water

Beat the egg whites until they are frothy. Gradually beat in the sugar until the mixture is stiff and glossy. Fold in the cream, strawberry purée, lemon juice and gelatine. Spoon into a rinsed mould and chill for 3 hours or until set.

Serves 4-6

Strawberries Romanoff

½ kg./1 lb. strawberries,
 hulled
75 ml./3 fl. oz. brandy or
 orange liqueur
150 ml./5 fl. oz. double
 cream, stiffly whipped
2.5 ml./½ teaspoon vanilla
 essence

Put the strawberries in a serving bowl and pour over the brandy or liqueur. Chill for 1 hour. Beat the cream and vanilla together and spoon over the strawberries.

Serves 4

Apple and Mincemeat Flan

350 g./12 oz. digestive
 biscuits, crushed
75 g./3 oz. butter, melted
30 ml./2 tablespoons golden
 syrup
5 ml./1 teaspoon ground
 cinammon
600 ml./1 pint thick custard
2 dessert apples, cored and
 thinly sliced
23 ml./1½ tablespoons lemon
 juice
75 g./3 oz. mincemeat
30 ml./2 tablespoons apricot
 jam, warmed

Mix the biscuits, butter, syrup and cinammon together. Press over the bottom and sides of a 20 cm./8 in. springform flan tin. Chill for 30 minutes, or until set.

Spread the custard over the biscuit crust, then arrange the apple slices, slightly overlapping, around the edge. Brush lightly with the lemon juice to avoid discolouration. Put the mincemeat into a small saucepan and heat until warm. Spoon into the centre of the flan. Gently brush the apple slices with the warmed jam.

Serves 6

Cassata Ice-Cream

1 × 575 g./1¼ lb. can
  evaporated milk, chilled
  overnight
30 ml./2 tablespoons sherry
15 ml./1 tablespoon sugar
5 ml./1 teaspoon gelatine,
  dissolved in 15 ml./1
  tablespoon hot water
50 g./2 oz. chopped glacé
  cherries
50 g./2 oz. chopped almonds
50 g./2 oz. sultanas

Pour the milk into a chilled bowl and beat until stiff, then stir in the sherry, sugar and gelatine. Beat for 1 minute, then pour into ice-cube or freezer trays. Put in the freezer compartment of the refrigerator and freeze for 30 minutes or until half set.

Beat in the remaining ingredients and continue to freeze for at least 1 hour, or until set.

Serves 8-10

Orange Sorbet

75 g./3 oz. castor sugar
300 ml./10 fl. oz. water
1 × 175 g./6 oz. can
  undiluted frozen orange
  juice, thawed
1 egg white, stiffly beaten

Put the sugar and water in a saucepan and bring slowly to the boil, stirring until the sugar has dissolved. Cool, then stir in the orange juice. Pour into ice-cube trays or freezer trays. Cover and put in the freezing compartment of the refrigerator. Freeze for 30 minutes.

Spoon into a bowl and beat until smooth and creamy. Fold in the egg white. Return to the trays and freeze for at least 1 hour longer or until set.

Serves 4

Vanilla Ice-Cream

15 ml./1 tablespoon gelatine
125 g./4 oz. sugar
60 ml./4 tablespoons water
225 g./8 oz. full cream
  powdered milk
1¼ l./2 pints milk
10 ml./2 teaspoons vinegar
10 ml./2 teaspoons vanilla
  essence

Put the gelatine, sugar and water in a saucepan. Heat gently, stirring, until the sugar and gelatine have dissolved. Pour into a large bowl. Beat in the powdered milk, then gradually beat in the milk. Pour into ice-cube or freezer trays. Put in the freezing compartment of the refrigerator and freeze for 1½ hours, or until almost set. Spoon into a bowl, add the vinegar and vanilla and beat until thick and creamy. Return to the trays and freeze for a further 1 hour, or until the ice-cream is set. **Note:** For an even richer ice-cream, beat in 150 ml./5 fl. oz. of double cream with the milk.

Serves 6-8

Praline Ice-Cream

50 g./2 oz. castor sugar
30 ml./2 tablespoons water
50 g./2 oz. unblanched
  almonds
Ice-Cream
4 eggs, separated
125 g./4 oz. castor sugar
300 ml./10 fl. oz. double
  cream, lightly whipped

Put the sugar and water into a saucepan and stir to dissolve the sugar. Stir in the almonds and boil until the praline is a deep golden brown. Pour on to a well-greased baking sheet and leave to set. Pulverize the praline in a blender, or put it between layers of greaseproof paper and crush with a rolling pin.

Beat the egg yolks until they are blended. Beat the egg whites until they are frothy, then beat in the sugar until the mixture is stiff and glossy. Fold the egg yolks and cream into the egg white mixture. Spoon into ice-cube or freezer trays, cover and put in the freezing compartment of the refrigerator. Freeze for 2 hours. Spoon into a bowl and beat until smooth and creamy. Stir in the praline. Return to the trays and freeze until the ice-cream is set.

Serves 8

Austrian Dessert Cake

3 eggs, separated
75 g./3 oz. castor sugar
50 g./2 oz. self-raising flour
25 g./1 oz. cocoa powder
30 ml./2 tablespoons cooking
  oil
300 ml./10 fl. oz. double
  cream
45 ml./3 tablespoons rum or
  orange juice

Put the egg yolks and sugar in a heatproof bowl over a pan of hot water over low heat and beat until the mixture thickens. Remove the bowl from the pan. Sift the flour and cocoa together, then fold into the egg yolk mixture with the oil. Beat the egg whites until they are stiff, then fold them into the batter.

Line a deep 18 cm./7 in. cake tin with a double thickness of greased greaseproof paper. Spoon the batter into the tin and put into the oven preheated to moderate (180°C/350°F or Gas Mark 4). Bake for 40 minutes, or until it springs back when lightly pressed in the centre. Cool on a wire rack.

Beat the cream and rum or orange juice together until stiff. Cut the cake into two layers and put the bottom one on a plate. Generously spread over the cream and cover with the remaining layer.

Serves 4-6

Coffee Cream Pie

225 g./8 oz. ginger biscuits,
  crushed
125 g./4 oz. butter, melted
425 ml./15 fl. oz. double
  cream, stiffly whipped
30 ml./2 tablespoons strong
  black coffee
15 ml./1 tablespoon coffee
  liqueur (optional)
5 ml./1 teaspoon gelatine,
  dissolved in 15 ml./1
  tablespoon hot water
50 g./2 oz. flaked almonds
2 egg whites, stiffly beaten

Mix the biscuits and melted butter together and use to line a well-greased 20 cm./8 in. flan tin. Chill for 30 minutes or until set and firm.

Beat the cream, coffee and liqueur, if you are using it, together. Stir in the gelatine, then half the flaked almonds. Fold in the egg whites. Spoon into the biscuit case and chill for 1 hour or until set. Decorate with the remaining flaked almonds.

Serves 6

Banana Cream Pie

225 g./8 oz. rich shortcrust
  pastry *
25 g./1 oz. butter
125 g./4 oz. brown sugar
150 ml./4 fl. oz. water
300 ml./10 fl. oz. milk
15 ml./1 tablespoon gelatine
2 eggs, separated
150 ml./5 fl. oz. double
  cream, lightly whipped
4 bananas
15 ml./1 tablespoon lemon
  juice
extra whipped cream to
  decorate

Line a 20 cm./8 in. flan tin with the pastry dough. Prick the case with a fork and put into the oven preheated to fairly hot (190°C/375°F or Gas Mark 5). Bake blind for 15 minutes, or until golden brown.

Meanwhile, put the butter, sugar and half the water in a saucepan. Heat, stirring until the butter has melted and the sugar dissolved. Cool slightly, then stir in the milk. Dissolve the gelatine in the remaining water over low heat, stirring constantly, then fold into the milk mixture. Beat in the egg yolks and cool.

Beat the egg whites until they are stiff. When the milk mixture is half set, quickly fold in the cream, then the egg whites. Slice the bananas and dip the slices in lemon juice. Reserve a few slices for decoration and arrange the rest over the pastry case. Cover with the milk mixture. Chill until completely set. Decorate with the remaining banana slices and cream.

Serves 6

Cream Cheese and Fruit Flan

150 g./5 oz. flour
pinch of salt
75 g./3 oz. butter
50 g./2 oz. sugar
1 egg
Filling
125 g./4 oz. cream cheese
50 ml./2 fl. oz. double cream,
  stiffly whipped
½ kg./1 lb. fresh fruit, such as
  strawberries or cherries
60 ml./4 tablespoons
  redcurrant jelly, warmed

Sift the flour and salt into a bowl. Rub in the butter until the mixture resembles fine breadcrumbs. Beat in the sugar and egg to form a firm dough. Roll out into a circle and line a 20 cm./8 in. flan tin. Prick the case with a fork and put into the oven preheated to fairly hot (190°C/375°F or Gas Mark 5). Bake blind for 15 minutes, or until golden brown. Cool.

To make the filling, beat the cream cheese and cream together. Spread over the pastry case. Arrange the fruit on top, then brush with the melted jelly.

Serves 6

Layered Hazelnut Cream Meringue

3 egg whites
pinch of cream of tartar
200 g./7 oz. castor sugar
Filling
50 g./2 oz. hazelnuts, finely
  chopped
300 ml./10 fl. oz. double
  cream, stiffly whipped
30 ml./2 tablespoons grated
  chocolate

Line three baking sheets with non-stick silicone or greased greaseproof paper. Draw a circle, about 18 cm./7 in. in diameter on each sheet.

Beat the egg whites and cream of tartar until frothy. Gradually beat in the sugar until the mixture is stiff and glossy. (You should be able to turn the bowl upside-down without the mixture falling out.) Spoon the meringue into a piping bag with a plain nozzle and pipe one-third of the mixture into each circle on the baking sheets. Put into the oven preheated to very cool (130°C/250°F or Gas Mark ½) and bake for 1½ to 2 hours or until pale cream and slightly crisp on the outside. Remove the paper and return the meringues, upside-down, to the oven to dry out completely for a further 20 minutes.

To make the filling, fold the nuts into the cream. Put one meringue layer on a plate and generously spread with the filling. Continue making layers until the filling and meringues are finished. Decorate with the grated chocolate.

Serves 6

Pumpkin Pie

225 g./8 oz. rich shortcrust
    pastry*
125 g./4 oz. brown sugar
5 ml./1 teaspoon ground
    ginger
5 ml./1 teaspoon ground
    allspice
1 × 675 g./1½ lb. can
    pumpkin purée
2 eggs, lightly beaten
225 ml./8 fl. oz. single
    cream, lightly whipped

Line a 20 cm./8 in. flan tin with the pastry dough. Mix the sugar and spices together. Beat into the pumpkin purée, with the eggs. Gradually stir in the cream. Spoon into the dough case and put into the oven preheated to fairly hot (190°C/375°F or Gas Mark 5). Bake for 40 to 45 minutes, or until the filling has set and the pastry is golden brown.

Serves 6-8

Strawberry Flan

225 g./8 oz. rich shortcrust
    pastry*
300 ml./10 fl. oz. double
    cream, stiffly whipped
675 g./1½ lb. strawberries,
    hulled
125 g./4 oz. redcurrant jelly
15 ml./1 tablespoon
    cornflour, blended with 15
    ml./1 tablespoon cold
    water
juice of 1 orange

Line a 20 cm./8 in. flan tin with the pastry dough. Prick the case with a fork and put into the oven preheated to fairly hot (190°C/375°F or Gas Mark 5). Bake blind for 15 minutes, or until golden brown. Cool.

Spread the cream over the pastry base, then arrange the strawberries attractively on top. Put the redcurrant jelly into a saucepan and melt gently. Stir in the cornflour and bring to the boil, stirring until the mixture thickens. Stir in the orange juice. Brush over the strawberries. Chill the flan for at least 30 minutes or until set.

Serves 8

Fruit Trifle

4 sponge trifle squares,
    quartered
125 ml./4 fl. oz. sweet sherry
1 × 450 g./1 lb. can apricot
    or peach halves, drained
425 ml./15 fl. oz. thick
    custard
50 g./2 oz. flaked almonds
225 ml./8 fl. oz. double
    cream, stiffly whipped
chocolate curls to decorate

Put the sponge squares on the bottom of a deep serving bowl and pour over the sherry. Leave until it is absorbed. Cover with half the apricot or peach halves, then top with the custard. Chill for 15 minutes or until set.

Sprinkle over half the almonds, then the remaining fruit halves. Spread over the cream and decorate with the remaining almonds and chocolate curls. Chill for 1 hour.

Serves 4

Elizabethan Flan

45 ml./3 tablespoons clear
    honey
150 ml./5 fl. oz. water
2 large, thin-skinned
    oranges, thinly sliced
225 g./8 oz. rich shortcrust
    pastry*
150 ml./5 fl. oz. double
    cream, stiffly whipped
50 g./2 oz. sugar

Mix the honey and water together in a shallow dish. Stir in the oranges and marinate at room temperature for 8 hours or overnight. Transfer the oranges and syrup to a saucepan and simmer gently for 30 minutes.

Meanwhile, line a 20 cm./8 in. flan tin with the dough. Prick the case with a fork and put into the oven preheated to fairly hot (190°C/375°F or Gas Mark 5). Bake blind for 15 minutes or until golden brown. Cool.

Drain the oranges from the syrup and cool slightly. Reserve the syrup. Spread the cream over the bottom of the pastry case and top with the orange slices. Add the sugar to the reserved syrup and stir until it has dissolved. Bring to the boil and simmer for 3 to 5 minutes, or until the mixture is thick. Spoon over the orange slices.

Serves 6

Lemon Meringue Pie

225 g./8 oz. rich shortcrust
    pastry*
Filling
125 g./4 oz. sugar
300 ml./10 fl. oz. water
60 ml./4 tablespoons lemon
    juice
30 ml./2 tablespoons finely
    grated lemon rind
50 g./2 oz. butter
40 g./1½ oz. cornflour
3 egg yolks
Meringue
3 egg whites
50 g./2 oz. castor sugar

Line a 20 cm./8 in. flan tin with the pastry dough. Prick the case with a fork and put into the oven preheated to fairly hot (190°C/375°F or Gas Mark 5). Bake blind for 15 minutes or until golden.

Meanwhile to make the filling, put the sugar, water, lemon juice and rind, and butter in a saucepan and bring to the boil, stirring constantly. Stir in the cornflour and cook, stirring, for 3 minutes or until the mixture is thick and smooth. Cool slightly, then beat in the egg yolks, one at a time. Cool, then spoon into the pastry case.

To make the meringue, beat the egg whites until they are frothy. Gradually beat in the sugar until the mixture is stiff and glossy. Spread the mixture over the filling, bringing it up into decorative peaks. Put into the oven preheated to moderate (180°C/350°F or Gas Mark 4) and bake for 10 to 15 minutes, or until the meringue is lightly brown.

Serves 6

Fruit Cream Pastry

450 g./1 lb. puff pastry*
30 ml./2 tablespoons custard
  powder
30 ml./2 tablespoons sugar
300 ml./10 fl. oz. milk
150 ml./5 fl. oz. double
  cream, lightly whipped
8 dessert plums, halved and
  stoned
1 red apple, cored and sliced
1 pear, peeled, cored and
  sliced
75 g./3 oz. apricot jam,
  warmed

Roll out two-thirds of the dough into a rectangle about 25 cm./10 in. × 20 cm./8 in. Transfer to a baking sheet. Roll out the remaining dough to two strips 25 cm./10 in. × 1.25 cm./½ in. and two strips 20 cm./8 in. × 1.25 cm./½ in. Wet the edges of the rectangle and press the bands into position along the sides, to make a basket. Brush the dough with a little milk or beaten egg and put into the oven pre-heated to fairly hot (200°C/400°F or Gas Mark 6). Bake for 20 to 25 minutes, or until puffed up and golden brown. Cool completely.

Meanwhile, mix the custard powder and sugar with a little of the milk to make a smooth paste. Heat the remaining milk until just boiling, then gradually stir in the custard paste. Cook, stirring constantly, until it is thick and smooth. Cool, stirring occasionally to prevent a skin from forming. When cold, beat in the cream, then spread the mixture over the bottom of the pastry basket. Arrange the plums, apple and pear decoratively over the cream, then glaze with the warmed jam.

Serves 4-6

Orange Refrigerator Pie

600 ml./1 pint evaporated
  milk
175 g/6 oz wholemeal
  biscuits, crushed
75 g/3 oz brown sugar
5 ml./1 teaspoon ground
  cinnamon
7.5 ml./1½ teaspoons ground
  allspice
75 g./3oz. butter, melted
2 eggs, separated
125 g./4 oz. castor sugar
finely grated rind and juice
  of 1 large orange
30 ml./2 tablespoons
  gelatine
orange jelly slices to
  decorate

Pour the milk into an ice-cube or freezer tray and chill in the freezing compartment until icicles form.

Meanwhile, mix the biscuits, brown sugar, spices and melted butter together. Press on to the bottom and sides of a well-greased 23 cm/9 in. flan tin.

Beat the egg yolks, castor sugar and orange rind together until pale and thick. Dissolve the gelatine in the orange juice over hot water and leave on one side to cool a little. Pour the evaporated milk into a chilled bowl and beat until thick and creamy. Beat in the egg mixture. Beat the egg whites until they are stiff. Beat the dissolved gelatine into the egg and milk mixture and quickly but gently fold in the egg whites. Spoon the filling into the biscuit case and chill for 1 hour or until set. Decorate with the jelly slices.

Serves 8-10

Sachertorte

175 g./6 oz. chocolate, cut
  into small pieces
175 g./6 oz. butter
150 g./5 oz. castor sugar
6 eggs, separated
175 g./6 oz. self-raising
  flour, sifted
Filling and Topping
50 g./2 oz. apricot jam
300 ml./10 fl. oz. double
  cream, stiffly whipped
175 g/6 oz. plain chocolate,
  cut into small pieces

Put the chocolate into a heatproof bowl over a pan of hot water over low heat and melt gently. Cool slightly.

Cream the butter and sugar together until fluffy. Beat in the melted chocolate, then the egg yolks. Fold in the flour. Beat the egg whites until they are stiff, then fold into the batter. Spoon into a well-greased 23 cm./9 in. cake tin and put into the oven preheated to cool (150°C/300°F or Gas Mark 2). Bake for 1¼ to 1½ hours, or until a knife inserted into the centre comes out clean. Cool in the tin for 15 minutes, then transfer to a wire rack to cool completely.

Cut the cake into two layers and put the bottom one on a plate. Spread with jam, then half the cream. Cover with the remaining layer. Melt the remaining chocolate as above, then spread smoothly over the top and sides. Set aside until firm and set. Put the remaining cream into a piping bag with a star nozzle and pipe decoratively over the icing.

Serves 6-8

Jelly Trifle

4 sponge trifle squares,
  quartered
125 ml./4 fl. oz. sherry
350 g./12 oz. strawberries,
  hulled and sliced
1 packet strawberry jelly
300 ml./10 fl. oz. boiling
  water
300 ml./10 fl. oz. single
  cream
225 ml./8 fl. oz. double
  cream, stiffly whipped

Put the sponge squares on the bottom of a deep serving bowl and pour over the sherry. Leave until it is absorbed. Cover with about one-third of the strawberries.

Dissolve the jelly in the boiling water, stirring constantly. Cool until the mixture stiffens slightly, then beat in the single cream. Pour half the mixture over the strawberries and chill for about 30 minutes or until almost set. Cover with another third of the strawberries and pour over the remaining jelly. Chill until completely set. Decorate with whipped cream and the remaining strawberries.

Serves 4

Baked Apples

4 apples, cored
60 ml./4 tablespoons brown sugar (approximately)

Arrange the apples in an ovenproof dish. Fill the centres with sugar and put into the oven preheated to moderate (180°C/350°F or Gas Mark 4). Bake for about 1 hour, or until the apples are tender but still firm.

Serves 4

Apple and Raisin Crumble

1 kg./2 lb. apples, peeled, cored and sliced
175 g./6 oz. sultanas
15 ml./1 tablespoon finely grated orange rind
50 g./2 oz. castor sugar
5 ml./1 teaspoon ground mixed spice
Topping
150 g./5 oz. flour
75 g./3 oz. castor sugar
75 g./3 oz. butter
5 ml./1 teaspoon ground mixed spice

Arrange the apples and sultanas in a well-greased ovenproof dish. Sprinkle over the orange rind, sugar and spice.

To make the topping, sift the flour and sugar into a bowl. Rub in the butter until the mixture resembles fine breadcrumbs. Stir in the spice. Spoon over the filling to cover completely. Put into the oven preheated to moderate (180°C/350°F or Gas Mark 4) and bake for 40 minutes, or until the topping is crisp and golden.

Serves 4

Creamy Apple Crunch

125 g./4 oz. castor sugar
150 ml./5 fl. oz. water
5 medium cooking apples, peeled, cored and sliced
300 ml./10 fl. oz. sour cream
30 ml./2 tablespoons brown sugar
75 g./3 oz. gingernut biscuits, crushed
45 ml./3 tablespoons chopped almonds

Put the sugar and water in a saucepan and bring to the boil, stirring to dissolve the sugar. Simmer for 3 minutes. Carefully stir in the apple slices and simmer for 5 to 8 minutes, or until they are tender but still firm. Drain the apples and mix with the sour cream and sugar. Spoon into a shallow ovenproof dish.

Mix the biscuits and almonds together and scatter over the apples. Grill for 3 minutes or until the topping is crisp.

Serves 4

Dutch Apple Flan

175 g./6 oz. flour
5 ml./1 teaspoon baking
  powder
75 g./3 oz. butter
1 small egg
75 g./3 oz. castor sugar
5 ml./1 teaspoon vanilla
  essence
Filling
125 g./4 oz. golden syrup
1 large egg
3 large cooking apples,
  peeled, cored and thinly
  sliced
50 g./2 oz. dates, chopped
25 g./1 oz. butter, cut into
  small pieces

Sift the flour and baking powder into a bowl. Add all the remaining pastry ingredients and mix to a soft dough. Roll it out to a rectangle about .75 cm./¼ in. thick. Line a shallow 30 cm./12 in. × 20 cm./8 in. baking tin with the dough, bringing it halfway up the sides of the tin.

Warm the syrup in a saucepan. Remove from the heat and beat in the egg. Pour half the mixture into the dough case and arrange the apple slices in it in overlapping rows. Cover with the remaining syrup mixture. Sprinkle over the dates and butter pieces. Put into the oven preheated to hot (220°C/425°F or Gas Mark 7) and bake for 35 minutes, or until the filling is set and the pastry golden brown. Serve warm.

Serves 8

Apple Sponge Pudding

4 apples, peeled, cored and
  sliced
125 g./4 oz. sugar
60 ml./4 tablespoons water
5 ml./1 teaspoon finely
  grated lemon rind
2.5 ml./½ teaspoon ground
  cloves
Topping
2 eggs
2.5 ml./½ teaspoon vanilla
  essence
50 g./2 oz. castor sugar
50 g./2 oz. self-raising flour,
  sifted
pinch of salt
15 ml./1 tablespoon brown
  sugar

Put the apples, sugar, water, lemon rind and cloves in a saucepan and simmer until the apples are tender. Transfer the mixture to a well-greased pie dish.

To make the topping, beat the eggs and vanilla together, then beat in the sugar. Fold in the flour and salt. Pour over the apple mixture and sprinkle over the brown sugar. Put into the oven preheated to moderate (180°C/350°F or Gas Mark 4) and bake for 30 to 35 minutes or until the topping is golden brown and firm.

Serves 4

Caramel Dumplings

150 g./5 oz. self-raising flour
pinch of salt
25 g./1 oz. butter
50 g./2 oz. sugar
60 ml./4 tablespoons milk
5 ml./1 teaspoon vanilla
essence
Sauce
25 g./1 oz. butter
225 g./8 oz. brown sugar
pinch of salt
400 ml./15 fl. oz. water

Sift the flour and salt into a bowl. Rub in the butter until the mixture resembles fine breadcrumbs. Stir in the sugar, milk and vanilla to form a smooth dough.

To make the sauce, put all the ingredients into a saucepan and bring to the boil, stirring constantly. Drop tablespoonfuls of the dough into the sauce and simmer for 20 minutes, or until they are cooked through.

Serves 4

Baked Alaska

1 × 20 cm./8 in. stale sponge
cake
1 × 225 g./8 oz. can
peaches, drained
1 large block neapolitan or
other ice-cream
6 egg whites
350 g./12 oz. castor sugar

Place the sponge on a lightly greased baking sheet. Arrange the peaches decoratively over the top, pressing them in gently. Put the ice-cream on top and trim it to the same size as the cake. Chill in the freezing compartment of the refrigerator.

Beat the egg whites until they are frothy. Gradually beat in the sugar until the mixture is stiff and glossy. (You should be able to turn the bowl upside-down without the mixture falling out.) Cover the ice-cream and cake completely with the meringue mixture, bringing it up into decorative peaks. Put into the oven preheated to very hot (230°C/450°F or Gas Mark 8) and bake for 5 minutes, or until the meringue is set and lightly browned. Serve at once.

Serves 6

Bread and Butter Pudding

4 large slices buttered bread,
  crusts removed and
  quartered
125 g./4 oz. sultanas
30 ml./2 tablespoons brown
  sugar
Custard
3 eggs
1 egg yolk
50 g./2 oz. castor sugar
600 ml./1 pint milk

Arrange the bread slices in an ovenproof dish. Scatter over the sultanas and sugar.

Beat the eggs, egg yolk and sugar together. Heat the milk to scalding point, then cool slightly. Stir into the egg mixture and strain over the bread slices. Put the dish into a deep baking tin, half-filled with hot water. Put the tin into the oven pre-heated to cool (150°C/300°F or Gas Mark 2) and bake for 45 minutes, or until set.

Serves 4

Chocolate Soufflé

75 g./3 oz. plain chocolate,
  cut into small pieces
300 ml./10 fl. oz. milk
75 g./3 oz. butter
50 g./2 oz. flour
50 g./2 oz. castor sugar
4 egg yolks
4 egg whites, stiffly whipped

Put the chocolate and milk in a saucepan and heat gently until the chocolate melts.

Melt the butter in a saucepan. Stir in the flour to form a smooth paste. Gradually stir in the chocolate mixture. Bring to the boil, then simmer for 2 to 3 minutes, stirring, or until the sauce has thickened. Stir in the sugar, then the egg yolks. Cool, then fold in the egg whites. Spoon into a well-greased soufflé dish and put into the oven pre-heated to fairly hot (190°C/375°F or Gas Mark 5). Bake for 35 to 40 minutes or until well risen.

Serves 4-6

Choux Fritters with Cherry Sauce

1 × 450 g./1 lb. can Morello
  cherries, drained
150 ml./5 fl. oz. water
50 g./2 oz. sugar
5 ml./1 teaspoon arrowroot
60 ml./4 tablespoons cherry
  brandy
225 g./8 oz. choux pastry*
oil for deep frying

Put the cherries, water and sugar into a saucepan and heat, stirring until the sugar has dissolved. Mix the arrowroot and cherry brandy together and stir into the pan. Bring to the boil and cook for 2 to 3 minutes, stirring constantly, or until the sauce thickens. Set aside and keep hot.

Deep-fry tablespoonfuls of the choux dough for 6 to 8 minutes, or until crisp and golden brown. Drain on kitchen towels and serve with the hot sauce.

Serves 4-6

Clafoutis

675 g./1¼ lb. black cherries
75 g./3 oz. castor sugar
15 ml./1 tablespoon brandy
225 g./8 oz. flour
pinch of salt
3 eggs, separated
300 ml./10 fl. oz. milk
15 ml./1 tablespoon butter,
  cut into very small pieces

Put the cherries into a shallow dish and sprinkle with 30 ml./2 tablespoons of sugar and the brandy. Set aside for 30 minutes, stirring occasionally.

Sift the flour and salt into a bowl. Gradually add the egg yolks and enough milk to make a smooth, pouring batter. Beat the egg whites until they are frothy. Gradually beat in the remaining sugar until the mixture is stiff and glossy. Fold into the batter. Pour into a well-greased 1½ l./3 pint ovenproof dish and spoon over the cherry mixture. Dot with the butter pieces. Put into the oven preheated to fairly hot (190°C/375°F or Gas Mark 5) and bake for 40 minutes, or until risen and golden brown.

Serves 6

Crème Brulée

60 ml./4 tablespoons castor
  sugar
45 ml./3 tablespoons water
300 ml./10 fl. oz. milk
4 eggs
300 ml./10 fl. oz. double
  cream, lightly whipped
30 ml./2 tablespoons
  chopped almonds
30 ml./2 tablespoons icing
  sugar

Put 3 tablespoons of sugar and water in a saucepan and bring to the boil, stirring to dissolve the sugar. Boil, without stirring, until the syrup turns a caramel colour. Cool slightly, then gradually stir the milk into the caramel. Return to low heat and stir until the ingredients are thoroughly blended. Remove from the heat and gradually beat in the eggs, remaining sugar and cream. Strain into a flameproof dish. Put the dish into a deep baking tin, half-filled with hot water. Put the tin into the oven preheated to cool (150°C/300°F or Gas Mark 2) and bake for 45 minutes, or until set.

Sprinkle over the almonds and icing sugar and grill for 2 minutes or until lightly glazed and brown.

Serves 4-6

Cornflake Brown Betty

675 g./1½ lb. rhubarb, cut into pieces
60 ml./4 tablespoons orange juice
5 ml./1 teaspoon ground allspice
75 g./3 oz. brown sugar
75 g./3 oz. butter
150 g./5 oz. cornflakes
50 g./2 oz. castor sugar

Put the rhubarb, orange juice, allspice and brown sugar into a saucepan. Simmer for 15 minutes, or until the rhubarb forms a thick purée.

Meanwhile, melt the butter in a frying-pan. Add the cornflakes and fry for 3 minutes. Remove from the heat and stir in the sugar. Put about one-third of the rhubarb mixture in an ovenproof dish. Top with one-third of the cornflakes, and continue making layers until all the ingredients are finished. Put into the oven preheated to moderate (180°C/350°F or Gas Mark 4) and bake for 35 minutes.

Serves 4

Crêpes Suzette

125 g./4 oz. castor sugar
125 g./4 oz. butter
juice of 2 oranges
finely grated rind of 1 orange
8 crêpes, made with French crêpe batter*
30 ml./2 tablespoons orange liqueur
30 ml./2 tablespoons brandy

Put the sugar, butter, orange juice and rind in a large, wide saucepan. Simmer, stirring constantly, until the butter has melted and the sugar dissolved. Continue to simmer for 10 minutes. Put a crêpe in the pan, then fold it in four and transfer to a warmed serving dish. Keep hot while you repeat the process with the remaining crêpes.

When all the crêpes have been folded, stir the liqueur and brandy into the pan, then arrange the folded crêpes in the sauce. Reheat gently, then serve.

Serves 4

Curried Fruit with Sour Cream

1 × 900 g./2 lb. can fruit cocktail, drained
125 g./4 oz. butter
175 g./6 oz. brown sugar
10 ml./2 teaspoons garam masala
5 ml./1 teaspoon curry powder
225 ml./8 fl. oz. sour cream

Arrange the fruit cocktail in a shallow ovenproof dish. Melt the butter in a saucepan and add the sugar. Heat, stirring until the sugar has dissolved. Stir in the spices, then pour over the fruit. Put into the oven preheated to moderate (180°C/350°F or Gas Mark 4) and bake for 25 minutes. Stir in the sour cream.

Serves 4-6

Soufflé Omelet with Apple Purée

6 eggs, separated
50 g./2 oz. castor sugar
*5 ml./1 teaspoon ground
   cinnamon*
50 g./2 oz. butter
225 g./8 oz. thick apple purée

Beat the egg yolks, sugar and cinnamon together. Beat the egg whites until they are stiff. Fold the egg whites into the egg yolk mixture.

Melt the butter in an omelet pan. Pour in the egg mixture. Let it set for about 1 minute, then gently work the underside loose from the pan and tilt slightly so that the liquid runs into the pan. When the omelet is half-cooked, put the pan under the grill and grill until the top is golden. Spoon the apple purée into the centre of the omelet and flip over in a semi-circle.

Serves 3-4

Steamed Pudding

125 g./4 oz. butter
125 g./4 oz. sugar
2 eggs
*225 g./8 oz. self-raising
   flour, sifted*
pinch of salt
150 ml./5 fl. oz. milk
45 ml./3 tablespoons jam

Cream the butter and sugar together until fluffy. Beat in the eggs, then fold in the flour and salt, alternately with the milk.

Spoon the jam into the bottom of a well-greased heatproof basin, then spoon in the batter. Cover the basin, put it into a large pan half-filled with hot water and steam over low heat for 1½ to 2 hours, or until a knife inserted into the centre of the pudding comes out clean.

Serves 4

Chocolate Sauce Pudding

50 g./2 oz. butter
75 ml./3 fl. oz. milk
5 ml./1 teaspoon vanilla
  essence
125 g./4 oz. self-raising flour
175 g./6 oz. castor sugar
15 ml./1 tablespoon cocoa
  powder
425 ml./15 fl. oz. hot water
Topping
125 g./4 oz. brown sugar
15 ml./1 tablespoon cocoa
  powder

Put the butter and milk in a saucepan and heat until the butter has melted. Stir in the vanilla.

Sift the flour, sugar and cocoa into a bowl, then beat in the milk mixture. Pour into a deep, well-greased 1¼ l./2 pint ovenproof dish. Combine the topping ingredients and sprinkle over the mixture, then carefully pour over the hot water. Put into the oven preheated to moderate (180°C/350°F or Gas Mark 4) and bake for 45 minutes.

Serves 4

Christmas Pudding

125 g./4 oz. currants
225 g./8 oz. raisins
225 g./8 oz. sultanas
125 g./4 oz. chopped mixed
  peel
75 ml./3 fl. oz. ale
juice and grated rind of 1
  lemon
175 g./6 oz. butter
225 g./8 oz. brown sugar
2 eggs
225 g./8 oz. fresh
  breadcrumbs
10 ml./2 teaspoons ground
  mixed spice
5 ml./1 teaspoon grated
  nutmeg

Mix the fruit, ale and lemon juice and rind together. Cover and leave overnight.

Cream the butter and sugar together until fluffy. Beat in the eggs, then add all the remaining ingredients and mix well. Put in the centre of a floured pudding cloth and tie securely, allowing room for expansion. Put into a large pan half-filled with hot water and boil the pudding for 4 hours.

Serves 6

Ginger Pudding

50 g./2 oz. butter
30 ml./2 tablespoons golden
  syrup
5 ml./1 teaspoon ground
  ginger
2.5 ml./½ teaspoon
  bicarbonate of soda
75 ml./3 fl. oz. tepid milk
125 g./4 oz. self-raising
  flour, sifted
pinch of salt

Beat the butter, syrup and ginger together until fluffy. Dissolve the soda in the milk, then beat into the mixture. Stir in the flour and salt and mix well. Spoon into a well-greased heatproof basin. Cover the basin, put it into a large pan half-filled with hot water and steam over low heat for 1½ to 2 hours, or until a knife inserted into the centre of the pudding comes out clean.

Serves 4

Lemon Pudding

125 g./4 oz. butter
125 g./4 oz. sugar
23 ml./1½ tablespoons finely
  grated lemon rind
2 eggs
125 g./4 oz. self-raising
  flour, sifted
50 g./2 oz. castor sugar
juice of 2 lemons

Cream the butter, sugar and lemon rind together until fluffy. Beat in the eggs, then fold in the flour.

Mix the castor sugar and lemon juice together and pour into a well-greased heatproof basin. Spoon the batter on top. Cover the basin, put it into a large pan half-filled with hot water and steam over low heat for 1½ to 2 hours, or until a knife inserted into the centre of the pudding comes out clean.

Serves 4-6

Roly Poly

225 g./8 oz. flour
pinch of salt
30 ml./2 tablespoons castor
  sugar
10 ml./2 teaspoons baking
  powder
75 g./3 oz. shredded suet
150 ml./5 fl. oz. water
225 g./8 oz. sultanas
15 ml./1 tablespoon milk

Sift the flour, salt, sugar and baking powder into a bowl, then stir in the suet. Gradually beat in the water to form a light dough. Add a little more water if necessary. Roll out to a rectangle about .75 cm./¼ in. thick. Sprinkle the sultanas over the dough, then brush the edges with the milk. Roll up, like a Swiss roll, and seal the edges. Enclose the roly poly in foil, leaving room for expansion. Put it into a large pan half-filled with hot water and steam over low heat for 2½ hours, or until a knife inserted into the centre of the pudding comes out clean.

Serves 4-6

Cakes & Biscuits

Apple Shortcake

125 g./4 oz. butter
125 g./4 oz. castor sugar
1 egg
125 g./4 oz. self-raising flour
125 g./4 oz. flour
1.25 ml./¼ teaspoon salt
30 ml./2 tablespoons orange
  marmalade
3 eating apples, cored and
  coarsely grated
grated rind and juice of 1
  lemon
30 ml./2 tablespoons sugar

Cream the butter and castor sugar together until fluffy. Beat in the egg, then sift in the flours and salt, a little at a time, mixing well. Roll into two 20 cm./8 in. circles. Transfer one circle to a well-greased 20 cm./8 in. sandwich tin. Cover with marmalade, apples, lemon rind and juice, and half the sugar. Top with the remaining circle. Brush with water, then sprinkle over the remaining sugar. Put in the oven preheated to moderate (180°C/350°F or Gas Mark 4) and bake for 35 to 40 minutes, or until the top is golden brown.

Serves 6-8

Spiced Applesauce Cake

50 g./2 oz. butter
175 g./6 oz. brown sugar
5 ml./1 teaspoon ground
  allspice
2.5 ml./½ teaspoon grated
  nutmeg
2.5 ml./½ teaspoon ground
  ginger
pinch of ground cardamom
275 g./10 oz. thick apple
  purée
225 g./8 oz. flour, sifted
5 ml./1 teaspoon baking
  powder
75 g./3 oz. sultanas
25 g./1 oz. walnuts, finely
  chopped

Cream the butter and sugar together until fluffy, then beat in the spices, apple purée, flour and baking powder. Fold in the sultanas and walnuts. Spoon into a well-greased 18 cm./7 in. shallow cake tin and put into the oven preheated to moderate (180°C/350°F or Gas Mark 4). Bake for 1 hour, or until a knife inserted into the centre comes out clean.

Serves 6-8

French Apricot Tart

175 g./6 oz. rich shortcrust
    pastry*
45 ml./3 tablespoons custard
    powder
15 ml./1 tablespoon castor
    sugar
300 ml./10 fl. oz. milk
1 × 900 g./2 lb. can apricot
    halves, drained
50 g./2 oz. apricot jam,
    warmed
30 ml./2 oz. flaked almonds
    to decorate

Line a 20 cm./8 in. flan tin with the pastry dough. Prick with a fork and put into the oven preheated to fairly hot (190°C/375°F or Gas Mark 5). Bake blind for 15 minutes, or until golden brown.

Meanwhile, mix the custard powder and sugar with a little milk to make a paste. Boil the remaining milk, then pour over the custard mixture, stirring constantly. Return to the pan and cook, stirring constantly, for 2 to 3 minutes, or until thick. Cool, then spoon the custard into the pastry case. Arrange the apricot halves in concentric circles on the custard. Brush with the warmed jam and sprinkle over the almonds.

Serves 6-8

Blackberry and Apple Pie

350 g./12 oz. rich shortcrust
    pastry*
½ kg./1 lb. tart apples, cored
    and sliced
225 g./8 oz. blackberries
30 ml./2 tablespoons sugar
10 ml./2 teaspoons ground
    cinnamon
cinnamon sugar to decorate

Line a well-greased 20 cm./8 in. pie plate with half the dough. Arrange the apples, blackberries, sugar and cinnamon in the dough case. Roll out the remaining dough to a circle large enough to cover the pie and place it over the filling. Crimp the edges to seal. Brush the top with a little milk or beaten egg. Put into the oven preheated to fairly hot (200°C/400°F or Gas Mark 6) and bake for 40 minutes, or until the pastry is golden brown. Sprinkle with cinnamon sugar.

Serves 6-8

Bakewell Tart

225 g./8 oz. shortcrust
    pastry*
75 g./3 oz. butter
75 g./3 oz. sugar
75 g./3 oz. ground rice
1 egg yolk
75 g./3 oz. ground almonds
2.5 ml./½ teaspoon almond
    essence
2 egg whites, stiffly beaten
30 ml./2 tablespoons
    strawberry or raspberry
    jam

Line a well-greased 20 cm./8 in. flan tin with the pastry dough. Reserve the trimmings. Melt the butter in a saucepan. Add the sugar and stir until it dissolves. Remove the pan from the heat and beat in the rice, egg yolk, ground almonds and almond essence. Cool, then quickly fold in the egg whites.

Spread the jam over the bottom of the pastry shell. Spoon in the filling. Roll out the dough trimmings and cut them into 2 cm./¾ in. strips. Arrange the strips, lattice-fashion, over the filling. Put into the oven preheated to hot (220°C/425°F or Gas Mark 7) and bake for 30 minutes or until the filling is set and the pastry is golden.

Serves 6-8

Basque Cake

350 g./12 oz. self-raising
    flour
50 g./2 oz. cornflour
175 g./6 oz. butter
225 g./8 oz. castor sugar
2 eggs, beaten
1 egg yolk, beaten
10 ml./2 teaspoons finely
    grated lemon rind
15 ml./1 tablespoon fresh
    lemon juice
Filling
1 large egg
50 g./2 oz. castor sugar
20 ml./2 tablespoons
    cornflour
225 ml./8 fl. oz. milk
1 egg white, stiffly beaten
1.25 ml./¼ teaspoon vanilla
    essence

Sift together the flour and cornflour. Cream the butter and sugar together until fluffy, then gradually beat in the eggs, egg yolk and lemon rind. Fold in the flour, then the lemon juice and mix to a soft dough. Cover and chill in the refrigerator for 40 minutes.

Meanwhile to make the filling, beat the egg and sugar together until pale. Gradually beat in the cornflour and a little milk to make a paste. Boil the remaining milk, then pour over the egg mixture, stirring constantly. Return to the pan and cook, stirring constantly, for 3 minutes or until thick. Cool slightly, then quickly fold in the egg white and vanilla. Chill until cold.

Divide the dough in half. Roll out one half to a circle large enough to line a well-greased 25 cm./10 in. flan tin. Spread the filling in the pastry case. Roll out the remaining dough and cover the filling completely. Put into the oven preheated to moderate (180°C/350°F or Gas Mark 4) and bake for 45 minutes or until the pastry is golden brown.

Serves 6-8

Caramel Cake

125 g./4 oz. butter
125 g./4 oz. brown sugar
2 eggs
125 g./4 oz. self-raising
    flour, sifted
2.5 ml./½ teaspoon ground
    mixed spice
30 ml./2 tablespoons milk
Icing
50 g./2 oz. butter
125 g./4 oz. brown sugar
30 ml./2 tablespoons milk
225 g./8 oz. icing sugar

Cream the butter and sugar together until fluffy. Beat in the eggs. Fold in the flour, mixed spice and milk. Spoon into a well-greased, shallow 23 cm./9 in. cake tin. Put into the oven preheated to fairly hot (190°C/375°F or Gas Mark 5) and bake for 20 to 25 minutes, or until the cake springs back when lightly pressed in the centre. Cool on a wire rack.

To make the icing, melt the butter in a saucepan. Add the sugar and stir until it dissolves. Stir in the milk. Remove the pan from the heat and beat in half the icing sugar. Then gradually beat in the remaining icing sugar. Spread the icing generously over the top and sides of the cake.

Serves 6-8

Cider Crumble Cake

500 g./1 lb. 2 oz. self-raising
    flour
pinch of salt
125 g./4 oz. brown sugar
75 g./3 oz. dates, chopped
45 ml./3 tablespoons dark
    treacle
300 ml./10 fl. oz. dry cider
2 eggs, beaten
Topping
40 g./1½ oz. flour
40 g./1½ oz. castor sugar
40 g./1½ oz. butter, cut into
    small pieces
40 g./1½ oz. walnuts, chopped
2.5 ml./½ teaspoon ground
    cinnamon
60 ml./4 tablespoons plum
    jam

Sift the flour and salt into bowl. Add the sugar and dates. Put the treacle and cider into a saucepan and heat until they are well blended. Gradually beat the cider mixture into the flour, then stir in the eggs. Spoon the batter into a well-greased 23 cm./9 in. square cake tin and put into the oven preheated to warm (170°C/325°F or Gas Mark 3). Bake for 30 minutes.

Meanwhile to make the topping, rub the flour, sugar and butter together, then stir in the walnuts and cinnamon. Remove the tin from the oven and spread the jam, then the topping over the cake. Return to the oven and continue to bake for a further 20 minutes, or until a knife inserted into the centre comes out clean.

Serves 6-8

Lemon Cheesecake

175 g./6 oz. digestive
 biscuits, crushed
75 g./3 oz. butter, melted
5 ml./1 teaspoon ground
 cinnamon
225 g./8 oz. cream cheese
1 × 175 g./6 oz. can
 condensed milk
grated rind and juice of 2
 lemons
30 ml./2 tablespoons
 sultanas
150 ml./5 fl. oz. double
 cream, stiffly whipped

Mix the biscuits, butter and cinnamon together, then press into the bottom and sides of a well-greased 20 cm./8 in. flan tin. Chill in the refrigerator for 10 minutes.

Mix all the remaining ingredients, then spoon the mixture into the biscuit crust. Chill in the refrigerator for 30 minutes before serving.

Serves 6-8

Honey Cheesecake

225 g./8 oz. wholewheat
 biscuits, crushed
125 g./4 oz. butter, melted
5 ml./1 teaspoon ground
 allspice
350 g./12 oz. cottage cheese
125 g./4 oz. clear honey
10 ml./2 teaspoons brown
 sugar
2 eggs
pinch of salt
10 ml./2 teaspoons ground
 cinnamon

Mix the biscuits, butter and allspice together, then press into the bottom and sides of a well-greased 23 cm./9 in. flan tin. Chill in the refrigerator for 10 minutes.

Mix all the remaining ingredients, except the cinnamon, together. Spoon into the biscuit crust and dust with the cinnamon. Put into the oven preheated to warm (170°C/325°F or Gas Mark 3) and bake for 40 minutes, or until the filling is set.

Serves 6-8

Vanilla Chiffon Cake

125 g./4 oz. self-raising flour
150 g./5 oz. castor sugar
2.5 ml./½ teaspoon salt
60 ml./4 tablespoons corn oil
3 egg yolks
75 ml./5 tablespoons water
7.5 ml./1½ teaspoons vanilla
 essence
2.5 ml./½ teaspoon cream of
 tartar
3 egg whites, stiffly beaten

Sift the flour, sugar and salt into a bowl. Gradually beat in the oil, egg yolks, water and vanilla. Beat the cream of tartar into the egg whites, then quickly fold into the batter. Pour into an ungreased 20 cm./8 in. ring mould and put into the oven preheated to warm (170°C/325°F or Gas Mark 3). Bake for 1¼ hours or until a knife inserted into the centre comes out clean.

Serves 6-8

Italian Cream Cheesecake

1 sponge cake (about 15
   cm./6 in. × 7.5 cm./3 in.
   deep)
575 g./1¼ lb. ricotta cheese
175 g./6 oz. sugar
5 ml./1 teaspoon finely
   grated orange rind
50 g./2 oz. dessert chocolate,
   cut into small pieces
125 g./4 oz. candied peel,
   finely chopped
45 ml./3 tablespoons orange
   liqueur or orange juice

Cut the sponge cake into three layers. Rub the ricotta cheese through a strainer, then mix with the sugar and orange rind. Divide the mixture in half, and put one half in the refrigerator. Beat the chocolate and candied peel into the remaining cheese mixture.

Put the bottom layer of the sponge cake on a serving dish, and sprinkle over 15 ml./1 tablespoon of the liqueur or juice. Spread over half of the chocolate-cheese mixture. Cover with the second slice of cake, then the remaining ricotta chocolate mixture and third cake layer. Chill in the refrigerator for 1 hour, then spread the remaining ricotta mixture over the top and sides.

Serves 8-10

Chestnut and Chocolate Gâteau

4 eggs, separated
225 g./8 oz. sugar
75 g./3 oz. chocolate, cut into
   small pieces
30 ml./2 tablespoons strong
   black coffee
225 g./8 oz. unsweetened
   chestnut purée
Icing
75 g./3 oz. chocolate, cut into
   small pieces
30 ml./2 tablespoons strong
   black coffee
2 egg yolks
30 ml./2 tablespoons sugar
150 ml./5 fl. oz. double
   cream
marrons glacés to decorate

Beat the egg yolks with the sugar until pale. Melt the chocolate with the coffee over low heat, then stir into the egg yolks. Beat in the chestnut purée. Beat the egg whites until they are stiff, then fold into the egg yolk mixture. Spoon into two well-greased 15 cm./6 in. sandwich tins. Put into the oven preheated to moderate (180°C/350°F or Gas Mark 4) and bake for 35 minutes or until a knife inserted into the centres comes out clean. Cool on a wire rack.

Meanwhile to make the icing, melt the chocolate with the coffee over low heat. Add the egg yolks and sugar and stir to dissolve the sugar. Remove from the heat and cool, then beat in the cream.

Put one of the cakes on a plate. Cover with half the icing, then top with the second cake. Spread the remaining icing over the top and decorate with marrons glacés.

Serves 6-8

Butterscotch Cake

125 g./4 oz. butter
175 g./6 oz. brown sugar
1 large egg
225 g./8 oz. flour
15 ml./1 tablespoon baking
   powder
150 ml./5 fl. oz. milk
Butterscotch Icing
125 g./4 oz. dark brown
   sugar
45 ml./3 tablespoons milk
pinch of salt
25 g./1 oz. butter
75 g./3 oz. icing sugar, sifted

Cream the butter and sugar together until fluffy. Beat in the egg. Sift the flour and baking powder together, then add to the butter mixture with the milk, beating well. Spoon into a well-greased 20 cm./8 in. sandwich tin. Put into the oven preheated to moderate (180°C/350°F or Gas Mark 4) and bake for 45 minutes or until a knife inserted into the centre comes out clean. Cool on a wire rack.

Meanwhile to make the icing, put all the icing ingredients, except the icing sugar, in a saucepan and bring to the boil, stirring. Boil for 5 minutes, without stirring, then cool to warm. Gradually beat in the icing sugar. Add more icing sugar if necessary to make a spreading consistency. Cover the top and sides of the cake with the icing.

Serves 6-8

Devil's Food Cake

50 g./2 oz. butter
225 g./8 oz. sugar
2 eggs
175 g./6 oz. self-raising
   flour, sifted
50 ml./2 fl. oz. sour milk
75 ml./3 fl. oz. boiling black
   coffee
50 g./2 oz. plain chocolate,
   cut into small pieces
5 ml./1 teaspoon bicarbonate
   of soda
5 ml./1 teaspoon vanilla
   essence
melted chocolate to decorate
Filling
1 egg white
38 ml./2½ tablespoons cold
   water
200 g./7 oz. sugar
1.25 ml./¼ teaspoon cream of
   tartar
2.5 ml./½ teaspoon vanilla
   essence

Cream the butter and sugar together until fluffy. Beat in the eggs, then fold in the flour with the sour milk. Mix the coffee, chocolate and soda together until the chocolate has melted. Cool slightly, then stir in the vanilla. Add to the flour mixture and beat well. Divide the batter evenly between two well-greased 23 cm./9 in. sandwich tins. Put into the oven preheated to fairly hot (190°C/375°F or Gas Mark 5) and bake for 25 to 30 minutes, or until a knife inserted into the centres comes out clean. Cool on a wire rack.

Meanwhile to make the filling, beat all the ingredients, except the vanilla, together in a heatproof bowl. Put the bowl over a saucepan of hot water over low heat and whisk for 6 to 8 minutes, or until stiff. Put one of the cakes on a plate. Spread the filling liberally over the top and cover with the remaining cake. Dribble a little melted chocolate over the top to decorate.

Serves 6-8

Dark Chocolate Cake

125 ml./4 fl. oz. hot black
  coffee
50 g./2 oz. cocoa powder
275 g./10 oz. brown sugar
125 g./4 oz. butter, softened
3 eggs, separated
5 ml./1 teaspoon salt
5 ml./1 teaspoon vanilla
  essence
5 ml./1 teaspoon bicarbonate
  of soda
150 ml./5 fl. oz. sour cream
225 g./8 oz. flour, sifted
125 g./4 oz. sugar
225 ml./8 fl. oz. double
  cream, stiffly whipped
Frosting
125 g./4 oz. plain chocolate,
  cut into small pieces
150 ml./5 fl. oz. sour cream
pinch of salt
45 ml./3 tablespoons icing
  sugar, sifted

Mix together the coffee and cocoa. Beat half of the mixture with the brown sugar, butter, egg yolks, salt and vanilla. Mix together the soda and sour cream, then add to the butter mixture, with the remaining cocoa mixture and the flour. Beat the egg whites until they are soft. Beat in the sugar until the mixture is stiff and glossy. Fold into the batter.

Spoon the batter into a well-greased 23 cm./9 in. cake tin. Put into the oven preheated to moderate (180°C/350°F or Gas Mark 4) and bake for 1 to 1¼ hours, or until a knife inserted into the centre comes out clean. Cool on a wire rack.

Meanwhile to make the icing, melt the chocolate, then cool slightly. Beat in the remaining ingredients until the mixture is smooth. Cut the cake into two layers. Put the bottom layer on a plate and spread generously with the whipped cream. Top with the remaining layer and cover the top and sides with the frosting.

Serves 6-8

Easy Dundee Cake

275 g./10 oz. flour
5 ml./1 teaspoon baking
  powder
2.5 ml./½ teaspoon ground
  mixed spice
175 g./6 oz. butter, softened
175 g./6 oz. castor sugar
225 g./8 oz. currants
225 g./8 oz. sultanas
225 g./8 oz. raisins
50 g./2 oz. chopped mixed
  peel
50 g./2 oz. chopped glacé
  cherries
5 eggs
25 g./1 oz. blanched
  almonds to decorate

Sift the flour, baking powder and mixed spice together. Cream the butter and sugar together until fluffy. Beat in the flour mixture, fruit and eggs. Add a little milk if the batter is too stiff.

Line a 20 cm./8 in. cake tin with a double thickness of greased greaseproof paper. Spoon the batter into the tin. Decorate the top with the almonds. Put into the oven preheated to warm (170°C/325°F or Gas Mark 3) and bake for 2 to 2¼ hours, or until a knife inserted into the centre comes out clean.

Serves 8-10

Chocolate Orange Cake

175 g./6 oz. butter
175 g./6 oz. sugar
3 eggs
175 g./6 oz. self-raising
  flour, sifted
30 ml./2 tablespoons milk
grated rind of 2 oranges
Chocolate Icing
175 g./6 oz. icing sugar
15 ml./1 tablespoon cocoa
  powder
2.5 ml./½ teaspoon butter
water to blend

Cream the butter and sugar together until fluffy. Beat in the eggs, then fold in the flour with the milk and orange rind. Spoon the batter into a well-greased loaf tin and put into the oven preheated to moderate (180°C/350°F or Gas Mark 4). Bake for 1 hour, or until a knife inserted into the centre comes out clean. Cool on a wire rack.

Meanwhile to make the icing, sift the icing sugar and cocoa into a heatproof bowl. Add the butter and put the bowl over a pan of boiling water. Stir in enough water to make a spreading consistency. Spread the icing over the top and sides of the cake.

Serves 6-8

Cherry Cake

175 g./6 oz. butter
175 g./6 oz. castor sugar
3 eggs, beaten
75 g./3 oz. flour, sifted
75 g./3 oz. self-raising flour,
  sifted
45 ml./3 tablespoons milk
125 g./4 oz. glacé cherries,
  chopped
Snow Glaze
275 g./10 oz. icing sugar,
  sifted
5 ml./1 teaspoon butter,
  softened
2.5 ml./½ teaspoon vanilla
  essence
23 ml./1½ tablespoons milk

Cream the butter and sugar together until fluffy. Gradually beat in the eggs, then fold in the flours and milk. Mix in the cherries. Spoon into a well-greased 20 cm./8 in. cake tin. Put into the oven preheated to moderate (180°C/350°F or Gas Mark 4) and bake for 1 hour, or until a knife inserted into the centre comes out clean. Cool in the tin for 10 minutes, then transfer to a wire rack to cool completely.

To make the glaze, combine the sugar, butter and vanilla together, then beat in enough milk to make a thick, spreading consistency. Spread over the top and sides of the cake.

Serves 6-8

Marble Cake

125 g./4 oz. butter
175 g./6 oz. castor sugar
5 ml./1 teaspoon vanilla
 essence
2 eggs
225 g./8 oz. self-raising
 flour, sifted
pinch of salt
45-60 ml./3-4 tablespoons
 milk
2.5 ml./½ teaspoon red food
 colouring
30 ml./2 tablespoons cocoa
 powder dissolved in 30
 ml./2 tablespoons water

Cream the butter and sugar together until fluffy. Beat in the vanilla, then the eggs. Fold in the flour and salt with the milk. Divide the batter into three. Add the red food colouring to one, the cocoa mixture to the second and leave the third plain. Spoon the mixtures, in alternating spoonfuls, into a well-greased 18 cm./7 in. cake tin, then cut through and swirl the mixture a few times with a knife or skewer.

Put into the oven preheated to moderate (180°C/350°F or Gas Mark 4) and bake for 50 minutes to 1 hour, or until a knife inserted into the centre comes out clean.

Serves 6-8

Sultana Cake

225 g./8 oz. butter
225 g./8 oz. castor sugar
5 eggs
275 g./10 oz. flour
25 g./1 oz. self-raising flour
pinch of salt
675 g./1½ lb. sultanas,
 soaked in warm water for
 2 hours and drained
125 g./4 oz. flaked almonds
45 ml./3 tablespoons brandy
 (optional)
2.5 ml./½ teaspoon vanilla
 essence

Cream the butter and sugar together until fluffy. Beat in the eggs. Sift the flours and salt together, then add to the butter mixture with the sultanas, beating well. Fold in the almonds, reserving a few for decoration, then stir in the brandy, if you are using it, and the vanilla.

Line a 20 cm./8 in. square cake tin with a double thickness of greased greaseproof paper. Spoon the batter into the tin. Put into the oven preheated to warm (170°C/325°F or Gas Mark 3) and bake for 1¼ hours.

Decorate the top of the cake with the reserved almonds, return to the oven and bake for a further 30 minutes, or until a knife inserted into the centre comes out clean.

Serves 8-10

Farmhouse Fruit Cake

275 g./10 oz. self-raising
    flour
1.25 ml./¼ teaspoon salt
225 g./8 oz. butter
225 g./8 oz. castor sugar
15 ml./1 tablespoon finely
    grated orange rind
5 eggs
350 g./12 oz. sultanas
125 g./4 oz. raisins
175 g./6 oz. chopped glacé
    cherries
50 g./2 oz. chopped mixed
    peel
15 ml./1 tablespoon fresh
    orange juice

Sift the flour and salt together. Cream the butter and sugar together until fluffy, then beat in the orange rind. Beat in the eggs, then the fruit, orange juice and flour.

Line a 20 cm./8 in. cake tin with a double thickness of greased greaseproof paper. Spoon the batter into the tin. Put into the oven preheated to cool (150°C/300°F or Gas Mark 2) and bake for 2½ hours or until a knife inserted into the centre comes out clean.

Serves 8-10

Strawberry Cream and Almond Ring

125 g./4 oz. self-raising flour
pinch of salt
125 g./4 oz. butter
125 g./4 oz. castor sugar
5 ml./1 teaspoon vanilla
    essence
2 eggs, beaten
Filling
30 ml./2 tablespoons sweet
    sherry
15 ml./1 tablespoon orange
    juice
300 ml./10 fl. oz. double
    cream, stiffly whipped
30 ml./2 tablespoons milk
23 ml./1½ tablespoons icing
    sugar
½ kg./1 lb. strawberries,
    hulled
15 ml./1 tablespoon flaked
    almonds, toasted

Sift the flour and salt into a bowl. Cream the butter and sugar together until fluffy. Beat in the vanilla, then the eggs. Fold in the flour and beat well. Pour the batter into a well-greased 23 cm./9 in. ovenproof ring mould. Put into the oven preheated to fairly hot (190°C/375°F or Gas Mark 5) and bake for 30 to 35 minutes or until the cake springs back when lightly pressed in the centre. Cool in the mould for 10 minutes, then transfer to a plate. Prick with a fork. Mix the sherry and orange together and pour over the cake. Set aside until the liquid has been absorbed.

Beat the cream and milk together, then fold in the icing sugar. Spoon about one-quarter of the cream into a piping bag with a star nozzle. Spread the remaining cream over the top and sides of the cake to cover it completely. Pile the strawberries in the centre and sprinkle over the almonds. Pipe the remaining cream around the filling and serve.

Serves 6-8

346

Madeira Cake

175 g./6 oz. butter
150 g./5 oz. castor sugar
15 ml./1 tablespoon finely
  grated lemon rind
3 large eggs
225 g./8 oz. flour
10 ml./2 teaspoons baking
  powder
candied peel to decorate

Cream the butter and sugar together until fluffy. Beat in the lemon rind, then the eggs. Sift the flour and baking powder together, then lightly fold them into the butter mixture.

Line an 18 cm./7 in. cake tin with a double thickness of greased greaseproof paper. Spoon the batter into the tin and put into the oven preheated to moderate (180°C/350°F or Gas Mark 4). Bake for 45 minutes.

Decorate the top of the cake with the candied peel, return to the oven and bake for a further 20 to 30 minutes or until a knife inserted into the centre comes out clean.

Serves 8-10

Coffee Gâteau

3 large eggs
75 g./3 oz. castor sugar
75 g./3 oz. self-raising flour,
  sifted
50 g./2 oz. flaked almonds,
  toasted
chocolate balls or nuts to
  decorate
Icing
350 g./12 oz. icing sugar,
  sifted
30 ml./2 tablespoons strong
  black coffee
30 ml./2 tablespoons rum
175 g./6 oz. butter, softened
25 g./1 oz. crystallized
  ginger

Mix the eggs and sugar together in a heatproof bowl. Put the bowl over a pan of boiling water over low heat and beat until very thick. Remove the bowl from the pan and gradually beat in the flour. Divide between two well-greased 18 cm./7 in. sandwich tins and put into the oven preheated to fairly hot (190°C/375°F or Gas Mark 5). Bake for 20 to 25 minutes, or until the cakes spring back when lightly pressed in the centre. Cool on a wire rack.

Meanwhile to make the icing, beat the icing sugar, coffee and rum together. Gradually beat in the butter. Put about one-third of the mixture in another bowl and beat in the ginger.

Put one cake on a plate and spread the ginger icing mixture over the top. Cover with the remaining cake, and spread the remaining icing over the top and sides. Decorate the top and sides with flaked almonds, then arrange the chocolate balls or nuts on top.

Serves 6-8

Nutmeg Cake

225 g./8 oz. wholemeal flour
450 g./1 lb. brown sugar
10 ml./2 teaspoons baking
  powder
125 g./4 oz. butter
1 egg
5 ml./1 teaspoon freshly
  grated nutmeg
5 ml./1 teaspoon bicarbonate
  of soda dissolved in 225
  ml./8 fl. oz. milk
125 g./4 oz. shelled walnuts

Mix together the flour, sugar and baking powder. Rub in the butter until the mixture resembles breadcrumbs.

Line a 20 cm./8 in. cake tin with a double thickness of greased greaseproof paper. Put half the flour mixture on the bottom. Beat the egg, nutmeg and soda mixture together, then stir into the remaining flour mixture. Spoon into the tin. Scatter the walnuts over the top. Put into the oven preheated to moderate (180°C/350°F or Gas Mark 4) and bake for 1 hour, or until a knife inserted into the centre comes out clean.

Serves 6-8

Pineapple Upside-Down Cake

175 g./6 oz. butter, melted
350 g./12 oz. brown sugar
1 × 400 g./14 oz. can
  pineapple rings, drained
450 g./1 lb. wholemeal flour
5 ml./1 teaspoon ground
  cinnamon
5 ml./1 teaspoon grated
  nutmeg
2 eggs
125 ml./4 fl. oz. skimmed
  milk

Put 125 g./4 oz. of the melted butter in a flameproof baking dish, then add 225 g./8 oz. of the sugar. Stir over low heat until the sugar dissolves. Remove from the heat and arrange the pineapple rings in the dish.

Sift the flour, cinnamon and nutmeg into a bowl. Beat the eggs, remaining sugar and melted butter, and the milk together, then beat into the flour mixture to make a soft, dropping consistency. Spoon over the pineapple rings and put into the oven preheated to moderate (180°C/350°F or Gas Mark 4). Bake for 50 minutes.

Serves 6-8

Sponge Sandwich

3 large eggs, separated
125 g./4 oz. castor sugar
125 g./4 oz. self-raising
  flour, sifted
5 ml./1 teaspoon butter
45 ml./3 tablespoons boiling
  water
225 ml./8 fl. oz. double
  cream, stiffly whipped
icing sugar to decorate

Beat the egg whites until they are frothy. Beat in the sugar until the mixture is stiff and glossy, then quickly beat in the egg yolks until evenly coloured. Fold in the flour. Mix the butter and water together until the butter melts, then add to the cake batter.

Divide the batter evenly between two well-greased 18 cm./7 in. sandwich tins. Put into the oven preheated to moderate (180°C/350°F or Gas Mark 4) and bake for 20 to 25 minutes or until the cakes spring back when lightly pressed in the centre. Cool on a wire rack.

When cool, spread the top of one cake with the whipped cream and cover with the remaining cake. Dust the top with a little icing sugar.

Serves 6-8

Mocha Torte

6 egg yolks
125 g./4 oz. castor sugar
125 g./4 oz. plain chocolate,
  melted and cooled slightly
5 ml./1 teaspoon coffee
  powder
45 ml./3 tablespoons water
30 ml./2 tablespoons flour,
  sifted
6 egg whites, lightly beaten
Coffee Cream
10 ml./2 teaspoons coffee
  powder
300 ml./10 fl. oz. double
  cream, stiffly whipped
50 g./2 oz. castor sugar

Beat the egg yolks and sugar together until pale. Gradually beat in the melted chocolate, coffee powder and water. Quickly fold in the flour, then the egg whites. Divide between three well-greased 20 cm./8 in. sandwich tins and put into the oven preheated to warm (170°C/325°F or Gas Mark 3). Bake for 30 to 35 minutes, or until a knife inserted into the centres comes out clean. Cool on a wire rack.

Meanwhile to make the coffee cream, beat all the ingredients together until they are thoroughly blended. Chill in the refrigerator for 1 hour.

Put one cake on a plate and cover with a little of the coffee cream. Continue making layers, finishing with a layer of cream over the top and sides of the cake.

Serves 6-8

Fudge Cake

150 g./5 oz. butter
30 ml./2 tablespoons golden
  syrup
150 g./5 oz. plain chocolate,
  cut into small pieces
175 g./6 oz. lady finger
  biscuits, crushed
25 g./1 oz. sultanas
30 ml./2 tablespoons
  chopped glacé cherries
Fudge Icing
50 g./2 oz. plain chocolate,
  cut into small pieces
25 g./1 oz. butter
30 ml./2 tablespoons water
150 g./5 oz. icing sugar,
  sifted

Put the butter, syrup and chocolate in a saucepan and heat until the butter and chocolate have melted. Stir in the biscuits, sultanas and cherries. Spoon into a well-greased springform ½ kg./1 lb. loaf tin. Chill in the refrigerator for 30 minutes or until set. Remove the sides of the tin and transfer the cake to a plate.

To make the icing, melt the chocolate and butter with the water over low heat. Remove from the heat and gradually beat in the icing sugar until the mixture is of a thick spreading consistency. Spread generously over the top and sides of the cake and allow to set.

Serves 6-8

Strawberry Hazelnut Gâteau

4 egg whites
275 g./10 oz. castor sugar
125 g./4 oz. ground
  hazelnuts
2.5 ml./½ teaspoon vanilla
  essence
5 ml./1 teaspoon vinegar
45 ml./3 tablespoons black
  coffee
Filling
175 g./6 oz. plain chocolate,
  cut into small pieces
45 ml./3 tablespoons water
600 ml./1 pint double cream,
  stiffly whipped
½ kg./1 lb. strawberries,
  hulled and sliced

Beat the egg whites until they are frothy. Gradually beat in the sugar and continue beating until the mixture is stiff and glossy. Fold in the nuts, vanilla, vinegar and coffee. Spoon into two well-greased 20 cm./8 in. springform tins. Put into the oven preheated to moderate (180°C/350°F or Gas Mark 4) and bake for 35 to 40 minutes or until crisp on the outside and pale brown in colour. Release the sides of the tins and set the meringues aside to cool on the bases.

To make the filling, melt the chocolate with the water over low heat. Put one meringue on a plate. Spread a thin layer of chocolate over the top, then cover with a 2 cm./¾ in. layer of whipped cream. Top the cream with a layer of sliced strawberries. Place the remaining meringue on top of the strawberries and spread it with the remaining chocolate. Cover the top and sides of the cake with the remaining cream and decorate the top with the remaining strawberry slices. Chill in the refrigerator overnight before serving.

Serves 6-8

Easy Simnel Cake

175 g./6 oz. self-raising flour
pinch of salt
2.5 ml./½ teaspoon grated
 nutmeg
2.5 ml./½ teaspoon ground
 ginger
5 ml./1 teaspoon ground
 cinnamon
5 ml./1 teaspoon ground
 mixed spice
175 g./6 oz. butter
175 g./6 oz. brown sugar
3 eggs
225 g./8 oz. mixed dried fruit
125 g./4 oz. apricot jam
Almond Paste/Marzipan
450 g./1 lb. ground almonds
450 g./1 lb. icing sugar,
 sifted
2.5 ml./½ teaspoon vanilla
 essence
2.5 ml./½ teaspoon almond
 essence
15 ml./1 tablespoon lemon
 juice
2 egg yolks
1 egg white, beaten

Sift together the flour, salt and spices. Cream the butter and sugar together until fluffy. Beat in the eggs, then fold in the flour and fruit.

Line two 20 cm./8 in. sandwich tins with a double thickness of greased greaseproof paper. Divide the batter equally between the tins and put into the oven preheated to warm (170°C/325°F or Gas Mark 3). Bake for 45 minutes, or until a knife inserted into the centres comes out clean. Cool in the tins for 10 minutes, then transfer to a wire rack to cool completely. Spread the tops and sides with the apricot jam.

Meanwhile to make the almond paste, beat the almonds and icing sugar together, then beat in the vanilla and almond essences, lemon juice and egg yolks until a stiff paste is formed. (If the mixture is too wet, work in more icing sugar; if it is too dry, beat in more lemon juice.) Divide the paste into three. Lightly roll out two of the pieces, on a surface lightly dusted with icing sugar, to 20 cm./8 in. circles. Top one cake layer with a paste circle, then the remaining cake and second paste circle. Form the remaining paste into 12 small balls and arrange them around the top edge of the cake. Lightly glaze the top with the egg white and put the cake on a baking sheet. Put into the oven preheated to very hot (230°C/450°F or Gas Mark 8) and bake for 5 minutes to glaze the top.

Serves 8-10

Lemon Cream Pie

225 g./8 oz. digestive
   biscuits, crushed
5 ml./1 teaspoon ground
   mixed spice
125 g./4 oz. butter, melted
Filling
5 ml./1 teaspoon gelatine
45 ml./3 tablespoons boiling
   water
175 g./6 oz. lemon curd
300 ml./10 fl. oz. double
   cream, stiffly whipped

Mix the biscuits, mixed spice and butter together, then press into a well-greased 20 cm./8 in. flan tin. Chill in the refrigerator for 10 minutes.

Dissolve the gelatine in the water. Cool slightly, then beat in the lemon curd. Quickly fold in the whipped cream and pour the filling into the biscuit crust. Chill in the refrigerator for at least 5 hours, or until the filling is set.

Serves 6-8

Butterscotch Walnut Brownies

125 g./4 oz. butter
125 g./4 oz. brown sugar
2 eggs, beaten
5 ml./1 teaspoon vanilla
   essence
75 g./3 oz. self-raising flour,
   sifted
50 g./2 oz. walnuts, chopped

Cream the butter and sugar together until fluffy. Beat in the eggs, then the vanilla essence. Fold in the flour, then the walnuts and mix well. Spoon the batter into a well-greased 18 cm./7 in. square baking tin and put into the oven preheated to warm (170°C/325°F or Gas Mark 3). Bake for 35 to 40 minutes or until firm. Cut into squares to serve.

Makes about 16 brownies

Chocolate Nut Brownies

75 g./3 oz. flour
40 g./1½ oz. cocoa powder
2.5 ml./½ teaspoon baking
   powder
125 g./4 oz. butter
225 g./8 oz. brown sugar
5 ml./1 teaspoon vanilla
   essence
2 large eggs, beaten
50 g./2 oz. walnuts, chopped

Sift together the flour, cocoa powder and baking powder. Cream the butter and sugar together until fluffy. Beat in the vanilla, then the eggs. Fold in the flour mixture and walnuts and mix well. Spoon the batter into a well-greased 20 cm./8 in. square baking tin and put into the oven preheated to moderate (180°C/350°F or Gas Mark 4). Bake for 30 minutes or until firm. Cut into squares to serve.

Makes about 16 brownies

Yogurt and Orange Cake

175 g./6 oz. self-raising flour
pinch of salt
125 g./4 oz. butter
175 g./6 oz. castor sugar
2 eggs
75 g./3 oz. frozen
*   concentrated orange juice,*
*   thawed*
150 ml./5 fl. oz. plain yogurt
Orange Filling
50 g./2 oz. butter
175 g./6 oz. icing sugar,
*   sifted*
30 ml./2 tablespoons frozen
*   concentrated orange juice,*
*   thawed*
crystallized orange slices to
*   decorate*

Sift together the flour and salt. Cream the butter and sugar together until fluffy. Beat in the eggs, then fold in the flour with the orange juice and yogurt. Spoon the batter into two well-greased 20 cm./8 in. sandwich tins and put into the oven preheated to fairly hot (190°C/375°F or Gas Mark 5). Bake for 30 to 35 minutes or until a knife inserted into the centres comes out clean. Cool in the tins for 10 minutes, then transfer to a wire rack to cool completely.

To make the filling, cream the butter until it is pale, then gradually beat in the icing sugar and orange juice. Put one cake on a plate and spread with half of the filling. Cover with the remaining cake, and spread over the remaining filling. Decorate with crystallized orange slices.

Serves 6-8

Cheesecake Squares

125 g./4 oz. flour
125 g./4 oz. self-raising flour
50 g./2 oz. cornflour
50 g./2 oz. custard powder
40 g./1½ oz. icing sugar
175 g./6 oz. butter
45 ml./3 tablespoons water
10 ml./2 teaspoons lemon
*   juice*
125 g./4 oz. apricot jam
1 egg, beaten
icing sugar to decorate
Filling
75 g./3 oz. butter
50 g./2 oz. sugar
2 eggs, separated
50 g./2 oz. raisins
5 ml./1 teaspoon finely
*   grated lemon rind*
350 g./12 oz. cottage cheese
75 ml./3 fl. oz. sour cream

Sift all the dry ingredients into a large bowl. Rub in the butter until the mixture resembles fine breadcrumbs. Add the water and lemon juice and beat to a firm dough. Knead lightly for 3 minutes. Divide the dough in half and roll out one half to fit the bottom of an 18 cm./7 in. square greased baking tin. Carefully lay the dough in the tin, then spread it with the apricot jam.

To make the filling, cream the butter and sugar together until fluffy. Beat in the egg yolks, raisins, lemon rind, cottage cheese and sour cream. Beat the egg whites until they are stiff. Fold into the cheese mixture and spread over the jam in the tin.

Roll out the remaining dough to fit the tin, then carefully place it over the filling so that it is completely covered. Brush the dough with the beaten egg. Put into the oven preheated to moderate (180°C/350°F or Gas Mark 4) and bake for 30 to 40 minutes, or until the pastry is golden brown. Cut into squares and dust with icing sugar.

Makes about 16 squares

Continental Chocolate Slice

125 g./4 oz. butter
125 g./4 oz. sugar
30 ml./2 tablespoons cocoa
  powder
1 egg
5 ml./1 teaspoon vanilla
  essence
225 g./8 oz. wholemeal
  digestive biscuits, crushed
75 g./3 oz. desiccated
  coconut
75 g./3 oz. walnuts, finely
  chopped
Topping
50 g./2 oz. butter
275 g./10 oz. icing sugar,
  sifted
23 ml./1½ tablespoons
  custard powder
45 ml./3 tablespoons hot
  water
125 g./4 oz. plain chocolate,
  cut into small pieces

Put the butter, sugar and cocoa into a saucepan and heat until the butter has melted. Stir in the egg and vanilla essence and cook gently for 1 minute. Remove from the heat and stir in the biscuits, coconut and walnuts. Press the mixture on to the bottom of a well-greased 25 cm./10 in. × 20 cm./8 in. baking tin. Chill in the refrigerator for 15 minutes, or until set.

Meanwhile to make the topping, cream the butter until it is pale. Beat in the icing sugar, then gradually mix in the custard powder with the water. Beat until the mixture is thick and smooth.

Spread the topping over the biscuit base, then chill in the refrigerator for a further 15 minutes. Melt the chocolate over low heat, then carefully spread it over the topping. Cut into slices.

Makes about 24 slices

Réligieuses

450 g./1 lb. choux pastry*
Filling
2 eggs, separated
50 g./2 oz. castor sugar
25 g./1 oz. flour
300 ml./10 fl. oz. milk
2.5 ml./½ teaspoon vanilla
  essence
Glacé Icing
50 g./2 oz. plain chocolate,
  melted
15 g./½ oz. butter
175 g./6 oz. icing sugar,
  sifted
water to blend
Butter Icing
40 g./1½ oz. butter
75 g./3 oz. icing sugar
25 g./1 oz. plain chocolate,
  melted

Spoon the pastry dough into a piping bag with a plain nozzle. Pipe on to well-greased baking sheets in nine balls about 4 cm./1½ in. diameter and nine of about 1.25 cm./½ in. diameter. Put into the oven preheated to fairly hot (200°C/400°F or Gas Mark 6) and bake for 10 minutes. Reduce the oven temperature to moderate (180°C/350°F or Gas Mark 4) and continue to bake for 20 to 25 minutes, or until puffed up and golden brown. Make a slit in the side of each ball and, using a teaspoon, carefully scoop out any soft dough from inside. Return to the oven for 5 minutes to dry out. Cool on a wire rack.

To make the filling, beat the egg yolks and sugar together until pale. Gradually beat in the flour and enough milk to form a smooth paste. Boil the remaining milk, then stir into the egg mixture. Return to the pan and cook, stirring constantly, for 3 minutes or until very thick. Cool slightly. Beat the egg whites until stiff, then fold into the cream with the vanilla. Spoon the filling into the choux buns.

To make the glacé icing, cream the chocolate and butter together. Gradually beat in the icing sugar, then add just enough water to make a thick icing. Spread the icing over the large buns, then coat the tops of the small buns and place over the large ones.

To make the butter icing, beat all the ingredients together until they are thoroughly blended. Set aside until stiff enough to pipe. Spoon into a piping bag with a small star nozzle and pipe over and around the bases of each small bun.

Makes 9 buns

Vanilla Custard Slice

275 g./10 oz. puff pastry*
1¼ l./2 pints milk
175 g./6 oz. sugar
50 g./2 oz. butter
50 g./2 oz. cornflour
60 ml./4 tablespoons custard
   powder
10 ml./2 teaspoons vanilla
   essence
1 egg
Lemon Icing
350 g./12 oz. icing sugar,
   sifted
15 g./½ oz. butter, softened
lemon juice to blend

Roll out the dough to two 25 cm./10 in. squares. Carefully transfer the squares to ungreased baking sheets and put into the oven preheated to very hot (230°C/450°F or Gas Mark 8). Bake for 15 minutes. Cool, then trim the squares to about 20 cm./8 in. Transfer one square to an ungreased 20 cm./8 in. cake tin.

Put 1 l./1¾ pints of the milk, sugar and butter in a saucepan. Blend the cornflour and custard with the remaining milk, then add to the pan. Bring to the boil, stirring constantly, and simmer until smooth and thick. Cool, then beat in the vanilla essence and egg. Pour over the pastry in the tin, then cover with the remaining pastry square. Set aside to cool completely.

Meanwhile, to make the icing beat the icing sugar and butter together until the mixture is crumbly. Gradually beat in enough lemon juice to make a spreading consistency. Spread the icing over the pastry. Cut into slices to serve.

Makes about 16 slices

Cream Horns

350 g./12 oz. puff pastry*
1 egg, beaten
45 ml./3 tablespoons sugar
125 g./4 oz. jam
Filling
300 ml./10 fl. oz. double
   cream, stiffly whipped
5 ml./1 teaspoon vanilla
   essence
15 ml./1 tablespoon icing
   sugar
30 ml./2 tablespoons milk

Roll out the dough to about .75 cm./¼ in. thick. Cut into 12 long strips, about 2.5 cm./1 in. wide. Brush one side of each strip with water and carefully wind round the outside of 12 greased cream horn tins, overlapping slightly so that there are no gaps. Transfer the tins to a damp baking sheet, brush with the beaten egg and sprinkle over the sugar. Set aside for 30 minutes.

Put into the oven preheated to very hot (230°C/450°F or Gas Mark 8) and bake for 20 to 25 minutes, or until golden brown. Gently transfer to a wire rack to cool.

When cold, remove the tins from the pastry. Put a tablespoonful of jam into the bottom of the horns. Beat the filling ingredients together until thick, then spoon into the horns.

Makes 12 horns

Coffee Eclairs

275 g./10 oz. choux pastry*
Filling
150 ml./5 fl. oz. double
  cream, stiffly whipped
30 ml./2 tablespoons castor
  sugar
30 ml./2 tablespoons milk
Icing
250 g./9 oz. icing sugar,
  sifted
45 ml./3 tablespoons strong
  black coffee

Spoon the pastry dough into a piping bag with a plain tube nozzle. Pipe, in 5 cm./2 in. lengths, on to well-greased baking sheets. Put into the oven pre-heated to fairly hot (200°C/400°F or Gas Mark 6) and bake for 10 minutes. Reduce the oven temperature to moderate (180°C/350°F or Gas Mark 4) and continue to bake for 20 to 25 minutes, or until the éclairs are puffed up and golden brown. Make a slit in the side of each éclair and, using a teaspoon, carefully scoop out any soft dough from inside. Return to the oven for 5 minutes to dry out. Cool on a wire rack.

To make the filling, beat all the ingredients together until the mixture is very thick. Slice the éclairs in half, lengthways, and fill generously with the filling.

To make the icing, mix together the icing sugar and coffee. Dip the tops of the éclairs in the icing, or spread it with a knife.

Makes about 10 éclairs

Profiteroles

175 g./6 oz. choux pastry*
300 ml./10 fl. oz. double
  cream, stiffly whipped
225 g./8 oz. icing sugar
15 ml./1 tablespoon cocoa
  powder
23 ml./1½ tablespoons rum or
  brandy
23 ml./1½ tablespoons tepid
  water

Spoon the pastry dough into a large piping bag with a 1.25 cm./½ in. nozzle. Pipe on to a well-greased baking sheet in circles about 5 cm./2 in. in diameter and about 2.5 cm./1 in. deep. Keep the circles well spaced on the sheet. Put into the oven preheated to hot (220°C/425°F or Gas Mark 7) and bake for 10 minutes. Reduce the oven temperature to moderate (180°C/350°F or Gas Mark 4) and bake for a further 15 to 20 minutes or until golden brown.

Make a slit in the side of each puff and, using a teaspoon, carefully scoop out any soft dough from inside. Cool on a wire rack.

Cut the puffs in half and fill with the whipped cream. Sift the icing sugar and cocoa together, then stir in the rum or brandy and water. Gently dip the tops of the profiteroles in the icing, then replace them on top of the cream.

Makes about 8 profiteroles

Brandied Custard Tarts

175 g./6 oz. rich shortcrust
   pastry*
1 egg
15 ml./1 tablespoon sugar
150 ml./5 fl. oz. milk
15 ml./1 tablespoon brandy
10 ml./2 teaspoons grated
   nutmeg

Roll out the dough to about .75 cm./¼ in. thick. Cut into 8 cm./3 in. circles with a pastry cutter, then line 12 well-greased patty tins with the circles.

Beat the egg, sugar, milk and brandy together, then strain into the patty tins. Sprinkle each with a little nutmeg. Put into the oven preheated to fairly hot (190°C/375°F or Gas Mark 5) and bake for 20 to 30 minutes, or until the filling has set and the pastry is golden brown.

Makes 12 tarts

Rock Cakes

225 g./8 oz. self-raising flour
50 g./2 oz. sugar
pinch of salt
1.25 ml./¼ teaspoon ground
   cinnamon
75 g./3 oz. butter
75 g./3 oz. sultanas or raisins
25 g./1 oz. chopped mixed
   peel
1 egg, beaten
60 ml./4 tablespoons milk
60 ml./4 tablespoons castor
   sugar

Sift the flour, sugar, salt and cinnamon into a bowl. Rub in the butter until the mixture resembles fine breadcrumbs. Stir in the sultanas or raisins and mixed peel. Beat in the egg and milk. Spoon tablespoons of the batter on to well-greased baking sheets, well spaced apart. Sprinkle the castor sugar over the tops and put into the oven preheated to fairly hot (190°C/375°F or Gas Mark 5). Bake for 15 to 20 minutes, or until golden brown.

Makes about 15–18 cakes

Nougat Tarts

175 g./6 oz. rich shortcrust
   pastry*
60 ml./4 tablespoons
   raspberry jam
1 egg white, stiffly beaten
125 g./4 oz. sugar
50 g./2 oz. ground almonds
125 g./4 oz. desiccated
   coconut
15 ml./1 tablespoon milk
dash of almond essence
6 glacé cherries, halved

Roll out the dough to about .75 cm./¼ in. thick. Cut into 8 cm./3 in. circles with a pastry cutter, then line 12 well-greased patty tins with the circles. Spread a teaspoon of jam over the bottom of each tin. Combine all the remaining ingredients, except the glacé cherries. Divide the mixture among the cases and top each one with a cherry half. Put into the oven preheated to moderate (180°C/350°F or Gas Mark 4) and bake for 20 to 25 minutes, or until the filling has set and the pastry is golden brown.

Makes 12 tarts

Crunchy Treacle Squares

75 g./3 oz. butter
75 g./3 oz. sugar
75 g./3 oz. black treacle
75 g./3 oz. golden syrup
175 g./6 oz. rolled oats

Put the butter, sugar, treacle and syrup into a saucepan and heat until the butter has melted and the sugar dissolved. Do not allow to boil. Remove from the heat and stir in the oats. Press into a well-greased Swiss roll tin and put into the oven pre-heated to warm (170°C/325°F or Gas Mark 3). Bake for 30 minutes, or until firm. Cut into squares to serve.

Makes about 24 squares

Butterfly Cakes

75 g./3 oz. butter
125 g./4 oz. castor sugar
2 large eggs
125 g./4 oz. flour
5 ml./1 teaspoon baking
    powder
175 ml./6 fl. oz. double
    cream, stiffly whipped
12-15 pieces of angelica to
    decorate

Cream the butter and sugar together until fluffy. Gradually beat in the eggs. Sift the flour and baking powder together, then fold into the butter mixture. Spoon into 12 to 15 greased paper cases on a baking sheet. Put into the oven preheated to moderate (180°C/350°F or Gas Mark 4) and bake for 15 to 20 minutes, or until golden brown. Cool on a wire rack.

When the cakes are cold, carefully scoop out a small circle from the tops. Spoon whipped cream into the cavities, slice the circle in two and arrange on either side of the cream, to form 'wings'. Decorate with a piece of angelica.

Makes 12-15 cakes

Maids of Honour

175 g./6 oz. rich shortcrust
    pastry*
60 ml./4 tablespoons
    raspberry jam
50 g./2 oz. butter
50 g./2 oz. sugar
2.5 ml./½ teaspoon vanilla
    essence
1 egg
50 g./2 oz. self-raising flour,
    sifted

Roll out the dough to about .75 cm./¼ in. thick. Cut into 8 cm./3 in. circles with a pastry cutter, then line 12 well-greased patty tins with the circles. Put about 5 ml./1 teaspoon of jam into each tin.

Cream the butter and sugar together until fluffy. Beat in the vanilla and egg, then gradually fold in the flour. Spoon into the patty tins. Put into the oven preheated to moderate (180°C/350°F or Gas Mark 4) and bake for 20 to 25 minutes, or until the filling has set and the pastry is golden brown.

Makes 12 tarts

Iced Mince Pies

175 g./6 oz. rich shortcrust
  pastry*
450 g./1 lb. mincemeat
30 ml./2 tablespoons icing
  sugar
½ egg white, beaten
few drops of red food
  colouring (optional)

Roll out the dough to about .75 cm./¼ in. thick. Cut into 8 cm./3 in. circles with a pastry cutter, then line 12 well-greased patty tins with the circles. Prick with a fork and put into the oven preheated to fairly hot (190°C/375°F or Gas Mark 5). Bake blind for 10 to 15 minutes, or until golden brown.

Divide the mincemeat among the pastry cases. Beat the icing sugar and egg white together. Stir in the red food colouring, if you wish to have pink icing. Spread the icing thinly over the top of the mincemeat. Put into the oven preheated to moderate (180°C/350°F or Gas Mark 4) and bake for 5 to 10 minutes, or until the icing has set.

Makes 12 pies

Vanilla Buns

225 g./8 oz. flour
10 ml./2 teaspoons baking
  powder
125 g./4 oz. castor sugar
125 g./4 oz. butter
5 ml./1 teaspoon vanilla
  essence
2 eggs
15 ml./1 tablespoon milk

Sift the flour, baking powder and castor sugar into a bowl. Rub in the butter until the mixture resembles fine breadcrumbs. Beat in the remaining ingredients. Spoon tablespoons of the batter on to well-greased baking sheets, well spaced apart. Put into the oven preheated to hot (220°C/425°F or Gas Mark 7) and bake for 12 to 15 minutes, or until golden brown.

Makes about 12 buns

Butter-Oat Biscuits

125 g./4 oz. butter
125 g./4 oz. sugar
15 ml./1 tablespoon golden
  syrup
125 g./4 oz. self-raising
  flour, sifted
250 g./9 oz. rolled oats
5 ml./1 teaspoon bicarbonate
  of soda dissolved in 60
  ml./4 tablespoons boiling
  water

Cream the butter and sugar together until fluffy. Beat in the syrup, then gradually beat in the flour, oats and soda mixture to form a stiff dough. Roll the dough into walnut-sized balls and place them, well spaced apart, on well-greased baking sheets. Press the balls down flat, then put into the oven preheated to moderate (180°C/350°F or Gas Mark 4). Bake for 15 minutes, or until brown and crisp.

Makes about 40 biscuits

Pineapple and Cream Cheese Tartlets

175 g./6 oz. rich shortcrust
  pastry*
50 g./2 oz. full-fat cream
  cheese
10 ml./2 teaspoons lemon
  juice
1 × 125 g./4 oz. can crushed
  pineapple, drained
5 ml./1 teaspoon ground
  ginger
Glaze
5 ml./1 teaspoon arrowroot
150 ml./5 fl. oz. pineapple
  syrup (from can)
few drops of yellow food
  colouring

Roll out the dough to about .75 cm./¼ in. thick. Cut into 8 cm./3 in. circles with a pastry cutter, then line 12 well-greased patty tins with the circles. Prick with a fork and put into the oven preheated to fairly hot (190°C/375°F or Gas Mark 5). Bake blind for 10 to 15 minutes, or until golden brown.

Beat the cream cheese and lemon juice together until smooth. Beat in the pineapple and ginger. Spoon the mixture into the patty tins.

To make the glaze, mix the arrowroot and pineapple syrup together in a saucepan. Simmer until the mixture boils and thickens, then stir in food colouring. Cool slightly, then spoon over the filling.

Makes 12 tarts

Meringues

2 large egg whites
pinch of cream of tartar
150 g./5 oz. castor sugar
10 ml./2 teaspoons cornflour
150 ml./5 fl. oz. double
  cream, stiffly whipped

Beat the egg whites and cream of tartar together until they are frothy. Gradually beat in half the sugar until the mixture is stiff and glossy. (You should be able to turn the bowl upside-down without the mixture falling out.) Gently fold in the remaining sugar and the cornflour. Spoon into a piping bag with a plain nozzle. Pipe whirls on to baking sheets lined with a double thickness of greased greaseproof paper or non-stick silicone paper. Put into the oven preheated to very cool (130°C/250°F or Gas Mark ½) and bake for 1¼ to 1½ hours, or until pale cream and slightly crisp on the outside. Turn the meringues over and return to the oven to dry out completely for another 20 minutes.

Before serving, arrange half the meringues on a plate and cover the tops generously with the whipped cream. Top with the remaining meringues.

Makes about 8 meringues

Brandy Snaps

30 ml./2 tablespoons golden
  syrup
50 g./2 oz. butter
50 g./2 oz. brown sugar
50 g./2 oz. flour
10 ml./2 teaspoons ground
  ginger
pinch of salt

Put the syrup, butter and sugar into a saucepan. Heat until the butter has melted. Sift the flour, ginger and salt together, then stir in the syrup mixture. Drop tablespoons of the batter on to well-greased baking sheets, well spaced apart (don't put more than two or three on each sheet). Put into the oven preheated to moderate (180°C/350°F or Gas Mark 4) and bake for 7 minutes, or until golden brown. Cool for 1 minute, then carefully remove the brandy snaps from the sheets, one at a time, and immediately roll them around the handle of a wooden spoon. Allow to firm and cool on the handle. If they firm up before you have a chance to mould them into shape, return to the oven for a few minutes to soften.

Makes about 6 biscuits

Butter Coconut Crisps

175 g./6 oz. self-raising
  flour, sifted
225 g./8 oz. sugar
1 egg, beaten
125 g./4 oz. butter, melted
150 g./5 oz. desiccated
  coconut

Mix the flour and sugar together. Gradually beat in the egg, then the melted butter. Form into small balls, then roll in the coconut. Put on well-greased baking sheets, well spaced apart, and put into the oven preheated to moderate (180°C/350°F or Gas Mark 4).Bake for 10 to 15 minutes, or until lightly browned and firm to touch.

Makes about 30 biscuits

Chocolate Chip Cookies

75 g./3 oz. butter
50 g./2 oz. castor sugar
125 g./4 oz. self-raising
  flour, sifted
50 g./2 oz. plain chocolate,
  cut into very small pieces,
  or chocolate dots

Cream the butter and sugar together until fluffy. Fold in the flour, then the chocolate pieces. Roll the dough into small balls and put them, well spaced apart, on well-greased baking sheets. Flatten the balls slightly. Put into the oven preheated to moderate (180°C/350°F or Gas Mark 4) and bake for 15 minutes, or until lightly browned and firm to touch.

Makes about 14 biscuits

Currant Crisps

125 g./4 oz. butter
125 g./4 oz. castor sugar
1 egg yolk
125 g./4 oz. currants
225 g./8 oz. flour, sifted

Cream the butter and sugar together until fluffy. Gradually beat in the egg yolk, then the currants and flour to form a stiff dough. Knead gently for 3 minutes. Roll out to about .75 cm./¼ in. thick and cut into 5 cm./2 in. circles with a pastry cutter. Put the circles, well spaced apart, on a well-greased baking sheet. Put into the oven preheated to moderate (180°C/350°F or Gas Mark 4) and bake for 10 to 12 minutes, or until lightly browned and firm to touch.

Makes about 20 biscuits

Hazelnut Chocolate Biscuits

175 g./6 oz. butter
225 g./8 oz. castor sugar
1 egg
2.5 ml./½ teaspoon vanilla
  essence
225 g./8 oz. self-raising
  flour, sifted
50 g./2 oz. ground hazelnuts
50g./2 oz. plain chocolate,
  cut into very small pieces
75 g./3 oz. desiccated
  coconut

Cream the butter and sugar together until fluffy. Beat in the egg and vanilla, then the flour. Stir in the hazelnuts, chocolate pieces and coconut. Roll into walnut-sized balls and put them, well spaced apart, on well-greased baking sheets. Put into the oven preheated to moderate (180°C/350°F or Gas Mark 4) and bake for 15 minutes, or until golden brown and firm to touch.

Makes about 54 biscuits

Date Crunchies

225 g./8 oz. dates, chopped
30 ml./2 tablespoons water
15 ml./1 tablespoon lemon
  juice
15 ml./1 tablespoon clear
  honey
pinch of ground cinnamon
125 g./4 oz. wholewheat
  flour
175 g./6 oz. rolled oats
225 g./8 oz. butter

Put the dates and water in a saucepan and simmer until the dates are soft. Stir in the lemon juice, honey and cinnamon and cool.

Mix the flour and oats together, then rub in the butter. Divide in two and press one half on to the bottom of a well-greased 18 cm./7 in. square cake tin. Spread over the date mixture, then top with the remaining flour mixture. Put into the oven preheated to fairly hot (190°C/375°F or Gas Mark 5) and bake for 25 minutes. Cut into fingers to serve.

Makes about 14 biscuits

Almond Fingers

150 g./5 oz. butter
75 g./3 oz. sugar
175 g./6 oz. flour, sifted
Filling
150 ml./5 fl. oz. double
   cream, stiffly whipped
75 g./3 oz. flaked almonds
30 ml./2 tablespoons brown
   sugar
5 ml./1 teaspoon ground
   cinnamon
1 egg yolk, beaten
Icing
lemon juice
75 g./3 oz. icing sugar, sifted

Cream the butter and sugar together until fluffy. Gradually beat in the flour to form a smooth dough. Pat the dough out into a well-greased shallow 30 cm./1 ft. × 15 cm./6 in. baking tin. Put into the oven preheated to warm (170°C/325°F or Gas Mark 3) and bake for 20 minutes or until golden brown. Cool slightly.

To make the filling, beat all the ingredients together, then spread over the cooled pastry. Return to the oven and bake for a further 40 minutes. Cool, then chill in the refrigerator for 3 hours.

To make the icing, beat enough lemon juice into the icing sugar to make a thick spreading consistency. Spread over the top of the filling and cut into fingers to serve.

Makes about 24 biscuits

Florentines

50 g./2 oz. butter
50 g./2 oz. sugar
50 g./2 oz. walnuts, finely
   chopped
15 g./½ oz. chopped mixed
   peel
15 g./½ oz. chopped glacé
   cherries
15 g./½ oz. sultanas
15 ml./1 tablespoon single
   cream
75 g./3 oz. plain chocolate,
   melted

Melt the butter in a saucepan. Add the sugar and stir until it has dissolved. Add all the remaining ingredients, except the chocolate, and beat well. Drop teaspoons of the batter, well spaced apart, on well-greased baking sheets. Put into the oven preheated to moderate (180°C/350°F or Gas Mark 4) and bake for 10 minutes or until golden brown. Remove from the oven and quickly press into neat circles with a palette knife. Cool slightly, then transfer to a wire rack to cool completely.

Spread melted chocolate on the backs of the biscuits and mark with a fork in a wavy pattern. Leave to set before serving.

Makes about 20 biscuits.

Honey Raisin Bars

75 g./3 oz. butter
175 g./6 oz. clear honey
3 eggs
175 g./6 oz. flour
5 ml./1 teaspoon baking
  powder
175 g./6 oz. raisins
125 g./4 oz. chopped nuts

Beat the butter and honey together until soft. Beat in the eggs. Sift the flour and baking powder together, then gradually fold into the butter mixture, with the raisins and nuts. Press on to a well-greased 30 cm./1 ft. ×23 cm./9 in. shallow tin and put into the oven preheated to moderate (180°C/350°F or Gas Mark 4). Bake for 30 minutes, or until golden brown and firm to touch. Cut into bars to serve.

Makes about 18 biscuits

Ginger Nut Biscuits

225 g./8 oz. flour
225 g./8 oz. castor sugar
2.5 ml./½ teaspoon
  bicarbonate of soda
5 ml./1 teaspoon ground
  cinnamon
pinch of salt
10 ml./2 teaspoons ground
  ginger
125 g./4 oz. butter
1 small egg
5 ml./1 teaspoon golden
  syrup

Sift the flour, sugar, soda, cinnamon, salt and ginger into a bowl. Rub in the butter until the mixture resembles fine breadcrumbs. Beat the egg and syrup together, then gradually beat into the flour mixture to form a stiff dough. Roll into small balls and place them, well spaced apart, on well-greased baking sheets. Put into the oven preheated to warm (170°C/325°F or Gas Mark 3) and bake for 15 to 20 minutes, or until brown and crisp.

Makes about 36 biscuits

Jam and Nut Bars

125 g./4 oz. butter
125 g./4 oz. sugar
1 egg yolk
5 ml./1 teaspoon vanilla
  essence
1.25 ml./¼ teaspoon ground
  cinnamon
125 g./4 oz. self-raising
  flour, sifted
50 g./2 oz. walnuts, chopped
125 g./4 oz. jam

Cream the butter and sugar together until fluffy. Beat in the egg yolk and vanilla essence, then fold in the cinnamon and flour. Beat in the walnuts. Press half the mixture into a well-greased shallow baking dish. Cover with jam, then top with the remaining mixture. Put into the oven preheated to fairly hot (190°C/375°F or Gas Mark 5) and bake for 45 minutes, or until lightly browned and set. Cut into bars to serve.

Makes about 12 bars

...chen

...oz. flour
...2 teaspoons ground
  ...namon
2.5 ml./½ teaspoon cloves
2.5 ml./½ teaspoon ground
  allspice
2.5 ml./½ teaspoon cream of
  tartar
2 eggs, beaten
175 g./6 oz. brown sugar
45 ml./3 tablespoons very
  finely grated orange rind
50 g./2 oz. almonds, finely
  chopped

Sift the flour, spices and cream of tartar into a bowl. Beat in the eggs and sugar, then mix in the remaining ingredients. Roll out the dough until it is about .75 cm./¼ in. thick and cut into shapes or circles with a pastry cutter. Transfer to well-greased baking sheets. Put into the oven preheated to moderate (180°C/350°F or Gas Mark 4) and bake for 15 minutes, or until browned and firm to touch.

Note: Lebkuchen are sometimes iced with a plain or lemon topping before serving.

Makes about 15 biscuits.

Macaroons

2 egg whites
175 g./6 oz. castor sugar
75 g./3 oz. ground almonds
grated rind of 1 lemon

Beat the egg whites until they are frothy. Gradually add the sugar and continue beating until the mixture is stiff and glossy. Fold in the ground almonds and lemon rind. Carefully spoon the mixture on to well-greased baking sheets sprinkled with cornflour. Leave about 5 cm./2 in. between each macaroon. Put into the oven preheated to moderate (180°C/350°F or Gas Mark 4) and bake for 15 to 20 minutes, or until lightly browned and firm to touch.

Makes about 36 biscuits

Shortbread

225 g./8 oz. flour
40 g./1½ oz. icing sugar
15 ml./1 tablespoon ground
  rice
175 g./6 oz. butter

Sift the flour, icing sugar and ground rice into a bowl. Rub in the butter until it is well blended. Roll out the dough to about .75 cm./¼ in. thick. Cut into 5 cm./2 in. circles with a pastry cutter and transfer the circles to an ungreased baking sheet. Put into the oven preheated to moderate (180°C/350°F or Gas Mark 4) and bake for 15 to 20 minutes, or until lightly browned and firm to touch.

Makes about 24 biscuits

Viennese Fingers

225 g./8 oz. butter
50 g./2 oz. castor sugar
2.5 ml./½ teaspoon vanilla
  essence
225 g./8 oz. flour, sifted
pinch of salt
melted chocolate to decorate

Cream the butter and sugar together until fluffy. Beat in the vanilla essence, then gradually beat in the flour and salt. Spoon the mixture into a piping bag with a large star nozzle, and pipe on to well-greased baking sheets, in finger lengths, well spaced apart. Put into the oven preheated to fairly hot (190°C/375°F or Gas Mark 5) and bake for 15 to 20 minutes, or until lightly browned and crisp.

Cool the fingers on a wire rack. Just before serving dip one end of each finger into melted chocolate.

Makes about 36 biscuits

Flaky Cheese Biscuits

50 g./2 oz. butter
50 g./2 oz. Cheddar cheese,
  finely grated
½ egg yolk
pinch of salt
1.25 ml./¼ teaspoon paprika
50 g./2 oz. flour, sifted

Cream the butter until it is fluffy. Gradually beat in the cheese, egg yolk, salt and paprika. Fold in the flour until the mixture forms a dough. Chill in the refrigerator for 1 hour.

Knead for 3 minutes, then roll out to about .75 cm./¼ in. thick. Cut into 2.5 cm./1 in. circles with a pastry cutter. Transfer the circles to a lightly greased baking sheet, and put into the oven pre-heated to hot (220°C/425°F or Gas Mark 7). Bake for 10 minutes, or until browned.

Makes about 30 biscuits

Paprika Biscuits

75 g./3 oz. butter
75 g./3 oz. Cheddar cheese,
  grated
125 g./4 oz. flour
5 ml./1 teaspoon paprika
2.5 ml./½ teaspoon salt
2.5 ml./½ teaspoon dry
  mustard
10 ml./2 teaspoons poppy
  seeds

Beat the butter and grated cheese together until well blended. Sift the flour and seasonings (except the poppy seeds) together, then fold into the butter mixture. Form the mixture into small balls and place on well-greased baking sheets, well spaced apart. Flatten the balls slightly. Sprinkle over the poppy seeds. Put into the oven preheated to moderate (180°C/350°F or Gas Mark 4) and bake for 15 to 20 minutes, or until golden brown.

Makes about 18 biscuits

Breads & Tea Breads

White Bread

23 ml./1½ tablespoons sugar
15 g./½ oz. yeast
475 ml./16 fl. oz. tepid water
675 g./1½ lb. flour
10 ml./2 teaspoons salt

Mix 7.5 ml./1½ teaspoons of the sugar, the yeast and 30 ml./2 tablespoons of tepid water to a paste. Set aside in a warm place for 15 minutes or until the mixture is frothy. Sift the flour and salt into a large, warmed bowl. Add the yeast mixture, the remaining tepid water and sugar and mix to a smooth dough. Knead for about 10 minutes or until smooth and elastic. Set aside in a warm place for 1 to 1¼ hours or until the dough has doubled in size.

Knead the dough again for about 8 minutes. Shape into a loaf and put into a well-greased 1 kg./2 lb. loaf tin. Set aside in a warm place for 30 minutes or until the dough has risen to the top of the tin.

Put the tin into the oven preheated to very hot (230°C/450°F or Gas Mark 8) and bake for 15 minutes. Reduce the oven temperature to hot (220°C/425°F or Gas Mark 7) and continue to bake for 30 minutes. The bread is cooked if it sounds hollow when knocked on the bottom with your knuckle. Cool on a wire rack.

Wholewheat Bread

23 ml./1½ tablespoons brown
  ˉsugar
15 g./½ oz. yeast
475 ml./16 fl. oz. tepid water
675 g./1½ lb. wholewheat
  flour
10 ml./2 teaspoons salt
15 ml./1 tablespoon clear
  honey

Mix 7.5 ml./1½ teaspoons of the sugar, the yeast and 30 ml./2 tablespoons of tepid water to a paste. Set aside in a warm place for 15 minutes or until the mixture is frothy. Put the flour and salt into a large, warmed bowl. Add the yeast mixture, the remaining tepid water and sugar, and the honey, and mix to a smooth dough. Knead for about 10 minutes or until smooth and elastic. Set aside in a warm place for 1 to 1¼ hours or until the dough has doubled in size.

Knead the dough again for about 8 minutes. Shape into a loaf and put into a well-greased 1 kg./2 lb. loaf tin. Set aside in a warm place for 30 minutes or until the dough has risen to the top of the tin.

Put the tin into the oven preheated to very hot (230°C/450°F or Gas Mark 8) and bake for 15 minutes. Reduce the oven temperature to hot (220°C/425°F or Gas Mark 7) and continue to bake for 30 minutes. The bread is cooked if it sounds hollow when knocked on the bottom with your knuckle. Cool on a wire rack.

Quick Bread

5 ml./1 teaspoon sugar
15 g./½ oz. yeast
15 ml./1 tablespoon tepid
  milk
450 g./1 lb. stone ground
  flour
5 ml./1 teaspoon salt
300 ml./10 fl. oz. tepid water

Mix the sugar, yeast and milk to a paste. Set aside in a warm place for 15 minutes or until the mixture is frothy. Sift the flour and salt into a large, warmed bowl. Add the yeast mixture and tepid water and mix to a smooth dough. Knead for about 5 minutes or until smooth and elastic. Shape the dough into a loaf and put it into a well-greased 1 kg./2 lb. loaf tin. Cover and set aside for 1¼ hours or until the dough has risen to the top of the tin.

Glaze the top of the dough with a little milk or beaten egg and put into the oven preheated to very hot (230°C/425°F or Gas Mark 8). Bake for 15 minutes, then reduce the oven temperature to hot (220°C/425°F or Gas Mark 7) and continue to bake for 30 minutes. The bread is cooked if it sounds hollow when knocked on the bottom with your knuckle. Cool on a wire rack.

Rye Bread

5 ml./1 teaspoon sugar
15 g./½ oz. yeast
475 ml./16 fl. oz. tepid water
450 g./1 lb. rye flour
225 g./8 oz. flour, sifted
10 ml./2 teaspoons salt
10 ml./2 teaspoons brown
  sugar
10 ml./2 teaspoons cooking
  oil

Mix the sugar, yeast and 30 ml./2 tablespoons of tepid water to a paste. Set aside in a warm place for 15 minutes or until the mixture is frothy. Mix the flours, salt and brown sugar together in a large, warmed bowl. Add the yeast mixture, the remaining tepid water and the cooking oil and mix to a smooth dough. Knead for about 10 minutes or until smooth and elastic. Set aside in a warm place for 1½ hours or until doubled in size.

Knead the dough again for about 10 minutes. Shape into a loaf and put into a well-greased 1 kg./2 lb. loaf tin. Set aside in a warm place for 35 minutes or until the dough has risen to the top of the tin.

Put the tin into the oven preheated to fairly hot (200°C/400°F or Gas Mark 6) and bake for 40 minutes. The bread is cooked if it sounds hollow when knocked on the bottom with your knuckle. Cool on a wire rack.

Milk Sandwich Loaf

23 ml./1½ tablespoons sugar
15 g./½ oz. yeast
325 ml./11 fl. oz. tepid milk
50 g./2 oz. butter
450 g./1 lb. flour
5 ml./1 teaspoon salt
50 g./2 oz. butter, melted

Mix 5 ml./1 teaspoon of sugar, the yeast and 30 ml./2 tablespoons of tepid milk to a paste. Set aside in a warm place for 15 minutes or until the mixture is frothy. Sift the flour, salt and remaining sugar into a large, warmed bowl. Add the yeast mixture, the remaining milk and melted butter and mix to a smooth dough. Knead for about 10 minutes or until smooth and elastic. Set aside in a warm place for 1 hour or until the dough has doubled in size.

Knead the dough again for 5 minutes. Shape into a loaf and put into a well-greased 1 kg./2 lb. loaf tin. Set aside in a warm place for 30 minutes or until the dough has risen almost to the top of the tin.

Put the tin into the oven preheated to very hot (230°C/450°F or Gas Mark 8) and bake for 15 minutes. Reduce the oven temperature to hot (220°C/425°F or Gas Mark 7) and continue to bake for 25 minutes. The bread is cooked if it sounds hollow when knocked on the bottom with your knuckle. Cool on a wire rack.

Challah

23 ml./1½ tablespoons sugar
15 g./½ oz. yeast
175 ml./6 fl. oz. tepid milk
450 g./1 lb. flour
5 ml./1 teaspoon salt
3 eggs, beaten
Glaze
1 egg, beaten
30 ml./2 tablespoons poppy
   seeds

Mix 5 ml./1 teaspoon of sugar, the yeast and tepid milk to a paste. Set aside in a warm place for 15 minutes or until the mixture is frothy. Sift the flour and salt into a large, warmed bowl. Add the yeast mixture, eggs and remaining sugar, and mix to a smooth dough. Cover and set aside in a warm place for 1 hour or until the dough has doubled in size.

Knead the dough for 8 minutes or until it is smooth and elastic. Divide the dough into three pieces and roll out into three long ropes, about 30 cm./1 ft. long. Join the ropes together at one end and plait the three strands, joining the other end together when the plait is finished. Put the loaf on a well-greased baking sheet, cover and set aside in a warm place for 45 minutes.

Brush the bread with the egg for glazing and sprinkle over the poppy seeds. Put into the oven preheated to hot (220°C/425°F or Gas Mark 7) and bake for 15 minutes. Reduce the oven temperature to fairly hot (190°C/375°F or Gas Mark 5) and continue to bake for 20 to 25 minutes. The bread is cooked if it sounds hollow when knocked on the bottom with your knuckle. Cool on a wire rack.

Brioche

23 ml./1½ tablespoons castor
   sugar
15 g./½ oz. yeast
75 ml./3 fl. oz. tepid water
225 g./8 oz. flour
pinch of salt
2 eggs, beaten
125 g./4 oz. butter, melted
Glaze
1 egg, beaten
15 ml./1 tablespoon cold
   water

Mix 5 ml./1 teaspoon of sugar, the yeast and water to a paste. Set aside in a warm place for 15 minutes or until the mixture is frothy. Sift the flour, salt and remaining sugar into a warmed bowl. Add the yeast mixture, eggs and melted butter and mix to a very soft dough. Cover and set aside in a warm place for 1½ hours or until the dough has doubled in size.

Put into a well-greased brioche mould. Put the mould into the oven preheated to hot (220°C/425°F or Gas Mark 7) and bake for 10 minutes. Beat the glaze ingredients together, then brush generously over the brioche. Return to the oven reduced to fairly hot (190°C/375°F or Gas Mark 5) and continue to bake for a further 20 minutes, or until a knife inserted into the centre comes out clean. Cool in the mould for 30 minutes, then transfer to a wire rack to cool completely.

Soda Bread

1 kg./2 lb. flour
10 ml./2 teaspoons
   bicarbonate of soda
10 ml./2 teaspoons salt
350 ml./12 fl. oz. milk or
   buttermilk

Sift the flour, bicarbonate of soda and salt into a large, warmed bowl. Add the milk or buttermilk and mix to a smooth dough. Shape it into a large, deep circle. Transfer to a well-greased baking sheet, then cut a deep cross in the centre. Put the baking sheet into the oven preheated to hot (220°C/425°F or Gas Mark 7) and bake for 35 minutes or until the top is golden brown. Cool on a wire rack.

Savarin

5 ml./1 teaspoon sugar
15 g./½ oz. yeast
150 ml./5 fl. oz. tepid milk
225 g./8 oz. flour
2.5 ml./½ teaspoon salt
25 g./1 oz. castor sugar
4 eggs, beaten
125 g./4 oz. butter, softened
   and cut into small pieces
Rum Syrup
225 g./8 oz. sugar
425 ml./15 fl. oz. water
125 ml./4 fl. oz. rum
Filling
½ kg./1 lb. mixed fresh fruit,
   chopped
300 ml./10 fl. oz. double
   cream, stiffly whipped

Mix the sugar, yeast and 75 ml./3 fl. oz. of tepid milk to a paste. Set aside in a warm place for 15 minutes or until the mixture is frothy. Sift the flour, salt and castor sugar into a warmed bowl. Add the yeast mixture, remaining milk, eggs and butter and mix to a smooth dough. Set aside in a warm place for 45 minutes to 1 hour, or until the dough has doubled in size.

Put into a well-greased savarin or ovenproof ring mould. Set aside in a warm place for 30 minutes, or until the dough comes almost to the top of the mould.

Put the mould into the oven preheated to very hot (230°C/450°F or Gas Mark 8) and bake for 15 minutes. Reduce the oven temperature to fairly hot (190°C/375°F or Gas Mark 5) and continue to bake for 20 minutes, or until a knife inserted into the centre comes out clean. Set aside to cool to warm in the mould.

Meanwhile to make the syrup, bring all the ingredients to the boil, then simmer for 5 minutes. Prick the savarin all over, then pour over the syrup. Set aside until the syrup has been absorbed. Invert on to a wire rack to cool completely. Mix the fruit and cream together and pile into the centre of the savarin.

Stollen

175 g./6 oz. castor sugar
25 g./1 oz. yeast
200 ml./7 fl. oz. tepid milk
450 g./1 lb. flour
5 ml./1 teaspoon ground
    cinnamon
5 ml./1 teaspoon ground all-
    spice
2 eggs, beaten
125 g./4 oz. chopped mixed
    peel
125 g./4 oz. sultanas
75 g./3 oz. walnuts, chopped
Icing
25 g./1 oz. butter, melted
15 ml./1 tablespoon lemon
    juice
2.5 ml./½ teaspoon vanilla
    essence
225 g./8 oz. icing sugar

Mix 5 ml./1 teaspoon of sugar, the yeast and 30 ml./2 tablespoons of tepid milk to a paste. Set aside in a warm place for 15 minutes or until the mixture is frothy. Sift the flour and spices into a large bowl. Add the yeast mixture, the remaining sugar, the remaining milk and the eggs and mix to a smooth dough. Knead for about 10 minutes or until smooth and elastic. Set aside in a warm place for 1 hour or until the dough has doubled in size.

Knead the dough again for 5 minutes. Knead in the mixed peel, sultanas and walnuts until they are distributed throughout the dough. Shape the dough into an oval and put it on a well-greased baking sheet. Set aside in a warm place for 30 minutes.

Put into the oven preheated to fairly hot (200°C/400°F or Gas Mark 6) and bake for 10 minutes. Reduce the oven temperature to moderate (180°C/350°F or Gas Mark 4) and continue to bake for a further 35 minutes. Cool on a wire rack.

To make the icing, beat the butter, lemon juice and vanilla together. Gradually beat in the icing sugar until the mixture is of a thick spreading consistency. When the bread is cool, generously spread the icing over the top and sides.

Corn Bread

175 g./6 oz. corn meal
125 g./4 oz. flour, sifted
10 ml./2 teaspoons baking
    powder
5 ml./1 teaspoon salt
50 g./2 oz. butter
175 ml./6 fl. oz. milk
2 eggs, beaten

Put the corn meal, flour, baking powder and salt into a bowl. Rub in the butter until the mixture resembles fine breadcrumbs. Gradually beat in the milk and eggs. Spoon the batter into a well-greased 20 cm./8 in. square cake tin. Put the tin into the oven preheated to fairly hot (200°C/400°F or Gas Mark 6). Bake for 20 to 25 minutes, or until a knife inserted into the centre comes out clean. Cool, then cut into squares.

Coffee Walnut Buns

600 ml./1 pint milk
50 g./2 oz. sugar
50 g./2 oz. butter
25 g./1 oz. yeast
1 kg./2 lb. flour
2.5 ml./½ teaspoon salt
2 eggs, beaten
75 g./3 oz. sultanas
50 g./2 oz. walnuts, chopped
Icing
225 g./8 oz. icing sugar,
   sifted
5 ml./1 teaspoon coffee
   powder
15 g./½ oz. butter
milk to blend

Put the milk, sugar and butter in a saucepan and heat until the butter has melted and the mixture is lukewarm. Stir in the yeast. Sift the flour and salt together, then beat in the eggs and yeast mixture. Stir in the sultanas. Cover and set aside in a warm place for 40 minutes or until the dough has doubled in size.

Knead the dough for 3 minutes, then set aside in a warm place for a further 15 minutes. Knead gently for 2 minutes. Break off pieces of the dough, about the size of a lemon, and roll between your hands to form a long, thick roll. Tie the rolls in a knot and place on a well-greased baking sheet. Set aside in a warm place for 20 to 30 minutes or until almost doubled in size.

Put into the oven preheated to moderate (180°C/350°F or Gas Mark 4) and bake for 25 to 30 minutes, or until golden brown.

Meanwhile to make the icing, mix the icing sugar and coffee powder together in a heatproof bowl. Add the butter and put the bowl in a pan of boiling water. Heat gently and stir in enough milk to make a glossy spreading icing. While the buns are still warm, cover them with the icing, then sprinkle over the chopped walnuts. Cool on a wire rack.

Makes about 20 buns

German Potato Pancakes

25 g./1 oz. flour
7.5 ml./1½ teaspoons salt
1.25 ml./¼ teaspoon baking
   powder
pinch of white pepper
2 eggs, beaten
15 ml./1 tablespoon finely
   chopped onion
15 ml./1 tablespoon finely
   chopped fresh parsley
1 kg./2 lb. potatoes, grated
   and with the excess liquid
   squeezed out
50 g./2 oz. butter

Sift the flour, salt, baking powder and pepper into a bowl. Gradually beat in the eggs, onion, parsley and potatoes.

Melt the butter in a frying-pan. Drop about two tablespoons of the batter on to the pan and flatten slightly. Cook until the tops are bubbly and the undersides golden brown. Carefully turn and brown the other sides in the same way. Drain the pancakes on kitchen towels.

Makes about 6 pancakes

Spiced Almond Ring

5 ml./1 teaspoon sugar
15 g./½ oz. yeast
125 ml./4 fl oz. tepid milk
225 g./8 oz. flour
pinch of salt
15 g./½ oz. butter, melted
1 egg, beaten
Filling
15 g./½ oz. butter, melted
50 g./2 oz. brown sugar
7.5 ml./1½ teaspoons ground
    allspice
50 g./2 oz. chopped almonds
50 g./2 oz. icing sugar, sifted
7.5 ml./1½ teaspoons tepid
    water
glacé cherries and flaked
    almonds to decorate

Mix the sugar, yeast and 30 ml./2 tablespoons of the tepid milk to a paste. Set aside in a warm place for 15 minutes or until the mixture is frothy. Sift the flour and salt into a warmed bowl. Add the yeast mixture, butter, remaining milk and egg and mix to a smooth dough. Knead for about 10 minutes or until smooth and elastic. Set aside in a warm place for 1 hour or until the dough has doubled in size.

Knead the dough again for 5 minutes. Roll it out to a rectangle about 30 cm./1 ft. × 23 cm./9 in. Brush the butter over the dough, then sprinkle over the sugar, spice and almonds. Roll up like a Swiss roll, sealing the edge. Put the roll on a well-greased baking sheet, then bring round the ends to form a ring. Carefully cut into the ring at about 4 cm./1½ in. intervals to within 1.25 cm./½ in. of the centre. Separate the slices from one another by turning each piece sideways very gently Set aside in a warm place for 30 minutes.

Put into the oven preheated to fairly hot (190°C/375°F or Gas Mark 5) and bake for 35 minutes. Cool on a wire rack.

Meanwhile, mix the icing sugar and water together. Carefully spread over the top and sides of the ring and decorate with glacé cherries and almonds.

Wholemeal Scones

200 g./7 oz. wholemeal flour
25 g./1 oz. soya flour
1.25 ml./¼ teaspoon salt
5 ml./1 teaspoon baking
    powder
25 g./1 oz. butter
25 g./1 oz. brown sugar
175 ml./6 fl. oz. sour milk or
    buttermilk

Put the flours, salt and baking powder into a bowl. Rub in the butter until the mixture resembles fine breadcrumbs. Add the sugar, then the milk and beat until a soft dough is formed. Knead gently for 3 minutes. Pat the dough out until it is about 2 cm./¾ in. thick, then cut into 5 cm./2 in. circles with a pastry cutter. Transfer the circles to a well-greased baking sheet and lightly brush the tops with a little milk or beaten egg.

Put into the oven preheated to very hot (230°C/450°F or Gas Mark 8) and bake for 10 to 15 minutes, or until golden brown.

Makes 8-10 scones

Garlic Bread

1 French loaf
50 g./2 oz. butter
2 garlic cloves, crushed
salt and black pepper

Cut the loaf, at about 2.5 cm./1 in. intervals, almost through to the bottom. Mix the butter, garlic, salt and pepper to taste together, beating until smooth. Spread the mixture generously between the loaf slices. Wrap in aluminium foil and put into the oven preheated to hot (220°C/425°F or Gas Mark 7). Bake for 20 minutes.

Serves 4-6

Chelsea Buns

140 g./4½ oz. sugar
15 g./½ oz. yeast
15 ml./1 tablespoon tepid
   water
450 g./1 lb. flour
pinch of salt
2.5 ml./½ teaspoon ground
   cloves
175 g./6 oz. butter, melted
125 ml./4 fl. oz. tepid milk
2 eggs, beaten
125 g./4 oz. raisins
50 g./2 oz. chopped mixed
   peel
5 ml./1 teaspoon ground
   cinnamon

Mix 15 g./½ oz. of sugar, the yeast and water to a paste. Set aside in a warm place for 15 minutes or until the mixture is frothy. Sift the flour, half the remaining sugar, the salt and cloves into a large, warmed bowl. Gradually beat in the yeast mixture, 150 g./5 oz. of melted butter, the milk and eggs and mix to a smooth dough. Knead for about 5 minutes or until smooth and elastic. Set aside in a warm place for 1¼ hours, or until the dough has doubled in size.

Knead the dough again for about 4 minutes. Roll out into a rectangle about .75 cm./¼ in. thick. Brush the rectangle with the remaining melted butter and sprinkle over the raisins, mixed peel and cinnamon. Roll up like a Swiss roll, sealing the edge. Cut into 3.75 cm./1½ in. slices and put the slices on a well-greased baking sheet. Set aside in a warm place for 20 minutes.

Put into the oven preheated to fairly hot (190°C/375°F or Gas Mark 5) and bake for 30 to 35 minutes, or until the buns are golden brown. Cool slightly, then sprinkle over the remaining sugar.

Makes about 8 buns

Hot Cross Buns

50 g./2 oz. sugar
15 g./½ oz. yeast
300 ml./10 fl. oz. tepid milk
450 g./1 lb. flour
5 ml./1 teaspoon salt
2.5 ml./½ teaspoon ground
*   mixed spice*
5 ml./1 teaspoon ground
*   cinnamon*
50 g./2 oz. butter
50 g./2 oz. sultanas
50 g./2 oz. currants
1 egg, beaten
Pastry
25 g./1 oz. flour, sifted
cold water to blend
Glaze
15 ml./1 tablespoon sugar
*   dissolved in 15 ml./1*
*   tablespoon hot water*

Mix 5 ml./1 teaspoon of sugar, the yeast and 30 ml./2 tablespoons of tepid milk to a paste. Set aside in a warm place for 15 minutes or until the mixture is frothy. Sift the flour, salt and spices into a large, warmed bowl. Rub in the butter. Stir in the remaining sugar and dried fruit. Add the egg, yeast mixture and remaining tepid milk and mix to a soft dough. Cover and set aside in a warm place for 40 minutes or until the dough has doubled in size.

Knead the dough for 8 minutes or until it is smooth and elastic. Roll and shape the dough into about 15 thick circles. Put the circles on a well-greased baking sheet and set aside in a warm place for 15 minutes.

To make the pastry, mix the flour to a soft paste with cold water, then spoon into a piping bag with a plain nozzle. Pipe crosses on each bun, then put the sheet into the oven preheated to hot (220°C/425°F or Gas Mark 7). Bake for 20 minutes. Brush the glaze over the tops of the buns. Cool on a wire rack.

Makes about 15 buns

379

Malt Bread

5 ml./1 teaspoon sugar
25 g./1 oz. yeast
30 ml./2 tablespoons tepid
    water
25 g./1 oz. butter
45 ml./3 tablespoons malt
    extract
45 ml./3 tablespoons treacle
450 g./1 lb. flour
5 ml./1 teaspoon salt
150 ml./5 fl. oz. tepid milk
175 g./6 oz. sultanas
50 g./2 oz. chopped nuts

Mix the sugar, yeast and water to a paste. Set aside in a warm place for 15 minutes or until the mixture is frothy. Put the butter, malt and treacle in a saucepan and heat until the butter melts. Remove from the heat.

Sift the flour and salt into a large, warmed bowl. Gradually beat in the yeast mixture, milk and malt mixture. Stir in the sultanas and nuts and mix to a smooth dough. Knead for about 10 minutes or until smooth and elastic. Set aside in a warm place for 1¼ hours or until the dough has doubled in size.

Knead the dough again for 5 minutes. Shape into a loaf and put into a well-greased 1 kg./2 lb. loaf tin. Set aside in a warm place for 40 minutes or until the dough has risen to the top of the tin. Put into the oven preheated to very hot (230°C/450°F or Gas Mark 8) and bake for 15 minutes. Reduce the oven temperature to fairly hot (200°C/400°F or Gas Mark 6) and continue to bake for 20 to 30 minutes. The bread is cooked if it sounds hollow when knocked on the bottom with your knuckle. Cool on a wire rack.

Barm Brack

425 ml./15 fl. oz. cold tea
200 g./7 oz. brown sugar
350 g./12 oz. mixed dried
    fruit
275 g./10 oz. self-raising
    flour
1 egg, beaten

Put the tea, sugar and mixed fruit into a bowl. Cover and leave overnight.

Sift the flour into a bowl, then gradually beat in the egg and tea mixture. Line a 1 kg./2 lb. loaf tin with a double thickness of greased greaseproof paper and spoon in the batter. Put into the oven preheated to moderate (180°C/350°F or Gas Mark 4) and bake for 1½ hours or until a knife inserted into the centre comes out clean. Cool to lukewarm in the tin, then transfer to a wire rack to cool completely. Remove the paper before serving.

English Muffins

5 ml./1 teaspoon sugar
15 g./½ oz. yeast
75 ml./3 fl. oz. tepid water
450 g./1 lb. flour
pinch of salt
150 ml./5 fl. oz. tepid milk
1 egg, beaten
25 g./1 oz. butter, melted

Mix the sugar, yeast and water to a paste. Set aside in a warm place for 15 minutes or until the mixture is frothy. Sift the flour and salt into a large, warmed bowl. Gradually add the yeast mixture, milk, egg and butter and mix to a soft dough. Knead for about 15 minutes or until smooth and elastic. Set aside in a warm place for 45 minutes or until the dough has doubled in size.

Knead the dough again for 3 minutes. Roll out the dough to about 1.25 cm./½ in. thick, then cut into 10 cm./4 in. circles with a pastry cutter. Transfer the circles to well-greased baking sheets sprinkled with a little flour. Set aside in a warm place for 20 minutes or until the circles have doubled in size.

Put into the oven preheated to very hot (230°C/450°F or Gas Mark 8) and bake for 5 minutes. Turn over and bake for 5 minutes on the other side or until the muffins are golden brown.

Makes about 10 muffins

Doughnuts

5 ml./1 teaspoon sugar
15 g./½ oz. yeast
75 ml./3 fl. oz. tepid milk
225 g./8 oz. flour
2.5 ml./½ teaspoon salt
15 g./½ oz. butter, melted
1 egg, beaten
75 g./3 oz. jam
oil for deep frying
75 g./3 oz. castor sugar
5 ml./1 teaspoon ground
   cinnamon

Mix the sugar, yeast and milk to a paste. Set aside in a warm place for 15 minutes or until the mixture is frothy. Sift the flour and salt into a warmed bowl. Add the butter, yeast mixture and egg and mix to a soft dough. Knead for 8 minutes or until smooth and elastic. Set aside in a warm place for 45 minutes or until the dough has doubled in size.

Knead the dough again for 5 minutes. Divide into about 12 pieces and roll them into balls. Make a depression in each ball, fill with some jam, then enclose the filling completely. Set aside in a warm place for 20 minutes or until the balls have doubled in size.

Deep fry the balls for 4 minutes or until they are golden brown. Drain on kitchen towels and roll in sugar and cinnamon.

Makes about 12 doughnuts

Drop Scones

125 g./4 oz. self-raising flour
pinch of salt
1.25 ml./¼ teaspoon
   bicarbonate of soda
45 ml./3 tablespoons sugar
150 ml./5 fl. oz. sour milk
1 egg, beaten
10 ml./2 teaspoons melted
   butter

Sift the flour, salt and soda into a bowl, then stir in the sugar. Pour in the milk, egg and butter and beat until it forms a batter.

Heat a greased griddle or heavy frying-pan. Drop tablespoons of the batter on to the griddle or pan, well spaced apart, and cook until the top is bubbly and the underside golden brown. Carefully turn and brown the other side in the same way.

Makes about 15 scones

Basic Scones

225 g./8 oz. self-raising flour
2.5 ml./½ teaspoon salt
5 ml./1 teaspoon sugar
25 g./1 oz. butter
75 ml./3 fl oz. milk
30 ml./2 tablespoons water

Sift the flour and salt into a bowl, then stir in the sugar. Rub in the butter until the mixture resembles fine breadcrumbs. Pour in the liquid and beat until a soft dough is formed. Knead gently for 3 minutes. Pat the dough out until it is about 2 cm./¾ in. thick, then cut into 5 cm./2 in. circles with a pastry cutter. Transfer the circles to a well-greased baking sheet and lightly brush the tops with a little milk or beaten egg. Put into the oven preheated to very hot (230°C/450°F or Gas Mark 8) and bake for 10 to 15 minutes, or until golden brown.

Makes about 12 scones

Apricot Coffee Bread

350 g./12 oz. self-raising
   flour
2.5 ml./½ teaspoon salt
75 g./3 oz. castor sugar
150 g./5 oz. dried apricots,
   soaked overnight, drained
   and chopped
50 g./2 oz. chopped almonds
finely grated rind of 1 orange
2 eggs, beaten
125 ml./4 fl. oz. milk
50 g./2 oz. butter, melted

Sift the flour and salt into a bowl. Stir in the sugar, apricots, almonds and orange rind. Mix the eggs, milk and melted butter together, then gradually beat into the flour mixture. Spoon into a well-greased 1 kg./2 lb. loaf tin. Put into the oven preheated to warm (170°C/325°F or Gas Mark 3) and bake for 1¼ to 1½ hours, or until a knife inserted into the centre comes out clean. Cool on a wire rack.

Treacle Scones

225 g./8 oz. flour
5 ml./1 teaspoon cream of
    tartar
5 ml./1 teaspoon bicarbonate
    of soda
pinch of salt
25 g./1 oz. butter
50 g./2 oz. treacle, warmed
50 ml./2 fl. oz. milk

Sift the flour, cream of tartar, soda and salt into a bowl. Rub in the butter until the mixture resembles fine breadcrumbs. Pour in the treacle and milk and beat until a soft dough is formed. Knead gently for 3 minutes. Pat the dough out to about 2.5 cm./1 in. thick, then cut into 5 cm./2 in. circles with a pastry cutter. Transfer the circles to a well-greased baking sheet and lightly brush the tops with a little milk or beaten egg.

Put into the oven preheated to fairly hot (200°C/400°F or Gas Mark 6) and bake for 10 to 15 minutes, or until golden brown.

Makes 8-10 scones

Nut Muffins

225 g./8 oz. self-raising flour
pinch of salt
50 g./2 oz. sugar
75 g./3 oz. walnuts, chopped
2 eggs, beaten
50 g./2 oz. butter, melted
150 ml./5 fl. oz. milk

Sift the flour and salt into a bowl. Gradually beat in all the remaining ingredients until a smooth batter is formed. Pour into 12 well-greased patty tins, put the tins into the oven preheated to fairly hot (190°C/375°F or Gas Mark 5) and bake for 20 to 25 minutes, or until a knife inserted into the centres comes out clean. Cool in the tins for 5 minutes, then transfer to a wire rack.

Makes 12 muffins

Apple Muffins

225 g./8 oz. self-raising flour
pinch of salt
50 g./2 oz. brown sugar
5 ml./1 teaspoon ground
    cinnamon
2 eggs, beaten
50 g./2 oz. butter, melted
150 ml./5 fl. oz. milk
2 eating apples, peeled, cored
    and grated

Sift the flour and salt into a bowl. Gradually beat in all the remaining ingredients until a smooth batter is formed. Pour into 12 well-greased patty tins, put the tins into the oven preheated to fairly hot (190°C/375°F or Gas Mark 5) and bake for 20 to 25 minutes, or until a knife inserted into the centres comes out clean. Cool in the tins for 5 minutes, then transfer to a wire rack.

Makes 12 muffins

Waffles

2 eggs, separated
10 ml./2 teaspoons sugar
175 ml./6 fl. oz. milk
150 ml./5 fl. oz. water
5 ml./1 teaspoon vanilla
essence
225 g./8 oz. self-raising flour
pinch of salt
30 ml./2 tablespoons
cornflour
125 g./4 oz. butter, melted

Beat the egg yolks and sugar together, then beat in the milk, water and vanilla. Gradually sift in the flour, salt and cornflour, beating constantly, then beat in the melted butter. Beat the egg whites until they are stiff, then quickly fold them into the batter. Set aside for 10 minutes.

Heat a greased waffle iron. Spoon a little of the batter into the iron and cook the waffle for 5 minutes, or until it stops steaming and is golden brown on both sides.

Makes about 6, depending on the size of the iron

Orange and Almond Loaf

350 g./12 oz. self-raising
flour
2.5 ml./½ teaspoon salt
5 ml./1 teaspoon ground
cinnamon
50 g./2 oz. flaked almonds
finely grated rind of 1 orange
75 g./3 oz. castor sugar
2 eggs, beaten
275 ml./9 fl. oz. milk
50 g./2 oz. butter, melted

Sift the flour, salt and cinnamon into a bowl. Add the almonds, orange rind and castor sugar and beat well. Gradually stir in the eggs, milk and butter, beating until the mixture forms a soft dough. Spoon into a well-greased 1 kg./2 lb. loaf tin and put into the oven preheated to moderate (180°C/350°F or Gas Mark 4). Bake for 1 hour, or until a knife inserted into the centre comes out clean. Cool on a wire rack.

Banana and Walnut Bread

50 g./2 oz. butter
150 g./5 oz. sugar
3 eggs
4 bananas, mashed
225 g./8 oz. self-raising flour
pinch of salt
125 g./4 oz. walnuts,
chopped
5 ml./1 teaspoon ground
cinnamon

Beat the butter and sugar together until they are fluffy. Gradually beat in the eggs, one at a time, then stir in the bananas. Sift the flour and salt together, then gradually beat into the bananas. Stir in the walnuts and cinnamon. Spoon into a well-greased ½ kg./1 lb. loaf tin and put into the oven preheated to moderate (180°C/350°F or Gas Mark 4). Bake for 1 hour, or until a knife inserted into the centre comes out clean. Cool on a wire rack.

Lardy Cake

5 ml./1 teaspoon sugar
15 g./½ oz. yeast
300 ml./10 fl. oz. tepid water
450 g./1 lb. flour
10 ml./2 teaspoons salt
125 g./4 oz. lard
60 ml./4 tablespoons castor
sugar
5 ml./1 teaspoon ground
mixed spice

Mix the sugar, yeast and 30 ml./2 tablespoons of tepid water to a paste. Set aside in a warm place for 15 minutes or until the mixture is frothy. Sift the flour and salt into a warmed bowl. Add the yeast mixture and remaining water and mix to a smooth dough. Knead for about 15 minutes or until smooth and elastic. Set aside in a warm place for 1 hour or until the dough has doubled in size.

Roll the dough out into a large oblong. Cut half the lard into flakes and sprinkle over the dough. Sprinkle over half the castor sugar and spice. Fold the dough into three, seal the edges with the rolling pin and knead until the ingredients are thoroughly blended. Repeat this process with the remaining lard, sugar and spice. Finally, roll the dough into an oval, about 2.5 cm./1 in. thick. Put on a well-greased baking sheet and set aside in a warm place for 35 minutes.

Put into the oven preheated to hot (220°C/425°F or Gas Mark 7) and bake for 30 minutes. Cool on a wire rack.

Spiced Date Bread

450 g./1 lb. dates, chopped
175 ml./6 fl. oz. milk
50 g./2 oz. butter
350 g./12 oz. self-raising
flour
pinch of salt
7.5 ml./1½ teaspoons baking
powder
5 ml./1 teaspoon grated
nutmeg
5 ml./1 teaspoon ground
allspice
50 g./2 oz. sugar
1 egg

Put the dates, milk and butter into a saucepan and heat gently until the butter has melted. Sift the flour, salt, baking powder and spices into a bowl. Gradually beat in the sugar, egg and date mixture. Spoon into a well-greased 1 kg./2 lb. loaf tin and put into the oven preheated to moderate (180°C/350°F or Gas Mark 4). Bake for 1 to 1¼ hours, or until a knife inserted into the centre comes out clean. Cool on a wire rack.

Date and Walnut Loaf

125 g./4 oz. self-raising flour
125 g./4 oz. sugar
2.5 ml./½ teaspoon
   bicarbonate of soda
10 ml./2 teaspoons ground
   cinnamon
50 g./2 oz. dates, chopped
50 g./2 oz. walnuts, chopped
25 g./1 oz. butter
150 ml./5 fl. oz. water

Sift the flour, sugar, soda and cinnamon into a bowl. Stir in the dates and walnuts. Bring the butter and water to the boil, then gradually stir into the flour mixture. Spoon into a well-greased ½ kg./1 lb. loaf tin and put into the oven preheated to moderate (180°C/350°F or Gas Mark 4). Bake for 45 to 50 minutes, or until a knife inserted into the centre comes out clean. Cool on a wire rack.

Walnut Loaf

225 g./8 oz. flour
10 ml./2 teaspoons baking
   powder
125 g./4 oz. castor sugar
125 g./4 oz. walnuts, finely
   chopped
175 g./6 oz. golden syrup
125 ml./4 fl. oz. milk
1 egg, beaten

Sift the flour and baking powder into a bowl. Stir in the sugar and walnuts. Simmer the syrup and milk together until the syrup has melted, then gradually beat into the flour mixture, with the egg. Spoon into a well-greased 1 kg./2 lb. loaf tin and put into the oven preheated to warm (170°C/325°F or Gas Mark 3). Bake for 1¼ hours, or until a knife inserted into the centre comes out clean. Cool on a wire rack.

Gingerbread

125 g./4 oz. butter
50 g./2 oz. brown sugar
175 g./6 oz. dark treacle
50 g./2 oz. golden syrup
150 ml./5 fl. oz. milk
2 eggs
225 g./8 oz. flour
5 ml./1 teaspoon ground
   mixed spice
10 ml./2 teaspoons ground
   ginger
5 ml./1 teaspoon bicarbonate
   of soda

Put the butter, sugar, treacle and syrup into a saucepan. Heat until the butter has melted. Remove from the heat, add the milk and set aside to cool. When cool, beat in the eggs. Sift the flour, spices and soda into a bowl. Add the butter mixture and stir well.

Line a 1 kg./2 lb. loaf tin with a double thickness of greased greaseproof paper. Spoon in the batter and put the tin in the oven preheated to cool (150°C/300°F or Gas Mark 2). Bake for 1¼ to 1½ hours, or until a knife inserted into the centre comes out clean. Cool on a wire rack, and keep overnight before serving.

Pineapple Coffee Bread

350 g./12 oz. self-raising
  flour
2.5 ml./½ teaspoon salt
75 g./3 oz. castor sugar
1 × 225 g./8 oz. can
  pineapple rings, drained
50 g./2 oz. walnuts
2 eggs, beaten
150 ml./5 fl. oz. milk
50 g./2 oz. butter, melted
Icing
175 g./6 oz. icing sugar,
  sifted
warm water to blend

Sift the flour and salt into a bowl. Add the sugar and mix well. Reserve and halve two pineapple rings and four walnut halves, then chop the remainder and add them to the flour. Gradually, beat in the eggs, milk and butter. Spoon into a well-greased 1 kg./2 lb. loaf tin and put into the oven preheated to warm (170°C/325°F or Gas Mark 3). Bake for 1¼ to 1½ hours, or until a knife inserted into the centre comes out clean. Cool in the tin for 5 minutes, then transfer to a wire rack to cool completely.

To make the icing, beat the icing sugar with enough warm water to form a thick spreading consistency. Pour over the bread, allowing it to trickle down the sides. When the icing is half set, arrange the reserved pineapple slices and walnut halves decoratively over the top.

Fruit Gingerbread

125 g./4 oz. butter
75 g./3 oz. brown sugar
125 g./4 oz. dark treacle
3 eggs
225 g./8 oz. flour
5 ml./1 teaspoon bicarbonate
  of soda
10 ml./2 teaspoons ground
  ginger
2.5 ml./½ teaspoon grated
  nutmeg
50 g./2 oz. rolled oats
75 g./3 oz. sultanas
25 g./1 oz. flaked almonds
175 ml./6 fl. oz. sour cream

Put the butter, sugar and treacle into a saucepan. Heat until the butter has melted. Set aside to cool slightly, then beat in the eggs, one at a time. Sift the flour, soda and spices into a bowl, then stir in the oats, sultanas and almonds. Add the butter mixture and the sour cream and stir well.

Line an 18 cm./7 in. square baking tin with a double thickness of greased greaseproof paper. Spoon in the batter and put the tin into the oven preheated to moderate (180°C/350°F or Gas Mark 4). Bake for 50 minutes to 1 hour, or until a knife inserted into the centre comes out clean. Cool on a wire rack.

Chutneys Pickles & Relishes

Apple Chutney

3 kg./6 lb. apples, peeled,
  cored and chopped
1 kg./2 lb. shallots or small
  pickling onions, chopped
1½ kg./3 lb. brown sugar
1¼ l./2 pints malt vinegar
¾ kg./1½ lb. sultanas
50 g./2 oz. mustard seeds
10 ml./2 teaspoons salt
2.5 ml./½ teaspoon cayenne
pepper

Put all the ingredients in a saucepan and bring to the boil. Simmer for 1½ hours, or until the chutney is thick. Pour into hot, sterilized jars and seal.

Makes about 4 kg./8 lb. chutney

Gooseberry Chutney

1 kg./2 lb. gooseberries,
  topped and tailed
3 onions, chopped
350 g./12 oz. raisins
2.5 ml./½ teaspoon red pepper
  flakes
pinch of salt
1¼ l./2 pints vinegar
225 g./8 oz. brown sugar
30 ml./2 tablespoons ground
  ginger
1.25 ml./¼ teaspoon mustard
  seeds

Put all the ingredients into a saucepan and bring to the boil. Simmer for 1 hour, or until the mixture is thick. Pour into hot, sterilized jars and seal.

Makes about 1½ kg./3 lb. chutney

Mango Chutney

3 large mangoes, skinned
  and chopped
1 onion, chopped
1 chilli, chopped
5 ml./1 teaspoon mustard
  seeds
5 ml./1 teaspoon celery seeds
50 g./2 oz. raisins
50 g./2 oz. currants
15 ml./1 tablespoon chopped
  mixed peel
5 ml./1 teaspoon finely
  chopped green ginger
1 garlic clove, crushed
5 ml./1 teaspoon salt
2.5 ml./½ teaspoon ground
  cinnamon
2.5 ml./½ teaspoon ground
  nutmeg
2.5 ml./½ teaspoon ground
  allspice
50 g./2 oz. brown sugar
75 g./3 fl. oz. malt vinegar
75 ml./3 fl. oz. lemon juice

Put the mangoes, onion and chilli in a bowl. Tie the mustard and celery seeds in a cheesecloth bag and add to the bowl, with all the remaining ingredients. Cover and set aside for 24 hours. Transfer to a large saucepan. Bring to the boil, then simmer for 30 minutes, or until the chutney has thickened. Remove the cheesecloth bag and pour the chutney into hot, sterilized jars. Seal at once.

Makes about 675 g./1½ lb. chutney

Oriental Chutney

1¼ kg./2½ lb. dried apricots,
  chopped
675 g./1½ lb. dried peaches,
  chopped
675 g./1½ lb. dates, chopped
1 kg./2 lb. sultanas
675 g./1½ lb. raisins
675 g./1½ lb. currants
3¾ kg./6½ lb. brown sugar
50 g./2 oz. salt
125 g./4 oz. garlic, chopped
25 g./1 oz. ground cloves
25 g./1 oz. ground cinnamon
5 ml./1 teaspoon cayenne
  pepper
1¼ l./2 pints vinegar

Put the fruit into a saucepan and just cover with water. Bring to the boil, then simmer for 10 to 15 minutes, or until the fruit is tender. Add the remaining ingredients and bring to the boil. Simmer for about 30 to 45 minutes, or until the chutney is very thick. Pour into hot, sterilized jars and seal. Store for 6 months before using.

Makes about 5 kg./10 lb. chutney

Marrow Chutney

4 kg./8 lb. marrow, peeled and cubed
50 g./2 oz. salt
3¼ l./6 pints vinegar
350 g./12 oz. sugar
50 g./2 oz. turmeric
8 chillis, chopped
12 shallots, chopped
5 ml./1 teaspoon ground ginger
50 g./2 oz. dry mustard

Put the marrow cubes in a bowl and sprinkle over the salt. Set aside for 24 hours, then drain off any liquid and rinse under cold running water. Put the marrow into a large saucepan and add 3 l./5 pints of vinegar, sugar, turmeric, chillis and shallots. Stir to dissolve the sugar. Mix the remaining ingredients with the remaining vinegar, then stir into the pan. Bring to the boil and simmer for 30 to 45 minutes, or until the marrow is very soft. Pour into hot, sterilized jars and seal.

Makes about 5 kg./10 lb. chutney

Peach Chutney

16 medium peaches, skinned and sliced
175 g./6 oz. raisins
225 g./8 oz. brown sugar
175 ml./6 fl. oz. cider vinegar
5 ml./1 teaspoon ground cinnamon
2.5 ml./½ teaspoon ground cloves
10 ml./2 teaspoons mustard seeds
50 g./2 oz. chopped nuts

Put all the ingredients, except the nuts, into a saucepan and bring to the boil. Simmer for 45 minutes, or until the chutney has thickened. Stir in the nuts and simmer for a further 2 minutes. Pour into hot, sterilized jars and seal. Use within 2 to 3 weeks of making, and store in the refrigerator.

Makes about 2 kg./4 lb. chutney

Sweet Fruit Chutney

1 kg./2 lb. tomatoes, skinned and chopped
3 large onions, chopped
2 large cooking apples, peeled, cored and chopped
675 g./1½ lb. sugar
125 g./4 oz. sultanas
125 g./4 oz. currants
15 ml./1 tablespoon salt
15 ml./1 tablespoon cloves
pinch of cayenne pepper
1¼ l./2 pints malt vinegar

Put all the ingredients into a saucepan and bring to the boil. Simmer for 2½ hours, or until the chutney is very thick. Pour into hot, sterilized jars and seal.

Makes about 1½ kg./3 lb. chutney

Quince and Lemon Chutney

1½ kg./3 lb. quinces, peeled
  and cored
1 large lemon, chopped
5 ml./1 teaspoon ground
  allspice
5 ml./1 teaspoon ground
  coriander
4 cloves
6 peppercorns
5 cm./2 in. cinnamon stick
5 cm./2 in. piece fresh root
  ginger, peeled
5 ml./1 teaspoon salt
1 onion, chopped
1 garlic clove, crushed
225 g./8 oz. sultanas
125 g./4 oz. stem ginger

Put the quinces and lemon in a saucepan. Tie the spices in a cheesecloth bag and add to the pan with all the remaining ingredients. Bring to the boil, then simmer for about 45 minutes, or until thick and reduced by about half. Remove the cheesecloth bag. Pour into hot, sterilized jars and seal.

Makes about 1½ kg./3 lb. chutney

Bread and Butter Pickles

4 large cucumbers, thinly
  sliced
50 g./2 oz. salt
600 ml./1 pint cider vinegar
150 ml./5 fl. oz. hot water
30 ml./2 tablespoons sugar
10 ml./2 teaspoons mustard
  seeds
5 ml./1 teaspoon salt
4 red pepper strips

Arrange the cucumber slices, in layers, in a wide, shallow dish, sprinkling each layer generously with the salt. Cover and set aside overnight. Drain, then rinse in cold running water.

Put all the remaining ingredients, except the pepper strips, into a saucepan and bring to the boil. Simmer for 5 minutes, then add the cucumber. Bring to the boil again, then remove from the heat. Transfer the cucumbers to hot, sterilized jars and top with pepper strips. Pour over enough vinegar mixture to come within 1.25 cm./½ in. of the top and seal.

Makes about 2 kg./4 lb. pickle

Mixed Pickle

1 cauliflower, broken into
    flowerets
1 large carrot, cut into strips
2 cucumbers, cut into
    quarters, lengthways
¼ white cabbage, chopped
4 green peppers, pith and
    seeds removed and
    chopped
350 g./12 oz. sugar
1½ l./2½ pints white malt
    vinegar
10 ml./2 teaspoons salt
2 chillis, seeds removed and
    cut into strips

Cook the cauliflower and carrot in boiling salted water for 10 minutes, or until they are just tender. Drain and transfer to a large bowl. Stir in the remaining vegetables.

Mix the sugar, vinegar and salt together and bring to the boil. Pour over the vegetables, cover and set aside for 24 hours.

Transfer the mixture to sterilized jars and top each one with strips of chilli. Seal.

Makes about 3 kg./6 lb. pickle

Pickled Beetroot

300 ml./10 fl. oz. malt
    vinegar
150 ml./5 fl. oz. water
125 g./4 oz. sugar
1.25 ml./¼ teaspoon ground
    cinnamon
1 bay leaf
2 cloves
4 peppercorns
4 medium cooked beetroots,
    sliced

Put all the ingredients, except the beetroots, into a saucepan and bring to the boil. Simmer for 5 minutes. Set aside to cool. Pack the beetroots into hot, sterilized jars, then strain over the vinegar mixture to within 1.25 cm./½ in. of the tops. Seal. Because of the high sugar content of the beetroots, this pickle should be used as soon as possible.

Makes about 1 kg./2 lb. pickle

Pickled Cucumbers

1 kg./2 lb. small pickling
    cucumbers, pricked all
    over
900 ml./1½ pints malt vinegar
15 ml./1 tablespoon mustard
    seeds
5 ml./1 teaspoon celery seeds
30 ml./2 tablespoons salt
5 ml./1 teaspoon cloves
15 ml./1 tablespoon dill
    seeds

Pack the cucumbers into hot, sterilized jars. Put all the remaining ingredients into a saucepan and bring to the boil. Simmer for 10 minutes. Set aside to cool. Pour over the cucumbers to within 1.25 cm./½ in. of the top and seal.

Makes 1 kg./2 lb. pickle

Chow-Chow

1 white cabbage, shredded

4 green peppers, pith and
    seeds removed and
    chopped

4 celery stalks, chopped

6 onions, chopped

2 tomatoes, skinned and
    chopped

1 cucumber, chopped

23 ml./1½ tablespoons celery
    seeds

15 ml./1 tablespoon turmeric

10 ml./2 teaspoons ground
    ginger

15 ml./1 tablespoon ground
    cloves

23 ml./1½ tablespoons salt

75 g./3 oz. mustard seeds

½ kg./1 lb. brown sugar

900 ml./1½ pints brown
    vinegar

Parboil the cabbage, peppers, celery and onions separately in boiling, salted water, then drain. Layer the vegetables into hot, sterilized jars, with the remaining vegetables. Put all the remaining ingredients in a saucepan and bring to the boil. Simmer for 15 minutes. Pour over the vegetables, to within 1.25 cm./½ in. of the top, and seal.

Makes about 4 kg./8 lb. pickle

Green Tomato Pickle

1 kg./2 lb. green tomatoes,
    skinned and chopped

½ cauliflower, broken into
    flowerets

675 g./1½ lb. onions, chopped

50 g./2 oz. salt

1½ l./2½ pints malt vinegar

1¼ kg./2½ lb. brown sugar

150 g./5 oz. flour

10 ml./2 teaspoons turmeric

10 ml./2 teaspoons dry
    mustard

10 ml./2 teaspoons curry
    powder

2.5 ml./½ teaspoon grated
    nutmeg

2.5 ml./½ teaspoon ground
    cloves

2.5 ml./½ teaspoon ground
    ginger

Arrange the vegetables, in layers, in a bowl, sprinkling each layer generously with the salt. Cover with water and set aside overnight. Drain and rinse under cold running water.

Put 1¼ l./2 pints of vinegar and the sugar into a saucepan and bring to the boil. Stir in the vegetables, then bring to the boil again. Mix all the remaining ingredients with the remaining vinegar, then stir into the pan. Bring back to the boil, then simmer for 10 minutes or until the pickle is thick. Pour into hot, sterilized jars and seal.

Makes about 4 kg./8 lb. pickle

Pickled Onions

2 kg./4 lb. pickling onions
675 g./1½ lb. salt
1¼ l./2 pints white vinegar
10 ml./2 teaspoons salt
10 ml./2 teaspoons ground
  ginger
7.5 ml./1½ teaspoons allspice
  berries
7.5 ml./1½ teaspoons cloves
5 cm./2 in. cinnamon stick
6 peppercorns

Put the unpeeled onions in a large bowl and sprinkle over the salt. Cover with water, cover and set aside for 2 days, stirring occasionally. Drain and peel the onions. Cover with boiling water, set aside for 3 minutes, then drain again. Repeat the process twice more, then pack the onions into hot, sterilized jars.

Put all the remaining ingredients into a saucepan and bring slowly to the boil. Simmer for 10 minutes, then strain over the onions to within 1.25 cm./½ in. of the top. Seal.

Makes about 2 kg./4 lb. pickle

Pimientos

1 kg./2 lb. red peppers, pith
  and seeds removed and
  halved
600 ml./1 pint vinegar
600 ml./1 pint cooking oil

Put the peppers in a large bowl and pour over boiling water to cover. Set aside for 2 minutes, then drain. Pour over iced water to cover, then drain again. Pack the peppers into hot, sterilized jars.

Put the vinegar into a saucepan and bring to the boil. Boil for 2 minutes, then pour in the oil and bring to the boil again. Pour over the peppers, making sure they are completely covered with liquid, and seal.

Makes about 1¼ kg./2½ lb. pickle

Piccalilli

2 kg./4 lb. mixed vegetables
  (including cauliflower
  flowerets, chopped
  cucumber, pickling onions
  and small French beans)
25 g./1 oz. salt
25 g./1 oz. flour
25 g./1 oz. dry mustard
900 ml./1½ pints malt vinegar
30 ml./2 tablespoons
  turmeric
4 chillis, chopped
50 g./2 oz. sugar

Spread the vegetables in a large, shallow dish and sprinkle over the salt. Set aside for 24 hours, then drain off any liquid and rinse in cold running water. Set aside to dry.

Mix the flour and mustard to a paste with a little of the vinegar. Put the remaining vinegar and remaining ingredients into a saucepan and bring to the boil. Stir in the vegetables and flour mixture and bring back to the boil. Simmer for 15 minutes or until thick. Set aside to cool. Pour into sterilized jars and seal.

Makes about 2 kg./4 lb. piccalilli

Spiced Pears

1 kg./2 lb. firm pears, peeled,
  cored and sliced
300 ml./10 fl. oz. water
1 kg./2 lb. brown sugar
juice and rind of 2 oranges
125 g./4 oz. preserved ginger,
  chopped

Cook the pears in the water until they are tender but still firm. Stir in the remaining ingredients and bring to the boil. Simmer for 20 to 30 minutes, or until the mixture is thick. Pour into hot, sterilized jars and seal.

Makes about 1½ kg./3 lb. pickle

Apricot and Orange Relish

½ kg./1 lb. dried apricots,
  soaked overnight in cold
  water
2 chillis, seeds removed and
  chopped
2 garlic cloves, chopped
2 shallots, chopped
15 g./½ oz. preserved ginger
300 ml./10 fl. oz. white wine
  vinegar
5 ml./1 teaspoon salt
½ kg./1 lb. brown sugar
grated rind and juice of 1
  large orange
6 shredded almonds

Pour the apricots and their soaking liquid into a saucepan and simmer for 10 to 15 minutes, or until soft. Drain and chop the apricots.

Put the chillis, garlic, shallots, ginger, vinegar, salt, sugar and orange rind and juice into a saucepan and bring to the boil. Stir in the apricots and simmer for 20 to 30 minutes or until the mixture has thickened. Stir in the almonds and simmer for a further 5 minutes. Pour into hot sterilized jars and seal.

Makes about 1 kg./2 lb. relish

Spiced Peaches

½ kg./1 lb. peaches, skinned
  and halved
225 g./8 oz. sugar
5 ml./1 teaspoon ground
  cinnamon
5 ml./1 teaspoon ground
  allspice
5 ml./1 teaspoon ground
  coriander
2.5 ml./½ teaspoon ground
  cloves
1.25 ml./¼ teaspoon grated
  nutmeg
75 ml./3 fl. oz. cider

Put the peach halves into a large saucepan. Mix the sugar and spices together and sprinkle over the peaches. Pour over the cider and bring to the boil. Simmer gently for 3 minutes. With a slotted spoon, carefully transfer the peaches to wide-necked sterilized jars. Boil the syrup for 5 to 10 minutes, or until it starts to thicken. Pour over the peaches and seal.

Makes about ½ kg./1 lb.

Pickled Green Beans

1 kg./2 lb. green beans
425 ml./15 fl. oz. brown
  vinegar
½ kg./1 lb. sugar
425 ml./15 fl. oz. water
5 ml./1 teaspoon salt

Cook the green beans in boiling, salted water until they are tender. Drain and pack into hot, sterilized jars.

Put all the remaining ingredients into a saucepan and bring to the boil. Simmer for 10 minutes. Set aside to cool. Pour over the beans to within 1.25 cm./½ in. of the top and seal.

Makes about 1 kg./2 lb. pickle

Pickled Red Cabbage

1 red cabbage, shredded
50 g./2 oz. salt
2½ l./4 pints white vinegar
15 ml./1 tablespoon cloves
15 ml./1 tablespoon allspice
  berries
5 cm./2 in. cinnamon stick
6 peppercorns
1.25 ml./¼ teaspoon grated
  nutmeg

Arrange the cabbage, in layers, in a wide bowl, sprinkling each layer generously with the salt. Cover and set aside overnight. Drain, then rinse in cold running water.

Put the remaining ingredients in a heatproof bowl and put the bowl in a pan half-filled with hot water. Bring the water to the boil, then remove the pan from the heat. Set aside and allow the vinegar and spices to steep for 2 hours.

Pack the cabbage into hot, sterilized jars and strain over the vinegar to within 1.25 cm./½ in. of the top. Seal.

Makes about 1½ kg./3 lb. pickle

Cucumber Relish

4 large cucumbers, diced
50 g./2 oz. salt
1 red pepper, pith and seeds
  removed and chopped
1 green pepper, pith and
  seeds removed and
  chopped
225 g./8 oz. onions, chopped
3 celery stalks, chopped
15 ml./1 tablespoon mustard
  seeds
350 g./12 oz. sugar
425 ml./15 fl. oz. white
  vinegar

Arrange the diced cucumber in a bowl and sprinkle over the salt. Cover and set aside overnight. Drain, then rinse in cold running water. Put the cucumber into a saucepan with the remaining ingredients. Bring to the boil, then simmer for 30 minutes, or until the relish has thickened. Pour into hot, sterilized jars and seal.

Makes about 1½ kg./3 lb. relish

Cabbage Relish

1 small white cabbage,
    shredded
3 carrots, thinly sliced
½ kg./1 lb. onions, chopped
4 green peppers, pith and
    seeds removed and
    chopped
30 ml./2 tablespoons salt
½ kg./1 lb. sugar
15 ml./1 tablespoon mustard
    seeds
pinch of cayenne pepper
1¼ l./2 pints white vinegar
15 ml./1 tablespoon celery
    seeds
bay leaves

Arrange the vegetables in a bowl and sprinkle over
the salt. Cover and set aside overnight. Drain, then
pack into hot, sterilized jars.

Put all the remaining ingredients, except the bay
leaves, into a saucepan and bring to the boil.
Simmer for 5 minutes. Pour over the vegetables
and set aside to cool. Add a bay leaf to each jar and
seal when cold.

Makes about 2 kg./4 lb. relish

Corn Relish

725 ml./1¼ pints white
    vinegar
225 g./8 oz. sugar
2 × 275 g./10 oz. cans
    sweetcorn, drained
1 onion, chopped
50 g./2 oz. celery, chopped
2 green peppers, pith and
    seeds removed and
    chopped
1 large red pepper, pith and
    seeds removed and
    chopped
45 ml./3 tablespoons
    cornflour
15 ml./1 tablespoon dry
    mustard
5 ml./1 teaspoon mustard
    seeds

Put 600 ml./1 pint of vinegar and the sugar into a
saucepan and bring to the boil. Stir in the vegetables and simmer for 20 minutes.

Mix the cornflour with the remaining vinegar
and stir into the mixture, with the mustard seeds.
Bring to the boil and simmer for 5 minutes or until
the relish thickens. Pour into hot, sterilized jars
and seal.

Makes about 1 kg./2 lb. relish

Drinks

Fresh Lemon Drink

3 large whole lemons,
  washed and cubed
125 g./4 oz. sugar
1¼ l./2 pints boiling water
3 mint sprigs
4 lemon slices
ice cubes

Put the lemon cubes in a large stoneware jug, add the sugar and pour over the boiling water. Leave for 20 minutes, then strain. Add the mint, lemon slices and ice cubes. Allow the ice to cool the drink before serving.

Serves 6

Ginger Beer

225 g./8 oz. sugar
50 g./2 oz. fresh root ginger,
  crushed
15 ml./1 tablespoon cream of
  tartar
grated rind and juice of 1
  lemon
3 l./5 pints boiling water
7 g./¼ oz. fresh yeast
2.5 ml./½ teaspoon extra
  sugar

Mix together the sugar, ginger, cream of tartar, lemon rind and boiling water. Stir well and cool to lukewarm. Crumble the yeast and mash in the extra sugar. Add the yeast mixture to the lukewarm liquid and leave in a warm, draught-free place for two days or until the yeast stops frothing.

Strain into a large jug and stir in the lemon juice. Pour into airtight bottles and secure.

About 3¼ l./5¼ pints

Strawberry Whip

½ kg./1 lb. strawberries
900 ml./1½ pints milk
225 g./8 oz. ice-cream
50 g./2 oz. sugar
2.5 ml./½ teaspoon vanilla
  essence
ice cubes
75 ml./3 fl. oz. double cream,
  whipped
4 whole strawberries to
  garnish

Rub the strawberries through a strainer into a bowl. Beat in the milk, ice-cream, sugar and vanilla essence. Alternatively mix to a purée in an electric blender. Put some ice cubes into each of four tall glasses. Pour over the puréed mixture and top with a generous swirl of cream. Put one strawberry on the top of each glass.

Serves 4

Tomato Juice

1 kg./2 lb. tomatoes, skinned
and chopped
1 small green pepper, pith
and seeds removed and
chopped
1 small onion, chopped
15 ml./1 tablespoon chopped
fresh basil
15 ml./1 tablespoon
Worcestershire sauce
50 ml./2 fl. oz. lemon juice
15 ml./1 tablespoon olive oil
salt and pepper

Place all the ingredients in the jar of an electric blender and blend until they form a purée. Strain and season to taste. Serve chilled.

Serves 4

Iced Coffee

50 g./2 oz. instant coffee
powder
300 ml./10 fl. oz. hot water
900 ml./1½ pints cold water
sugar
150 ml./5 fl. oz. double
cream, stiffly whipped
50 g./2 oz. chocolate, grated

Put the coffee powder and hot water in a large jug and stir to dissolve. Add the cold water and sweeten to taste with sugar, if desired. Chill, then pour into four chilled glasses and top with the whipped cream. Sprinkle over the grated chocolate.

Serves 4

Iced Tea

sugar
1 l./1¾ pints freshly brewed
tea, cooled
ice cubes
4 lemon slices
4 mint sprigs

Sweeten the tea to taste if desired and strain into four glasses. Add the ice cubes. Garnish each glass with a lemon slice and a sprig of mint.

Serves 4

Egg Flip

175 ml./6 fl. oz. milk
1 egg
10 ml./2 teaspoons sugar
25 ml./1 fl. oz. rum, whisky
    or brandy (optional)

Blend together the milk, egg, sugar and alcohol if used. Pour into a glass.

Serves 1

Hot Toddy

thinly pared rind of 2 lemons
15 ml./1 tablespoon clear
    honey
175 ml./6 fl. oz. water
125 ml./4 fl. oz. dark rum

Simmer the lemon rind, honey and water for 5 minutes. In a separate saucepan, gently warm the rum. Strain the honey mixture into the rum and pour into two small heatproof mugs.

Serves 2

Irish Coffee

4 sugar lumps
175 ml./6 fl. oz. Irish
    whiskey
300 ml./10 fl. oz. strong
    boiling coffee
125 ml./4 fl. oz. double
    cream

Put a sugar lump in each of four stemmed, heatproof glasses of about 200 ml./7 fl. oz. capacity. Pour over the whiskey, then top up with the hot coffee. Pour cream over the back of a teaspoon into each glass so it floats on top.

Serves 4

Sloe Gin

½ kg./1 lb. sloes
1¼ l./2 pints gin
125 g./4 oz. sugar
2-3 drops almond essence

Prick the sloes all over with a sharp needle. Pour over the gin and stir in the sugar and almond essence. Pour into a large airtight container, such as a corked storage jar, and fasten tightly. Leave in a dark place for about 15 weeks to allow the mixture to infuse. Shake the container occasionally.

Strain through a funnel lined with muslin or cheesecloth and pour into clean, dry bottles. Seal the bottles and keep for at least 6 months before drinking.

2 l./3½ pints

Gluhwein

3 bottles dry red wine
½ bottle brandy
300 ml./10 fl. oz. water
300 ml./10 fl. oz. orange
   juice
juice of 2 lemons
thinly pared rind of 1 lemon
   and 1 orange
6 sticks of cinnamon
1 orange stuck with 12 cloves

Combine all the ingredients in a large flameproof serving pot and simmer gently for 20 minutes. Serve in small mugs.

Serves 20

Mulled Wine

1 bottle red wine
50 ml./2 fl. oz. sherry
30 ml./2 tablespoons clear
   honey
5 ml./1 teaspoon ground
   allspice
1.25 ml./¼ teaspoon grated
   nutmeg
1 dessert apple, studded with
   10 cloves and baked for
   10 minutes

Pour the wine and sherry into a large saucepan and stir in the honey, allspice and nutmeg. Add the apple and bring to the boil, stirring occasionally. Simmer for 10 minutes. Serve hot, straight from the saucepan.

Serves 8-10

Party Punch

1 bottle red wine
300 ml./10 fl. oz. port
150 ml./5 fl. oz. brandy
150 ml./5 fl. oz. orange juice
juice of 2 lemons
90 ml./6 tablespoons sugar
15 ml./1 tablespoon grated
   orange rind
10 ml./2 teaspoons grated
   lemon rind
175 ml./6 fl. oz. soda water
ice cubes
1 orange, thinly sliced to
   garnish

Mix the wine, port, brandy, orange and lemon juice together in a large serving bowl. Stir in the sugar. Add the orange and lemon rind and soda. Chill for 20 minutes.

Add ice cubes and serve garnished with the floating slices of orange.

Serves 8-10

Tea Punch

15 ml./1 tablespoon grated
    lemon rind
175 g./6 oz. brown sugar
1.25 l./2 pints freshly made
    tea, strained
300 ml./10 fl. oz. dark rum
175 ml./6 fl. oz. brandy
600 ml./1 pint soda water
    (optional)

Put the lemon rind and sugar in a large bowl and crush together with the back of a spoon. Pour in the tea and stir until the sugar has dissolved. Cool, then strain into a large serving bowl. Stir in the rum and brandy. If you wish to dilute the punch, stir in the soda water just before serving.

Serves 12-15

Cider Cup

2 l./3½ pints dry cider
2 oranges stuck with 12
    cloves
5 ml./1 teaspoon ground
    cinnamon
2 dessert apples, sliced
60 ml./4 tablespoons sugar
50 ml./2 fl. oz. brandy

Pour the cider into a large saucepan and simmer for 5 minutes. Add the oranges, cinnamon, apple slices and sugar. Bring to the boil, stirring occasionally, and stir in the brandy. Remove the oranges and pour the cider into a warmed serving bowl. Remove the cloves from the oranges, slice and return to the cider. Serve immediately.

Serves 12-15

Sangria

60 ml./4 tablespoons sugar
juice of 1 lemon
1½ l./2½ pints red wine
300 ml./10 fl. oz. water
ice cubes
Garnish
1 orange, sliced
1 lemon, sliced

Dissolve the sugar in the lemon juice in a large serving bowl or jug. Add the wine and stir well. Pour in the water and add about 10 ice cubes. Float the orange and lemon slices on the top and chill.

Serves 12

Basic Recipes

Beef Stock

1 kg./2 lb. shin bone,
  chopped
1 marrow bone
3½ l./6 pints water
2 onions, halved
2 carrots, chopped
2 celery stalks
5 ml./1 teaspoon peppercorns
salt
10 ml./2 teaspoons dried
  mixed herbs

Put the bones and water in a large saucepan and bring to the boil. Skim off any scum. When the scum stops rising, add the rest of the ingredients. Cover and simmer for 3½ to 4 hours or until the liquid is reduced by about half. Strain the stock. If you wish to use it immediately, cool then remove the fat from the surface. Otherwise leave the fat intact, cover and keep in the refrigerator.

Makes about 1¾ l./3 pints

Chicken Stock

carcass and giblets of a raw
  or cooked chicken
1¾ l./3 pints water
1 onion, halved
2 carrots, chopped
2 celery stalks, chopped
5 ml./1 teaspoon peppercorns
salt
5 ml./1 teaspoon dried mixed
  herbs

Put the chicken carcass and giblets in a saucepan and pour over the water. Add the remaining ingredients and bring to the boil. Skim off any scum. Cover and simmer for about 2 hours or until the liquid is reduced by about half. Strain the stock. If you wish to use it immediately, cool then remove the fat from the surface. Otherwise leave the fat intact, cover and keep in the refrigerator.

Makes about ¾ l./1½ pints

Fish Stock

1 kg./2 lb. fish bones and
  trimmings
1¼ l./2¼ pints water
175 ml./6 fl. oz. white wine
1 onion, halved
2 carrots, chopped
2 celery stalks, chopped
5 peppercorns
salt
2.5 ml./½ teaspoon dried
  mixed herbs

Put the fish bones and trimmings in a saucepan and pour over the water and wine. Add the remaining ingredients and bring to the boil. Skim off any scum. Cover and simmer for 30 minutes or until the liquid is reduced by about one-third. Strain the stock. If the stock is not to be used immediately, it should be covered in foil and put in the refrigerator.

Makes about 1 l./2 pints

Vegetable Stock

50 g./2 oz. vegetable oil
1 large onion, chopped
4 carrots, chopped
4 celery stalks, with leaves,
   chopped
1 turnip, peeled and chopped
2½ l./4 pints water
2 bouquet garni
8 black peppercorns
salt

Heat the oil in a saucepan. Add the vegetables and cook for about 10 minutes, or until the onion is brown. Pour in the water and add the bouquet garni, peppercorns and salt. Bring to the boil and simmer for 45 minutes. Strain before using.

Makes about 1¾ l./3pints

Chestnut Stuffing

½ kg./1 lb. chestnuts, slit
300 ml./10 fl. oz. chicken or
   turkey stock
125 g./4 oz. ham, diced
225 g./8 oz. pork
   sausagemeat
salt and pepper

Boil the chestnuts in water for about 8 minutes and remove the skins while still warm. Put the skinned chestnuts in a saucepan with the stock and simmer for 20 minutes, or until the chestnuts are tender and nearly all the stock is absorbed. Chop the chestnuts very finely or rub them through a strainer. Blend with the ham and sausagemeat and season with salt and pepper. If the mixture is too dry, moisten with a little extra stock.

Makes about ¾ kg./1½ lb.

Parsley and Thyme Stuffing

125 g./4 oz. fresh
   breadcrumbs
30 ml./2 tablespoons
   chopped fresh parsley
50 g./2 oz. shredded suet
10 ml./2 teaspoons chopped
   fresh thyme or a good
   pinch of dried thyme
grated rind and juice of 1
   lemon
1 egg, beaten
salt and pepper

Blend together the breadcrumbs, parsley, suet and thyme. Stir in the lemon rind and juice and bind together with the egg. Season with salt and pepper and mix well.

Makes about 175 g./6 oz.

Sage and Onion Stuffing

3 medium onions, chopped
150 ml./5 fl. oz. water
75 g./3 oz. fresh
   breadcrumbs
10 ml./2 teaspoons chopped
   fresh sage, or 2.5 ml./½
   teaspoon dried sage
50 g./2 oz. shredded suet
salt and pepper
1 egg, beaten

Cook the onions in the water for about 10 minutes or until slightly tender. Drain and mix with the breadcrumbs, sage and suet. Season with salt and pepper to taste and mix well. Bind the mixture with the egg. If it is too dry, moisten with a little of the onion stock.

Makes about 350 g./12 oz.

Veal and Apricot Stuffing

30 ml./2 tablespoons
   vegetable oil
½ kg./1 lb. minced veal
1 small onion, grated
salt and pepper to taste
2.5 ml./½ teaspoon dried sage
1 × 225 g./8 oz. can apricots,
   drained
25 g./1 oz. flaked almonds

Heat the oil in a large frying-pan. Add the veal and onion and fry until the meat loses its pinkness. Stir in seasoning to taste and sage, then add the apricots and flaked almonds. Cook for a further 10 minutes, stirring frequently.
   The stuffing is now ready to use.

Makes about ½ kg./1 lb.

White Sauce

25 g./1 oz. butter
25 g./1 oz. flour
300 ml./10 fl. oz. milk, or
   milk and fish, meat or
   vegetable stock
salt and pepper

Melt the butter in a saucepan. Stir in the flour to form a smooth paste. Cook gently for about 1 minute or until the mixture is pale brown. Remove from the heat and gradually stir in the milk or milk and stock. Return to the heat and bring to the boil, stirring constantly. Cook for about 3 minutes or until the sauce thickens. Season to taste with salt and pepper.

Makes about 300 ml./10 fl. oz.

Mint Sauce

15 ml./1 tablespoon sugar
15 ml./1 tablespoon boiling
   water
30 ml./2 tablespoons vinegar
30 ml./2 tablespoons
   chopped fresh mint leaves

Put the sugar and water in a small saucepan and boil for 1 minute. Add the vinegar and pour over the mint leaves. Soak for 15 minutes. Stir well before serving.

Makes about 50 ml./2 fl. oz.

Bread Sauce

300 ml./10 fl. oz. milk
15 g./½ oz. butter
75 g./3 oz. fresh
   breadcrumbs
1 onion, stuck with 2 cloves
30 ml./2 tablespoons double
   cream
salt and pepper

Put the milk, butter, breadcrumbs and onion in the top of a double boiler over boiling water. Stir in the cream and season with salt and pepper. Heat slowly until the sauce has thickened. Remove the onion and cloves and stir well before serving.

Makes about 350 ml./12 fl. oz.

Mornay Sauce

50 g./2 oz. cheese, grated
   (Parmesan, Cheddar or
   Gruyère)
300 ml./10 fl. oz hot
   béchamel sauce*
pinch of paprika
salt and pepper

Stir the cheese into the sauce with the paprika, salt and pepper. Continue mixing until the cheese has melted. Do not reheat or the cheese will become stringy.

Makes about 300 ml./10 fl. oz.

Apple Sauce

3 tart apples, peeled and
   sliced
15 ml./1 tablespoon water
15 ml./1 tablespoon sugar
pinch of salt
squeeze of lemon
5 ml./1 teaspoon butter

Put the apple slices, water and sugar in a small saucepan. Add the salt, lemon juice and butter and cook until the apple slices are soft. Beat with the back of a wooden spoon until the sauce is smooth. Serve hot or cold.

Makes about 150 ml./5 fl. oz.

Béarnaise Sauce

60 ml./4 tablespoons
   tarragon vinegar
6 peppercorns, crushed
1 shallot, chopped
1 bay leaf
3 egg yolks
125 g./4 oz. butter, melted
   and cooled
salt and pepper

Simmer the vinegar, peppercorns, shallot and bay leaf together until the liquid is reduced by half. Strain and cool. Beat the egg yolks lightly in the top of a double boiler over simmering water. Gradually stir in the strained vinegar. Add the butter, in small pieces, stirring constantly until the sauce thickens. Season with salt and pepper.

Makes 150 ml./5 fl. oz.

Hollandaise Sauce

45 ml./3 tablespoons wine
   vinegar
6 peppercorns
½ bay leaf
2 egg yolks
125 g./4 oz. butter, softened
salt and pepper
lemon juice

Simmer the vinegar, peppercorns and bay leaf together until the liquid is reduced by half. Cool and strain. Beat the egg yolks with a knob of the butter and a pinch of salt and pepper in the top of a double boiler. Gradually stir in the strained vinegar. Stir over simmering water until the sauce has just begun to thicken. Add the remaining butter in small pieces, stirring constantly. When all the butter has been added, add lemon juice to taste.

Makes about 150 ml./5 fl. oz.

Béchamel Sauce

1 bay leaf
15 ml./1 tablespoon chopped
   fresh parsley
½ small onion, chopped
4 peppercorns
sprig of thyme
1 carrot, sliced
1 celery stalk, sliced
300 ml./10 fl. oz. milk
15 ml./1 tablespoon butter
15 g./½ oz. flour
salt and pepper

Put the bay leaf, parsley, onion, peppercorns, thyme, carrot, celery and milk in a saucepan. Simmer for 30 minutes. Leave to cool and strain.

Melt the butter in a saucepan and stir in the flour to form a smooth paste. Cook for 1 minute or until the mixture is pale gold. Remove from the heat and gradually stir in the strained milk. When thoroughly blended, return to the heat and stir until the sauce boils and thickens. Season to taste with salt and pepper.

Makes about 300 ml./10 fl. oz.

Tomato Sauce

30 ml./2 tablespoons oil
1 small onion, finely
   chopped
2 × 400 g./14 oz. can
   tomatoes, chopped
30 ml./2 tablespoons tomato
   purée
10 ml./2 teaspoons chopped
   fresh basil or 2.5 ml./½
   teaspoon dried basil
5 ml./1 teaspoon sugar
pepper

Heat the oil in a frying-pan. Add the onion and fry for 5 minutes. Add the tomatoes, and can juice, and all the remaining ingredients. Partially cover the pan and simmer gently for about 40 minutes, stirring occasionally. Rub the sauce through a strainer, return to a clean pan and reheat gently.

Makes about 300 ml./10 fl. oz.

Devilled Sauce

3 large onions, finely
  chopped
150 ml./5 fl. oz. oil
30 ml./2 tablespoons
  Worcestershire sauce
5 ml./1 teaspoon Tabasco
  sauce
pinch of cayenne pepper
pinch of curry powder
salt
150 ml./5 fl. oz. red wine
150 ml./5 fl. oz. beef stock

Mix the onions with the oil and sauces. Add the cayenne, curry powder and salt to taste. Brush whatever meat you are cooking with this mixture during cooking, then baste with the mixture during cooking. Add the wine and stock towards the end of the cooking time, stir well and heat through to make a sauce.

Makes about 300 ml./10 fl. oz.

Tartare Sauce

175 ml./6 fl. oz.
  mayonnaise*
30 ml./2 tablespoons capers,
  finely chopped
30 ml./2 tablespoons
  gherkins, chopped
2.5 ml./½ teaspoon chopped
  chives
15 ml./1 tablespoon chopped
  fresh parsley
salt and pepper

Combine the mayonnaise, capers, gherkins, chives and parsley. Season with the salt and pepper.

Makes about 175 ml./6 fl. oz.

Orange Sauce

425 ml./15 fl. oz. duck stock,
  made by simmering the
  giblets
grated rind and juice of 2
  large oranges
15 g./½ oz. cornflour
15 ml./1 tablespoon sugar
30 ml./2 tablespoons port
  (optional)
salt and pepper

Strain the stock well. Add the grated orange rind and simmer for 10 minutes. Strain carefully. Blend the orange juice with the cornflour and stir into the stock until it becomes clear. Allow the sauce to simmer gently until it has thickened. (This takes some time but improves the flavour.) Add the sugar and port, if used, and season with salt and pepper. Simmer for 3 minutes longer.

Makes about 400 ml./15 fl. oz.

Cumberland Sauce

thinly pared rind and juice of
  2 oranges
150 ml./5 fl. oz. cold water
10 ml./2 teaspoons arrowroot
  or cornflour
150 ml./5 fl. oz. ham or
  chicken stock
juice of 1 lemon
10 ml./2 teaspoons mustard
30 ml./2 tablespoons port
75 g./3 oz. redcurrant jelly
salt and pepper

Cut the orange rind into very thin strips and put in a saucepan with the water. Soak for 1 hour, then cover and simmer gently for 15 to 20 minutes, or until the rind is tender. Remove the lid for the last 10 minutes of the cooking time so that the liquid is reduced to about 45 ml./3 tablespoons. Blend the arrowroot or cornflour with the ham or chicken stock and add to the saucepan. Stir in the orange and lemon juice, mustard, port and jelly. Stir over low heat until the sauce is thick and clear. Season to taste with salt and pepper. Serve hot or cold.

Makes about 400 ml./15 fl. oz.

Chinese Plum Sauce

75 g./3 oz. butter
1 onion, finely chopped
225 g./8 oz. plum jam,
  strained
30 ml./2 tablespoons soy
  sauce
15 ml./1 tablespoon wine
  vinegar
2.5 ml./½ teaspoon ground
  ginger
pinch of mustard

Melt the butter in a saucepan. Add the onion and fry for 5 minutes. Stir in the remaining ingredients. Heat gently, stirring constantly.

Makes about 350 ml./12 fl. oz.

Chocolate Sauce

175 g./6 oz. plain cooking
  chocolate
15 ml./1 tablespoon water
15 g./½ oz. butter

Break the chocolate into pieces and put in a heat-proof basin with the water and butter. Use twice the amount of water if you are serving the sauce cold. Place the bowl over a saucepan of simmering water and stir until the ingredients are combined. Serve hot or cold.

Makes about 125 ml./4 fl. oz.

Mayonnaise

2 egg yolks
2.5 ml./½ teaspoon dry
  mustard
2.5 ml./½ teaspoon salt
1.25 ml./¼ teaspoon pepper
300 ml./10 fl. oz. oil
30 ml./2 tablespoons wine
  vinegar or lemon juice

If possible have all the ingredients at room temperature, as eggs taken straight from the refrigerator tend to curdle. Beat the egg yolks with the mustard, salt and pepper until they become creamy in colour. Gradually beat in half the oil, drop by drop, until the sauce is thick and shiny. Beat in half of the vinegar or lemon juice, then beat in the remaining oil, a little more quickly. Beat in the remaining vinegar or lemon juice. If you want to thin the mayonnaise down a little, add some lemon juice, a little single cream or 15-30 ml./1-2 tablespoons hot water.

Thick mayonnaise may be stored in an airtight container in the refrigerator for about two weeks.

Note: If the mayonnaise does curdle, beat another egg yolk in a clean bowl and beat in the curdled mixture a teaspoon at a time.

Makes about 350 ml./12 fl. oz.

Aioli

2 egg yolks
2 garlic cloves, crushed
300 ml./10 fl. oz. oil
15 ml./1 tablespoon lemon
  juice
salt and pepper

Beat the egg yolks with the garlic, until they become creamy in colour. Gradually beat in half the oil, drop by drop, until the sauce is thick and shiny. Beat in half of the lemon juice, then beat in the remaining oil, a little more quickly. Season with salt and pepper and beat in the remaining lemon juice.

Makes about 325 ml./11 fl. oz.

French Dressing or Vinaigrette

125 ml./4 fl. oz. oil
50 ml./2 fl. oz. wine vinegar
1.25 ml./¼ teaspoon dry
  mustard
1 garlic clove, crushed
  (optional)
2.5 ml./½ teaspoon sugar
salt and pepper

Put all the ingredients into a screw-topped jar and shake well until thoroughly blended. This will keep for several weeks. Always shake well before using.

Makes about 175 ml./6 fl. oz.

410

Thousand Island Dressing

350 ml./12 fl. oz.
   mayonnaise*
5 ml./1 teaspoon Tabasco
   sauce
30 ml./2 tablespoons sweet
   pickle
2 hard-boiled eggs, chopped
2 spring onions, chopped
45 ml./3 tablespoons French
   dressing*

Combine all the ingredients and beat until they are thoroughly blended. Chill well.

Makes about 350 ml./12 fl. oz.

Blue Cheese Dressing

50 g./2 oz. blue cheese, such
   as Danish Blue
150 ml./5 fl. oz. yogurt
salt and pepper

Rub the cheese through a strainer and mix with the yogurt. Season to taste with salt and pepper and chill well.

Makes about 175 ml./6 fl. oz.

Green Goddess Dressing

225 ml./8 fl. oz.
   mayonnaise*
2 anchovy fillets, chopped
2 spring onions, chopped
15 ml./1 tablespoon chopped
   fresh parsley
5 ml./1 teaspoon chopped
   fresh thyme
10 ml./2 teaspoons vinegar
salt and pepper to taste
125 ml./4 fl. oz. sour or
   double cream

Put the mayonnaise in a serving bowl or jug and gradually beat in all the remaining ingredients until they are thoroughly blended.

Chill in the refrigerator for 30 minutes before serving.

Makes about 400 ml./15 fl. oz. dressing

Coleslaw Dressing

175 ml./6 fl. oz.
   mayonnaise*
5 ml./1 teaspoon dry mustard
10 ml./2 teaspoons lemon
   juice
salt and pepper
pinch of cayenne pepper
45 ml./3 tablespoons cream

Combine all the ingredients and beat until they are thoroughly blended. Chill well.

Makes about 200 ml./7 fl. oz.

Shortcrust Pastry

225 g./8 oz. flour
pinch of salt
125 g./4 oz. butter,
   margarine or cooking fat
about 45-60 ml./3-4
   tablespoons cold water

Sift the flour and salt into a mixing bowl. Rub in the fat until the mixture resembles fine breadcrumbs. Add the water and mix to a dough. (Too much water will result in tough pastry.) Chill for 15 minutes before using for the best results.

Note: When a recipe states 225 g./8 oz. of shortcrust pastry, it means pastry made with 225 g./8 oz. of flour

Makes 225g./8 oz.

Flaky Pastry

225 g./8 oz. flour
pinch of salt
75 g./3 oz. butter
75 g./3 oz. lard
cold water to mix

Sift the flour and salt into a mixing bowl. Mix the fats together on a plate with a knife and shape into a square block. Rub one-quarter of the fat into the flour and mix to a firm dough with cold water. Knead the dough lightly until smooth, then roll out to an oblong. Put a second quarter of the fat, in small pieces, on the top two-thirds of the dough. Fold in three, folding the bottom third up and the top third down. This gives you even layers of dough and fat. Half turn the dough so that an open end faces you, and roll out again to an oblong. Repeat the flaking, folding and rolling of the dough twice more. Chill the dough at any stage when it becomes too soft and greasy to handle. Fold the dough into three once more and chill for 30 minutes before using for best results.

Makes 225 g./8 oz.

Rough Puff Pastry

225 g./8 oz. flour
pinch of salt
75 g./3 oz. butter
75 g./3 oz. lard
cold water to mix

Sift the flour and salt into a mixing bowl. Cut the fat into walnut-sized pieces and drop into the flour, tossing each piece well to coat it with flour. Mix in enough cold water to make a soft dough. Roll out the dough to an oblong, fold in three and make a half turn so that an open end faces you. Repeat the rolling, folding and turning twice more. Chill the dough at any stage when it becomes too soft and greasy to handle. Chill for 30 minutes before using for best results.

Makes 225 g./8 oz.

Rich Shortcrust Pastry

225 g./8 oz. flour
salt
125 g./4 oz. butter
5 ml./1 teaspoon sugar
1 egg, beaten
cold water to mix

Sift the flour and salt into a mixing bowl. Rub in the butter until the mixture resembles fine bread-crumbs. Stir in the sugar. Add the egg with a spoonful of cold water and mix to a dough. Add more water if the dough is too dry. Chill for 30 minutes before using for the best results.

Makes 225 g./8 oz.

Puff Pastry

225 g./8 oz. flour
salt
225 g./8 oz. unsalted butter
125 ml./4 fl. oz. iced water

Sift the flour and salt into a mixing bowl. Rub in half the butter until the mixture resembles fine breadcrumbs. Add the water and mix to a firm dough. Chill for 15 minutes. Put the other half of the butter between two sheets of greaseproof paper and beat until it forms an oblong shape about 1.5 cm./¾ in. thick. Roll out the dough into a rectangle .75 cm./¼ in. thick. Place the butter in the centre and fold the dough over it to form a parcel. Chill for 10 minutes. Roll the dough, with the folds downwards, away from you into a rectangle. Fold in three. Turn once, so that an open end is towards you. Roll out again and fold as before. Chill for 15 minutes. Repeat this process twice more, then chill for at least 30 minutes before using for best results.

Makes 225 g./8 oz.

Choux Pastry

300 ml./10 fl. oz. water
75 g./3 oz. butter, cut into
   pieces
2.5 ml./½ teaspoon salt
275 g./10 oz. flour, sifted
5 standard eggs

Heat the water, butter and salt in a saucepan. When the butter has melted, remove from the heat and beat in the flour. Beat in the eggs, one at a time, until the mixture is thick and glossy.

Makes 275 g./10 oz.

Flan or Quiche Case

175 g./6 oz. shortcrust or rich
   shortcrust pastry*
haricot beans, rice or dried
   peas

Roll out the dough to .75 cm./¼ in. thick. Use to line a 23 cm./9 in. flan ring, placed on a baking sheet, or a flan tin. Prick the base lightly with a fork. If the flan case is to be **baked blind**, place a circle of greaseproof paper over the dough and half fill with the beans, rice or dried peas. Put into the oven preheated to moderate (180°C/350°F or Gas Mark 4) and bake for 15 minutes, or until the pastry is set in shape. Remove the beans or peas and greaseproof paper and return to the oven. Bake for a further 10 to 15 minutes or until the pastry is golden.

Crêpes

125 g./4 oz. flour
pinch of salt
1 egg
300 ml./10 fl. oz. milk
oil for frying

Sift the flour and salt into a bowl. Make a well in the centre and add the egg and a little milk. Beat thoroughly to give a smooth batter. Gradually beat in the rest of the milk. Leave for at least 1 hour before using.

For each crêpe, put about 10 ml./2 teaspoons of oil into the frying-pan. Heat the oil until a faint blue haze is visible. Pour or spoon in a little batter, then tilt the pan so that the batter flows over the bottom; it should give a paper thin layer. Cook fairly quickly until set on the bottom. This takes about 1½ to 2 minutes. To test if ready to toss or turn, shake the pan; the crêpe should move easily. Toss or turn carefully and cook for about the same time on the other side. Lift or slide the crêpe out of the pan.

Makes about 8 crêpes

Vanilla Sugar

1 vanilla pod
½ kg./1 lb. sugar

Break the vanilla pod into pieces and put in a bowl with one-quarter of the sugar. Using a wooden spoon, crush the pod and sugar together until the pod is reduced to very small specks. Alternatively, put the pod and one quarter of the sugar in the jar of an electric blender and blend until the pod is reduced to small specks. Stir in the remaining sugar. Keep in an airtight container.

Makes ½ kg./1 lb.

Chutney Butter

50 g./2 oz. butter
50 g./2 oz. chutney
1.25 ml./¼ teaspoon lemon juice
salt and pepper

Cream the butter until it is fluffy. Beat in the chutney and lemon juice. Season with salt and pepper to taste.

Makes about 125 g./4 oz.

Aspic Jelly

300 ml./10 fl. oz. chicken stock
15 g./1 tablespoon gelatine
75 ml./3 fl. oz. white wine

Bring the stock to the boil and remove from the heat. Mix 60 ml./4 tablespoons of the stock with the gelatine and stir until the gelatine has dissolved. Add to the rest of the stock. Mix in wine and leave to cool. Chill until required.

Makes about 375 ml./13 fl. oz.

Index